FORTUNE TELLING

FORTUNE TELLING

This edition published and distributed by Siena, 1998

Siena
13 Whiteladies Road
Clifton
Bristol BS8 1PB

First published in the UK as *The Mammoth Book of Fortune Telling*,
by Robinson Publishing, London, 1997

A copy of the British Library Cataloguing-in-Publication Data
is available from the British Library

ISBN 0-75252-826-2

Compiled by Peter Thorndike

Produced by Book Packaging and Marketing, Silverstone

Typeset by White Horse Graphics, Charlbury

Printed and bound in the EC

CONTENTS

ASTROLOGY

The Foundations of Astrology

Astrology has been around for many centuries. Archaeologists tell us that the earliest etchings and scratchings on cave wall and parchment reveal primitive renditions of planetary symbols – the ancient Chaldeans, for instance, watched the night sky religiously, and through this observation built up a detailed astrological understanding.

Despite such a long history, Astrology remains a much misunderstood philosophy. Most people, for instance, believe that it is all about *predicting the future* – tall dark strangers, crocks of gold, etc. This is certainly not the case, and Astrology is only presented in this distorted light by amateurish dabblers of the worst kind.

Astrology – the science of interpreting the movements of the planets and their relationship to human destiny – is actually about *potential*. It is about calculating whether or not a particular course of action is advisable, for instance, or calculating whether or not this is the right time to begin a new project. True Astrology is never dogmatic or scaremongering; it merely presents the individual concerned with a list of possibilities. Any planetary set-up can be either positive or negative – the trick lies in understanding the aspects involved, and acting accordingly. Thus Astrology, far from being something which circumscribes, as some believe, is actually something which opens the door of opportunity, and presents the individual with real choices. It follows then that the only people who are limited by Astrology are those who are blind to its advice.

The 12 Signs In Brief

ARIES: The Ram – Dynamic, impulsive, innovative, quick to anger.

TAURUS: The Bull – Steady, persevering, conservative, materialistic.

GEMINI: The Twins – Versatile, quick-witted, communicative, imaginative.

CANCER: The Crab – Sensitive, home-loving, protective, moody.

LEO: The Lion – Proud, aggressive, gregarious, generous.

VIRGO: The Virgin – Enterprising, focused, perfectionist, intellectual.

LIBRA: The Scales – Harmony-loving, affable, indecisive, self-indulgent.

SCORPIO: The Scorpion – Intense, shrewd, unforgiving, creative healing.

SAGITTARIUS: The Archer – Extrovert, forward-thinking, wayward, humorous, wasteful.

CAPRICORN: The Goat – Inhibited, ambitious, staid, perservering.

AQUARIUS: The Water Carrier – Eccentric, ahead-of-their-time, high-strung, inventive.

PISCES: The Fishes – Enigmatic, romantic, impractical, compassionate, easy-going.

How The Planets Work

SUN – rules Leo
creative dynamic – commanding – fun-loving

MOON – rules Cancer
nurturing – imaginative – changeable – responsive

MERCURY – rules Gemini, Virgo
intelligent – communicative – versatile – go-between

VENUS – rules Taurus, Libra
charming – diplomatic – pleasure-loving – co-operative

MARS – rules Aries, co-rules Scorpio
fast – decisive – assertive – energetic

JUPITER – rules Sagittarius, co-rules Pisces
expansive – cheerful – freedom-loving – honest

SATURN – rules Capricorn, co-rules Aquarius
hardworking – disciplined – organized – ambitious

URANUS – co-rules Aquarius
Original – unpredictable – exciting – surprising

NEPTUNE – co-rules Pisces
imaginative – deceptive – unreliable – confusing

PLUTO – co-rules Scorpio
transforming – penetrating – deep – intense

WESTERN ASTROLOGY

INTERPRETING A BIRTHCHART

The Three Options

Sooner or later, anyone with a developing interest in astrology wants to interpret their birth chart – and probably other people's too! But how do you get one drawn up?

Today, there are three options, each of which has its pros and cons. Option 1 involves getting someone else to do it for you, Option 2 is only feasible if you own a computer. Option 3 involves calculating the chart yourself, which is time-consuming but not as difficult as some people think. This chapter takes you through the process in easy-to-manage stages.

Option 1

Nowadays it is possible to have your chart calculated (and usually interpreted, too) by one of the many computer 'read-out' companies. The cost of a basic calculation can be offset against the time taken and books needed to do it yourself.

Computer interpretations are fun, and very accurate as far as they go. The drawback is that computers can only ever give a standard description of what the various planetary combinations in your chart mean.

For a deeper understanding of the way these combinations refer specifically to you and your life, you must either learn to interpret them youself or visit a professional astrologer.

Option 2

If you own a personal computer and you want to study astrology seriously, a chart calculation program could prove an excellent investment. Most practising astrologers find them indispensable, since they will draw up and print out all kinds of charts at the touch of a button and save the details on file.

A good program should cost you between £30 and £50 ($40-$70), though some have interpretation programs which you can add on at extra cost. All these programs are widely advertized in the specialist computer or astrology press.

CONSULTING AN ASTROLOGER

Plenty of astrologers advertise in the specialist magazines, but if you know someone who has been before, and whose judgement you trust, personal recommendation is probably the most reliable way to choose one.

The astrologer will need to know your date, time and place of birth. If you do not know your time of birth, it is possible to have a reading based on a chart set up for noon on the day you were born. This will not be as precise as a proper chart, but should still reveal some of your basic personality traits. It may even provide a platform for the astrologer to deduce your birth time by working back through the major events in your life. However, this process – called rectification – is time-consuming, and therefore costly.

Most chart readings take the form of face-to-face interviews. Remember that astrology is not the same as clairvoyance, although all good astrologers are highly intuitive. Your chart is not a record of all your thoughts and deeds, but a coded list of your potential strengths and limitations.

In order to crack the code, an astrologer has to establish which areas of your personality you have developed, and which seem to be as yet untapped. Most astrologers charge a sum equivalent to the cost of a computer program.

Option 3

This is the old method – calculating and drawing up the chart by hand. At first sight it can appear a little daunting, but in fact the maths are not that complicated. The only serious drawback is the number of reference books you need to obtain before you can start drawing up the chart. The essential books are:

An Ephemeris for the positions of the planets for each day, either at noon or midnight. You can buy general ones covering periods of around 50 years, or detailed ones for one year only.

A Table of Houses for working out where the Ascendant (Asc), Midheaven (MC) and House cusps fall.

An Atlas giving the longitude and latitude of major cities and towns around the world.

A Book of Time Changes around the world. There are in fact three – one for the USA, one for Canada and Mexico, and one for the rest of the world. With any luck, you should find some of these books in the second hand section of a reasonable occult bookshop. You also need:

- Some blank charts (these are easily available from occult bookshops; it is very tedious drawing up your own).
- A calculator (ideally one that works in hours and minutes).

The Essential Data

Having decided to calculate a birth chart yourself and assembled the necessary equipment, start by sorting out the data.

The Birth Place

If this is a large city or town, look it up in an atlas and find its *latitude* (expressed as degrees/minutes – °/' – North or South of the Equator) and *longitude* (expressed as degrees/minutes East or West of the Greenwich Meridian). If you cannot find the exact place, take the nearest town and then 'guesstimate'.

The Birth Date

Note this down, writing the name of the month out in full to avoid confusion – e.g. 25 April 1970. Note, when only digits are used, the month may be given before the day – e.g. in the USA, 4/12/73 means 12 April, not 4 December.

The Birth Time

Write this down using the 24 hour clock to avoid confusion – e.g. 5.30pm = 17:30. **Now double-check your data.**

Stage 1 – Converting the Time

The first stage of birth chart calculation is to convert the time given in the birth data to Greenwich Mean Time (GMT) – the standard on which all world times are based, and the time quoted in all astrological tables.

Step 1: Establish time of birth

If you were born in the UK you are lucky. Britain has worked on GMT since 1880, so all you have to do is make an allowance for *Daylight Saving* (see step 3).

Most other countries work on zone standards based on GMT (see map). Thus, the time in Bangkok is seven hours **ahead** of GMT (+7); the time in New York is five hours **behind** GMT (-5). However, some countries only switched to zone standard time relatively recently. Before that they used *Local Mean Time* (LMT), based on the sun's position relative to their own country (as did the UK before 1880). Some states in the USA (and even countries) have changed their time zones from year to year. Because of this confusing situation, the only way to be absolutely sure what time standard was in force for places abroad is to consult the various time change books mentioned above. There is one for the USA, one for Canada and Mexico, and another covering the rest of the world.

Step 2: Convert to GMT

If your birth time is in a zone standard **ahead** of GMT, then all you need do to convert it is **subtract** the number of hours quoted for that zone.

Example: Bangkok is 7hr ahead of GMT. A time of 14.34 Bangkok local time thus becomes 07.34 GMT (14.34 – 7hr).

If your birth time is in a zone standard **behind** GMT, then to convert it **add** the number of hours quoted for that zone.

Example: New York is 5hr behind GMT. A time of 14.34 New York local time thus becomes 19.34 GMT (14.34 + 5hr).

If your birth time is quoted as LMT, you can calculate the GMT on the basis that the sun moves 1° of longitude every 4 minutes.

Example: for a time of 14.34 LMT Moscow on 30 December 1925:

- *Find the longitude for Moscow (= 37°42'W)*
- *Use the table in your time change book to find out how long the sun takes to travel from Moscow to Greenwich (= 2hr 30min 48sec).*
- *Subtract 2hr 30min 48sec from LMT (14.34.00). This gives a final result of 12.03.12 GMT.*

Step 3: Check Daylight Saving

Daylight Saving (e.g. 'British Summer Time') has been in force on and off around the world for years. The table given below shows British Daylight Saving dates. For other countries, check your time change books.

Where the tables say '=1', this means local time was one hour ahead of the zone standard time for the date shown. So if a '+' figure is given, subtract it from the adjusted time. In certain

DATE PLACE AND TIME

DATE/PLACE	d m y
Birth Date	
Birth Place	
Latitude (N/S)	
Longitude (E/W)	

TIME	h m s
Birth Time as given	
Zone Standard (+E –W LMT)	
Allowance for Daylight Saving	
GMT Time	
(Adjusted GMT Date)	

Use the blank chart above as a guide when converting the time (or photocopy this page). Shown below is an example for Paris.

DATE/PLACE	d m y
Birth Date	25 April 1970
Birth Place	Paris, France
Latitude (N/S)	48° 50′ N
Longitude (E/W)	2° 20′ E

TIME	h m s
Birth Time as given	18 . 48
Zone Standard (+E -W LMT)	+ 1 (subtract)
Allowance for Daylight Saving	(not used in 1970)
GMT Time	17. 48
(Adjusted GMT Date)	—

U.K. DAYLIGHT SAVING TIMES

Change at 2 a.m. except *= change at 3 a.m. **= change at 12 a.m.
1916-1920: Daylight Saving only observed in England and Scotland
1921-onwards: Daylight Saving also observed by N. Ireland, Channel Islands, Isle of Man and Wales

1916 (+1) 21/5-1/10
1917 (+1) 8/4-17/9
1918 (+1) 24/3-30/9
1919 (+1) 30/3-29/9
1920 (+1) 28/3-25/10
1921 (+1) 3/4-3/10
1922 (+1) 26/3-8/10
1923 (+1) 22/4-16/9
1924 (+1) 13/4-21/9
1925 (+1) 19/4-4/10
1926 (+1) 18/4-3/10
1927 (+1) 10/4-2/10
1928 (+1) 22/4-7/10
1929 (+1) 25/4-6/10
1930 (+1) 13/4-5/10
1931 (+1) 19/4-4/10
1932 (+1) 17/4-2/10
1933 (+1) 9/4-8/10
1934 (+1) 22/4-7/10
1935 (+1) 14/4-6/10
1936 (+1) 19/4-4/10
1937 (+1) 4/4-3/10
1938 (+1) 10/4-2/10
1939 (+1) 10/4-19/11
1940 (+1) 25/2-31/12**
1941 (+1) 1/1-31/12
1941 (+2) 4/5-10/8*
1942 (+1) 1/1-31/12
1942 (+2) 5/4-9/8*
1943 (+1) 1/1-31/12
1943 (+2) 4/4-15/8*
1944 (+1) 1/1-31/12
1944 (+2) 2/4-17/9*
1945 (+1) 1/1-7/10
1945 (+2) 2/4-15/7*
1946 (+1) 14/4-6/10
1947 (+1) 16/3-2/11
1947 (+2) 13/4-10/8
1948 (+1) 14/3-31/10
1949 (+1) 3/4-30/10
1950 (+1) 16/4-22/10
1951 (+1) 15/4-21/10
1952 (+1) 20/4-26/10
1953 (+1) 19/4-4/10
1954 (+1) 11/4-3/10
1955 (+1) 17/4-2/10
1956 (+1) 22/4-7/10
1957 (+1) 14/4-6/10
1958 (+1) 20/4-5/10
1959 (+1) 19/4-4/10
1960 (+1) 10/4-2/10
1961 (+1) 26/3-29/10
1962 (+1) 25/3-28/10
1963 (+1) 31/3-27/10
1964 (+1) 22/3-25/10
1965 (+1) 21/3-24/10
1966 (+1) 20/3-23/10
1967 (+1) 19/3-29/10
1968 18/2-1971 31/10 (+1)
1972 (+1) 19/3-29/10
1973 (+1) 18/3-28/10
1974 (+1) 17/3-27/10
1975 (+1) 16/3-26/10
1976 (+1) 21/3-24/10
1977 (+1) 20/3-23/10
1978 (+1) 19/3-29/10
1979 (+1) 18/3-28/10
1980 (+1) 16/3-26/10
1981 (+1) 29/3-25/10
1982 (+1) 28/2-24/10
1983 (+1) 27/3-23/10
1984 (+1) 25/3-28/10
1985 (+1) 31/3-27/10
1986 (+1) 30/3-26/10
1987 (+1) 29/3-25/10
1988 (+1) 27/3-23/10
1989 (+1) 21/3-29/10
1990 (+1) 25/3-29/10

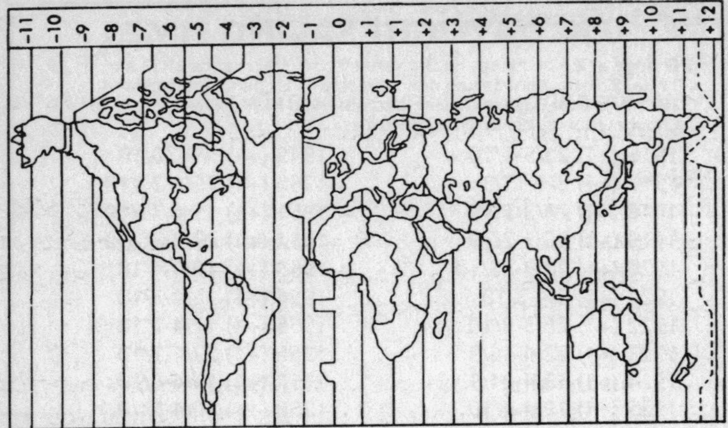

Time zones

cases (e.g. World War 2) some countries adopted 'Double Summer Time'. **Subtract** 2 hours from the adjusted time.

Example: on 19 June 1955, British Summer Time (+1) was in force. Therefore, for a local time of 05.45, subtract 1hr = 04.45 GMT.

Note: After performing these calculations, you may find that the GMT time carried the Birth Date back to the day before or forward to the day after. Either way, be sure to use this new GMT date for all further calculations – not the given birth date.

You find the Ascendant and Midheaven for the birth chart by looking up the Birth Time in a Table of Houses and reading off the relevant degrees. But there is just one snag.

All astrological tables use *Sidereal Time*, which is based on the rotation of the earth relative to the fixed stars and has been used by navigators for centuries. Your adjusted GMT Birth Time is *Tropical Time* ('Clock Time'), which is based on the rotation of the earth relative to the sun.

The difference between a day of Sidereal Time and a day of Tropical Time is 3min 54sec. The two are now so 'out of sync' that they bear no relation to one another, so the next step is to convert the *GMT Time at Birth* to the *Local Sidereal Time at Birth.*

Stage 2 – Convert GMT to Sidereal Time

Step 1:

Write down the GMT Time at Birth, then below it write the Latitude and Longitude of the Birth Place.

Step 2:

Turning to your Ephemeris, look up the Sidereal Time for Midnight (00.00) or Noon (12.00) at Greenwich on the Date of Birth, depending on which one the Ephemeris gives. If you had to adjust the Birth Date, use the adjusted date.

Step 3:

Work out the time difference in hours and minutes between the GMT Time at Birth and Midnight (or Noon, if you are using a Noon Ephemeris). This is called the *Interval.*

For a **Midnight** Ephemeris, **add** the Interval to the Sidereal time you have just looked up.

For a **Noon** Ephemeris, **subtract** the Interval if the GMT Time at Birth is **before** midday; if it is **after** midday, **add** it.

Step 4:

To allow for the slight variation between Sidereal and Tropical time during the Interval you have to make one further calculation – astrologers call it the *Acceleration on the Interval.*

Allow 1sec for every 6min of the Interval (i.e. 10sec per hour). As in Step 3, if you are using a **Midnight** Ephemeris, **add** this to your existing time. If you are using a **Noon** Ephemeris, **subtract** it for a time **before** midday; **add** it for a time **after** midday.

Step 5:

What you have before you is the *Sidereal Time at Greenwich at Birth.* This figure must now be adjusted to the *Local Sidereal Time at Birth.*

- First work out the distance in degrees Longitude between the Birth Place and Greenwich (0°).
- The sun takes 4min to move through 1° of Longitude. So, if you multiply the distance in degrees and minutes by 4, you get the time difference (in minutes and seconds) between the *Sidereal Time at Greenwich* and the *Local Sidereal Time.*

SOUTHERN LATITUDES

Tables of Houses are normally only given for Northern latitudes. If the Birth Place is in the Southern Hemisphere, find the Local Sidereal Time at Birth as if it were for the equivalent Northern Latitude, then:

- Add 12 hours. If the total comes to over 24, subtract 24.
- Turn to your Table of Houses and find the column giving the equivalent Northern Latitude.
- Look up the Ascendant and Midheaven, then simply change the signs to their opposites in the zodiac. Thus 3° 4' Gemini becomes 3° 4' Sagattarius; 23° 25' Leo becomes 23° 25' Aquarius.

This is called the *Longitude Equivalent in Time* (LET). (Time Change books have tables which get around the need to make this calculation.)

Example: To convert 112° 40' E to hours, minutes and seconds east of Greenwich:
112° x 4 = 448min = 7hr 28min
40' x 4 = 160sec = 2min 40sec
TOTAL = 7hr 30min 40sec

- If the Longitude of the Birth Place is West of Greenwich, **subtract** the LET from your adjusted GMT Time (see Stage 1); if the Longitude is East of Greenwich, **add** it.
- If the figure in front of you is over 24 hours, subtract 24.

You now have the *Local Sidereal Time at Birth.*

Stage 3 – Find Ascendant

Step 1:

Turn to your Table of Houses. Most Tables only give whole degrees of latitude, so pick the column that most nearly matches the Latitude of the Birth Place (e.g. for Paris, 48° 50'N = 49°N). This will give you the Ascendant to within 20', accurate enough for most purposes.

Work down the column to find the Local Sidereal times

TIME CALCULATION CHECKLIST

	H	M	S
STEP 1:			
• GMT Time at Birth			
• Latitude/Longitude of Birth Place			
STEP 2:			
• Sidereal Time at Midnight (Noon)			
STEP 3:			
• Interval between Sidereal time and Birth Time (+ or –)			
Result:			
STEP 4:			
• Acceleration on Interval (+ or –)			
STEP 5:			
• Sidereal Time at Greenwich at Birth			
• Longitude Equivalent in Time (+ or –)			
• Local Sidereal Time at Birth (subtract 24 hr if necessary)			

Use the checklist as a guide to completing Stage 2.

A filled in example is shown here.

	h	m	s
STEP 1:			
• GMT Time at Birth	17	48	
• Latitude/Longitude of Birth Place	48°50'N 2°20'E		
STEP 2:			
• Sidereal Time at Midnight (Noon)	2	12	21
STEP 3:			
• Interval between Sidereal Time and Birth Time (+ or –)	+5	48	00
RESULT:	8	00	21
STEP 4:			
• Acceleration on Interval (+ or –)	+0	00	58
STEP 5:			
• Sidereal Time at Greenwich at Birth	8	01	19
• Longitude Equivalent in Time (+ or –)	0	09	20
• Local Sidereal Time at Birth (subtract 24 hr if necessary)	8	10	39

immediately **preceding** and **following** the Local Sidereal Time at Birth. Then, work across and note the Ascendant and Midheaven degrees given for **both** times.

Step 2:

Subtract the earlier Sidereal Time from the later one and convert the result to seconds. Call this **A**.

Example:				
		08	*12*	*54*
	–	*08*	*08*	*44*
	=		*4*	*10 = 250sec*

Step 3:

Subtract the earlier Sidereal Time from the Local Sidereal Time at Birth and convert the result to seconds. Call this **B**.

Example:				
		08	*10*	*34*
	–	*08*	*08*	*44*
	=		*2*	*55 = 175sec*

Step 4:

Subtract the earlier Ascendant degree from the later one and convert the result to minutes ('). Call this **C**.

Example:				
		24°	*05'*	*Libra*
	–	*23°*	*20'*	*Libra*
	=	*0°*	*45'*	*Libra*

Step 5:

Subtract the earlier Midheaven degree from the later one and convert the result to minutes (as the Midheaven is given a degree at a time, the result is always 60). Call this **D**.

Step 6:

Using a calculator, multiply **B** x **C** and divide by **A**. Add the result to the earlier Ascendant degree (converted to minutes) to find the **approximate Ascendant degree at birth.**

Example (as above): If A = 250sec,
B = 175 sec and C = 45',
then 175(B) x 45(c)/
250(a) = 31.5' (say 32'). Add
this to the earlier Ascendant
degree (23° 20' Libra) = Asc 23° 52'.

Step 7:

Multiply **B** x **D** and divide by **A**. Add to the earlier Midheaven degree for the **exact Midheaven degree at Birth.**

> *Example (as above):*
> *175(B) x 60(D)/250(A) = 42°.*
> *Add this to the earlier Midheaven degree (0° Capricorn) = MC 5° 42' Capricorn.*

Once you have found the Ascendant and Midheaven degrees, all you need to complete the birth chart are the positions of the planets. You look these up against the Date of Birth (or the Adjusted Date of Birth, if you have had to adjust it after converting the time) in your Ephemeris. But because the planetary positions will be given for Midnight or Noon (depending on the Ephemeris), you must adjust them for the exact Time of Birth.

The outer planets, from Jupiter onwards, move so slowly that these adjustments are hardly critical. But the inner planets – especially the Moon – move at a much faster rate, and their motions through the day must be worked out more carefully if the birth chart is to give a true picture.

The method shown here does not give the exact positions (which involves a lot of complicated maths) but is accurate to within a few minutes of a degree.

The examples used are again based on the data entered in Stage 1, for a Birth Time of 18.48 (17:48 GMT) on 25 April 1970 in Paris.

Stage 4 – To find a Planet's position

Step 1:

Take a large sheet of paper and write down the Interval between the Time of Birth and Midnight (if you are using a Midnight Ephemeris) or Noon (for a Noon Ephemeris).

Step 2:

Consult the page in the Ephemeris for the Date of Birth and write down each planet's position on that date. To avoid confusion, note whether they are for Midnight or Noon.

Step 3:

So that you can work out how far each planet moves in one day, consult the Ephemeris again and write down the planets' positions for the following day.

> *Example - 25 April 1970:*
> *• At Noon on 25 April the Moon was at 22° 47' Sagittarius*
> *• At Noon on 26 April the Moon was at 6° 44' Capricorn*

Step 4:

For each planet, subtract the higher figure from the lower one to find the planet's Daily Motion for the day (remember, there are 60 minutes to a degree). Add 30° if the Moon moves into an adjacent sign.

> *Continuing the example:*
> *36° 44'*
> *– 22° 47'*
> *= 13° 57' (or 837')*

Step 5:

Using a calculator, divide the planet's Daily Motion by 24 to find its Hourly Motion.

> *Continuing the example:*
> *837'/24 = 34.9' per hour*

Step 6:

Using a calculator again, multiply the planet's Hourly Motion by the Interval between the Time of Birth and Midnight (Noon) to find its Motion During the Interval. (To avoid complex sums, round off the interval to the nearest quarter of an hour – e.g. 22min goes to 15min = 0.25hr; 23min goes to 30min = 0.5hr).

> *Continuing the example:*
> *• Interval = 5hr 48min (say, 5.75hr)*
> *• Hourly motion = 34.9'*
> *• Motion During Interval = 5.75 x 34.9 = 201' = 3° 21'*

PLANETARY POSITION CHECKLIST

Interval between Midnight (Noon) and Time of Birth	________
________'s position at End of Day (or Noon on day after/before birth)	________
________'s position at Start of Day (or Noon on day of birth)	________
________'s Daily Motion	________
________'s Hourly Motion	________
Motion During interval	________
Position at Start of Day (or Noon on Day of Birth)	________
Position at Time of Birth	________

PLANETARY POSITION CHECKLIST

Interval between Midnight (Noon) and Time of Birth	5hr 49 min (say 5.75hr)
VENUS 's position at End of Day (or Noon on day after/before birth)	27° 07' Taurus
VENUS 's position at Start of Day (or Noon on day of birth)	25° 54' Taurus
VENUS 's Daily Motion	1° 13' (73')
VENUS 's Hourly Motion	73/24 = 3' (approx)
Motion During interval	5.75 x 3' = 17.25' say 17
Position at Start of Day (or Noon on Day of Birth)	25° 54' Taurus
Position at Time of Birth	25°54' + 17' = 26° 11' Taurus

Continuing the example:

- *Position of the Moon at Noon on D.O.B = 22° 47' Sagittarius*
- *Add Motion During Interval (3° 21') = 26° 08' Sagittarius at exact Time of Birth (17.48 GMT on 25 April 1970)*

Step 7:

Returning to the planet's position for the Date of Birth, adjust it to allow for the Motion During the Interval. For a **Midnight** Ephemeris, **add** the Motion During the Interval; for a **Noon** Ephemeris, **subtract** it for a birth **before** noon, and **add** it for a birth after noon.

Repeat for Mercury, Venus and Mars not forgetting that where the Ephemeris shows a planet to be 'retrograde', you work backwards through the sign instead of forwards. You will notice that the remaining planets move such a small distance in a day that for most purposes there is no need to work out their Motion during the Interval.

Stage 5 - Complete the Birthchart

Having found all the planets' positions, enter them on the birth chart. At the same time, it is a good idea to check the aspects between the planets and fill these in on an *aspect* grid. Aspects are discussed in detail in the sections starting on page 34, 80 and 170. This helps to 'register' the aspects in your mind, which makes birth chart interpretation much easier to understand.

Aspect Grid

PLANET	POSITION		ASPECTS ☉	☽	☿	♀	♂	♃	♄	♅	♆	♇	ASPECT SYMBOLS
Sun		☉											Conjunction (0°) ☌
Moon		☽											Semi-sextile (30°) ⚺
Mercury		☿											Semi-square (45°) ∠
Venus		♀											Sextile (60°) ⚹
Mars		♂											Square (90°) □
Jupiter		♃											Trine (120°) △
Saturn		♄											Sesquiquadrate (135°) ⚼
Uranus		♅											Quincunx (150°) ⚻
Neptune		♆											Opposition (180°) ☍
Pluto		♇											
Asc		Asc											
MC		MC											

Calculating Transits

There is no limit to the scope of the study of transiting planets. For example, they can be used to look at important one-off events such as a wedding, or the start up of a business.

To find out what is in store, make a note of the exact time and place of the 'event' and draw up a chart as you would a birth chart. The new chart – which shows the positions of the transiting planets and house cusps – can be interpreted on its own, but it will be much more revealing if it is also compared with the birth charts of the people involved.

If, on the other hand, you simply want to know how the transiting planets will affect you on a given day, simply make a note of their positions from the Ephemeris, then compare these with the planetary positions and Angles in the birth chart.

Since the Moon can move up to 14° each day, you may want

to plot its position more accurately – especially if it changes sign during the day in question. In this case, simply repeat the procedure for working out its natal position.

Long-term Forecasting

Transits are also employed to look at long-term future trends. Single transits – when only one planet aspects a sensitive natal point – are not normally reliable indicators of major change. What you must look for are *complexes of transits* – build-ups of astrological activity around natal planets or Angles (p. 40), over say, a period of about a year.

Over any 12-month period there will usually be several dates when this activity is at its most intense. These dates mark the times when significant events are most likely to occur.

However, in any single month, the transiting planets can make anything from 30 to 40 aspects to the natal planets and Angles, and most of these – involving the inner planets – will be only fleeting. Since it is extremely time-consuming to work out all the transits for a year, the usual procedure is to plot the transits of the slower-moving outer planets (from Jupiter to Pluto) and then see how transits from the inner planets tie in.

If you have a computer, all the commercial astrology programmes offer transit calculation as an optional – and indispensable – extra. Calculating transits by hand is not difficult, but it most certainly requires a fair amount of time and patience!

Step 1

Turn to your Ephemeris and on a separate piece of paper note the distances travelled by the outer planets over the next 12 months. Many astrologers also mark the positions of the transiting planets on the outside of the birth chart wheel (writing the letter 'T' before their symbols), as this reminds them which houses the planets are transiting at any one time of the year. (See pages 30 and 35 for symbols.)

Remember that when planets go retrograde, their positions at that moment may be further around the zodiac than at the end of the chosen 12-month period. Make a note if this is the case.

Example – movement of
outer planets Jan – Dec 1991

♃: 11°♌56' – 14°♍38'

♄: 25°♑43' – 5°♒55'
(Retrograde 17 May @ 6°♒50')

♅: 9°♑46' – 13°♑43'
(Retrograde 18 April @ 13°♑49')

♆: 14°♑ 8' – 16°♑14'
(Retrograde 19 April @ 16°♑46')

♇ 19°♏36' – 22°♏6'

Step 2

Work out the aspects (p. 34) that each transiting outer planet will make to the natal planets and Angles over this period. If you have a computer, you will be able to calculate the minor aspects as well; if not, concentrate on the major aspects and only turn to the minor ones if you need additional information.

Example – major aspects of
transiting Saturn only
Jan – Dec 1991

T♄ : □ ♆ ;
☍ ♅ ;
☍ ♃ ;
△ ♇
then T♄ turns
retrograde and
returns to ☍ ♃

Step 3

Returning to your Ephemeris, check through it to find out on which dates these aspects occur and how long they last. Allow an average orb of 1° each side of the exact aspect, but increase this slightly if several transiting planets combine to aspect a sensitive natal point at roughly the same time.

Example – dates of transiting
Saturn's major aspects
Jan – Dec 1991

T♄□♆ (22/12/90) – 8/1/91
T♄☍♅ (27/12/90) – 12/1/91
T♄☍♃ 8/2/91 – 27/2/91
T♄△♀ 18/4/91 – 15/6/91
T♄℞ ☍♃ 13/8/91 – 27/9/91
T♄D ☍ 12/10/91 – 24/11/91

NB ℞ = retrograde

Step 4

By this stage you should have a clear picture of the general pattern and timing of outer planet transits to the birth chart. Now check your Ephemeris to see if any of the transiting inner planets join forces with the transiting outer planets during these times. Pay particular attention to the Sun and Mars, as these two seem to play a critical role in the precise timing of events.

Example – trigger aspects
involving transiting Saturn
for January 1991

Between Jan 1–2
T☽ : 25°–26° ♋
T♀ : 25°–26° ♑

T♀ ☌ T♄ □ ♆ ☍ ♅

[T☽ ☍ T♀
☍ T♄
☌ ♅] □♆

Here, you can see that although transiting Saturn squares natal Neptune while opposing natal Uranus during early

January, the critical time is the 1st, when the transiting Moon conjuncts natal Uranus, squares natal Neptune and opposes transiting Saturn, and is also joined by an opposition from transiting Venus.

Calculating Progressions

Once you are familiar with the notion that, astrologically speaking, 24 hours equals one year, 'day-for-year' progressions are fairly easy to calculate.

Stage 1 – Find Progressed Date

Before you draw up a progressed chart for a particular year, you must establish the Progressed Date – the day equivalent to the year in question. For example, if you want to find the positions of the progressed planets for the 21st year (that is, between the 20th and 21st birthday) of someone born on 25 April 1970, you convert the subject's age in years (20) into days (20) and then add them to the original date of birth to give a Progressed Date of 15 May 1990.

Stage 2 – Progress the Chart

Once you have established the Progressed Date, the simplest way of calculating progressions by hand is to use a technique called the *Solar Arc Method.*

Step 1: Find Perpetual Date

Although the planetary positions given in the Ephemeris for the Progressed Date apply to the year in question, unless you were born at Noon (Midnight) at that date, they do not correspond exactly to your birthday but to a date some time before or after (remember, in the day-for-year method 1 day = 1 year, so 1 hour of time = 15 days and 4 minutes = 1 day).

The simple way round this problem is to convert the GMT time interval between Noon (or Midnight, depending on the Ephemeris) on your birthday into days (see box 'Interval Conversion, p. 26), then add or subtract the result from your birthday to find what astrologers call the *Perpetual Date.*

Having done this, you can look up the planetary positions given in the Ephemeris for Noon (or Midnight) on any Progressed Date, knowing exactly what date of the year (the Perpetual Date) these positions correspond to.

> *Example – to convert 17.48 GMT on 25 April to its Perpetual Noon Date:*
> *Interval after Noon = 5hr 48min*
> *(Consulting table) 5hr = 75 days;*
> *48min = 12 days*
> *Total Difference = 87 days*
> *For p.m. Birth Time, subtract from Birth Date (25 April) to give a Perpetual Noon Date of 28 January.*

Step 2: Progress the Angles

Although the Perpetual Date takes care of the positions of the progressed planets, it does not progress the Angles (p.40). Using the Solar Arc Method, all you have to do is progress the Midheaven by the distance *(arc)* travelled by the Sun from its natal position to its noon position on the Progressed Date.

> *Example – to calculate the progressed MC and Ascendant for the twentieth year of someone born on 25 April 1970*
> *Progressed Date = 15 May 1990*
> *Sun's position at Noon GMT on 15 May 1990 = 24° 14' Taurus*
> *Sun's position at Noon GMT on 25 April 1970 = 4° 51' Taurus*
> *Difference = 19° 23'*

Add the difference to the natal Midheaven degree to find the progressed Midheaven.

Now turn to your Table of Houses. Find the degree of the progressed Midheaven, and under the latitude of the Birth Place, read off the corresponding Ascendant degree. This is the progressed Ascendant for the year in question.

Step 3: Progress the Moon

The Moon covers from 12 to 14° in a day which means that in a progressed year, it will make several aspects to both the natal

INTERVAL CONVERSION

Use the table below to convert the time interval between Noon (or Midnight) and the Time of Birth into months and days:

24 hours = 12 months

2 hours = 1 month

1 hour = 15 days

4 minutes = 1 day

1 minute = 6 hours

Remember, for a Birth Time **before** Noon, **add** the converted total to the Date of Birth to find the Perpetual Noon Date; for a Birth Time **after** Noon, **subtract** the total.

and the progressed planets and Angles. To find out when these occur, you must calculate the Moon's average motion, month by month over the progressed year.

For example, to find the progressed Moon's monthly positions for the year in question:

- Enter the Moon's Noon position on 15 May 1970 = 16° 48' Virgo
- Enter the Moon's Noon position for the next day, 16 May 1970 = 28° 57' Virgo
- Subtract the first figure from the second to find the distance travelled by the Moon in one day (i.e. one year) = 12° 09'
- Convert the degrees to minutes = 729'
- Divide by 12 to find the Moon's average monthly motion: = 60,75'
  = roughly 1° 01' per month.
- Bearing in mind that the Noon position of the Moon on 15 May 1970 corresponds to January 28 1990, calculate its position for the 28th of each month by adding 1° 01' to each previous total: 28 January 1990: 16° 48' Virgo 28 February 1990: 17° 48' Virgo 28 March 1990: 18° 49' Virgo and so on through to 28 January 1991: 28° 57' Virgo.

ANOTHER METHOD

Another way of drawing up a progressed chart – known as the *Sidereal Time Method* – is to replace the Sidereal Time at Noon (or Midnight if you are using a Midnight Ephemeris) on your day of birth with the Sidereal Time at Noon (or Midnight) on the day of your Progressed Date and then draw up the chart as you would an ordinary birth chart.

This produces very detailed results, since it allows you to progress the house cusps, but it is extremely laborious to do by hand. Unless you have a computer, it is advisable to stick to the Solar Arc Method.

Calculating the Aspects

Once you have worked out and entered the positions of the progressed planets and Angles on the birth chart, you can plot the aspects in the usual way. Remember, you are looking for aspects from progressed planets and Angles to other progressed planets, as well as aspects from progressed planets and Angles to their natal counterparts.

The Birthchart: Basic Concepts

Birth chart interpretation is very similar to detective work. A large number of clues need to be sifted through and analysed before they can be assembled into a pattern of possible trends.

However, unlike the detective, the astrologer cannot hope to come up with a final solution to a problem. The birth chart is best seen as a blueprint of your potential, but it is up to you how that potential is expressed. It is, of course, possible to work out your own birth chart, using tables of planetary positions and various mathematical calculations; but many people find the process laborious, and prefer to send off their birth details to a company that offers a computerized birth chart service. For those who have personal computers, there are a number of software programmes, available through specialist shops and magazines, that will do all the necessary calculations.

Whether you have had your birth chart cast by a professional astrologer, sent off for a computerized chart, or set it up yourself, it is well worth trying your hand at astrological interpretation. Not only will it help you make sense of your own chart and give you the chance to compare your skills with those of the professionals, but you may well progress to interpreting the birth charts of other people.

Unlike astronomy, which takes the Sun as the centre of our solar system, astrology looks at the skies purely from the point of view of the Earth, tracing the apparent movements of the planets around it.

This does not mean that astrology dismisses the findings of astronomy. It simply asks us to look at the cosmos through a different lens; one through which our thoughts and actions are seen as part of a larger pattern of events.

The Concept of the Zodiac

As seen from Earth, the journey of the Sun across the heavens appears to steer a course through a broad circular band – approximately 18° of latitude wide – which encircles our planet. This imaginary wheel is referred to as the 'zodiac belt', and contains the 12 constellations of stars that give their names to the astrological signs. It is these constellations which form the visible backcloth to the Sun's apparent path through the zodiac.

Astrology divides this path – known as the 'ecliptic' – into 12 equal sections of 30°, which are referred to as the signs of the zodiac. These divisions do not correspond to the size or the positions of the constellations bearing the zodiac names, however. They are purely symbolic, marking out the seasonal cycles of the Sun.

While the Sun acts as the astrological timekeeper, taking a year to pass through all the signs of the zodiac, the Moon and the eight planets also have their own cycles. They appear to move through the heavens very close to the ecliptic, so that the zodiac is also a reference grid for their positions. Their speeds vary enormously: the Moon takes approximately 28 days to pass through all the signs; while Pluto, the slowest-moving planet, takes about 210 years.

Map of the Heavens

The birth chart is a personal map of the heavens as they were at the exact time and place of your birth. It is drawn as a circle divided into 12 segments and shows the precise positions, in degrees, of the Sun, the Moon and the planets in the signs. The areas where the planet-sign combinations fall in the chart – known as Houses – are determined by the Ascendant or rising sign, which is the degree of the ecliptic that was rising on the eastern horizon when you were born. Once this point or angle has been established, all the positions of planets and Houses can be entered on the chart.

Principles of Interpretation

There are four fundamental components which make up the basis for chart interpretation.

1. The eight planets, the Sun and the Moon, each of which represents a particular kind of energy which manifests itself in the individual as instinctive drives.
2. The 12 Sun signs, which modify the way a planetary energy expresses itself. For example, Venus in a birth chart signifies the way in which an individual forms close relationships with others. If it is placed in Aries the sign will bring out spontaneous and fiery qualities in friendship and love affairs. But Venus in Taurus will manifest itself in a slower, more sensual manner.
3. The 13 Houses, which indicate the main areas of the individual's life where all this activity will find an outlet. As with the signs, not all houses share the same level of importance in a chart. Some are 'empty' with no planets in them, others may be occupied by more than one planet. The Ascendant marks the beginning of the first house and, according to the commonly used 'Equal House' system, the other houses follow on at intervals of 30°. So if, for example, your Ascendant is 25° Libra, your second house will begin at 25° Scorpio, your third house at 25° Sagittarius, and so on through the zodiac.
4. The Aspects, which represent the geometrical angles that

the planets make to one another as seen from Earth. In the birth chart, they signify dynamic points of contact between two different types of energy, bringing either harmony or challenge to those areas of life connected with the planets concerned.

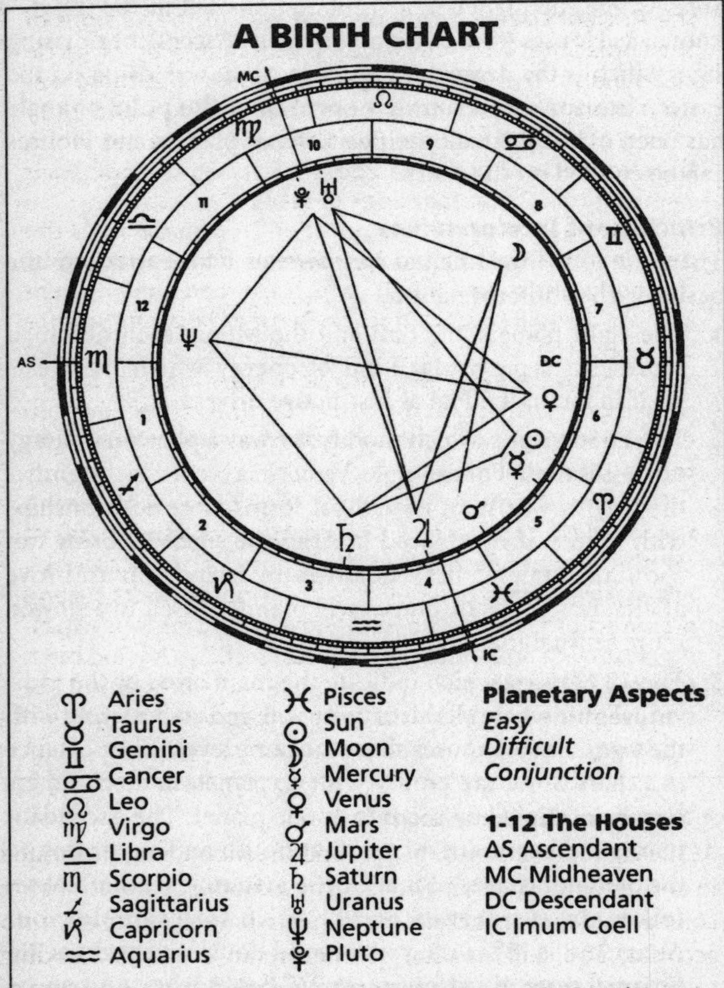

You can learn to fill in your own birth chart, placing the planets in the signs and houses, and drawing in the Ascendant and Midheaven.

ASTROLOGY SINCE ANCIENT TIMES

While the earliest astrological records are some 5,000 years old, the earliest known horoscope, or astrological chart, is a Babylonian one dating from 409 BC.

But it was not until the 3rd and 2nd centuries BC that the Ancient Greeks developed the idea of the 12 signs of the zodiac that we know today. (Zodiac is Greek for 'circle of animals'). The Greeks of this time noted that there was a relationship between people's personalities and their season of birth. They identified 12 types of character, which they connected to the 12 zodiac signs which took their names from 12 constellations of stars.

The influence of astrology faded in Europe with the decline of the classical world, however. It was attacked by the early Christian Church, which claimed that it went against the will of God. But the Persians kept the science alive. By the 8th and 9th centuries AD, it had been absorbed by the expanding Islamic cultures and was in turn passed on, via Spain, to the rest of Europe. Astrology then enjoyed a revival which lasted from the early Middle Ages to the 16th century.

The scientific discoveries of the 'Age of Reason', during the late 17th century and 18th century, conspired against anything that smacked of mysticism. And astrology's association with the occult arts contributed to its second major eclipse. Yet by the mid-19th century, serious astrology was once again popular, interest possibly having been sparked off by the discovery of the planets Uranus in 1781 and Neptune in 1848. This revival prepared the ground for today's reawakened interest in astrology.

A Picture of the Personality

As the eight planets, and the Sun and the Moon, may be located in any of the 12 signs and houses, the various permutations are considerable, even before the aspects have been taken into account. The skill and fun of interpretation lies in blending together all these various factors to form a complete picture of the personality; and you will learn more of how to set about this in the next section about analysing the birth chart.

Zodiac Wheel

If you visit an astrologer for a chart reading or write off for a computer analysis, you are unlikely to receive a copy of the zodiac wheel itself. You may be given a list of planet positions on the front page of the computer character analysis, or these may appear as marginal annotations in the text. However, this can be very frustrating if you decide you would like to learn more about your own chart and the workings of astrology in general, for the zodiac wheel provides a very graphic and compact picture of all the information you need.

One solution to the problem is to transfer the information to a birth chart yourself. There are many different ways to present information on a zodiac wheel, but the method described here is probably the simplest for the beginner.

Blank Charts

You can start with blank birth chart sheets, which are easily bought from 'occult' bookshops, and are very cheap. Alternatively, you can make up your own chart by copying the drawing below. You will need a ruler, a compass to draw the various circles, and a 5-6 inch/cm protractor to mark off the degrees of the outer circle – 360 in all, with every fifth one emphasized to make it easier when working out the positions of the Ascendant, Midheaven and House divisions (cusps). Remember that each sign takes up exactly 30° of the zodiac wheel, although these cusps are usually marked in the blank birth charts.

Step 1: The Signs

It is simplest to fill in the details of your chart by entering the signs first in the outer section of the wheel. Traditionally, astrologers begin with the Ascendant, or Rising sign – Scorpio, in our example – placing it in the first section below the horizontal line to the left of the zodiac wheel.

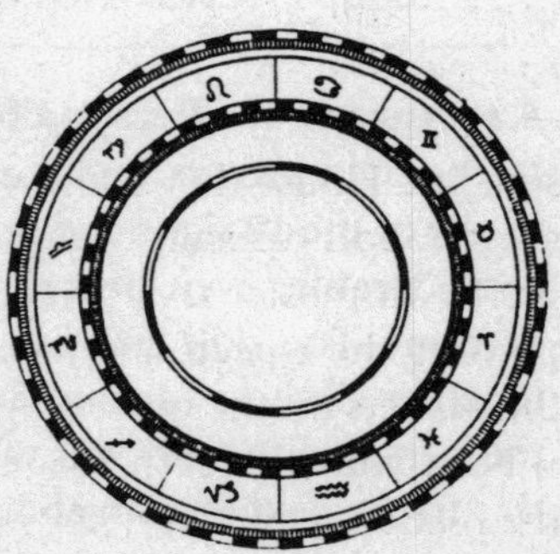

The other signs are then filled in anti-clockwise in their chronological order, so the second section is Sagittarius, the third Capricorn and so on.

Step 2: The Houses

The next stage is to draw in the Houses. Again, you should start with the Ascendant, which marks the beginning, or cusp, of the First House, and in our chart is at 17 degrees and 50 minutes of Scorpio – written 17° 50'. Place your ruler as near to the 17–18 point of this sign as possible and line it up with exactly the same degree in the opposite sign of Taurus. You can check that you are doing this correctly, as the ruler should pass directly across the central point of the wheel.

Start to draw a line between these two points, but leave the space in the centre blank. This process can be repeated for the remaining Houses, and for the sake of clarity, it helps to number the Houses as you go along in the inner ring. As we are using the Equal House System, each House cusp is 30° from the last, so the cusp for the Second House is at 17° 50' Sagittarius, and its opposite – the Eighth – at 17° 15' Gemini. When the Houses have been entered, fill in the Midheaven and its opposite point the IC, in the same way. This axis and the Ascendant–Descendant axis are very important in a birth chart interpretation and most astrologers give them a strong visual emphasis by adding arrow heads to the Ascendant and Midheaven to make them easy to find.

Step 3: The Planets

In our sample chart (p.30), the Sun, for instance, is at 19° 33' Aries and in the Sixth House. You should place this and the other planets in the largest ring of the wheel, so that both the sign and House they fall in can be easily identified. If you find the symbols difficult to draw, practise on a note pad and you will soon master their shapes. It also helps when it comes to plotting the aspects if you mark approximately the position of the planets on the inner ring of the wheel.

Next you will learn how to determine the aspects between the planets, and what they mean.

The Aspects

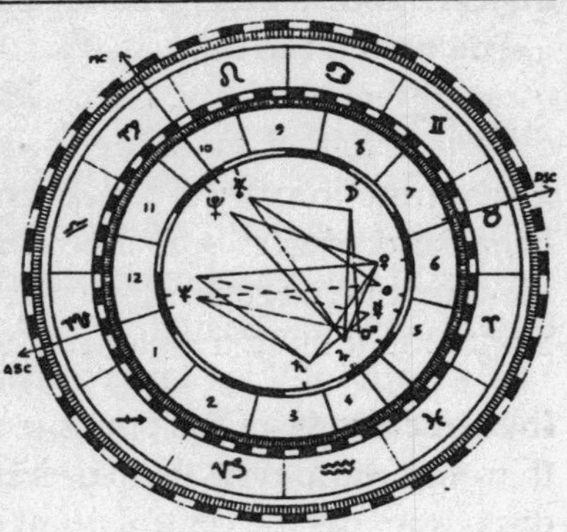

The final stage in preparing your chart is to determine the aspects. These are angular relationships between the planets, which combine their energies to create dynamic patterns of expression. They point to areas of potential harmony or tension in your personality. If the birth time is known to be accurate, aspects to the Ascendant and Midheaven are also important. Not all the planets make aspects to each other – just the ones that are certain distances apart.

Some computerized birth charts give the aspects in a box diagram, while others will list them as marginal annotations. Like the signs and planets, they have their own set of symbols. In the blank birth chart forms that can be bought from specialist bookshops, an aspect grid is provided for the aspect symbols to be filled in against the appropriate planets.

At this stage we will deal only with the category traditionally known as the 'major' aspects (see also p. 80). The following descriptions opposite show the symbol, the exact degree and the distance in degrees (known as the 'orb') allowed either side of the exact degree for each aspect. For example, in our sample chart (above) the Sun and Mercury are both in Aries, about 7.5° apart. They do not make an exact aspect – they would both have to occupy the same degree and minute of the sign to do that – but they fall within the allowable orb for a 'conjunction'.

Understanding Aspects

These are the general rules for interpreting the aspects, although the nature of the planets in aspect to each other must also be considered. Any contact between Saturn and Pluto, for example, whether a conjunction, trine or square is regarded by most astrologers as very testing. Yet the 'difficult' aspects (i.e. square, or opposition) between, say, Venus and Jupiter – two planets that harmonize well – are not thought to be too serious.

The aspects can be plotted across the centre of the birth chart using different coloured pens. Planets opposite or square each other are joined by a line in one colour (usually red); the in-conjunctions by a broken line in the same colour. For trines and sextiles you should use a different coloured pen (perhaps blue or green). Conjunctions can be marked by a small black loop joining the planets.

Interpreting the Chart

It is important to remember that what you are aiming for in a

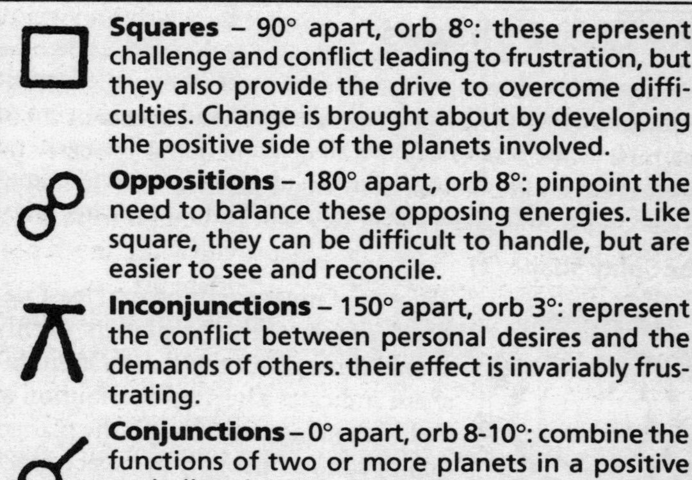

Squares – 90° apart, orb 8°: these represent challenge and conflict leading to frustration, but they also provide the drive to overcome difficulties. Change is brought about by developing the positive side of the planets involved.

Oppositions – 180° apart, orb 8°: pinpoint the need to balance these opposing energies. Like square, they can be difficult to handle, but are easier to see and reconcile.

Inconjunctions – 150° apart, orb 3°: represent the conflict between personal desires and the demands of others. their effect is invariably frustrating.

Conjunctions – 0° apart, orb 8-10°: combine the functions of two or more planets in a positive or challenging way, according to sign and house position, the planets involved and the type of aspects these planets make to any others, if any.

Trines – 120° apart, orb 8°: usually considered to be a helpful combination, but can also indicate the path of least resistance in people who find it difficult to motivate themselves.

Sextiles – 60° apart, orb 8°: like the trines they usually emphasize the constructive qualities of the planets, although they do require some effort.

chart interpretation is an understanding of what makes the person concerned behave the way he or she does. This can be a fascinating and, at times, baffling exercise, for you have to bring together the often contradictory data supplied by the planets in the signs, their house positions, and the aspects between the planets into a recognisable and coherent whole. Like the detective gathering forensic evidence, you are looking for motives.

It is always helpful to look at the general impression a chart creates before breaking it down into its component parts. There are in fact several patterns that emerge at first sign which can tell you a great deal about the basic personality type of the individual under the astrological microscope.

The Chart Shapes

Once you have drawn up a chart, the most immediate impact is the shape that the planets in their signs and houses seem to form. There are seven principal shapes and they offer a general insight into the psychological make-up and expected life experiences of the individual. Most charts fall into these categories.

The Splay Shape (1)

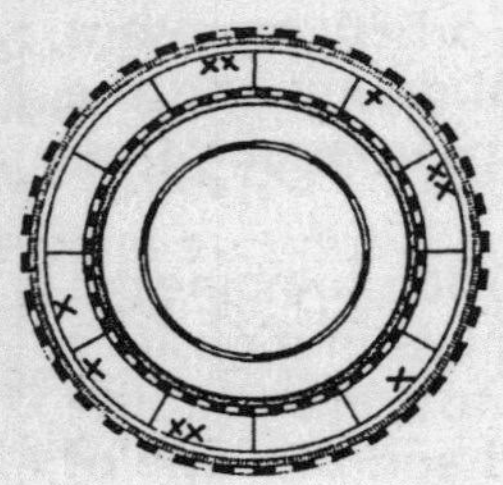

This is the most common and least defined shape, with the planets evenly spread throughout the chart. Often this shape indicates a healthy distribution of abilities and activities, but if the planets do not connect strongly by aspect, especially to the Ascendant and Midheaven, the individual may have difficulty in bringing them out.

The Bowl Shape (2)

All the planets fall within one half of the chart. If the planets are placed in the top half of the chart – taking the Ascendant–Descendant axis as the dividing line – the focus is on the conscious, external activities of the individual. In the bottom half, the experiences are much more subjective, bringing personal, unconscious issues to the surface.

The left side hemisphere – divided by the Midheaven-IC axis – is concerned with taking direct control of one's destiny, while the right side is associated more with the influence others have on your life.

The Bucket Shape (3)

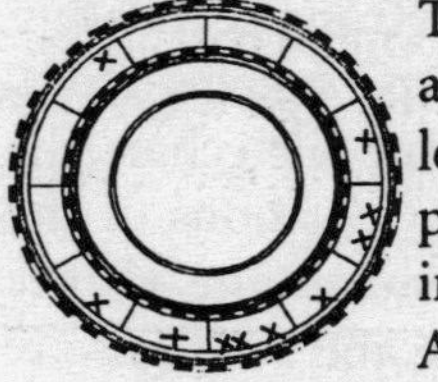

This is like the Bowl except that one planet, or a conjunction of planets, forms a 'handle'. It is less one-sided than the Bowl, as the handle provides access to the empty half, often creating a funnel of highly concentrated energy. Aspects from the other planets to the handle will show how and where this energy will manifest itself.

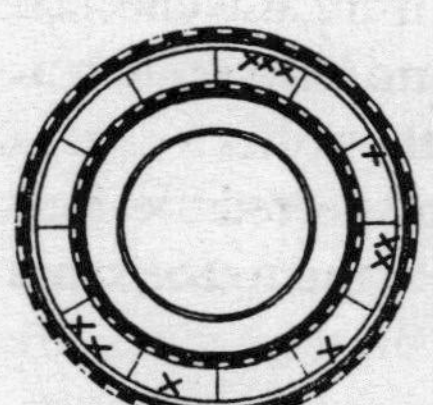

The Locomotive Shape (4)

One-third of the chart or the equivalent of four consecutive signs, contains no planets. The empty section indicates the vulnerable part of the personality which may need careful attention.

The Bundle Shape (5)

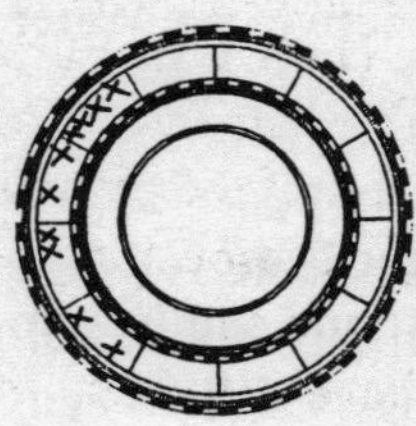

This is the opposite to the Locomotive with all planets contained within one-third, or 120°, of the chart. This is a fairly rare combination, but people with this shape tend to have highly focused objectives at the expense of any others. It can be the mark of the highly-strung genius, or the obsessive personality!

The Sling Shape (6)

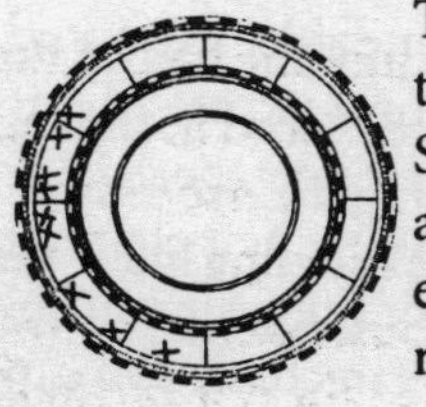

This is the Bundle with a planet, or conjunction, outside the concentrated section. The Sling is similar to the Bucket, except that the attention on the separate planet or planets is even more intense. People with this configuration are often driven by a vocational calling.

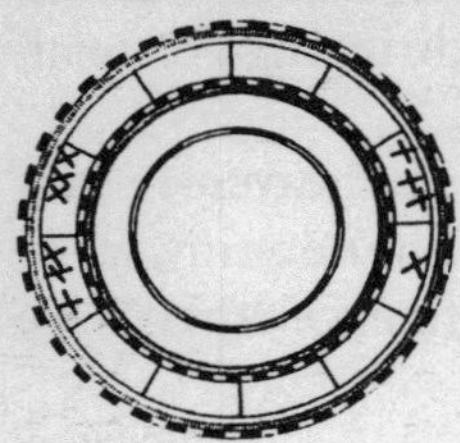

The See Saw Shape (7)

As the name suggests, this shape consists of two planetary groupings opposite each other. Behaviour patterns can fluctuate abruptly from one group to the other, often resulting in contradictory actions.

Positive and Negative

Psychology tests have shown that there is a strong correlation between the positive signs and the extrovert personality types, the negative signs and introverted types. In the birth chart, the planets in the signs, together with the sign positions of the Ascendant and Midheaven, are counted to find out the balance between introversion and extroversion. Fire and Air signs are positive, while the Earth and Water signs are negative.

The planets, the Ascendant and Midheaven are also checked to see how they break down into the elements (also known as Triplicities) and qualities (or Quadruplicities).

The elements – Fire, Earth, Air and Water – describe four basic psychological types and the signs belonging to the same element all share something in common: the Fire signs are restless, energetic, optimistic and assertive; the Earth signs, practical, sensual, persevering and reserved; the Air signs, objective, sociable, independent and mentally active; the Water signs, emotional, sensitive and intuitive.

The Qualities

The three qualities – Cardinal, Fixed and Mutable – define how we act and react to situations, although this will be coloured by the element to which each sign belongs. Cardinal signs are enterprising, self-motivated and like to initiate and involve themselves in projects. Fixed signs consolidate what the Cardinal signs begin: they are determined, dependable, loyal and often resistant to change. Mutable signs, by contrast, are adaptable, flexible, unpredictable and stimulated by new ideas.

Once you have accounted for all the planets by their element and quality you will have a strong overview of the distribution of the basic psychological categories in the birth chart. You can look immediately to see whether there is, for instance, an undue emphasis on planets in Negative, Earth, or Fixed signs. This would suggest a purposeful, reflective and probably stubborn individual who might find it hard to change his or her ways. Similarly, you may find that there are few or no planets belonging to a particular element or quality. Without going into any detailed chart analysis, you can establish early on likely strengths and weaknesses by looking at these patterns.

	FIRE	**EARTH**	**AIR**	**WATER**
CARDINAL	Aries	Capricorn	Libra	Cancer
FIXED	Leo	Taurus	Aquarius	Scorpio
MUTABLE	Sagittarius	Virgo	Gemini	Pisces
	POSITIVE	**NEGATIVE**	**POSITIVE**	**NEGATIVE**

Positive and Negative signs

The Distribution of Elements

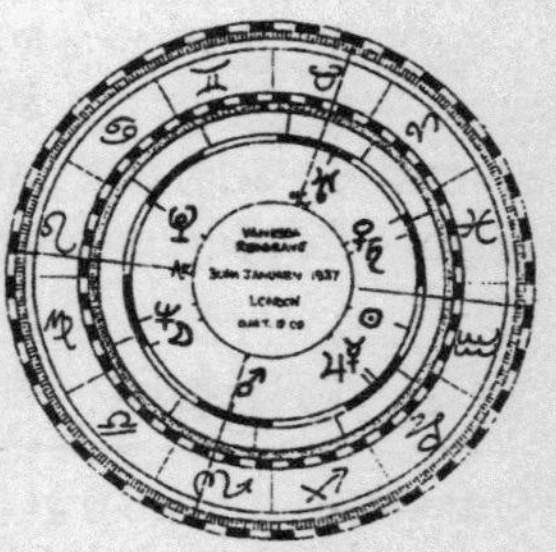

Vanessa Redgrave's chart shows a heavy emphasis on Earth (five planets plus the MC) and Water (four planets), with a corresponding lack of Fire and Air. Known as much for her politics as her acting, the distribution of Elements suggest that she is motivated more by unconscious personal feelings than by the high-minded idealism associated with her rational Aquarian Sun.

The Locomotive Shape

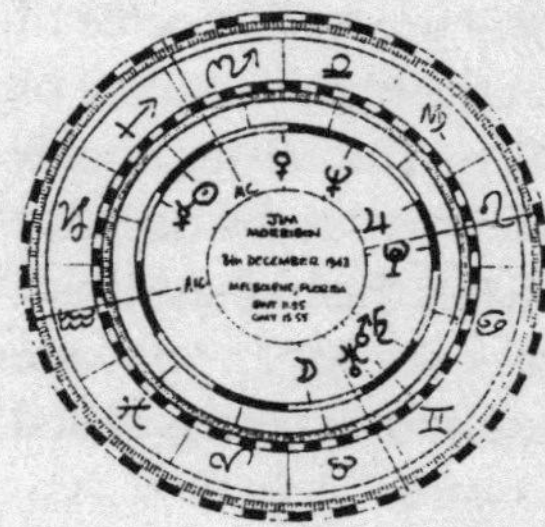

The late Jim Morrison, who was lead singer of the Doors, has a dynamic Locomotive shaped chart with restless Mercury leading the other planets. The empty quarter between his Third and Eleventh Houses suggests that in spite of his talent and huge zest for life, he lacked any sense of destiny and could never quite come to terms with who he was or what he was supposed to be doing.

The Distribution of Qualities

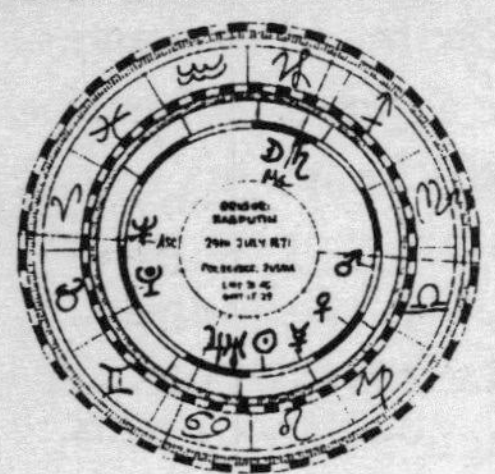

In keeping with his reputation, Rasputin's date, time and even place of birth are shrouded in mystery. The most reliable data available shows five planets plus the Ascendant and MC in Cardinal signs, revealing a high degree of self-motivation. It would certainly account for his remarkable rise from Siberian peasant to healer and political adviser to the Russian court.

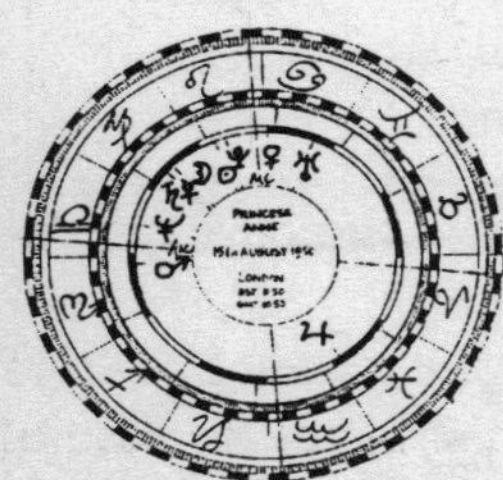

The Sling Shape

Princess Anne has a sling shape chart with Jupiter as the focus for the other planets. This signifies a powerful need to find a specific outlet for her highly charged personality – almost as if what she does chooses her, rather than the other way round! Clearly, her passion for horses and dedication to the plight of children in need reflect this 'driven' quality.

The Angles

Our time and place of birth are vital pieces of data for astrologers. As well as enabling them to plot precisely where the planets and signs fall in our birth chart, they establish the positions of four especially sensitive points – commonly known as the *angles*.

The first two angles are the *Ascendant* – the exact degree of the sign rising over the eastern horizon at the time and place of birth – and the *Descendant* – its opposite on the western horizon. The third is the *Midheaven* (often referred to by its Latin name *meridian coeli* or simply MC), which is the highest point directly above the horizon. The fourth is the MC's opposite number on the lowest point between the horizon, and is called the *IC* (*immeum coeli*).

Traditionally the Ascendant is held to be the most significant, followed by the Midheaven. But it is also worth considering

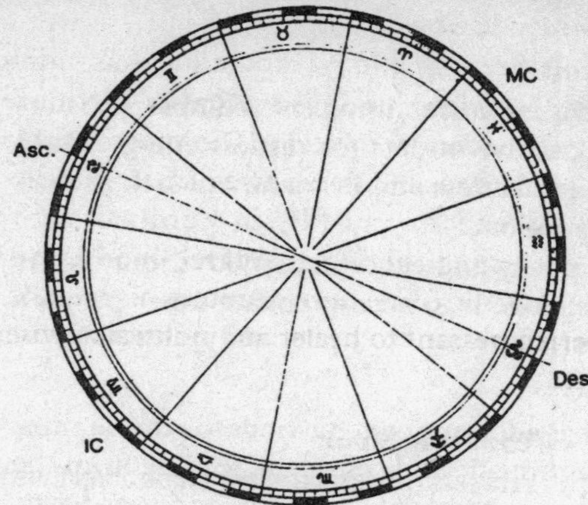

The four Angles of the birth chart – Ascendant, Descendant, Midheaven and IC. Together, they represent the chart's most sensitive points.

the other angles, as together they seem to symbolize heightened points of self-awareness.

The Ascendant represents our instinctive sense of self and also the way that we try to express it – the image we have of ourselves and how we present it to others. This applies particularly to the first impressions we create. Generally, the Ascendant governs the most visible aspects of our personality – and according to some astrologers, our physical appearance too.

The Descendant represents our sense of self in relation to others. It shows what we seek – whether consciously or otherwise – from relationships, and determines which side of our personality will be brought out through them. It also governs how we react to relationships, and the environment in which they are likely to take place.

The Midheaven represents our sense of self as we would want to impress it on the outside world. It shows the qualities we admire and strive to develop as we mature; the direction we wish to take; our need for status, recognition and achievement; our ideal career or vocation.

The IC signifies the exact opposite: our innermost, least consciously acknowledged sense of self, and where we are coming from. In adults it often points to past influences such as home and family background, defining our sense of 'belonging' and deepest motivations.

Aries

Ascendant/Descendant

Typical traits: decisive, impatient, impulsive, combative, assertive. Needs to find creative outlets for restless energy. Once channelled, actions are fearless and inspired, but lack of purpose can lead to frustration.

Dangers: being too pushy and egocentric. With Libra on the Descendant, the challenge is to accommodate other people's feelings and points of view.

Midheaven/IC

Looks to take initiative, adopting own methods to achieve aims. Likes to be seen as optimistic and confident, leading from the front. Can come across as arrogant, impulsive and over-hasty. With a Libra IC, the family background may provide the equilibrium for Arian individuality to flower.

Taurus

Ascendant/Descendant

Typical traits: cautious, purposeful, practical, reliable, industrious. Needs to create a secure framework within which to achieve aims. Enormously patient and persevering, but can become overly fond of routine.

Dangers: lazy habits and possessiveness. Scorpio on the Descendant calls for outmoded patterns of behaviour to be transformed.

Midheaven/IC

Seeks dignity, tangible results and often public recognition. Sees patience, hard work and, above all, professional security as virtues. Can be too conservative, inflexible or stubborn. Scorpio IC stresses the need to look inwards – possibly to face childhood issues – to gain emotional security.

Gemini

Ascendant/Descendant

Typical traits: inquisitive, sociable, versatile, ingenious, analytical. Needs constant and varied stimuli to occupy the mind. Excellent at communicating and people-handling, but can be too talkative and superficial.

Dangers: diffusing energies by being too easily diverted. Sagittarius on the Descendant teaches the value of breadth and depth of vision.

Midheaven/IC

Drawn by an urge to explore as many outlets as possible. Likes to be at the centre of activity without being tied to it. Often accused of a butterfly mentality and lack of purpose. Sagittarius IC can supply enough breadth of vision – either through travel or from childhood influences – to fuel big ambitions.

Cancer

Ascendant/Descendant

Typical traits: intuitive, tenacious, protective, sympathetic, shrewd. Needs to use acute sensitivity in a nurturing rather than a defensive way. Supportive when helping others, but may be reluctant to unburden own emotions.

Dangers: excessive irascibility and moodiness. Capricorn Descendant provides the strength to contain wildly fluctuating feelings.

Midheaven/IC

Tends to develop a tough outer shell to protect sensitivity, and is intensely aware of public reputation. Wants responsibility, but is wary of limelight. Tenacious and supportive, but may cling to outworn values and harbour resentment. Capricorn IC may mean that true vocation is shaped by limitations of one's background.

Leo

Ascendant/Descendant

Typical traits: authoritative, generous, dramatic, enthusiastic, dignified. Must feel appreciated to make most of creative flair. Lack of recognition of leadership qualities may sap confidence.

Dangers: self-importance and tyranny. Aquarius Descendant brings a wider lens to self-centred views, plus the ability to give without expecting any return.

Midheaven/IC

Seeks admiration, but can devote enormous energy and organising abilities to realising ambitions. Believes in self-promotion and glamour, but others may see it as rampant egotism. Aquarius IC suggests aspects of the home background are unconventional. Eventually, human issues must be included in personal ambitions.

Virgo

Ascendant/Descendant

Typical traits: discriminating, reserved, analytical, methodical, conscientious. Needs to acquire practical, detailed knowledge of how things work. Good at learning but often unable to 'let go'.

Dangers: hypercritical, obsessed with correctness. Pisces Descendant invites greater spontaneity and breaks down over-rigid boundaries.

Midheaven/IC

Strives for an orderly career in which intellectual abilities are employed. Fussy about image, and prefers to be thought efficient. May be seen as aloof and lacking spontaneity. Pisces IC can romanticize home and family environment, weakening one's sense of individuality. Spiritual yearnings may emerge later in life.

Libra

Ascendant/Descendant

Typical traits: tactful, charming, perfectionist, idealistic, considerate. Needs to establish balance and harmony in all interactions. Finely tuned sense of co-operation can lead to 'people pleasing' just to keep the peace.

Dangers: indecisiveness and insincerity. Aries Descendant encourages the instinct to stand up and fight for what is sought.

Midheaven/IC

Cultivates charm, diplomacy and fortunate contacts in pursuit of aims. Indecision often masks the need to gain co-operation of others, especially those offering professional advancement. Seen as unctuously calculating by some. Aries IC may present the challenge to find a sense of purpose free from family ties.

Scorpio

Ascendant/Descendant

Typical traits: loyal, secretive, penetrative, passionate, steadfast. Needs to channel intense emotions constructively. Has ability to draw on hidden resources, but does not always know when to pull back.

Dangers: destructive, manipulative and vengeful tendencies. Taurus Descendant can temper more extreme urges.

Midheaven/IC

Desires the independence to follow own path, and can be fiercely anti-establishment. More interested in the potential for transformation than in establishing a reputation. Often destroys to rebuild, which can be seen as needlessly ruthless. Taurus IC stresses the importance of traditional values in building lasting structures.

Sagittarius

Ascendant/Descendant

Typical traits: opportunist, freedom-seeking, frank, utopian, jovial. Needs to feel free to experience life as an adventure. Optimistic when energy and enthusiasm are directed, otherwise may be depressed and restless.

Dangers: taking others for granted, arrogance and self-pity. Gemini Descendant should help to ride less roughshod over others.

Midheaven/IC

Aims for high standards and fulfilment, rather than material success. Hates routine and may be hopelessly impractical. Views self as natural leader, often with high minded goals, but can be loud-mouthed and self-inflated. Gemini IC hints at a need to reach a precise understanding of one's deepest motives to realize ideals.

Capricorn

Ascendant/Descendant

Typical traits: resourceful, cautious, disciplined, reserved, cool. Needs to feel self-sufficient and in control. Has tremendous

ability to withstand hardship in pursuit of ambition, but can become trapped by conformity.
Dangers: selfish, calculating and unfeeling. Cancer Descendant may soften inflexible emotions and lack of sensitivity to others.

Midheaven/IC

Sensitive to how others react, but ploughs a solitary, cautious furrow. Driven by worldly ambition and equipped with patience and determination to succeed – eventually. May be seen as self-centred and obsessed with status. Cancer IC stresses the need for a sense of belonging.

Aquarius

Ascendant/Descendant

Typical traits: independent, original, humanitarian, sociable, progressive. Needs to experience the human condition as a totality rather than from a personal viewpoint. Thinks in broad concepts which can verge on the dogmatic.
Dangers: naive and dismissive of personal emotions. Leo Descendant calls for warmth and respect of individuals' rights.

Midheaven/IC

Is fascinated by innovation, and likes to work in unconventional or future-orientated areas. A need to feel part of the 'winds of change' sometimes fails to take account of the virtues of tradition and individuality. Leo IC shows that sense of self can grow without having to reject background.

Pisces

Ascendant/Descendant

Typical traits: compassionate, impressionable, imaginative, sensitive, visionary. Needs freedom from inflexibility. Selflessness can result in acts of great service or creativity, though sometimes at the expense of individuality.
Dangers: self-victimisation and drowning of sorrows destructively. Virgo Descendant gives power to live within one's own limits.

Midheaven/IC

May indicate a longing to be revered by the public which, more often than not, results in hard work for little recognition. Ability to be all things to all people leads to confusion about personal identity and ambition. Virgo IC shows a need to develop a more conscious sense of one's deepest motivations.

The Houses

If the planets in a birth chart represent particular energies, or modes of action, and the signs show the way in which these energies are expressed, then the House describes the areas of life in which all this activity is most likely to occur.

Regardless of which method is used to calculate the houses (and there are several – see House Systems, page 51), there are always twelve in a birth chart. They are counted anti-clockwise, beginning at the Ascendant.

Just as the twelve signs each embrace different human qualities under the same banner, so the twelve houses each encompass several different areas of life experience. Sagittarius, for example, is associated both with a love of freedom and with a desire to explore deeper philosophical concepts.

Similarly, the Sagittarius-ruled Ninth House may refer equally to adventure in foreign lands, or to some form of higher education.

Deciding which meanings apply is never easy, as it depends on the complex interrelationship between the planets. Often astrologers must rely on their own intuition; it is here that astrology changes from science to art.

Traditional Meanings of the Houses

Traditional house meanings lump together what at first sight appears to be a motley assortment of unconnected definitions. The Third house, for example, encompasses all forms of communication, mental abilities, early education, short-distance travel, neighbours, and brothers and sisters.

The explanation, according to American astrologer Robert Hand, is that planetary energies within the houses can operate simultaneously on three levels as demonstrated in the list for the Third House shown on page 48.

THE TRADITIONAL MEANINGS OF THE HOUSES

1st House: The front door to one's world: the self-image; reaction to one's environment; how others see one; physical characteristics; outer personality; how one initiates action; beginnings

2nd House: The process of valuing; self-worth; body-awareness; how one develops one's natural resources; attitudes towards money and possessions; emotional attachments to objects

3rd House: Communications; the analytical mind; early and immediate environment; school years; relatives; brothers and sisters; early peer group; short journeys

4th House: Home and family issues; one's sense of belonging; psychological foundations; how one is in private; the 'background' parent; childhood conditioning; later years of life

5th House: Creative instincts; the urge to express oneself spontaneously; children; how one gives love; love affairs; leisure; speculation

6th House: Daily routine; work; practical skills; techniques; relations with employer/employees; health issues

7th House: One-to-one encounters; partners; marriage; lawsuits; challenges; open enemies; how one co-operates or competes with others

8th House: Results of what one shares with others; intense relationship; sex; other people's money and possessions; legacies; death and re-birth; crises; change

9th House: The abstract mind; belief systems; higher education; teachers; foreign travel and connections with abroad; religion; the spirit of the law

10th House: Public role and status; career; ambition; influence; how one sets out to achieve aims; the dominant parent; relations with authority figures; one's tendency to be dominant or dominated

11th House: The need to make contact with others; how one receives love; friendships; social group; shared hopes and ideals; group activities

12th House: The unintegrated, unconscious self; what one projects on to intimate relationships; dreams; hidden fears and enemies; breakdowns; sacrifice and service to a greater cause

Meaning (as applied to 3rd house)	**Example**
1 The *internal* level, revealing our basic make-up	• skills in communication • thought patterns
2 The *relationship* level, how we relate to others and outside events.	• speech • writing • aptitude for school work
3 The *external* level, showing how other people and outside events can indirectly affect us.	• school • short journeys • neighbours • brothers and sisters

Linking all the meanings in the chart is a sense of how a person deals mentally with the routine of everyday life – the *essential* meaning of the Third House.

Hand's system of levels, which can be applied to the meanings of the other houses in exactly the same way, dispels the notion that astrology deals only with what is fated. By proving to people that their own psychological make-up is inextricably linked with the outside circumstances that can affect them, the system encourages them to take control of their own destiny, rather than simply be led by it.

House Relationships

Just as the various meanings ascribed to individual houses have common links, so the houses themselves are related to one another. They must never be considered purely in isolation.

The most obvious relationship is between opposite houses – the First and the Seventh, the Second and the Eighth, and so on. This becomes especially relevant when a planet in, say, the First opposes a planet in the Seventh.

This issue in this particular case focuses on the contrast between the person's urge to put themselves first and their need for close relationships. Does the person identify with one planet, while at the same time unconsciously causing others to act out the role of the opposing planet? Or does he or she flip erratically from one to the other?

Deciding which levels of meaning apply is largely a matter for the astrologer's own intuition. Questions like these are certainly beyond the scope of a computerized interpretation.

Another way to group the houses is to see them as stages in a persona's life. The journey begins at the Ascendant, the moment marking birth; Houses 1–3 then go on to represent the development of basic needs. Houses 4–6 show how the person acclimatizes to their surroundings in preparation for Houses 7–9, which are concerned with their response and adjustment to other people. Last are Houses 10–12, which reveal the nature of the person's involvement in the wider world.

Planets in Houses

There are several ways in which a planet can be seen to work through a house:

1 – The planet occupies the house. This is the most obvious way, and is generally agreed by astrologers to be the most powerful.

2 – The planet aspects another planet in another house, thereby affecting the other house. This is a development of (1), and is not always accurate. Sometimes such an aspect between two planets bears no apparent relation to the houses in which the planets fall.

3 – The planet makes an aspect to the house cusp. This is particularly important when the cusp, the point at which houses meet, is one of the Angles (Ascendant, Midheaven, Descendant, IC). Most astrologers agree that planets in these positions have a very strong bearing on the chart, while the other house cusps appear to be less critical.

4 – The planet rules the sign on the house cusp, or the sign following it. Unless a persons's Ascendant is 0°, each house will embrace the sign on the cusp and part of the sign which follows. So if the Ascendant is 15° Aries, both Mars (ruler of Aries) and Venus (ruler of Taurus, which follows) are involved, and their aspects, signs and house positions will all have a bearing on First House matters. For a full interpretation, this complex procedure must be applied to all the houses.

'Empty' Houses

Houses with no planets in them will naturally have less emphasis in the chart than houses that do. But this does not necessarily mean, for example, that an 'empty' Seventh House rules out the chance of close relationships.

To find out how such a house will be energized, the astrologer looks to the sign on the cusp and the sign following on. He or she then notes the planetary rulers of the two signs and checks their positions in the chart.

The Chart Ruler

Most astrologers agree that of all the planets' 'ruling' houses, the one ruling the sign on the First House cusp is the most important because it modifies the way the Ascendant is expressed. For example, Cancer rising calls for the Moon's position by sign and house and aspect to be given special prominence in the interpretation; the chart is said to have a 'lunar' flavour which will colour the whole picture.

HOUSE SYSTEMS

There are several systems for dividing up the birth chart into houses. Astrologers still argue about which is the most accurate, and the astronomical arguments for preferring one to another are extremely complicated. The two most commonly used are Equal House and Placidus.

The Equal House is the simplest to operate, since it divides the zodiac into houses of exactly 30° each, starting from the degree of the Ascendant. However, it also allows the Midheaven/IC axis to 'float' anywhere between the Eighth-Second and Eleventh-Fifth Houses. Critics point out that given their significance as Angles, the MC and IC should always mark the cusps of the Tenth and Fourth Houses respectively.

The Placidus system answers this criticism, but in doing so raises another problem. Because it works out the house divisions according to the observed movement of the heavens, calculations for latitudes near the Poles cause some houses to grow exceptionally large, while others disappear altogether! And even where it does work the Placidus system creates houses of unequal size, allowing planets to fall in houses different from those calculated when using the Equal House system.

For the aspiring astrologer, there is no solution to this dilemma. The only answer is to spend some time experimenting with both systems until you find the one which appears to work best for you. Or you may make your own choice according to the individual chart.

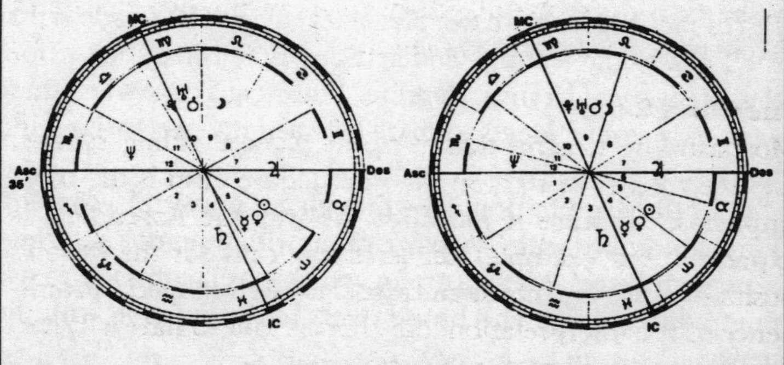

The Natural Zodiac

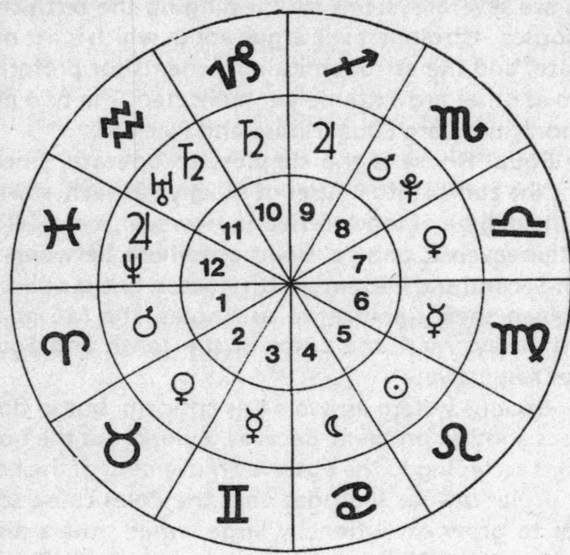

The basic links between the signs, planets and Houses are symbolized by what is called the Natural Zodiac, which takes 0° Aries as its Ascendant, 0° Taurus as the cusp of the Second House, and so on. Both Aries and the First House have an affinity with Mars and are said to be 'ruled' by this planet. The same applies to the other signs, houses, and planets, as shown above.

Some confusion exists as to why Scorpio, Aquarius and Pisces should each have two planetary rulers. The reason is that the links in the Natural Zodiac were established long before the discovery of Uranus, Neptune, Pluto – at a time when there were only seven planets to share between the twelve signs and houses.

Over the years, by popular – though not universal – consent, Pluto was linked with Scorpio, Uranus with Aquarius and Neptune with Pisces. Many astrologers, however, continue to use the traditional sign and house rulers in conjunction with the new.

The Planets

The Sun

In the birth chart the Sun, by sign, house position and – above all – the aspects it makes to the Angles and other planets, describes a person's motivating force; what essentially that person is seeking to become. This is reflected in the Sun's glyph – a dot, representing potential, in a circle signifying completeness or maturity.

On other levels the Sun also corresponds to the masculine principles – willpower, courage, creativity, purpose, growth, one's sense of uniqueness, authority, the father, the ruler.

This last image is particularly helpful to an understanding of the Sun's astrological function. In life, the ruler is the figurehead under which the disparate social groups of the nation either unite or divide. Similarly, the Sun symbolizes the process by which other planetary energies in the birth chart are integrated, or wasted.

The Sun through the Signs

ARIES – Assertive, impulsive, independent, pioneering, enthusiastic, insensitive, direct, aggressive, impatient, self-centred.

TAURUS – Calm, determined, patient, even-tempered, deliberate, inflexible, industrious, hedonistic, possessive, grasping.

GEMINI – Mentally agile, inquisitive, adaptable, restless, stimulating, fickle, superficial, dishonest, apt to scatter energies.

CANCER – Emotional, nurturing, protective, touchy, outwardly tough, shrewd, intuitive, changeable, sentimental, possessive.

LEO – Spontaneous, generous, theatrical, creative, dignified, overbearing, passionate, intolerant, snobbish, haughty.

VIRGO – Reserved, practical, analytical, methodical, critical, pedantic, conscientious, anxious, lacks self-worth, emotionally repressed.

LIBRA – Diplomatic, congenial, co-operative, idealistic, romantic, perfectionist, narcissistic, over-amenable, indecisive, lacking confidence.

SCORPIO – Intensely emotional, secretive, wilful, penetrative,

THE SUN THROUGH THE HOUSES

FIRST – The urge to leave one's mark; natural qualities of leadership; may radiate infectious enthusiasm or appear overbearing and proud.

SECOND – Acquires money and possessions as a mark of individuality; able to manage material resources; the need to develop a unique sense of self-worth.

THIRD – Achieving distinction through knowledge; wanting to be respected for one's mental abilities; 'streetwise' skills; intellectual arrogance; the need to develop depth of understanding.

FOURTH – Establishing a strong, sometimes tyrannical sense of self through the home; often indicates early struggles against the family background, especially the father figure.

FIFTH – A spontaneous need to express oneself through romantic or creative pursuits; a desire to prove one's strengths and abilities; extravagant self-confidence leading to recklessness.

SIXTH – Distinguishing oneself through hard work; a need to be of useful service and to be recognized for one's skills; focus on employment issues, or on health and dietary habits.

SEVENTH – Enhancing individuality through close partnerships; striking a balance between independence and reliance on others; a danger of inflicting one's will on partners.

EIGHTH – Learning to share resources and possessions with partners; intense emotional and sexual bonds; transforming oneself through inner development or the outer accumulation of wealth.

NINTH – A need to create one's own set of moral or spiritual values; an intellectual appetite for learning; bigoted views; identity often expanded through contact with foreign lands or cultures.

TENTH – A need to be taken seriously professionally, or to be seen as authoritative in some areas; dependent on the outward trappings of success; drawn to a prestigious partner; a powerful parent, often an ambitious mother.

ELEVENTH – Seeking recognition via group activities, or organizations; needing to cultivate own beliefs as distinct from group ideas; influential friends; selfish exploitation of friendships or groups.

TWELFTH – Sacrificing personal identity to collective needs; recognition through service to others; work behind the scenes; yearnings for approval often thwarted; powerful secret enemies; own worst enemy.

transformative, extremely jealous, perceptive, imaginative, suspicious, vindictive.

SAGITTARIUS – Freedom-loving, idealistic, deep-thinking, sincere, outspoken, benevolent, moralistic, optimistic, undisciplined, arrogant.

AQUARIUS – Individualistic, sociable, detached, humanitarian, intuitive, dogmatic, progressive, rebellious, cranky, erratic.

PISCES – Highly sensitive, compassionate, impressionable, receptive, imaginative, submissive, escapist, self-sacrificing, impractical, gullible.

The Moon

Just as the Moon reflects the Sun's light, so in astrology it signifies a person's instinctive, emotional response to their environment. Where the Sun is connected with action, the Moon's domain is reaction.

These feelings are largely unconscious in childhood, only coming to light as we become aware of our true selves as signified by the Sun. As a result, the Moon by sign, house position and aspects can reveal a great deal about a person's emotional development as a child, and how these patterns are likely to re-emerge in later life.

The Moon also corresponds to the 'feminine' principle – the protective instinct; the home environment; our sense of 'belonging'; natural habits; eating patterns and preferences; attitudes to the past; changing moods and fortunes (reflecting the cycles of the Moon); the imagination; the ability to reach the public; and women, especially the mother.

The Moon through the Signs

ARIES – Hasty reactions; a short-fused temper which quickly burns out; independent; intolerant of interference; may possibly seek to dominate others emotionally.

TAURUS – Instinctively finds emotional stability in material security; stimulated by beauty and the good life; often lazy, acquisitive and habit-bound.

GEMINI – An ability to rationalize emotions can lead to

THE MOON THROUGH THE HOUSES

FIRST – The feeling nature is heightened, especially the ability to tune into immediate surroundings; highly subjective; difficulty in distinguishing between own and others' needs.

SECOND – Material values endorse emotional security; difficulty in releasing emotional attachments; greedy; strong family ties; liable to experience changeable financial fortunes.

THIRD – Thought processes coloured by moods; intuitive about what others think; learning equals security; an ability to influence through writing or speaking.

FOURTH – A strong sense of belonging within the family framework; the need to create a home as a sanctuary; childhood patterns or issues may reemerge in later life.

FIFTH – An instinctive need to be creative; natural artistic ability; the possibility of reliving aspects of the 'mother' through love affairs or children; public appeal.

SIXTH – The need to be emotionally fulfilled by work; dealing with other people's emotions; working to perfect daily habits, especially how to handle stress; needing to be needed.

SEVENTH – Seeking a partner for 'completeness'; nurturing relationships; sometimes looking for 'mother' in the partner; family issues affecting the marriage.

EIGHTH – A subtle awareness of how to use other people's resources; responsive to partner's sexuality; emotional crises leading to a renewed sense of worth.

NINTH – A fascination with concepts that broaden the mind; travel; foreign connections; an ability to tune into future trends and to gauge public opinion; 'gut' convictions.

TENTH – Blending in with the status quo; seeking public approval; sensitivity to public reputation; intuitive feeling for public taste; unresolved issues with parents, especially the mother.

ELEVENTH – A sense of belonging through friends or organizations; falling in with the crowd; supporting emotive causes; female friendships; fluctuating goals throughout life.

TWELFTH – Susceptibility to others' emotions; the need to withdraw to find a sense of self; hidden or repressed emotions; vivid dreams; deep-rooted phobias; caring for the less fortunate.

losing touch with feelings; restless spirit may week stimulus through constantly changing surroundings; superficial.

CANCER – Great emotional strength and sensitivity; highly responsive to the moods of others, though easily wounded by imaginary slights; brooding; smothering affections.

LEO – Proud feelings and dramatic reactions; feels 'at home' in the limelight; powerful instinct to give and receive; loyal in affections; can be stubborn and self-centred.

VIRGO – Tendency for the head to govern the heart; difficulty in 'letting go' results in concern for order and correctness; shy; over-anxious; prudish; driven by a need to be useful.

LIBRA – Sensitivity to others means that emotional responses may be unduly influenced by partners; hates disharmony; loves beauty and elegance; can be fickle and hypercritical.

SCORPIO – Intense emotions, which can range from total self-denial to compulsive indulgence; capable of noble sacrifice or bearing deep grudges; stubborn; brooding and unforgiving.

SAGITTARIUS – A strong emotional attachment to childhood moral values; optimism and high ideals give a child-like innocence to responses; lacks objectivity; intuitive; restless.

CAPRICORN – Reluctant to express emotions for fear of exposing vulnerability; cautious, reserved and practical; reactions to others tend to be guided by material considerations.

AQUARIUS – Detached concern for others resulting from a dread of being restricted by personal involvements; intuitive; difficulty in dealing with emotions; needs freedom at home.

PISCES – Hypersensitivity can lead to unconscious absorption of other people's emotions; highly imaginative; easily wounded, has difficulty accepting worldly reality; escapist; addictive.

Mercury

Mercury, in his mythological role as Messenger of the Gods, was responsible for conveying information between mortals and the deities residing on Mount Olympus. In the birth chart, his planetary counterpart fulfils a similar function; Mercury carries the torch of conscious thought to the rest of the chart, offering the opportunity of greater self-awareness along the way.

More specifically, Mercury by sign, house position and aspects to other planets reveals the mental frequency on which we operate – how we think and generally communicate. He also shows our aptitude for learning, and – especially through the contact he makes to other planets – whether our opinions are likely to be based on logic or feelings and habits.

In his highest expression, Mercury symbolizes the power of wisdom and self-knowledge; in his lowest, the mind of the trickster, full of deceit and low cunning. On other levels Mercury corresponds to the workings of the rational, objective mind; early school experiences; reading and writing; languages; debate and discussion; transport; commerce; short-distance travel; and the tools of communication – books, newspapers, telephones, television and computers.

Mercury through the Signs

ARIES – A quick decisive mind, capable of producing highly intuitive ideas; impulsive decisions, often ill-thought out; lacking patience and attention to detail; argumentative.

TAURUS – Slow, deliberate thought processes; reluctant to change mind; shrews and practical head for business; strong powers of concentration; commonsensical; opinionated.

GEMINI – A logical, versatile mind, capable of processing a lot of information quickly; often articulate and witty; good at problem-solving; easily distracted; fickle opinions.

CANCER – Thoughts shaped by emotional responses; retentive memory; imaginative; susceptible to what others think; good business acumen; sentimental.

LEO – Strong-minded with a good overview, but poor grasp of details; slow to form and change opinions; thoughts expressed authoritatively, sometimes arrogantly; good at selling ideas.

VIRGO – An analytical, rational mind that concerns itself with the practical application of ideas; efficient and attentive to detail; can be over-fussy and obsessed with order.

LIBRA – A sharp, active mind capable of weighing all options

MERCURY THROUGH THE HOUSES

FIRST – Restless mental activity, always seeking to communicate, observant, perhaps with a gift for mimicry; may be over-talkative, even argumentative.

SECOND – Communication skills can be deployed to earn money; a sharp understanding of the value of things – either objects, such as antiques, or abstract activities, such as economics.

THIRD – A need for constant mental stimulation, especially through study, or work which involves travel; the ability to exploit knowledge commercially; strong mental ties with siblings.

FOURTH – A background where learning is important; how one develops a rational perspective on one's upbringing and family environment; may indicate frequent changes of home.

FIFTH – The urge to identify with one's 'rational' mind; a need to express one's thoughts creatively; independent or narrow-minded thinking; communication with children often emphasized.

SIXTH – Developing communication skill in one's work; seeking mentally stimulating work; learning how to synthesize detailed and varied information; an interest in health issues.

SEVENTH – Seeking a strong mental affinity in close relationships, especially marriage; how one adjusts to the opinions of others; the ability to sell an idea; possibly a younger partner.

EIGHTH – An interest in subjects that penetrate the mind, such as psychology, mysticism, and sex; handling other people's resources in business; intense mental contact in close relationships.

NINTH – An attraction to interests that broaden the mind, such as religion, philosophy, politics and foreign cultures; travel and further education are highlighted; possibly dogmatic opinions.

TENTH – May indicate the need for public speaking skills; educational qualifications as a means of furthering one's career; wanting to be taken seriously for one's ability with words.

ELEVENTH – Intellectual concern with humanitarian or social issues; thoughts shaped by friends or group organisations; the ability to be a group spokesperson; groups of like-minded people.

TWELFTH – A highly active imagination stirred by deeply felt, often unconscious, thought patterns; possible 'psychic' abilities; can indicate mental blocks stemming from early learning difficulties.

and reaching balanced decisions; may try to please others and compromise own opinions; good for business planning.

SCORPIO – An intuitive mind which can penetrate the most insoluble problems; communicates only when necessary, hence seen as secretive and scheming; instinctive business sense; may be sharp-tongued.

SAGITTARIUS – A philosophical mind, finely tuned to dominant social attitudes; can overlook facts for the sake of an idea; may either have almost visionary insight or bigoted beliefs.

CAPRICORN – An organized, practical mind, capable of great concentration; thinking is slow, often skeptical, but thorough; drawn to ideas that are well tested; resourceful in business.

AQUARIUS – A free-thinking, inventive mind, always seeking mental stimulation, humanitarian views can be either benevolent or dogmatic; obsession with objective truth may obscure subjective values.

PISCES – A highly sensitive mind with a vivid imagination, but prone to being overwhelmed by fluctuating and unconscious emotions; difficulty in communicating deepest thoughts; artistic leanings.

Venus

Named after the goddess of love, beauty and sensuality, the planet Venus traditionally refers to our need for relationship, affection and harmony. At a more fundamental level, however, Venus is concerned with what attracts and repels us, and how we respond to these influences.

The process involved is one of weighing up – of trying to decide what is good or bad according to how we perceive our needs. More often than not, this results in sharing or co-operative behaviour, since most people find dealing with others preferable to being lonely and unpopular.

In terms of love, Venus reveals our reaction when we meet it, rather than how we express ourselves emotionally (which is more a function of Mars). Venus rarely gives without expecting something in return, hence our ability to attract harmonious relationships will depend on its sign and house position, and more specifically on the nature of the planets it aspects.

On other levels, matters which fall within Venus' portfolio include the arts; style; taste; physical attraction; close partnerships of all kinds; women and feminine sexuality; physical wellbeing; money and all means of exchange; diplomacy and vanity.

Venus through the Signs

ARIES – Socially dynamic and openly flirtatious; affectionate, but prone to impulsive attractions; competitive instinct is sharpened by the chase, but can lead to overbearing, self-centred behaviour.

TAURUS – Can be passionate and loyal in love, though also possessive if emotional security is uncertain; highly sensual; artistic ability a common feature.

GEMINI – Seeks variety in both romantic and social spheres; needs space and a strong mental rapport in a relationship; fear of strong emotional contacts may lead to fickleness and superficiality.

CANCER – May be moody and hypersensitive in relationships; compassionate and highly protective – is not smothering – regarding partners or children; preoccupied with financial and domestic security.

LEO – Delights in courtship and in being the centre of attention; passionate and loyal, but expects due recognition in return; a natural talent for dramatising feelings; a strong sense of colour.

VIRGO – May undervalue self, both socially and romantically, leading to shyness; standards may be too high in relationships; a practical approach to love based on shared work and mental compatibility.

LIBRA – Usually romantic, affectionate and companionable; need for beauty may be projected on to partner; desire to accommodate others may lead to over-conformity and suppression of true desires.

SCORPIO – Passions run high and sexual desire is at its most

VENUS THROUGH THE HOUSES

FIRST – Refined; needs harmonious surroundings; prone to instant attractions; over-accommodating for the sake of peace; charming, but needs flattering in return; expects things to fall into place.

SECOND – Sets a high premium on beauty and material possessions; a strongly marked sensuality; tendency for indulgent and expensive habits; powerful emotions which can lead to possessiveness.

THIRD – Sensitive to the immediate environment; a sympathetic listener who can communicate easily; inclined to say what people want to hear; a sparkling love of words; an elusive magnetism.

FOURTH – Creates beauty and harmony in the home; clings to ancestral values; emotional stability; tied to parental influences; may romanticize about one parent; a need for dependency in relationships.

FIFTH – An urge to be popular and desirable; a passionate need to be 'in love'; liking for style and luxury; creative talents developed for the enjoyment they bring; easy contact with children.

SIXTH – Acquiring practical values; refining techniques and skills; learning to accept spontaneous desires; close relationships might develop through, or interfere with work.

SEVENTH – An attraction for social gatherings and the 'good life'; finds own sense of worth in a partner; too great a dependency on others; possible disappointments in search of 'ideal' partners.

EIGHTH – A need to share at the deepest level, especially through sex; crises in relationships which are destructive or transformative; possible benefits through marriage or inheritance.

NINTH – Developing an idealistic set of values, able to inspire others through own enthusiasm; a love of adventure, travel or foreign cultures; one to one relationships may be seen as restricting.

TENTH – Natural gifts used to advance career; places status and security above romance; seeks recognition for own style, taste, or beauty; possible loneliness in love by appearing too aloof.

ELEVENTH – Brings a spirit of co-operation to friendships or social contacts; many acquaintances; finds love through friendship and mutual interests.

TWELFTH – Yearns to submerge self in partner; strong subconscious emotional and sexual urges; falling for the unavailable; finding love at enormous personal sacrifice; often denotes strong artistic leanings.

intense; capacity for self-sacrifice can lead to great bitterness if loyalty is betrayed; feelings in love are either all or nothing.
SAGITTARIUS – Enthusiastic nature needs room to explore fun-loving relationships; many contacts often preferred to deep commitments; may try to mould partner to own outlook; love of high living.
CAPRICORN – Emotional stability linked to material status, so love and marriage may be used to advance socially or professionally; reserved but loyal in affections; objects of beauty seen as investments.
AQUARIUS -- Resistance to being conventionally 'tied down'; detached emotions may confuse friendship with love; need for unorthodox contacts may result in disappointment if experiment does not succeed!
PISCES – Must temper compassionate nature with a sense of discrimination; vulnerable to seduction and exploitation; tendency to become emotionally dependent on partner, or to play the martyr.

Mars

At an instinctive level, Mars represents our determination to battle for survival. When threatened, we can either confront a likely aggressor or flee. As we will only fight for what we value, the implications of Mars in our birth chart have to be seen in conjunction with Venus.

While Venus describes what we value, Mars shows how we obtain or preserve it. Consequently, Mars symbolizes all those qualities which help us achieve our desires and therefore enhance our self-image, such as initiative, courage, physical strength and stamina.

It is through the impulse Mars gives us to assert ourselves that it has acquired its reputation for conflict. In the birth chart, Mars's sign, house position and aspects show how we arouse ourselves to conscious action and reveals the way we spontaneously express our emotions.

On other levels, Mars is associated with athleticism and sport; war and all military affairs; all forms of coercion; men and male sexuality; selfish desires; anger; passion; panic; frustration; guns, iron and all sharp metal instruments; machines and mechanics; technicians; engineers; explosives; fire; fever; inflammation and accidents and operations.

Mars through the Signs

ARIES – An urge to take the initiative; courageous; determined to achieve desires; infectious enthusiasm; lack of consideration for others; erratic energy levels; aggressive under pressure.

TAURUS – Slow, but purposeful; deep reserves of strength; a capacity for hard work; practical, conservative aims, possessive emotions may lead to acquisitiveness; obstinate, even prejudiced, views.

GEMINI – Mentally assertive and competitive, though argumentative if threatened; good at problem-solving; an often biting wit; restlessness leading to a lack of consistency and purpose.

CANCER – Actions motivated by deeply felt emotions; lack of self-control in headlong confrontations; indirect approach to aims; moody when thwarted; repressed anger; an aptitude for DIY.

LEO – Tirelessly and consistently enterprising; can uplift others through self-confidence; tremendous vitality and passion; impractical schemes; a tendency to be self-publicising and extremely vain.

VIRGO – Cautious and methodical; precise; analytical; often critical of own or others' actions; highly strung; overly controlled emotions; moralistic.

LIBRA – Able to act strategically, but may be too dependent on others' support; indecisive; can confuse own aims with those of others; handling others' conflicts; quarrelsome relationships.

SCORPIO – Tenacious and sometimes ruthless pursuit of goals, stamina in adversity; secretive methods; overbearing with others emotionally and sexually; destructive; power-conscious; intense grudges.

SAGITTARIUS – A crusading spirit; pitching own strengths against others; extravagant, ill-conceived actions; seeking fulfilment through an unfettered sense of freedom.

MARS THROUGH THE HOUSES

FIRST – Finding outlets for self-expression; taking control of own destiny; competitive situations; impulsive actions; gratifying one's desires; a strong physical presence.

SECOND – Learning about the power of money; possessions as a reflection of self; fighting for what is valued; business initiative; rash use of financial resources; strongly expressed sensuality.

THIRD – Tuning the mind to perfection; speaking one's mind force-fully or bluntly; a restless mentality which needs relaxing outlets; fighting for survival in early childhood; possible tension with siblings.

FOURTH – Emotional issues concerning the family; an urge to dominate and finding ways to let off steam at home; abilities or resentments which slowly surface; conflicts with the father.

FIFTH – Expressing vitality through creative pursuits; passionate and spontaneous love affairs; impulsive speculation; a love of sport; an ability to work with the young; egotistical attitudes.

SIXTH – Learning skills which enhance pride in work; fighting for recognition of worth; punishing the body through over-exertion; possible conflicts with co-workers; obsessed with details; self-sufficient.

SEVENTH – Cultivating contacts in pursuit of aims; a partner who takes the initiative; needing others to confirm one's worth; rashness and disharmony in relationships; defending the down-trodden.

EIGHTH – Thriving on close emotional ties and joint enterprises; dealing with deep emotional and sexual instincts; meeting life as a series of crises and transformations; exploiting others' resources.

NINTH – A love of contests; grappling with belief systems or cultural issues; challenging higher authorities; invoking moral principles to justify actions; pioneering travel; religious bigotry.

TENTH – Wanting to be seen as influential and assertive; choosing a career for personal status; ambitions influenced by parents; clashes with people in authority; ruthless in achieving ends.

ELEVENTH – Finding confidence through group activities; competitive and possibly off-hand with friends; championing causes; clear-cut objectives.

TWELFTH – Finding a higher sense of purpose; trouble discriminating between own and other people's aims; covert operations; feeling ineffectual; self-destructive; passive resentments; violent dreams.

CAPRICORN – Well orchestrated plans and realistic ambitions; decisive actions calculated to bring tangible results; preserving; exploitative; controlled emotions for fear of seeming vulnerable.

AQUARIUS – Needs to act rationally; unorthodox methods; contributing to teamwork or to the betterment of the human condition; stubbornness born of a fierce need to act in one's own way.

PISCES – Passive attitude to aims; struggles for acknowledgement; works behind the scenes; self-confidence eroded by hypersensitivity; avoids confrontations; escapist; unreliable emotions.

Jupiter

As the largest planet in the solar system, it is perhaps not surprising that Jupiter has long been associated astrologically with growth and expansion.

This can be taken in the physical sense, in that Jupiter corresponds to the growth of the body – in particular, cellular development and digestion. But the main significance of Jupiter in the birth chart is its function as a 'social' planet – a role it shares with Saturn. The Sun, Moon, Mercury, Venus and Mars all deal with strictly personal aspects of our character without any reference to inherited or environmental factors. Jupiter, by contrast, shows how we grow throughout life to fulfil the potential of our birthright.

Growth in this context means how we develop in response to the prevailing beliefs in society, and to what extent we blend in with, or challenge them. In our quest to find a place in the world, Jupiter by sign, house and, above all, aspect, shows our social expectations and ideals, and also how we go about creating opportunities to realize them.

On other levels, Jupiter corresponds to religious faith, wisdom, our understanding of God; the spirit of the law, philosophy and all theoretical thought. It also embraces, politics, higher education, morality, travel, exploration, anything to do with places abroad, spiritual or material prosperity, overconsumption, obesity and wastefulness.

Jupiter through the Signs

ARIES – Learning to take the initiative to earn success; leading by example; inspiring others with one's faith; thoughtless and over-hasty actions; exaggerated optimism; inflated self-importance.

TAURUS – A sense of power through financial security; exploring the social uses to which money can be put; realistic expectations; over-indulgent habits; self-gratification; snobbish values; conventional.

GEMINI – Seeking breadth of experience; improving one's mental abilities; a need to keep abreast of social issues; many social contacts; wide, though superficial, knowledge; intellectual conceit.

CANCER – A strong sense of family; seeking to create a comfortable environment; supporting others in need; powerful emotions which cloud reason; faith based on 'gut' feeling; sentimental about the past.

LEO – Driven by a mission to achieve; radiating self-confidence; needing to feel important or popular; inspiring optimism in others; a tendency to sensationalize; reckless gambling; ostentatious.

VIRGO – Practical service to a social ideal; a hunger for information; tension from taking on too much responsibility; learning to delegate; technical excellence; skeptical of 'spiritual' values.

LIBRA – A wide range of personal contacts; influence through popularity and social prestige; a strong sense of fair play; a philosophical outlook; too dependent on others; companionship at all costs.

SCORPIO – Digging for the truth; obsessive or unbending beliefs; acquiring power over others; the drive for wealth and pleasure; an accentuated sexuality; delusions of invincibility.

SAGITTARIUS – Spiritual quests; far-sighted aims; expanding horizons through travel and study; slavishly following social trends; moral preaching.

CAPRICORN – A preoccupation with social responsibilities;

JUPITER THROUGH THE HOUSES

FIRST – Drawn to social, moral or spiritual issues; actions and gestures on a grand scale; the need for an adventurous environment; a dignified bearing; self-important; an authoritative presence.

SECOND – Searching for stability in a material or spiritual creed; the ability to realize one's ideals; money-consciousness; financial luck; complacency; powerful desires; hedonistic.

THIRD – Developing one's mental faculties; analytical abilities; understanding prevailing social trends; over-emphasising the power of the rational mind; intellectual arrogance; many 'streetwise' contacts.

FOURTH – Powerful moral or religious issues around one's upbringing; finding one's true home; burdensome family ties; focusing on one's need for inner growth; a spirit of adventure in later life.

FIFTH – A pressing need to express one's natural abilities; involvement in large scale ventures; lusty romantic adventures; pushing beliefs on to children; many interests; living life to the full.

SIXTH – Perfecting skills which are of practical use; over-dutiful in one's work; excessive or obsessive dietary habits; understanding the relationship between a healthy mind and body; healing abilities.

SEVENTH – Striking a balance between independence and security in relationships; issues around infidelity and jealousy; investing a partner with larger-than-life qualities; expectations others have of one.

EIGHTH – Deep sexual unions, or an insatiable appetite; reconciling beliefs with instinctive drives; intuitive touch with money; benefits through other people; probing hidden meanings.

NINTH – Expanding one's understanding of life through religion, philosophy, travel or higher education; communicating truth to others; inflated belief in one's own mission or importance.

TENTH – Seeking high office or prominence in career; wanting a reputation for integrity and hard work; a sense of duty; hypocritical posturing.

ELEVENTH – Expanding one's influence through friendships and groups; an active social life; influencing others to support personal goals; foresight into future trends; parasitical friends.

TWELFTH – Evolving an inner optimism in life; periods of confinement for self-examination; working in the healing professions; over-supportive of others; escapism through over-indulgent habits.

finding a philosophy to justify ambitions; a high regard for reputation; executive skills; concern with correct behaviour.

AQUARIUS – Philanthropic ideals; crossing the barriers of class or race; insight into human nature; progressive view on society; detached personal commitments; dissipating energies.

PISCES – Powerful spiritual yearnings; looking for a spiritual figurehead; service of humanity; visionary; indiscriminate altruism; enjoyment of solitude and tranquillity; lack of discipline.

Saturn

In counterbalance to Jupiter's expansive nature, Saturn's astrological function is to restrict. This is often a painful but nonetheless vital part of our development, for Saturn keeps Jupiter's urge to grow within manageable bounds.

Saturn's position in the birth chart shows where and how we most want to make our mark in society. The aspects it makes to the Angles and other planets focus on the obstacles we are likely to meet on the way. These may be self-inflected or brought about by events which appear to be beyond our control.

In both cases, Saturn teaches us – through harsh confrontation with reality and through limiting circumstances – what we must change in ourselves before we can achieve our ambitions. Since few of us accept delays or hardship gracefully, these lessons are seldom learned without pain.

At its most constructive Saturn imparts wisdom born of a true understanding of the virtues of patience, hard work, tradition and self-discipline. But if the Saturnian energy is ignored or becomes too dominant, it may also be repressive – inhibiting our self-confidence and frustrating our aims.

Saturn's rule extends among other things to all rules and regulations, the government and all authority figures, exams and teachers, the physical laws of the universe, economic recession, time, the aging process, depression, fear and loneliness.

Saturn Through The Signs

ARIES – Strong ambitions which require great effort to realize; developing patience and self-discipline in actions;

self-reliant; struggling to find motivation; repressive; the path of the loner.

TAURUS – Practical, long-term aims which are methodically executed; a dogged sense of purpose; inflexible principles; frugal to the point of self-denial; preoccupation with what one owns.

GEMINI – A well-ordered, sometimes calculating mind; an aptitude for research; good concentration; a distrust of the irrational; precise, or inhibited expression; an intellectual inferiority complex.

CANCER – Strong attachments to people or places; sensitive to the demands of others; shrewd business ability; performing to high family expectations; emotional inhibition from a fear of rejection.

LEO – A steady, self-assured pursuit of goals; a compulsive need to be in charge, or to have one's own way; easily slighted; resentful of external restrictions; high-handed, possibly autocratic.

VIRGO – A laborious concern for detail and order; over-conscientious about duties; a fear of the unknown; prone to excessive worrying.

LIBRA – Ambitions realized through teamwork; responsibility through organizing others; putting a great deal of effort into close partnerships to make them work; harsh on the failings of others.

SCORPIO – The urge to exploit every resource in pursuit of success; an ability to unravel insoluble problems; a fear of being betrayed; stubborn, even extreme principles; guarded emotions.

SAGITTARIUS – A conflict between grand ideas and the need for detail; practical application of concepts; coming to terms with everyday reality; strict moral or ethical views; intellectual arrogance.

CAPRICORN – Striving for worldly achievements and public recognition; putting self-reliance above all else; grafting for long-term aims; faith in traditional views of authority; a fear of failure.

SATURN THROUGH THE HOUSES

FIRST – Reluctant to assert oneself; a serious approach to life; feeling one's early environment to be unsupportive; pessimistic expectations.

SECOND – Insecurity about self-worth may lead to proving one's earning power; feeling restricted by material commitments; worry over finance may give rise to meanness; secure long-term investments.

THIRD – A fear of being ignorant, or mentally inadequate; early childhood, especially school, as a restrictive experience; a serious attitude to learning or diminishing its value altogether.

FOURTH – A deep feeling of being hemmed in by, or a need for, tradition; an absence of family support; a frosty or disciplinarian parent; a sense of alienation from one's background.

FIFTH – Spontaneity limited by fear of disapproval; frustration from feelings of blocked creativity; inhibited in love out of a dread of rejection; may find child-rearing a burdensome issue.

SIXTH – Dissatisfaction in one's work; suffocating routines; acquiring skills which have a useful social function; health issues which force one to work within one's mental and physical limitations.

SEVENTH – Picking holes in partners when relationships turn faulty; lessons in mutual responsibility; a reluctance to become too close or dependent; burdensome or infrequent relationships.

EIGHTH – A distrust of letting go emotionally; resisting change; a reluctance to probe beneath the surface; inhibited sexuality; controlling or being burdened with other people's assets or liabilities.

NINTH – Learning the value of discipline and self-denial; giving practical meaning to abstract concepts; puritanical beliefs; oppressive moral or religious influences; a frustrated urge to travel.

TENTH – The need for social acceptability; making one's mark in society; a slow progress to the top with many delays and obstacles; fulfilling parental expectations; the need to become self-reliant.

ELEVENTH – Lasting, or onerous friendships; a preference for older friends; the loner who finds friendship and group activities difficult; administrative abilities; dogmatic beliefs.

TWELFTH – Meeting unpleasant aspects of oneself in other people; hidden doubts and fears; feelings of loneliness; or being alienated from society; the need for a clearly defined self-image.

AQUARIUS – The ability to test new ideas; distrusting change or progressive views; mental self-discipline; placing too much value on the rational mind; insensitive to emotions; highly dogmatic.

PISCES – Requiring great self-discipline to be effective in the world; a feeling of being restricted by invisible forces; the need to develop an objective view of oneself.

THE OUTER PLANETS

The three planets beyond Saturn – Uranus (1781), Neptune (1846) and Pluto (1930) – are relatively recent additions to the planetary picture. Because of the length of time they spend in each sign (an average of 7, 14 or 21 years respectively), they are thought to apply more to generations, or to mankind as a whole, than to individuals.

Traditionally, it is their house positions and the aspects they make to the Angles and personal planets which give the outer planets significance in the birth charts; the impact of their energies is most evident when they appear on the Ascendant. Contrary to custom, some of the likely personal meanings of Uranus, Neptune and Pluto through the signs have been included in the course.

Uranus

Discovered in 1781, at a time of great social unrest and upheaval, Uranus has come to symbolize unexpected and traumatic change. Usually this happens when the Saturnian principles of order and control become too rigid – either in either our personal lives or in society as a whole.

Some people in life display powerful Uranian drives, either by spearheading progressive reforms, or – less constructively – by standing out from the crowd through shocking or anti-social behaviour. Whatever the level of expression. Uranian individuals seem to crackle with mysterious force that generates excitement, eccentricity or danger.

For most of us, though, the influence of Uranus is not so consistently evident. It tends to take us by surprise when it is activated in our personal lives, for few of us are receptive to the wholesale change it often demands.

As a result Uranus is often felt to work disruptively, breaking down attitudes or situations which have become fossilized. Yet no matter how painful these rude awakenings may be, they offer us the chance to take control of our destinies and live our lives in accordance with our deepest wishes. In this sense, Uranus can be seen as a truly liberating agent.

On other levels it corresponds to electricity; lightning; any sudden illumination or original discovery; eccentricity; all innovative technologies; the abstract sciences; revolutionary ideals; reforms; anarchy; democracy and civil liberties.

Uranus through the Signs

ARIES – Pioneering change and new ideas; a marked spirit of adventure; highly self-willed; an often disruptive impulse to act one's own way; a thoughtless disregard for past values.

TAURUS – Dogged persistence, or extreme impatience in working for change; inventive ways of resolving practical issues; breaking free from materialism.

GEMINI – Independent thinking; innovative ideas and methods; love of new or unusual social contacts; restlessness leading to uncompleted projects; poor mental self-discipline; unreliable; impractical.

CANCER – Emotional independence; highly intuitive, or cutting off from feelings; difficulty in asking for support; erratic mood swings; a need for space; emotionally excitable; sudden rebellious outbursts.

LEO – The urge to be seen as different or unconventional; championing radical causes; breaking free from authority; overbearing self-importance; stubborn refusal to take advice.

VIRGO – Upheavals through resistance to change; breaking away from inflexible methods; rigid adherence to principles; extreme points of view; outspoken criticism; anti-disciplinarian.

LIBRA – Unconventional or exciting relationships; sudden attractions and repulsions; self-reliant or self-centred; resisting mutual responsibility; rebelling against accepted social standards.

SCORPIO – Electrically charged emotions; generating or

URANUS THROUGH THE HOUSES

FIRST – An exciting, highly individualistic personality; the need to find a true role in life; sudden or drastic events, especially if personal environment is felt to be stifling.

SECOND – Breaking with conventional values; using money as a means to freedom, or renouncing its accepted value; unexpected gains and losses; realising special talents; an off-beat lifestyle.

THIRD – Sudden, intuitive insights; frustration with orthodox schooling; mental acrobatics; restless for constant stimulation; original, inventive mind.

FOURTH – Rebelling against one's background, or the need to look at it in a new light; unusual views on family values; an unorthodox parent; sudden changes in residence; radical change in later years.

FIFTH – A heightened need to express individuality; dissatisfaction with the fruits of one's labours; explosive or unusual love affairs; looking for constant excitement; erratic with children.

SIXTH – Seeking fulfilment in work; avoiding numbing routines; disruptive working relations; sudden illnesses; nervous disorders; innovative ways of addressing the balance between mind and body.

SEVENTH – Difficulty in settling into conventional relationships; learning to respect one another's needs; looking for a stimulating or charismatic partner; attracting people who force one to change.

EIGHTH – Exposure to deep or murky passions; the need to release oneself from unstable emotions; breaking through sexual taboos; inconsistent sex drive which may lead to experimentation.

NINTH – Evolving beliefs from personal experience rather than received wisdom; rebelling against tradition; far-reaching but not always practical aims; the ability to sense future trends.

TENTH – An agent for social change; radical views which touch the public; finding one's particular vocation; sudden career changes brought on by unforeseen events; success on one's own terms.

ELEVENTH – Sudden friendships that catalyse change; drawn to groups or people sharing the same ideals; the ability to bring fresh ideas into an organisation, or too independent to fit in.

TWELFTH – Fearful of facing changes necessary for inner growth; a need to free what is buried in the subconscious; experiencing or seeking heightened states of consciousness; predictive dreams.

seeking intense sexual excitement; ruthless, decisive action; sudden, violent outbursts which may be wilfully destructive; extreme courage.

SAGITTARIUS – Shaking others out of outmoded beliefs; fanatically non-conformist; exposing religious humbug, or hypocrisy in social morals; challenging educational values; radical thinking; skepticism.

CAPRICORN – A fear of rapid change; making new ideas work; rebelling against authority and tradition, or resisting progress; cautious reform, or forcing change through.

AQUARIUS – A progressive mind; breaking down social barriers; fighting for individual rights and freedoms; lack of thought for emotional issues in pursuit of the truth or a cause; individualistic.

PISCES – Heightened receptivity; sudden inspiration; escaping from unpalatable truths or situations, leading to unexpected upheavals; impractical idealism; emotionally erratic; mystical leanings.

Neptune

As the planet of unreality – of unlimited possibilities and things we cannot touch or see – Neptune's function is to break down the boundaries that keep us contained within the realities of the physical universe.

Both personally, and in society as a whole, the effect is to undermine the limitations imposed by harsh, practical Saturn. Neptune offers us the promise of other realities, and in so doing, fueled our dreams of transcending the routine and the humdrum.

In its positive expression, Neptune enables us to shift the focus of our lives from purely selfish concerns to a vision of the Greater Whole of which each of us is a part. It can heighten perception, inspire the imagination and deepen our understanding of other people. The ideals it spawns are both universal and spiritual.

The darker side of Neptune emerges when our wishes bear little relation to what we are capable of achieving. If, for whatever reason, we are reluctant to face undesirable qualities in

NEPTUNE THROUGH THE HOUSES

FIRST – Heightened awareness of surroundings and others; uncertainty about the boundaries between oneself and others resulting in impressionability or self-victimisation; a confused self-image.

SECOND – Experiencing the illusory nature of money and possessions; learning to value one's natural abilities; intuitive at earning money; confused or fluctuating finances; glamorising money.

THIRD – Difficulties with analytical thought; inspired sense of imagery and story-telling; embroidering the facts; highly receptive to other people's thinking; vague or weak-minded.

FOURTH – Sensitivity to atmospheres in the home; a romanticized memory of childhood; an idealized or 'absent' parent; a need to loosen family ties; searching for one's spiritual home.

FIFTH – The ability to play roles; susceptible to other people's approval; finding creative outlets that release the imagination; highly idealistic or falling for the unavailable in love.

SIXTH – Dissatisfaction with humdrum practicalities; looking for ideal working conditions; confusion or deception with working colleagues; either neglectful of health or else preoccupied with it.

SEVENTH – A yearning for the perfect relationship leading to disappointments; playing the martyr in relationships; understanding the meaning of selfless love; addictive or inspirational partners.

EIGHTH – The urge to lose oneself through physical intimacy; vulnerability to other people's values; encouraging others to develop their talents.

NINTH – Looking the salvation in a belief system or a spiritual leader; the ability to act as mouthpiece for others; the eternal student or wanderer; spiritually drawn to foreign countries or cultures.

TENTH – Catching the public's imagination; either worshipped by the public, or working for little recognition; fantasizing about glamour and fame; sacrificing career for a more fulfilling path.

ELEVENTH – Submerging oneself in, or being overwhelmed by the group identity; an indulgent social life; acts of altruism; supportive or deceitful friends; chasing elusive dreams.

TWELFTH – Swamped by strong unconscious emotions; an active dream life; feeling ineffective in the outer world; seeking to escape the harshness of reality; letting go through transcendental experiences.

ourselves, then our Neptunian values become distorted. When this happens, Neptune brings confusion, self-deception, greed, deceit, loss, disillusionment and a flight from reality through drugs, alcohol or idle fantasy.

Other correspondences to Neptune include water in all its forms; shipping oil; chemical gasses; leaks; scandal; films; photography; mysticism; altruism; martyrdom; spiritual salvation; artistic inspiration; altered states of consciousness; and illusion or confusion.

Neptune through the Signs

LEO (1914/16-1928/9) – Struggling to find a clear self-image; needing to follow one's own ideals; strong charitable instincts; attracted to the glamorous or the fashionable; false optimism; delusions of grandeur; unattainable standards.

VIRGO (1928/9-1942/3) – Mental sensitivity and a powerful imagination which need practical outlets; highly perceptive or intuitive; easily influenced by those with strong beliefs; false judgments; disorganisation due to a confused state of mind.

LIBRA (1942/3-1955/7) – A need to refine one's emotions, especially in close relationships; idealistic or unrealistic expectations of partnership; an intense desire for peace; lacking self-motivation; artistic inspiration.

SCORPIO (1955/7-1970) – A need to suppress intense desires; fluctuating between extremes of self-denial and self-gratification; an awareness of other people's true motives; confused or misled by others; misinterpreted ambitions.

SAGITTARIUS (1970-1984) – Looking for spiritual meaning or inspiration in life; grand schemes which come to nothing; a tendency to escape from reality; aimless wandering in pursuit of elusive dreams; unreal values or beliefs; extremely intuitive.

CAPRICORN (1984-1998) – Mixing practicality with idealism; shrewd foresight; the need to incorporate spiritual values in one's life; allowing fantasies to over-ride common sense; dissatisfaction with over-materialistic life-style; dedication to duty.

Pluto

Most astrologers now agree that tiny, distant Pluto represents in the birth chart the process of fundamental transformation – of death and rebirth. In contrast to Uranus – which disrupts the Saturnian structures we create in both society and our personal lives – and Neptune – which turns them inside out – Pluto breaks them down completely so that a new level of awareness can be brought into being.

Like the other slow-moving planets, the effect of Pluto in any particular sign is to raise issues which are experienced by a generation. In the birth chart, it is Pluto's house position and the contacts it makes to the Angles and personal planets which show in what area of life we are most likely to respond or contribute to these collective pressures.

Pluto's domain in the birth chart is the subconscious mind, where primitive instincts often lie buried because we have been taught they are socially undesirable. If we refuse to recognize them, they can result in negative Plutonian patterns of behaviour such as compulsions and obsessions, or give rise to events beyond our control which threaten our very survival.

Yet if we can bring these instincts to the surface, Pluto will enable us to refine them so that eventually all aspects of our personality can be brought under conscious control. Such a process of change may be extremely testing, since it involves breaking down old self-images before a new and more complete self is able to emerge.

Pluto also governs any aspect of society that is potentially undermining but which we are unwilling to face – the criminal underworld, subversive groups, taboos, urban decay and corruption; earthquakes and volcanic eruptions; self-transforming therapies and healers; charlatans; any form of uncontrolled power; nuclear energy; depth psychology; sexual reproduction; and the orgasm.

Pluto through the Signs

CANCER (1912/3-1938/9) – Emotional intensity; hiding emotions from view, or trying to suppress them; family upheavals; skeletons in the family cupboard; the need to rebuild one's notion of family or country; understanding the darker side of human nature.

PLUTO THROUGH THE HOUSES

FIRST – A powerful personality that can reach out to influence many, or turn inwards to create continual crises in personal life; the need to face one's buried instincts; life as a fight for survival.

SECOND – The ability to transform something of little worth into something valuable; over-concern about finances for fear of losing everything; financial crises forcing one to change one's material values.

THIRD – A laser-like mind, suited to research; a cutting tongue; revolutionary ideas; mental breakdown leading to changes in the way one thinks.

FOURTH – Wrestling with one's deepest feelings, bringing inner turmoil, or release from unconscious behaviour-patterns; a family background which is disruptive; domineering in the home.

FIFTH – A profound need to express creative instincts spontaneously; the need to overcome creative blocks; impulsive, passionate love affairs; driven by the need to be someone special.

SIXTH – The ability to transform one's working conditions; power struggles in the workplace; a tendency to bury oneself in one's work; illnesses that transform one's attitude to life.

SEVENTH – Relationships that force drastic personal changes, or that tap buried feelings of vulnerability; projecting one's more primitive nature on to partners; a powerful partner.

EIGHTH – Either repressing or learning to master one's instinctive nature; pent-up energy which may be expressed as sexual frustration; emotional crises which bring change; manipulating others.

NINTH – Crises of conviction which make one reassess one's beliefs; an overbearing belief in one's own views; an intense search for the meaning of existence, or a denial of spiritual values.

TENTH – A desire to be influential, or to hide from public attention; asserting one's will in order to succeed; crises in career which may result in new directions; struggles with authority figures.

ELEVENTH – Ideals or groups that have a deep effect on one's thinking; powerful friends that help one achieve objectives; using friends or groups for selfish motives; highly competitive friendships.

TWELFTH – A need to confront unpleasant aspects of oneself deeply buried in the unconscious; a fear of being unacceptable; transforming other people's circumstances, for better or worse.

LEO (1938/9-1957/8) – Prone to excessive pride; re-evaluating one's understanding of what power means, perhaps leading to misuse; fighting for one's individuality by resisting tyranny or mass ideologies; using arrogance to disguise lack of confidence.

VIRGO (1957/8-1971/2) – Intense dissatisfaction with meaningless routines, forcing one to find more fulfilling methods; redefining the quality of life; the need for increased awareness of one's environment; ideas that transform one's attitude to the relationship between mind and body.

LIBRA (1971/2-1983/4) – Emotional disappointments through inharmonious relationships; the need to face the real issues of commitment to another; clinging to outworn relationships out of a deep fear of being unlovable; learning to trust another person's love for what it is; new awareness of the power of appearance.

SCORPIO (1983/4-1995) – Intense desire for intimate unions; penetrating the surface of life to find the common thread that unites everything, yet also learning to tolerate individual differences; the exposure of the abuse of power, especially sexual power; breaking down sexual taboos.

Major & Minor Aspects

The aspects between planets are one of the most important areas of modern chart interpretation

When astrologers speak of *aspects* in a birth chart, they mean the relationships that are constantly forming and reforming between the planets.

While astronomy tells us that the planets of the solar system are in perpetual orbit around the Sun (and that the Moon is in orbit around the earth), from earth itself it seems as if all ten of the other bodies follow the circular path through the sky – the 360° of the zodiac. When a birth chart is drawn up for a certain time and place, each of these bodies is at a different point on the circle.

Astrologers came to discover that there were certain distances between the ten 'planets' – expressed as degrees of the zodiac

ASPECTS TO THE ANGLES

Just as planets can form aspects to one another, so they can form aspects to the Angles in the chart – the Ascendant and Midheaven (and by definition, their opposite numbers – the Descendent and IC). In this respect the Angles can be seen as extremely important outlets for the other planetary energies – but only if the exact time of birth is known.

circle – which corresponded to certain patterns of behaviour in people on earth. These distances, which became known as *aspects*, now form a significant part of the foundation of modern birth chart interpretation.

While the planets signify particular kinds of energy and the signs show the way in which those energies will be expressed, it is the aspects which indicate whether the energies will flow easily or with difficulty.

Good or Bad?

Once it was thought that certain aspects between the planets were 'good' and helped to make life easy, while others were 'bad' and hindered progress or brought misfortune. Modern astrologers no longer believe this. Instead, they classify the aspects as 'hard' and 'soft' (or sometimes, 'easy' and 'difficult').

If you imagine planetary energies as flows of traffic, then the aspects are the traffic lights. 'Hard' aspects are the red lights that cause congestion or hold-ups; 'soft' aspects allow the traffic to flow more easily.

Continuing the example, if the traffic were to flow too easily there would be chaos – things would be almost as bad as if the traffic were permanently snarled up. The same happens in the birth chart. A free flow of aggressive Martian energy might be fine for achieving goals, but at what and whose expense? To be easily moved to tears might seem on the surface to imply weakness, yet it may also denote compassion and depth of feeling.

The fact is that most charts contain both hard and soft aspects, which is just as well. The hard aspects create the tensions in the personality that urge us to get moving and go somewhere; the soft aspects help us to get there, but only if we know where that 'somewhere' is.

As well as the hard and soft aspects there is the conjunction (0°), which is often described as 'neutral'. In other words it can be hard or soft or both, according to the planets involved and depending on the aspects they make to other planets.

ORBS OF ASPECT

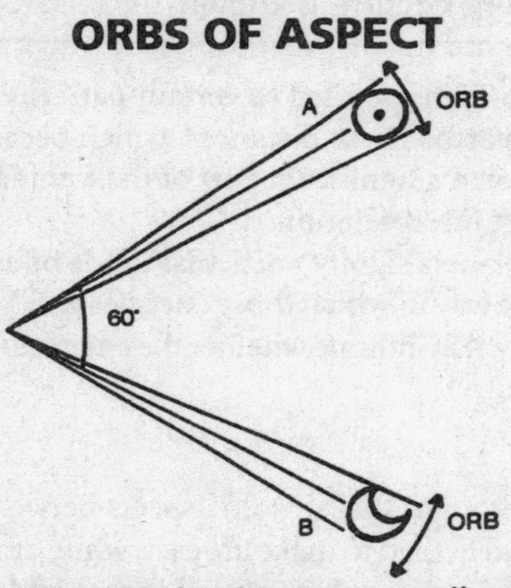

Although each aspect has its own prescribed distance – expressed in degrees of the zodiac – this distance does not have to be exact for the aspect to take effect. There is a 'margin for error' of a few degrees either side – commonly known in astrology as the orb.

Generally speaking, major aspects have a wider orb than minor ones. It is also customary to add a couple of extra degrees to the orbs of aspects involving the Sun and the Moon, since the influences exerted by these planets are so important.

When two planets are moving towards an aspect with each other they are said to be 'applying' – in other words, the aspect can only become stronger. After making an exact aspect, the planets then move apart and are said to be 'separating' – the aspect can only get weaker.

There are also the 'subtle' aspects, so-called because their effects show themselves in a much more subtle way. While the conjunction is very important, even for beginners, subtle aspects are generally only used by professional astrologers.

Major and Minor

Traditionally, the various types of aspect were classified as 'major' and 'minor' according to the importance they were believed to have. But most astrologers now agree that 'minor' aspects which are nearly exact are every bit as (if not more) significant as 'major' aspects which only just fall within their prescribed distance.

Defenders of the old view maintain that 'major' aspects relate to the issues central to a person's life, while the 'minor' ones are only at work below the surface. Generally speaking, though, any aspect which is close to being exact is likely to be important and warrants being looked at carefully.

Lack of Aspects

Many charts appear to have no aspects at all – at least, no major ones – but this does not mean that the subject is a 'non-person'. A closer look will reveal a host of minor aspects, which naturally take on greater significance than they might otherwise have had.

Professional astrologers today use this example to underline their argument that minor aspects are in fact an important part of the birth chart.

THE MAJOR ASPECTS

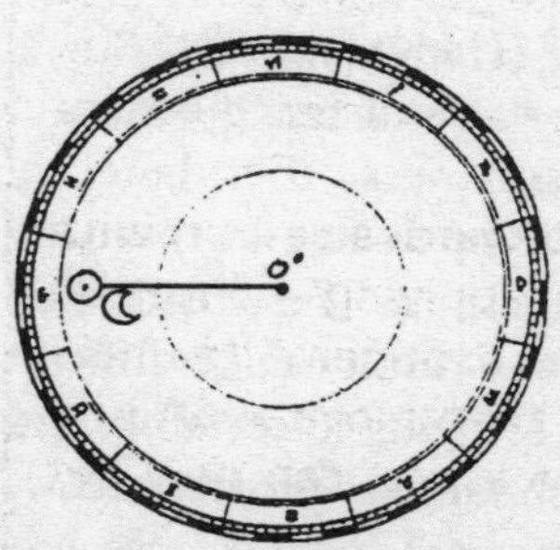

Conjunction 0° (Neutral) Orb: 8°

When two or more planets are in conjunction there is a union or coming together of the principles represented by those planets. They function as one, and yet each gains the support of its neighbour. They do not lose their individuality but provide a powerful focus of energy in the birth chart.

The natures of the planets involved in the conjunction will determine whether this is likely to be hard and challenging or soft and harmonious.

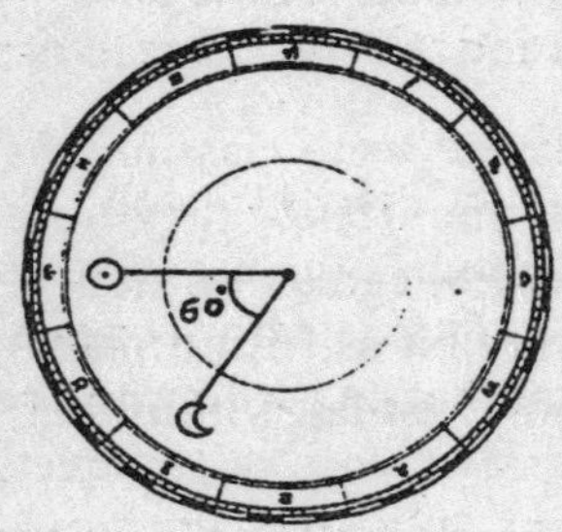

Sextile 60° (Soft) Orb: 4-5°

Sextiles link planets in signs of different but compatible elements. The flow of energy is similar to that of the trine, but not quite so easy – there is enough difference to create the kind of friction that stimulates effort and less risk of complacency. For this reason, the talents indicated by a sextile can be more valuable than those of a trine, though there may also be a tendency to live by one's wits.

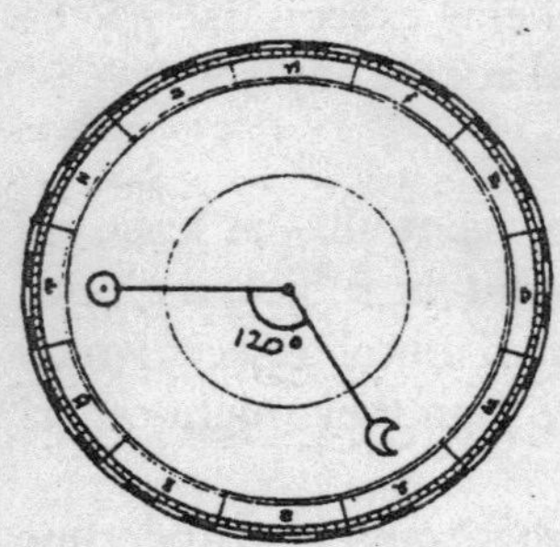

Trine 120° (Soft) Orb: 8°

Everyone has the potential to be creative. The trine shows how easily that creativity is expressed. Sometimes it comes too easily, in which case there is a danger that in-born talents are taken too much for granted and not developed as fully as they might be. It is often helpful to have hard aspects which link up with trines in a chart, as these can often generate the kind of inner tensions which tend to inject the creative instinct with the determination to succeed.

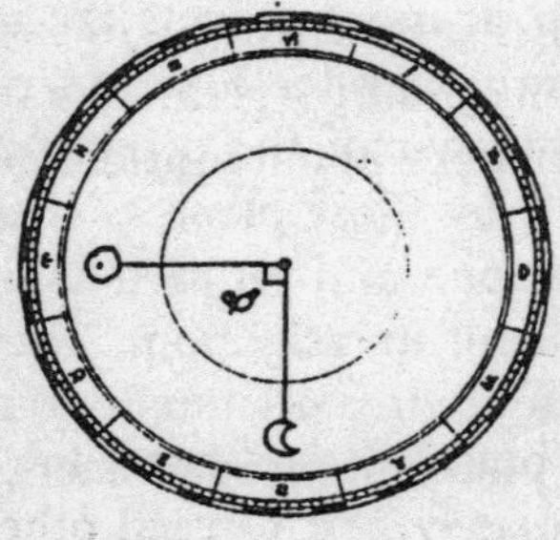

Square 90° (Hard) Orb: 8°

There is a sense of being boxed-in with the square, as the planetary energies are operating in mutually antagonistic signs. The tension that builds up as a result can be difficult to handle, bringing uncertainty and apparent obstacles to progress. However, squares are by and large less extreme than oppositions, forcing the kind of action that eventually leads to change – and to a new set of challenges. In fact without this aspect, the urge to push forward and prove oneself is considerably weakened. It is through the square that the individual acquires the determination and self-discipline to rise above their circumstances.

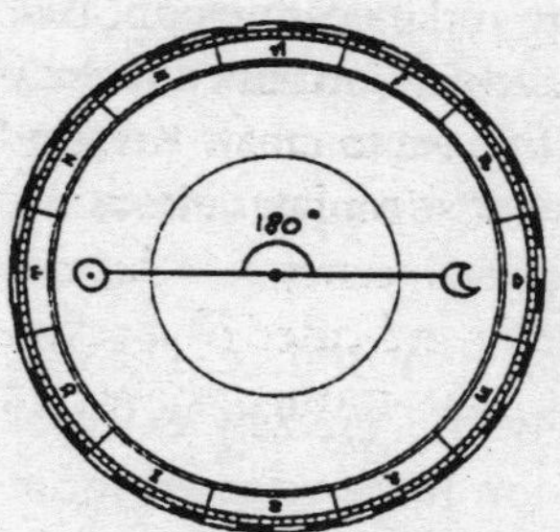

Opposition 180° (Hard) Orb: 8°

As its name implies, this aspect gives a tendency to fluctuate from one extreme to another, according to the energies represented by the planets and the signs. In early years, this is likely to be experienced as a feeling of being pulled apart, as if the individual is unable to satisfy themselves or anyone else. It is rather like trying to be in two places at the same time, one side of the opposition will always lose out. Even so, this aspect offers the chance to balance out the opposing factions so that with maturity and increasing self-awareness, what seem like incompatible facets of the personality can be reconciled. A supporting soft aspect can be helpful in creating openings in the conflicting energies and opportunities for personal growth.

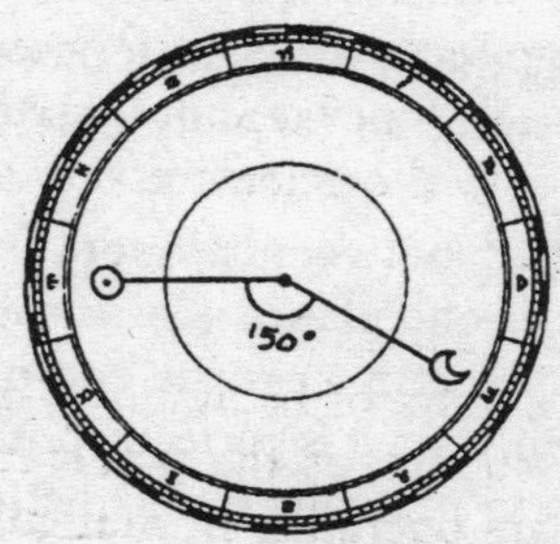

Quincunx 150° (Hard) Orb: 2–3°

This aspect implies tension which can prove very frustrating, since the planetary energies are working through signs that have little in common with one another. Out of such frustration can spring great achievement – but not without considerable effort.

THE MINOR ASPECTS

Semi-Sextile 30° (Neutral) Orb: 1–2°

This aspect could be described as both soft and hard, for it links the two zodiacal signs immediately next to each other.

Rather like neighbours, they have to learn to get along – which is not always easy! On its own the semi-sextile is not generally considered very important, but its significance grows when it acts as a 'bridge' between other aspects in a chart that would otherwise be unconnected.

Semi-Square 45° (Hard) Orb: 2–3°
Similar to the square, the semi-square indicates tension. But the changes it brings are often more sudden and unexpected, possibly because the conflict within the personality – represented by the planets involved in the aspect – are less conscious.

Sesquiquadrate 135° (Hard) Orb: 2–3°
This aspect is similar to the square and semi-square. The difference is that the changes are usually triggered by external events in a way that enables the tension to be released more easily than in the case with the square.

Quintile 72° (Subtle) Orb: 1–2°
Bi-Quintile 144° (Subtle) Orb: 1–2°
These aspects often reveal potential talents or gifts, although they may not show themselves unless there are some supporting hard aspects giving the individual the discipline and resolve to develop them.

Disassociation

There is one big difficulty concerning the aspects which those who study and practise astrology have so far only partly managed to resolve.

Hard aspects are usually formed between planets in mutually unsympathetic signs. But if one planet is near the beginning of a sign and the other planet is near the end of another sign as in the example shown, then it is perfectly possible for them to form a hard aspect in mutually sympathetic signs. Exactly the same condition may apply to soft aspects, which usually involve sympathetic signs but can equally embrace unsympathetic ones.

Astrologers disagree as to the significance of these so-called 'disassociate' aspects. For the beginner, the best advice is to think

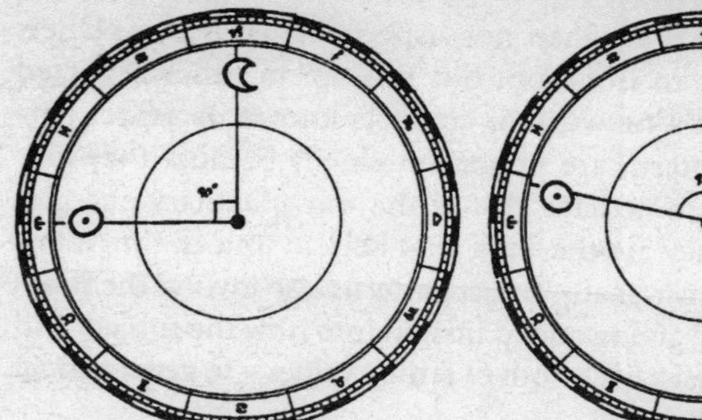

A normal square aspect: the planets fall in 'unsympathetic' Fire and Earth signs.

A disassociate square: the aspect is the same, but both planets fall in signs of the same element.

of a disassociate hard aspect as being 'softer' than it might otherwise be, and in the same way, to think of a disassociate soft aspect as being slightly 'harder'.

There is also a body of opinion which holds that any two planets in unsympathetic signs have something of a 'hard' connection between them whether they are in aspect or not, and that similarly, any two planets in sympathetic signs have some kind of 'soft' link. These subtle distinctions, however, are normally beyond the scope of the beginner.

Aspect Patterns

Every birth chart has its unique combination of aspects, assuming, of course, that the precise time of birth is known. Even if two people are born within minutes of each other in the same place, the Ascendant and Midheaven will have moved, along with the cusps of the other Houses. Over such a short time the aspects between the planets will stay virtually the same. Even so, the shift in the House cusps is often enough to alter the aspects to the all-important Angles, and for other planetary aspects to move into different Houses.

Yet in spite of each chart's uniqueness, people born on the same day, month or even year have certain planetary aspects in common. More often than not, aspects between two planets do not happen in isolation, but link up to other aspected planets to form a network of contacts known as aspect patterns. These patterns are important chiefly because they give astrologers an immediate idea of the way planetary energies are flowing – they are the 'keys' that help to unlock the rest of the chart. However, many aspect patterns also involve the slow-moving planets, giving added insight into how the subject will respond – against a backcloth of family values – to generational issues that affect us all.

Aspect patterns are divided into two categories: major and minor. The major patterns are the most powerful, pointing to complex and often conflicting attitudes within the subject's character. The minor patterns are more subtle, and symbolize less visible personality traits. As a general rule, however, the more planets involved in a pattern, the more intense are the effects.

No Aspect Patterns

Strictly speaking no chart is devoid of aspect patterns, since any aspected planets which also make contacts to other planets create a similar flow of energy. It is quite common for none of the major to minor aspect patterns to appear in a chart, but this does not mean that the subject is a weak or insignificant person – simply that for them the focus of planetary energies is different.

The Grand Cross

The Grand Cross, as its name implies, incorporates planets in square and opposition to each other and involves all four signs of a particular Quality – Cardinal, Fixed or Mutable. It is sometimes referred to as the 'Dilemma', in that when it is triggered – especially by a transiting planet – everything seems to happen at once. As a result, people with this tricky combination often seem to lurch from crisis to crisis as if their mettle is constantly being tested. But if and when they finally master their formidable energies, they may be capable of quite exceptional results. People with a Cardinal Grand Cross have tremendous

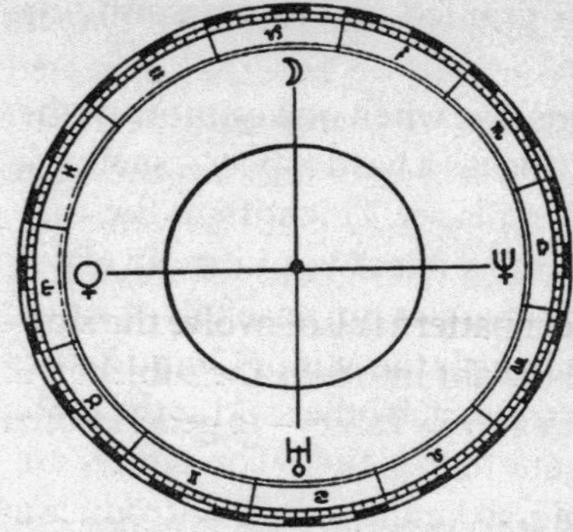

drive and energy, but also meet with a great deal of resistance in achieving their aims. While they may blame others for the frustration they experience, much of it is self-induced, for they seldom plan or think carefully before they act and insist on doing everything their own way. Those with a Fixed Grand Cross tend to do everything within their considerable power to keep things as they are. Valuing reliability and preservation above all else, they will passionately hold out against anything or anyone who tries to upset their sense of order; when change inevitably comes it is usually dramatic and sudden. Mutable Grand Cross types have no difficulty accepting change – in fact, this is their problem. Rather than face a challenge they tend to alter their course in the vain hope that by changing their external circumstances they can avoid unwanted difficulties. The lesson they have to learn is that their conflicts arise from within, as a result of a lack of consistency and a tendency to spread themselves too thinly.

The Grand Trine

The Grand Trine consists of a triangle of three or more planets – including sensitive points such as the Ascendant and MC – which all make trine aspects to each other in one of the Elements (Fire, Earth, Air, Water). Traditionally, the Grand Trine was thought to be extremely fortunate, but the modern view is that on its own it may be too fortunate. Since it shows natural talents which usually emerge early on in life, there may be a

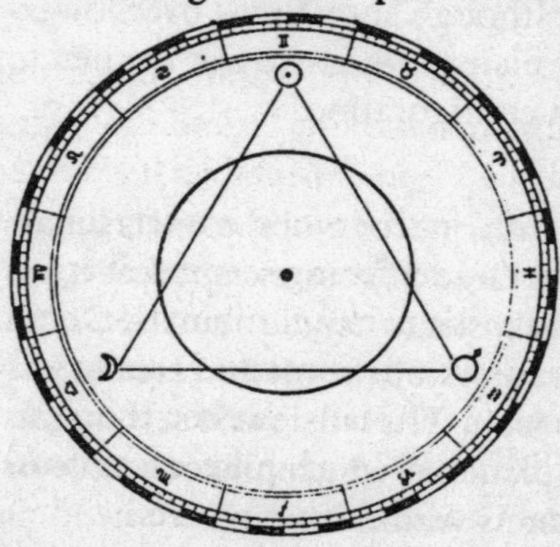

tendency to take these gifts for granted and a corresponding lack of resolve to develop them.

The effects are much more positive when one or more of the planets in the Grand Trine also makes a hard aspect – such as a square or opposition – to another planet. This stiffens the 'easy come, easy go' attitude, urging the subject to put more effort into channelling their planetary energies purposefully. A more common version of the Grand Trine is the Minor Grand Trine, which occurs when two planets trine each other and at the same time make a sextile aspect to another planet. The effects are similar, but often more dynamic, since the sextiles introduce a sense of perseverance that may otherwise be lacking.

The Stellium

A Stellium (also known as *Satellitium)* is an aspect pattern made up of three or more planets which are either in the same sign or in the same house (although if they are only in the same house and their signs are different, the effect is less intense). The group of planets form a chain of conjunctions, so that while the first and last planets in the chain may not be in aspect to each other, they are joined through their conjunctions to the planets in between. The effect is to exaggerate the qualities of the sign(s) and house(s) in which the stellium falls – although sometimes overpoweringly so, at the expense of any planets which do not happen to aspect this relatively common configuration.

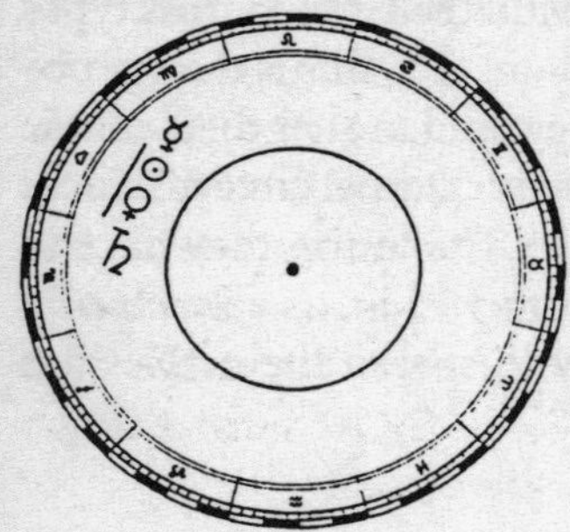

The T-Square

The T-Square – an opposition with one (or more) planets squaring both ends – is similar to the Grand Cross, except that it has one 'arm' missing. It is held to be easier to handle than the Grand Cross, for the empty arm offers an escape route and creates less of a feeling of being torn four ways. The tensions it sets up can also be released through any planet(s) which makes sextile or trine aspects to one of the planets within it.

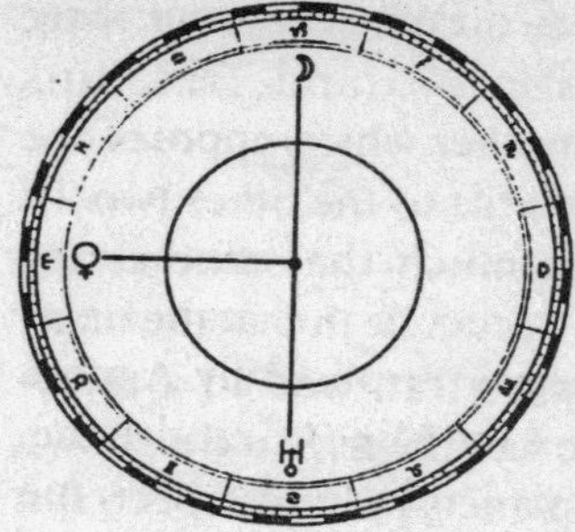

The same sort of dilemmas apply to the Cardinal, Fixed or Mutable qualities of the T-Square as to the Grand Cross. However, because the planetary energies are not as prone to being bottled up, people with this combination usually manage to sort out their inner problems more easily.

Minor Aspect Patterning

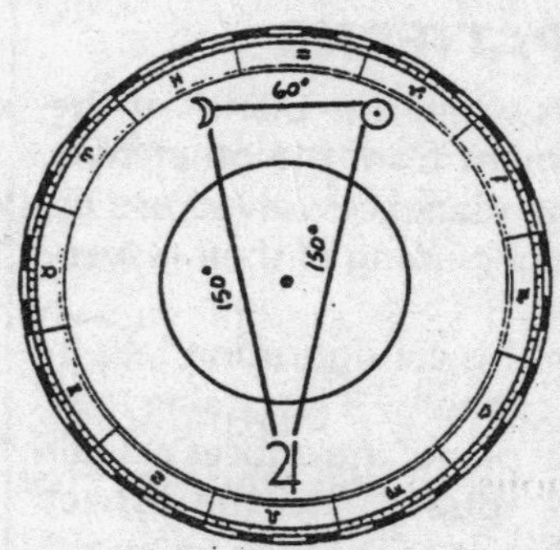

The Finger of Fate (Yod) is a rare pattern in which two planets in sextile to one another are both quincunx (150°) to a third. The Yod takes its name from the Hebrew meaning 'blessed' and is reputed to have a quality of fate about it – in other words, the planets and houses involved point to a certain direction in life. This is not an easy pattern to work with, but if the tensions it shows can be resolved, great achievements are possible.

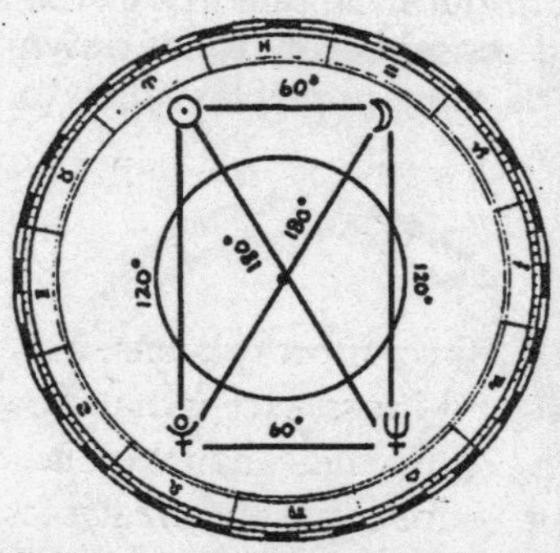

The Mystic Rectangle is a complex pattern consisting of two oppositions, the ends of which form sextiles or trines to each other. Because of its shape, the flow of energy may be limited to the soft aspects, missing out the hard ones altogether and leaving important issues unresolved, as with the Grand Trine. However, if the oppositions are integrated, the blend of hard and soft aspects can result in the kind of dynamic tension that enables people to develop their natural abilities to the full.

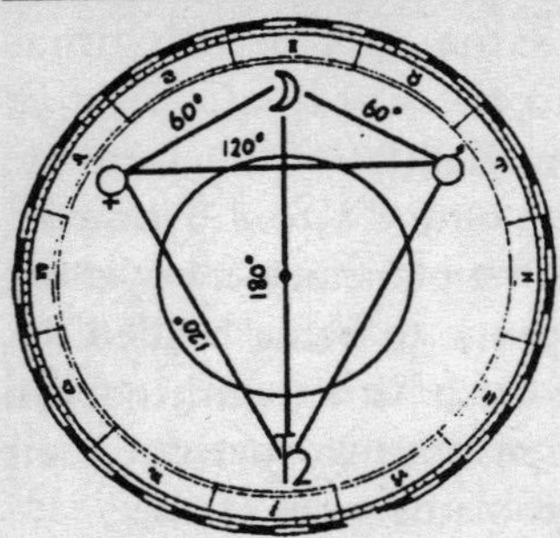

The Kite occurs whenever three planets in a Grand Trine link up to another which opposes one and is sextile to the other two. Its effect is much the same as the Mystic Rectangle in that the many soft aspects can lead to a reluctance to face the difficulties shown by the planets in hard aspect. But again, if the issues shown by the opposition are confronted, the potential rewards are high.

DISSOCIATE PATTERNS

A Dissociate Grand Trine occurs when one planet of the triangle falls in a different Element from the other two. This can only happen when the planets involved are either very near the end or at the beginning of their respective signs.

Because one of the planets in this configuration falls in an inharmonious sign, the flow of energy is less stable than the pure Grand Trine. The errant planet introduces a quality of tension – rather like a square – to the aspect pattern, and offers a greater chance of using the planets' collective energies assertively. Dissociate Grand Crosses and T-Squares are also softer versions of their pure forms.

At least one planet in the configuration falls in a different Quality to the others, and consequently tones down the overall level of tension. The same principles apply to all dissociate aspect patterns.

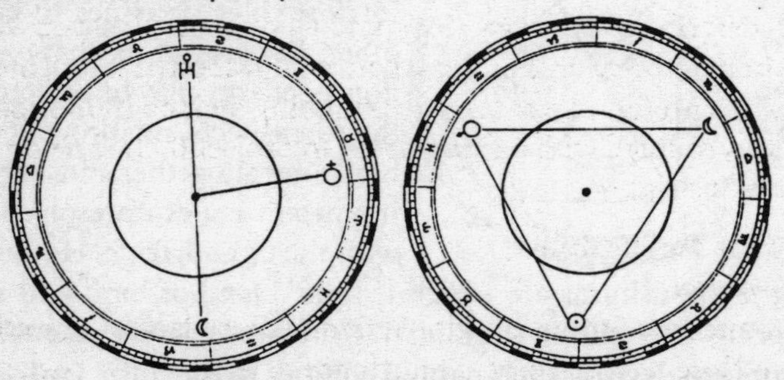

Planetary Aspects

Although aspects between planets are a key part of chart interpretation, this does not mean that unaspected planets are unimportant. In fact, they may be exceptionally revealing. If a planet has no aspects, or those present are very weak, then either its energy will be blocked and it will have trouble blending in with other planets, or it will take on a magnified importance.

People with an unaspected sun, for example, may struggle to find their purpose in life, or be excessively self-centred. An unaspected Moon can point to weak emotional ties in childhood for which the individual tries to compensate in later life. Mercury unaspected suggests trouble with self-expression, although people with this configuration may also be obsessed with developing their mental faculties.

Shyness often dominates those with an unaspected Venus; they may struggle to form close relationships, while at the same time hiding their inhibitions by being overly sociable. A lack of self-motivation commonly afflicts those with an unaspected Mars. It is not that they are short of energy; simply that they do not know what to do with it!

With Jupiter, weak or no aspects can lead to problems in creating opportunities, although much energy may be wasted through misplaced optimism. Those with an unaspected Saturn rarely know their own limitations, and often set themselves impossible tasks. A solitary Uranus suggests a person who has difficulty developing their individuality, mistaking frankness and anti-social behaviour for the same thing. Neptune on its own described people who may confuse their own feelings with spiritual inspiration. For those with an unaspected Pluto, there may be a profound resistance to plumbing their own emotional depths, coupled with a compulsion to project their fears on to others instead.

Aspects To The Sun

Sun-Moon

Conjunction: Strong emotional family ties; a lack of objectivity in close relationships; a reluctance to let go of the past.

Soft: A contented nature; good relations with family and partners; possibly too self-satisfied.
Hard: Argumentative and highly strung; difficulty in changing habits; may see family life as 'unsafe'; striving to overcome family patterns of behaviour.

Sun-Mercury
Conjunction: Independent-minded; mentally alert and talkative; may be opinionated while seeming rational. (Mercury is never more than 28° away from the Sun so only the conjunction is possible.)

Sun-Venus
Conjunction: An emphasized need for relationships; learning to love oneself; seeking popularity; refined and artistic; over-compromising; self-indulgent. (Venus is never more than 48° away from the Sun, so only a conjunction, semi-sextile or semi-square can occur. The semi-square is linked to breakdowns in relationships.)

Sun-Mars
Conjunction: A desire to achieve and be in charge; fiercely competitive and combative; hot-blooded, impulsive and full of energy.
Soft: Enormous vitality; channelling energy constructively; decisive; enterprising; vigorous.
Hard: Fluctuating energy levels; impetuous; argumentative; injury-prone; over-stressed; rash.

Sun-Jupiter
Conjunction: Optimistic; generous; fortunate contacts; visionary; humorous; high aspirations.
Soft: Tolerant; high expectations; benevolent; indulgent; easy-going; high expectations.
Hard: Wasteful; boastful; showy; restless; undisciplined; lazy; misplaced idealism; greedy.

Sun-Saturn
Conjunction: Serious; solitary; ambitious; self-denying; selfish; unsympathetic; undemonstrative.

Soft: Slow but steady progress; well organized; reliable; patient; cautious; dedicated; enduring.
Hard: Feeling inferior; self-conscious; pessimistic; inhibited; austere.

Sun-Uranus
Conjunction: Original; over-powering; stubborn; eccentric; magnetic; unorthodox; independent.
Soft: Progressive; a leader; frank; dramatic; seeking change; zestful; supporting the underdog.
Hard: Anarchic; rebellious; compelled to change things; self-destructive; domineering.

Sun-Neptune
Conjunction: Sensitive; dreamy; impractical; a weak sense of self; gullible; artistic; receptive.
Soft: Inspired ideas; visionary; compassionate; idealistic; strong creative potential.
Hard: Confused identity; highly emotional; self-victimising; impressionable; open to deception.

Sun-Pluto
Conjunction: A power complex; many upheavals; extreme ambition; a need for self-knowledge; tyrannical.
Soft: Notable achievements; forceful; crises may prove beneficial; creative potential.
Hard: Obsessed with self; ruthless; dynamic; stressed; fanatical.

JANE FONDA (SUN IN SAGITTARIUS)

Jane's birth chart contains a disassociated Grand Trine in Fire and Earth involving the Sun, Moon and Midheaven. This is indicative of her privileged, supportive upbringing and of her capacity to turn creative ideas into reality through the sheer force of her personality. However, her Sun in a Mutable T-Square with Saturn opposite Neptune suggests that in spite of the many favours which have come her way, she has been dogged by feelings of insecurity and a confused identity.

Aspects to the Moon

Moon-Mercury

Conjunction: A retentive memory; imaginative; intuitive; full of common sense; perceptive; talkative.

Soft: Expressive; language skills; shrewd; sensible; adaptable; reasonable; humorous.

Hard: Devious; quick-witted; scornful; hypersensitive; highly strung; erratic; gossiping.

Moon-Venus

Conjunction: Great charm; peaceful; cooperative; fair-minded; a love of beauty; tender.

Soft: Social graces; a strong sense of taste; supportive; popular; diplomatic; pleasure-seeking.

Hard: Struggles to express feelings; misunderstandings with partners; shy; moody; frustrated in love.

Moon-Mars

Conjunction: Fiery emotions; thoughtless courage; direct; strong-willed; a fighting spirit.

Soft: Vigorous health; candid; energetic; independent; fond of dare-devil pursuits; warm-hearted.

Hard: Poor health, exaggerated reactions; irritable; intolerant; short-tempered; ambitious; pushy.

Moon-Jupiter

Conjunction: Generous; protective; an urge to travel; emotionally demanding; self-indulgent; selfish.

Soft: Warm-hearted; benevolent; optimistic; generally fortunate; a keen social conscience; a traveller.

Hard: Harshly critical; careless; lazy; faulty judgment; wasteful; greedy.

Moon-Saturn

Conjunction: Powerful concentration; a poor mother image; self-denying; hardworking; dutiful; inhibited; mean.

Soft: Loyal, reliable; industrious; organising skills; controlled; down-to-earth; traditional; limited.

Hard: Depressive; pessimistic; afraid of failure; looking for 'mother'; a sense of being hard done by; low self-esteem; lonely; worrying.

Moon-Uranus
Conjunction: Original; unorthodox; extremely independent; highly strung; erratic emotional reactions.

Soft: Highly intuitive; capable of making instant decisions; prone to sudden mood changes; progressive; ambitious; off-beat.

Hard: Extremely tense and prone to stress; demanding; difficult to live with; an exaggerated need for space.

Moon-Neptune
Conjunction: Highly romantic; selfless; extremely sensitive to surroundings; secluded; escapist.

Soft: Imaginative; visionary; kind; difficulty in understanding own limitations; idealising the family.

Hard: Prone to self-deception; impractical; addictive; seducible; confused emotions; misplaced ideals.

Moon-Pluto
Conjunction: Intense but buried feelings; extreme reactions; a powerful mother; skeletons in the cupboard.

Soft: Resilient; able to express and transform deepest feelings; a vivid unconscious mind; passionate.

Hard: Thwarted needs; bouts of jealousy; impulsive or even violent reactions; obsessive; fated events; emotional blackmail; crises in home life.

TWIGGY (SUN IN VIRGO)

Twiggy has a shy, retiring Sun in Virgo in the Twelfth House, but counterbalancing this is a powerful Stellium aspect pattern comprising the Moon, Mars and Pluto in Leo in the Eleventh. Such a configuration at least partly explained her public impact as fashion leader for an entire generation.

Aspects to Mercury

Mercury-Venus

Conjunction: An elegant way with words, charming; sociable; vain; amusing; superficial relationships. (Mercury and Venus are never more than 72° apart; so only the conjunctions, sextile, semi-sextile, semi-square and quintile are possible.) Soft aspects mirror the more amiable qualities of the conjunction, while the semi-square emphasizes the lazier (and more conceited side)!

Mercury-Mars

Conjunction: Mentally alert; needle-tongued; argumentative; a sharp mind; nervous tension; outspoken.
Soft: A skilled speaker, ready wit; common sense; courageous; decisive; determined; a strong nervous system.
Hard: Capable; tends to overwork; irritable; critical; sarcastic; litigious; cheeky; self-important.

Mercury-Jupiter

Conjunction: A need to expand the mind; travel-hungry; optimistic; a mass of ideas; conceited; popular.
Soft: A fertile mind; eager for information; humorous; articulate; constructive ideas; self-satisfied.
Hard: Over-confident; a lazy mind; arrogant; poor judgement; negligent; original; deceitful; indiscreet.

Mercury-Saturn

Conjunction: Concentration; patient; methodical; great mental effort; depressed; dull; slow-witted; inhibited expression; deep thoughts.
Soft: Organisational and practical skills; serious; reliable; honest; blunt speech; profound; ambitious.
Hard: Shy; over-concerned with detail; anxious; unconfident; harsh; lonely; inhibited; a rigid mentality.

Mercury-Uranus

Conjunction: The mind of the genus; great originality; intuitive; highly strung; erratic; misunderstood.
Soft: Forward-looking; inventive; adaptable; dramatic; a good memory; single-minded; self-reliant; astute.

Hard: Nervous tension; wasted energy; eccentric; selfish; inflated believe in own views; tactless.

Mercury-Neptune

Conjunction: Imaginative; sensitive; creative; self-deluding; vague; poetic; gullible; impractical.

Soft: Highly sympathetic; easily hurt; inspired; an interest in the spiritual; receptive to ideas.

Hard: An extremely rich but troubled imagination; lack of self-belief; worrying; dishonest; deceitful.

Mercury-Pluto

Conjunction: A penetrating mind; mental stress; critical of others; persuasive; vigorous.

Soft: Incisive understanding; fast thinking; a restless, intense mind; a black sense of humour; cunning.

Hard: Tense; rushed thinking; over-straining the mind; fits of temper.

Planet-by-Planet Aspect Guide

A tricky problem for any astrologer is how to interpret the likely strengths and weaknesses of two (or more) planets when they are in aspect to each other. The traditional approach is to follow a planetary pecking order, in which the planets furthest from the Sun are given more weight than those which are nearer. For example, when Venus is in aspect to Pluto (the most distant planet), it is Pluto's influence which takes precedence.

But although this is a helpful way to learn how the planets work, most astrologers today keep an open mind on which planet in an aspect plays the dominant role. They resist drawing any firm conclusions until they have considered the chart as a whole.

Returning to our example, Venus may be involved in other strong aspect patterns, or be prominent either through its position or as the chart ruler, in which case it will hold sway over Pluto. Equally, if Scorpio or Pluto are strong in the chart, then Pluto's energies will be to the fore.

Relative Strengths

Another delicate question is how to interpret the relative strengths of aspects. Aspects are strongest when they are exact, give or take one degree of orb. But it is usual for the orbs to be wider – up to eight degrees – in which case the aspect will either by *applying* or *separating.*

When an aspect is applying it has yet to reach exactitude and its full effects will be felt after birth. The opposite is true of a separating aspect, since it was exact before birth.

Some astrologers believe that applying aspects refer to conditions that will be met in the future, while separating aspects deal with circumstances that the subject is born into and so have an hereditary quality about them.

Aspects to Venus

Venus-Mars

Conjunction: Passionate in love; sensual; strong sex drive; sensitive feelings; tactless; lewd; impulsive.

Soft: Warm and affectionate; expressive; appetite for sex may lead to many love affairs; creative.

Hard: Easily offended; stressful sex life; lustful; blowing hot and cold; discontented; insatiable; impatient.

Venus-Jupiter

Conjunction: Popularity through charm and generosity; a taste for luxury; high expectations of partners.

Soft: Sociable; pleasure-seeking; an eye for quality; graceful; able to handle people; extravagant.

Hard: Over-dramatic; conflicts in love; lazy; vain; many love affairs through high ideals.

Venus-Saturn

Conjunction: Inhibited; slow to form relationships; sense of duty; cold; lonely or deprived; faithful.

Soft: Responsible; controlled feelings; lack-lustre social life; stable love; lacking spontaneity.

Hard: Love sacrificed to ambition; unhappy loves; low self-worth; undemonstrative; selfish.

Venus-Uranus

Conjunction: Emotionally independent; magnetic attractions; erratic feelings; highly strung; eccentric tastes.

Soft: Many friends; charismatic; romantic; free with affections; will not be tied down; creative talents.

Hard: Problems with commitment; troubled loves; nervous tension; sudden changes in finances.

Venus-Neptune

Conjunction: Highly idealistic and romantic; finding love confusing and disappointing; overly compassionate.

Soft: Imaginative; unworldly; sensitive; artistic flair; image-conscious; a tendency to daydream; highly musical.

Hard: Unrealistic ideals leading to disappointments; indecisive; easily deluded; victimized; escapist.

Venus-Pluto

Conjunction: Powerful and deep feelings; obsessive or destructive loves; intense sexuality; demanding.

Soft: Passionate nature; dynamic; financial ability; intensely loyal; dramatic; magnetic; highly creative.

Hard: Strong likes and dislikes; lusting after money or sex; upheavals in love.

GOLDIE HAWN (SUN IN SCORPIO)

One of the most powerful women in films today comes in a deceptively doll-like package. But Goldie's Venus in Scorpio in a difficult square aspect to her Sun-sign ruler, Pluto, reveals a deep need to have total control over her life and work.

Aspects to Mars

Mars-Jupiter

Conjunction: Driving physical energy; competitive; open and direct; decisive; self-important.

Soft: Positive and enterprising; confidence in own actions; high energy levels; capable; willpower.

Hard: Restless; unfocused energy; a dislike of routine; disruptive; hasty; arrogant; challenging authority.

Mars-Saturn
Conjunction: Accident-prone; physical suffering; hardships; learning to endure delays; hard-working; frugal.
Soft: Disciplined; persevering; strong survival instinct; organising skills once motivated; practical; possibly unimaginative.
Hard: Poor staying power; negative attitudes; a fear of being cowardly; lack of purpose; injuries; harsh.

Mars-Uranus
Conjunction: Individualistic; sharp reflexes; courageous; wilful; high tension may lead to breakdown.
Soft: Intuitive snap decisions; heightened awareness; aims achieved; a need to channel impulsive urges.
Hard: Tense; temperamental; hasty; undisciplined; argumentative; brash; stubborn; carrying a high risk of accidents.

Mars-Neptune
Conjunction: Impractical daydreams; strong sexual fantasies; compassion; inconsistent energy; escapist.
Soft: Inspired goals which are often achieved; charitable; idealistic; a rich imagination; powerful emotions.
Hard: Longing for the impossible; discontent; escape through drink or drugs; diffused energy; depraved.

Mars-Pluto
Conjunction: Explosive or destructive energy; ruthlessly determined; cruel; violent emotional outbursts.
Soft: Ambitious; a tireless worker; great courage; remarkable feats against the odds; self-confident.
Hard: Obsessive emotions; obstinate; riding roughshod over others to attain goals; over-reaching aims.

RICHARD GERE (SUN IN VIRGO)

With Mars in sensual Cancer opposing Jupiter in chilly Capricorn, the heart-throb who can safely count himself among Hollywood's biggest earners actually dislikes the trappings of wealth and much prefers the simple life.

Aspects to Jupiter

Conjunction: Slow progress; need to persevere in the face of opposition; optimism tested; brooding; tenacity.

Soft: Steady but sure advancement; realistic beliefs; highly motivated; conscientious; modest; constructive.

Hard: Easily discouraged; unstable; pessimistic; confused ambitions; a need to work within limitations.

Jupiter-Uranus

Conjunction: Forward-looking; grand-scale ambitions; a pressing need for independence; restless.

Soft: Leadership qualities; radical thinking; unconventional beliefs; unexpected luck; sudden insights.

Hard: Stubborn resistance to change; rebellious; wilful; dogmatic; argumentative; outspoken.

Jupiter-Neptune

Conjunction: Idealistic; perceptive; unrealistic dreams; inflated pride; spiritual longings; artistic talent.

Soft: Kind-hearted; championing the underdog; a need for solitude; visionary; effortless gains; sloppy.

Hard: Hypersensitive; confused spiritual ideas; muddled finances; aimless wandering; scandal.

Jupiter-Pluto

Conjunction: Power complex; extreme self-confidence; unflinching; major accomplishments; leadership.

Soft: Single-minded pursuits; desire to influence; organising skills; the ability to unearth the truth.

Hard: Fanatical beliefs; wasteful; self-destructive; militant; great gains and losses; scheming or manipulative.

SYLVESTER STALLONE (SUN IN CANCER)

'Sly' Stallone has his Sun and Saturn square Jupiter in Libra, indicating the numerous personal problems which he has encountered despite riding the crest of a wave of success in his career.

Aspects to Saturn

Saturn-Uranus

Conjunction: Conflict between radical change and convention; great inner struggles; depression; excitability.

Soft: Mixing initiative with caution; perseverance; sudden major changes late in life; administrative skills.

Hard: Extreme nervous tension; conflicts with authority figures; difficult separations; displays of rebellion.

Saturn-Pluto

Conjunction: Unpredictable; deeply ingrained obsessions; severe; suppressing pain.

Soft: Overcoming frustrations; remarkable powers of endurance; great dedication; eventual success.

Hard: Lack of compassion; self-centred; destructive; severe losses; physical hardship.

JOHN TRAVOLTA (SUN IN AQUARIUS)

John has his Moon in conscientious Virgo, and sextile Saturn in deep, penetrating Scorpio, telling of the hard-working and dedicated way he responds to the challenge of each new screen role.

Aspects to Uranus

Uranus-Neptune

Conjunction: Remarkable talents; unstable events; an original mixture of intuition and imagination.

Soft: Strong humanitarian instinct; visionary; intuitive; idealistic.

Hard: Fear of the unknown; bigoted; a need to make dramatic changes; chaos; emotionally strained.

Uranus-Pluto

Conjunction: An urge to transform environment or exploit it mercilessly; huge creative potential.

Soft: Dynamic; a desire for change and self-improvement; self-awareness through facing traumas.

Hard: Suffering through resistance to change; subversive; inner tension which explodes violently; impatient.

Aspects to Neptune

Neptune-Pluto

Conjunction: Happens about every 490 years; those born with this aspect during the 1890s were at the centre of the huge upheavals resulting from two World Wars.

Soft: From 1945 to 2036 these two planets remain more or less in sextile to each other, coinciding with adjustments that have to be made in society following the effects of the conjunction.

Hard: Will not happen in the lifetime of the reader! Historically connected with prolonged periods of crisis and extreme reactions.

The Planets in the Signs

One thing never to forget when interpreting a birth chart is that whatever the aspects the planets make to each other, they are also always profoundly affects by the sign which they occupy. Some planetary energies flow more smoothly in certain signs, while in others their expression is less harmonious.

In principle, planets are at their 'purest' when they occupy the sign they rule and are said to be in **dignity**. However, in traditional astrology every planet also has one sign in which it is believed to function most effectively, known as its sign of **exaltation**.

In these signs, planets seem to acquire an extra dimension which encourages a higher level of expression. For example Saturn is 'exalted' in Libra, and while this may point to difficult or inhibited relationships, it also inspires – through experience – a responsible attitude and sense of duty towards such commitments.

When a planet is in the sign opposite to its dignity, it is in **detriment**. This placement is considered to be weak since the sign is a poor vehicle for the planet's energies. Similarly, planets in the opposite signs to their exaltation are said to be in their **fall** – a position which restricts their free expression. The

PLANETARY STRENGTHS

Planet	*Dignity (Sign ruled)*	*Detriment*	*Exaltation*	*Fall*
Sun	Leo	Aquarius	Aries	Libra
Moon	Cancer	Capricorn	Taurus	Scorpio
Mercury	Gemini	Sagittarius	Virgo	Pisces
	Virgo	Pisces	(Aquarius)	(Leo)
Venus	Taurus	Scorpio	Pisces	Virgo
	Libra	Aries		
Mars	Aries	Libra	Capricorn	Cancer
	Scorpio	Taurus		
Jupiter	Sagittarius	Gemini	Cancer	Capricorn
	Pisces	Virgo		
Saturn	Capricorn	Cancer	Libra	Aries
	Aquarius	Leo		
Uranus	Aquarius	Leo	Scorpio	Taurus
Neptune	Pisces	Virgo	(Cancer)	(Capricorn)
Pluto	Scorpio	Taurus	(Pisces)	(Virgo)
			(Aquarius)	(Leo)

NB: Astrologers have yet to agree about the Exaltations and Falls given in brackets

planet Mars, for example, 'falls' in Cancer because the direct, assertive nature of this planet is camouflaged by the defensive, non-confrontational quality of the sign.

Occasionally, two planets are found in signs ruled by each other – for instance, Mercury in Aries or Mars in Gemini. In this case they are said to be in **mutual reception** – a combination similar to the conjunction, although not as powerful.

The full list of planetary dignities, exaltations, detriments and falls is shown above, though astrologers are not completely in agreement about the relatively newly discovered 'Outer Planets'.

In fact, many modern astrologers tend to disregard these planetary strengths altogether, while others only use them cautiously. Even so, for the beginner, they are a useful way of learning how the planets and signs interact.

Planetary Aspects to the Angles

> IMPORTANT: For aspects between planets and Angles to be of any relevance, the Birth Time must be exact to within a few minutes.

The Sun

Sun-Ascendant

Conjunction: A radiant personality; self-centred; happy; seeking fame.

Opposition: Looking for fulfilment through relationships and partners.

Soft: Likable; confident; desire to shine; well-adjusted; recognition.

Hard: Over-confident; unpopular; overcoming obstacles to ambition.

Sun-Midheaven

Conjunction: Powerful urge to be recognized; single-minded ambition.

Opposition: Need for privacy; self-conscious; resolving family issues.

Soft: Positive outlook; easily motivated; self-aware; successful.

Hard: Arrogant belief in own abilities; setbacks lead to loss of confidence; the hard road to success.

The Moon

Moon-Ascendant

Conjunction: Strong family ties; caring; moody; highly subjective.

Opposition: Strong contacts with women; over-dependent.

Soft: Adaptable; receptive; easy-going; emotional needs satisfied.

Hard: Touchy; over-reacting; emotional discord; changeable.

Moon-Midheaven

Conjunction: Instinct for what the public wants; women, especially the mother, influence direction in life.

Opposition: Powerful link with family tradition; sense of history.
Soft: Sentimental; well-balanced emotions; flexible; urge to nurture.
Hard: Restlessness leads to many career changes; unsettled home life.

> With the Moon in Cancer conjuncting her Ascendant, Aquarian Farah Fawcett made a name for herself projecting an image of wholesome femininity. Interestingly, her domestic affairs have never been far from the public eye!

Mercury

Mercury-Ascendant

Conjunction: Inquisitive; versatile; many contacts; articulate; restless.
Opposition: Looking for lively partners; sensitive nervous system.
Soft: Chatty; charming; business-minded; stimulating company.
Hard: Gossiping; hypercritical; nervous disorders; fickle; rude.

Mercury-Midheaven

Conjunction: A passion for learning; seeking recognition for mental abilities; influential contacts.
Opposition: Feeling mentally inferior; lack of self-motivation.
Soft: In tune with public; planning skills; a professional attitude.
Hard: Indecisive; unreliable; aimless; many career changes.

Venus

Venus-Ascendant

Conjunction: Personable and usually physically very attractive; a love of luxury; somewhat vain.
Opposition: Motivated by others' needs; high expectations of partner.
Soft: Diplomatic; kind-hearted; sociable; charming; creative.
Hard: Extravagant; self-indulgent; pretentious; inclined towards idle pleasure-seeking.

Venus-Midheaven

Conjunction: Drawn to an artistic career; a need for partnership.

Opposition: Conflict between home life and career may dull ambition.

Soft: Easy expression of feelings and talents, though often lazy.

Hard: Feelings of being unloved; rivalry in partnerships; vain.

Mars

Mars-Ascendant

Conjunction: Strong-bodied; highly energetic; competitive; imposing; a strong physical presence.

Opposition: Argumentative or bossy partners; over-exertion; abrasive.

Soft: Leadership qualities; dynamic; honest; practical; hard-working.

Hard: Stressful; a need to direct powerful emotions purposefully; rash.

Mars-Midheaven

Conjunction: Determined; fiercely ambitious; a love of challenge.

Opposition: Frustrated goals; struggling to become independent; disruptive influences at home.

Soft: Enterprising; organisational skills; resolute; realistic goals.

Hard: Conflicts with authority; overworked; many disputes; hasty.

Jupiter

Jupiter-Ascendant

Conjunction: Hugely optimistic; great flair; self-important; idle.

Opposition: Difficulty reconciling need for freedom with obligations to others; 'lucky' partnerships.

Soft: Easy-going; optimistic outlook, usually vindicated.

Hard: Arrogant; poor judgment; over-generous; hedonistic.

Jupiter-Midheaven

Conjunction: Career success; a need to influence; confident.

Opposition: Quietly optimistic, or exaggerated expectations of life due to parental influence.

Soft: Expansive; humanitarian interests; generous; achieving goals.

Hard: Inflated self-importance; drawn to get-rich-quick schemes.

> With Jupiter conjuncting his IC, it seems likely that Paul McCartney's rise to fame and wealth stemmed from feelings of optimism and expectation acquired as a child. Neptune on the Descendant shows a rather idealized view of relationships.

Saturn

Saturn-Ascendant

Conjunction: Serious; capable; feeling unsupported; ambitious.

Opposition: Difficulty in expressing emotions in relationships; partner's age or outlook may differ markedly.

Soft: Reserved; reticent; a late developer who eventually succeeds.

Hard: Underlying shyness prevents intimate contacts; self-conscious.

Saturn-Midheaven

Conjunction: Hardworking; a lonely position of authority; setbacks.

Opposition: Inhibited ambition; a desire to become self-sufficient.

Soft: Patient; practical; the slow road to success; conscientious.

Hard: Self-doubt; pessimistic; difficult challenges.

Uranus

Uranus-Ascendant

Conjunction: Erratic; excitable; scattered energies; temperamentally 'different'; independent; magnetic.

Opposition: Unusual partner; sudden change through relationships.

Soft: Ingenious; continually changing; thriving on the unusual.

Hard: Explosive; nervous tension; unpredictable; compulsive.

Uranus-Midheaven
Conjunction: Sudden twists of fate; eccentric choice of career; original.
Opposition: Unable to settle; cut off from or rebelling against family.
Soft: Fortunate though unexpected events; original methods; dynamic.
Hard: Hasty decisions; many career changes; unreliable; stubborn.

Neptune

Neptune-Ascendant
Conjunction: Hypersensitive; dreamy; confused; escapist; deluded; gentle.
Opposition: Highly idealistic about relationships leading to sacrifices or disappointments.
Soft: Compassionate; romantic; easily influenced; unrealistic.
Hard: Misled; betrayed; insincere; confused motives; poor sense of self.

Neptune-Midheaven
Conjunction: Longing for the ideal career; hard work for little reward.
Opposition: Idealized memories of childhood; lack of security/purpose.
Soft: Attracted to the artistic; yearning for the impossible.
Hard: Confused objectives; easily deceived; lacking confidence.

Pluto

Pluto-Ascendant
Conjunction: A complex personality; dramatic changes in life; intense; inner strength; domineering.
Opposition: Obsessive quality about relationships; dictatorial partner.
Soft: The ability to heal past wounds and begin anew; influential.

Hard: Drastic upheavals; inner turmoil; deep-rooted obsessions.

Pluto-Midheaven

Conjunction: Hungry for fame; career may seem 'fated'.
Opposition: A need to explore one's origins; rebuilding a sense of self.
Soft: Organizing abilities; staying power; visionary; authoritative.
Hard: Unforeseen events; foolhardy.

Hollywood star Jack Nicholson has Pluto on his Ascendant, Jupiter on the Descendant, and Venus sitting on the Midheaven. As well as ensuring career success, the combination endows him with a fatally attractive quality as far as women are concerned – though relationships may well be undermined by the force of his own compelling personality.

The Component Parts

At first sight, the sheer volume of information contained within a birth chart can be overwhelming. Even seasoned astrologers sometimes find it daunting, for the purpose of astrology is to unveil the complex, and often conflicting facets of the human personality – no easy task!

For those new to the art of interpretation, the secret lies in breaking down the chart into its component parts, then reassembling these parts in clear, manageable categories. Like driving, the process gets easier the more you do it; the golden rule is to practise as much as possible!

Breaking down the Chart

The sequence described below is designed to help you analyse the chart one step at a time so that no detail gets overlooked. Accompanying each step is a sample breakdown of the chart of Ms X – a world-famous personality whose identity you are left to guess. (Since a chart cannot reveal the sex of the subject, you must establish this before you start). You will also find references to the meanings given in earlier parts of the book where appropriate.

Before you begin, always make a point of drawing up the chart by hand – even if you are working from someone else's version or from a computer print-out. This helps to build up an overall impression and allows your mind to absorb many of the chart's most important features.

As you progress, some of the information may appear to be contradictory; for example, one planetary aspect could suggest an extrovert, easy-going personality while another hints at someone who is shy and intensely private. There is nothing unusual in this, for no-one is entirely one thing or the other, and many of us fluctuate between different sides of our personalities all the time.

The point of breaking down the chart so carefully is to isolate the different character traits and place them in their proper context. This way, there is no danger that they might be misinterpreted or – even worse – completely misunderstood.

STEP 1

Establish the chart's outstanding features – its overall shape, and any major aspect patterns such as a Grand Trine, T-Square, or Stellium of planets in a single sign or house.

Ms X's chart (pp. 114 and 116) has a Locomotive shape with most of the planets in the left half (the Eastern Hemisphere), leaving Houses V-VIII empty. The critical planet is Saturn (located in Sagittarius in the Fourth House) as it 'leads' the others through the signs.

Six planets are above the Horizontal and four below it, while only two occupy the Western Hemisphere. The only major aspect patterns are the three Stellia: three planets in Virgo clustered around the Ascendant; three planets in Leo (although technically speaking they are not really in conjunction with each other); and four planets in the Twelfth House.

Ms X: FIRST IMPRESSIONS

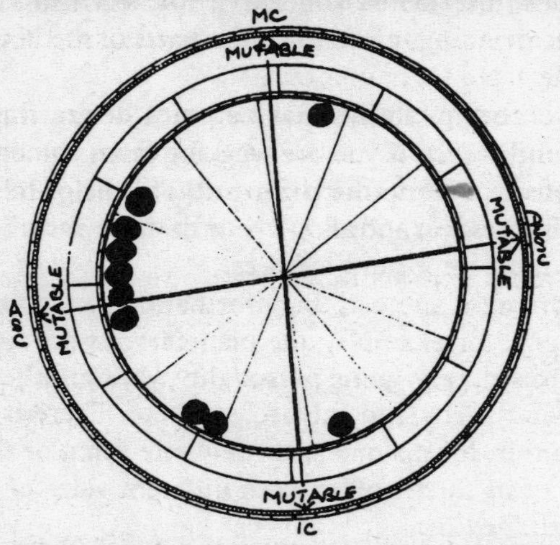

A helpful way of getting to grips with a chart without becoming swamped by information is to make a quick copy showing the planets as plain swirls of energy, plus the four Angles and their Elements/Qualities. This lets you see at a glance where the main focus of activity is, and which qualities colour the chart.

STEP 2

Assess the balance of planets in Positive (Fire/Air) and Negative (Earth/Water) signs. Likewise, assess the balance of planets in the various Elements and Qualities.

Is there a shortage or abundance of planets in any of them? Pay particular attention to the Element and Quality of the Ascendant and Midheaven.

Five planets are Positive and five Negative. The Elements break down: Fire 4, Earth 4 plus the Ascendant, Air 1 plus the Midheaven, and Water 1. The Qualities break down: Cardinal 1, Fixed 5 and Mutable 4 plus both the Ascendant and Midheaven.

This chart has a Fire-Earth, Fixed-Mutable emphasis which highlights the signs Virgo, Sagittarius, Leo and Taurus. There is a lack of Cardinal-Water – in other words, Cancer.

STEP 3

Make a note of the 'strong' planets. The most obvious ones are those which are Angular (conjunct the Ascendant, Descendant or IC), or Elevated (conjunct the MC).

Under this section you should also include the chart ruler (the planet ruling the Ascendant sign); planets in their own sign or House; planets which form the closest aspects; and planets in mutual reception.

Pluto, Mercury and the Moon are all rising (conjunct the Ascendant) which means that they are Angular and therefore very strongly placed.

Mercury also rules the Ascendant and is in its dignity, being in one of its own signs – Virgo. This makes it especially prominent (see chart overleaf).

The Sun in Leo is also in its dignity, whereas Mars and Uranus are both in their detriment and Pluto is in its fall – although with the outer planets these planetary 'weaknesses' are not thought to be very important.

Mars in Taurus in the Ninth House is the most 'elevated' planet, making its position important even though it does not conjunct the MC.

The closest aspects are formed by Neptune (inconjunct) and Pluto (square) to the Midheaven, and by Neptune to Pluto (sextile). No planets are in mutual reception.

STEP 4

Having noted the Ascendant and its ruling planet, focus attention on any aspects which they make to other planets in the chart. Remember, the Ascendant and Ascendant ruler represent the 'front door' of the personality. Their planetary contacts are especially significant, since they will colour the rest of the chart.

Virgo is on the Ascendant, and Pisces on the Descendant. As well as conjuncting Pluto, Mercury and the Moon, notice that the Ascendant also makes a wide (applying) trine to Mars and a sextile to Neptune.

Because Mercury – the Ascendant ruler – makes a close

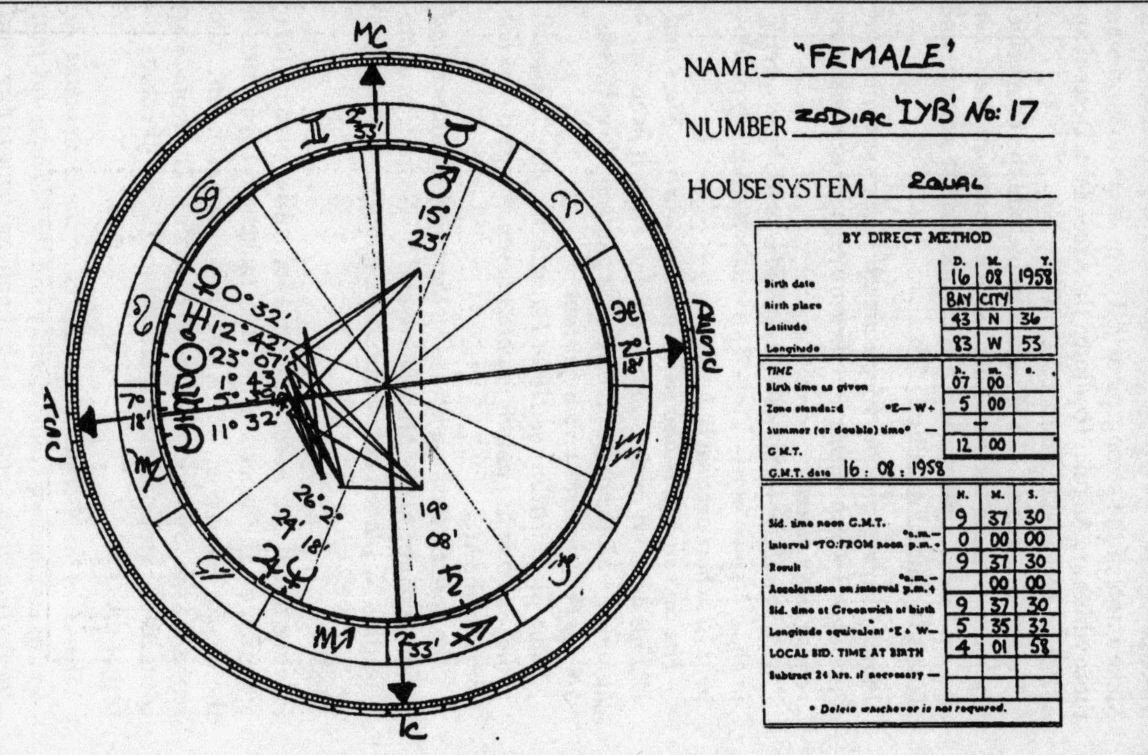
NAME "FEMALE'

NUMBER ZODIAC 'IYB' No: 17

HOUSE SYSTEM EQUAL

BY DIRECT METHOD	D.	M.	Y.
Birth date	16	08	1958
Birth place	BAY	CITY	
Latitude	43	N	36
Longitude	83	W	53
TIME	h.	m.	s.
Birth time as given	07	00	
Zone standard *E— W+	5	00	
Summer (or double) time* —		—	
G.M.T.	12	00	
G.M.T. date 16 : 08 : 1958			
	H.	M.	S.
Sid. time noon G.M.T.	9	37	30
Interval *TO/FROM noon *a.m.— p.m.+	0	00	00
Result	9	37	30
Acceleration on interval *a.m.— p.m.+		00	00
Sid. time at Greenwich at birth	9	37	30
Longitude equivalent *E+ W—	5	35	32
LOCAL SID. TIME AT BIRTH	4	01	58
Subtract 24 hrs. if necessary —			

* Delete whichever is not required.

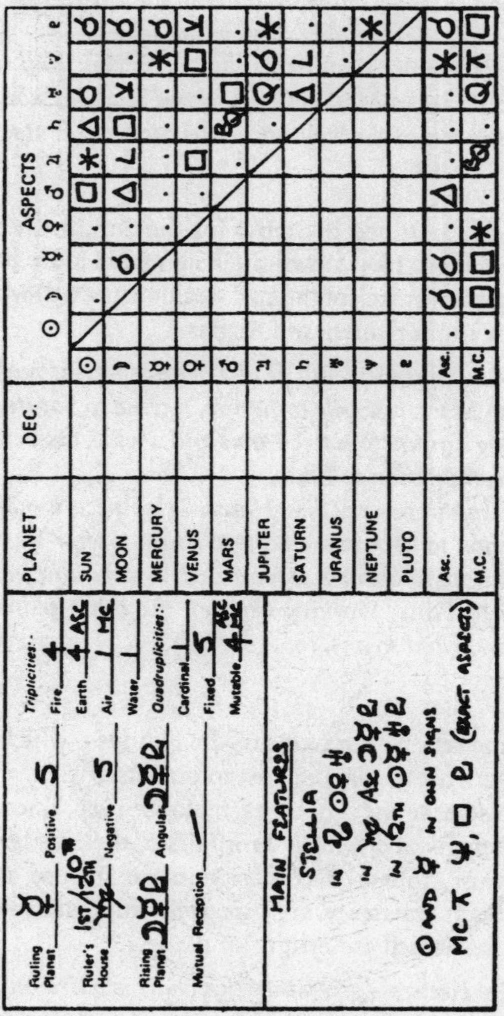

Ruling Planet ☿ Positive 5

Ruler's House 1st/12th/10th ♍ Negative 5

Rising Planet ☽☿♇ Angular ☽☿♇

Mutual Reception —

Triplicities:-
Fire 4
Earth 4 Asc
Air 1 Mc
Water 1

Quadruplicities:-
Cardinal 1
Fixed 5
Mutable 4 Asc Mc

MAIN FEATURES

STELLIA
in ♌ ☉♀♅
in ♍ Asc ☽☿♇
in 12th ☉☿♅♇

☉ and ☿ in own signs

Mc ⚻ ♆, □ ♇ (exact aspects)

PLANET	DEC.		☉	☽	☿	♀	♂	♃	♄	♅	♆	♇
SUN		☉		.	.	.	□	✱	△	☌		☌
MOON		☽			☌	.	△	L	□	⚺	.	☌
MERCURY		☿				.	.	.	.	.	✱	☌
VENUS		♀					.	□	.	.	□	⚺
MARS		♂						.	BQ	□	.	.
JUPITER		♃							.	Q	☌	✱
SATURN		♄								△	L	.
URANUS		♅									.	.
NEPTUNE		♆										✱
PLUTO		♇										
Asc.		Asc.	.	☌	☌	.	△	.	.	.	✱	☌
M.C.		M.C.	.	□	□	✱	.	BQ	.	Q	⚻	□

The fully drawn-up chart of mystery Ms X.

conjunction to the Ascendant, it shares the same aspects. Some astrologers would argue that the distance between Mars and Mercury (nearly 10°) is outside the allowable orb for a trine. But this is a good example of the need to use your discretion in such matters – the rules are only there as guidelines.

In this case, it is more than likely that the trines from the Moon and Ascendant to Mars set up a 'chain reaction' which also brings in the rest of the Stellium – Mercury and Pluto.

STEP 5

Repeat the process outlined in Step 4 for the Sun, the Moon and remaining planets. Note down their sign and House position, and any aspects (or lack of them, if weakly aspected) which they make to the other planets and Angles.

The Sun is in Leo in the Twelfth House. The aspects it makes are: a square to Mars, a sextile to Jupiter, a trine to Saturn, a wide, separating conjunction to Uranus and a wide, dissociate and applying conjunction to Pluto.

The Moon is in Virgo in the First House. The aspects is makes are: a conjunction to Mercury, a trine to Mars, a semi-square to Jupiter, a square to Saturn, a semi-sextile to Uranus, and a conjunction to Pluto. Working through the other planets: Mercury is in . . . (and so on).

STEP 6

Finally, assess the relative strengths of the Houses – which are most 'active' by virtue of playing host to planets?

You should also note the sign on each House cusp, since this sign's ruling planet is said to rule the affairs of the House.

At the same time, note the second sign in each House, along with its ruler. Such rulerships are especially important when looking at Houses which are 'empty' of planets.

The most active Houses – given that this chart is based on the Equal House System – are the Twelfth, Second and First (the First holds only one planets, but it is the Moon and it conjuncts the Ascendant).

Also important are the Fourth House (because Saturn, which sits there, 'leads' the other planets), and the Ninth House (because Mars, which sits there, is the most elevated planet).

As far as House rulerships go, and taking the Fifth House as an example, the sign on the cusp is Capricorn, which is ruled by Saturn. The second sign is Aquarius, which is co-ruled by Saturn and Uranus.

Therefore, when assessing Fifth House matters, the placement of Saturn and Uranus will be particularly important.

Conclusion

By the time you have completed Step 6 you will have done a lot of writing down! But in the process you will also have begun to form quite a clear impression of the subject, safe in the knowledge that you have not missed anything. Taking the elusive Ms X as an example:

Almost immediately, an impression emerges of someone who seeks to be very much her own person (I/XII House emphasis) – probably through fighting her own battles (Mars trine Ascendant Stellium). She is driven by a fierce need to be self-sufficient and in control of her own environment (Ascendant Virgo conjunct Pluto).

The empty part of her chart suggests that the whole area of love and relationships (Houses V-VIII) may take second place to personal ambition (Ascendant grouping contacting Mars, strong Saturn). There may be a longing for permanent intimacy, but Venus square to both Jupiter and Neptune suggests that this may elude her in the long run.

And who is Ms X? All is revealed in the next part of the course, which shows you in detail how to reorganize and interpret your notes to produce a detailed chart reading.

Basic Interpretation

In a way, the birth chart is like an alphabet of the personality. After all the astrological details have been broken down into their component parts, they are rather like a string of meaningless, unconnected sentences. So the next stage is to create a plot within which the story can be told.

For anyone new to the art of interpretation, the easiest way is to assemble the information under key 'areas' of experience or expression. Which areas you choose is, of course, entirely up to you. However, it is usual to begin with a general impression of the character, showing basic psychological attitudes and influences, and then to move on to wider issues – such as relationships, career and so on.

It is important not to see the areas simply as rigid categories which must be kept separate from one other; they are reference points and can be merged or added to according to personal preference. Never forget that your aim is to show how all the different (and often conflicting) parts of the personality combine.

Essential Feedback

Remember, too, that although it is perfectly possible to draw an accurate thumbnail sketch of someone's personality just from the birth chart, astrology is not a guessing game. The only way to give a meaningful interpretation is to set the chart against the subject's life – and this needs the participation of both parties.

For example, a Fourth House Saturn can be interpreted on many levels – such as an impoverished background or a lonely childhood. But apart from the general observation that family life was difficult in some way, the astrologer has no means of knowing about the specific circumstances without feedback from the subject. In this sense, a chart reading is a dialogue between astrologer and subject.

Now see how the process works in practice. The subject – if you haven't already guessed – is a lady by the name of Madonna.

General Impression

The overriding impression is of a woman with an exceptionally dynamic, wilful and charismatic personality.

There is, however, an essential contradiction in her nature between the independent 'anything goes' quality of the Sun–Uranus conjunction in Leo, and the enormous need for emotional and material security shown by the Moon on the Ascendant square Saturn in the Fourth House.

The position of the personal planets – the Sun, Moon and Mercury – together with the strong aspects they make to the 'generation' planets all point to a desire to reach out and influence the mass public.

The biquintile aspect between her elevated mars and Saturn, which leads the chart, suggests she is constantly driven to prove herself by showing that she is completely in control of her own destiny.

In all probability, her longing to be someone 'special' and make it in the world has been set by her experience of childhood; her family's hardships have given her a need for material and emotional security, maybe because one, if not both, of these qualities was felt to be missing as a child.

Mind

She is nobody's fool, nor does she suffer fools gladly.

With Mercury on her Virgo Ascendant, she is naturally observant with a sharp, analytical mind. There is a marked talent for business which, if exploited, will also satisfy her need to display her quite considerable mental abilities.

With her fondness for a challenge, she will find it difficult to resist full-blooded arguments. She may believe she is trying to convince others that they are wrong, but the force of her own – distinctively original – opinions is likely to meet strong resistance from other equally stubborn-minded people.

From an early age, she may have upset those in authority who refused to be steamrollered by her forthright views. On occasions her reaction will have been to lash out verbally when she did not get her way. She has a sharp tongue to assist her, though in her defence she is probably her own fiercest critic!

Knowledge, for her, must have a practical use, although she is by no means unimaginative. She has a fertile mind, teeming with hundreds of creative and humorous ideas – all of which she is quite capable of turning to her advantage.

Emotions

The Moon conjunct the Ascendant usually stresses the importance of close emotional ties. There is a side to her which can be extremely sympathetic, not just to the plight of those worse off than her, but also towards friends and those she is closely involved with in her career.

Although easily moved and affectionate, her emotional responses are likely to be extremely subjective and changeable, and at times she may be a bit too quick to criticize those she feels are not pulling their weight.

Occasionally, her emotional reactions will be exaggerated out of all proportion. In situations where she feels under pressure, everyone should watch out for her alarming temper tantrums!

Others may not always be sure where they stand with her, for it is likely she has an uncertain image of herself as a woman and may not find it easy to establish really close emotional ties.

Her tendency to periodic bouts of depression when she feels unloved or unsupported by those around her almost certainly stems from her childhood and a difficult relationship with her parents, whom she probably perceived as unsympathetic.

Perhaps there was too much emphasis at home on material matters, and not enough on emotional expression. As a result, if she cannot satisfy her craving for security on an emotional level, she may be tempted to look for it through material prosperity instead.

Her somewhat unstable sense of self-worth may also lead her to feel dissatisfied with the way she looks, and to experiment by constantly altering her personal appearance with her clothes, make-up and even changing the colour of her hair.

Body

This lady is tough, and she needs to be, since she tends to push herself to the limit.

She is blessed with a fast metabolic rate and recuperates quickly from illnesses. But she is prone to worry too much, especially if she hasn't got everything just as she wants it.

This could give rise to imaginary fears about her health, making her rather obsessive about her diet or level of fitness. Just as well, though, for there is also a part of her which if given free rein would happily indulge in the good life, or perhaps turn to alcohol or drugs.

The Venus sextile to the MC suggests she knows how to make the best of her looks; they are important to her. She is also fortunate in that she is likely to age well!

Relationships

Although she may appear to dominate others, she is something of a soft touch when it comes to love. Behind her guarded, self-contained exterior there is an incurable romantic straining at the leash.

Initially, she is likely to greet each romantic encounter as *the* great love of her life, only to be disappointed when she finds out about the true nature of her beloved. Part of the trouble is her fantasy of being swept off her feet by a knight in shining armour. It is a testing image for anyone to live up to, and problems are bound to emerge when each partner starts to blame the other for their own shortcomings. As a result, she is likely to stumble across many lovers in her quest for her romantic ideal. Given to extremes, she could flit from older partners – who may not be as mature as she secretly wishes – to younger ones who are exciting and 'different' but also inherently unstable.

The chances are that she will have at least two relationships of great significance – strongly Mercurial types usually 'marry' more than once. Deep down she yearns for a stable, dependable 'father figure' who she can respect and who can also control her wilder side.

Although it may take her longer than she likes to find her true partner, she has a sense of realism and the strength to learn from her love affairs. Her main challenge is to clarify what her own desires and needs are – and to stop confusing them with those with whom she is intimately involved.

Career

It is almost impossible to distinguish her personality from her career, for to all intents and purposes she is her career – everything about her is highly personalized, as well as almost overpoweringly dramatic!

Without doubt, her impoverished background and childhood

experiences have driven her to seek financial security in her career. But success for her is not measured solely by her earning power. She may seem supremely confident, independent and articulate, but deep down she is not so self-assured. She is hungry for the approval of her peers and her audience – probably as much as she is for fame; it is her way of knowing that she is loved, that she is someone 'special'.

As regards her choice of career there is a definite bias in favour of 'the arts', although with Mercury so prominent, it is highly likely that she will harness her undoubted artistic flair to a career in communications – especially the entertainment world.

This is confirmed by the position of, and aspects made to, Uranus (the media), which rules her Sixth House cusp (work). Mars elevated in Taurus highlights, among other things, the physical body as a vehicle for expressing her emotions, so singing, acting and any form of movement such as dancing should also play a part.

She has to be both the boss and the motivating force behind any business venture. She can be extremely egotistical, in the fashion of those born with a lot of Leo in their charts, but behind the show of pride she is extremely conscientious, hardworking and determined.

She *has* to work, partly because of the work ethic instilled in her by her parents. But work is also the vessel for her remarkable energy and inspired ideas – even though these may not always be in the best of taste! Her need for total control stems from her belief that when it comes down to it she is the only person she can truly depend on.

Yet at times she will be less sure of her direction her career is taking than she appears to be, and must take care not to overestimate her abilities by way of compensation.

Prospects

She has an extraordinary ability to endure hardship and turn setbacks to her advantage. She will put up with living in a rundown bedsitter if she believes it will lead her to a palace. Even though she may suffer from stage fright, she is prepared to put herself through any ordeal which she thinks will benefit her career. Such tenacity, allied to her talents, is bound to bring substantial rewards.

Later in life, once she is financially secure and the first flush of success has faded, she should become less compulsive about her career. At this point, she may turn her attention to more spiritual concerns.

In fact, she may use her earning power and her ability to gauge and influence popular opinion to put across an altogether different kind of message.

ADVANCED INTERPRETATION

Transits

An astrologer's work does not end with drawing up and interpreting a birth chart. In fact, it has only just begun. The birth chart is like a blueprint of our potential, but on its own it can only hint at how that potential may unfold during the course of a lifetime. This is where transits take over.

The birth chart is like a snap-shot of the solar system taken from a specific place at the exact moment of birth. Thereafter, the planets continue on their never-ending journeys, forming aspects to the natal planets and house cusps (the most important being the Angles). These aspects are called *transits*, and their effect is to transform the still photo of the birth chart into a running film.

Looking to the Future

Transits have long been employed as one of the main ways of predicting the future. Traditionally, they were believed to indicate events that happened to us during our lives – some good, some bad, according to the planets and aspects involved. But to astrologers of today, this smacks too much of a blind belief in Fate, and also implies that the planets are somehow 'responsible' for our lives.

This modern approach is to see nothing as inevitable unless

we make it so through our actions – or lack of actions. Transits are still used to look at future trends, but from a different perspective; depending on which planets are involved, they are thought to coincide with phases in our lives when certain issues are more likely to surface than others.

Nothing which happens during these phases is preordained, for the planets do not 'cause' anything; they are merely symbols for our inner energies. Transits simply show how, at specific times in our lives, we can use these energies in response to the issues at hand.

How to Interpret Transits

What orb should I allow for transits?

The orbs used for transits to natal planets and Angles are much tighter than those allowed in birth chart interpretation. Most astrologers use an orb of only one degree (1°), although this may be extended when a number of transiting planets gather around a key point in the natal chart.

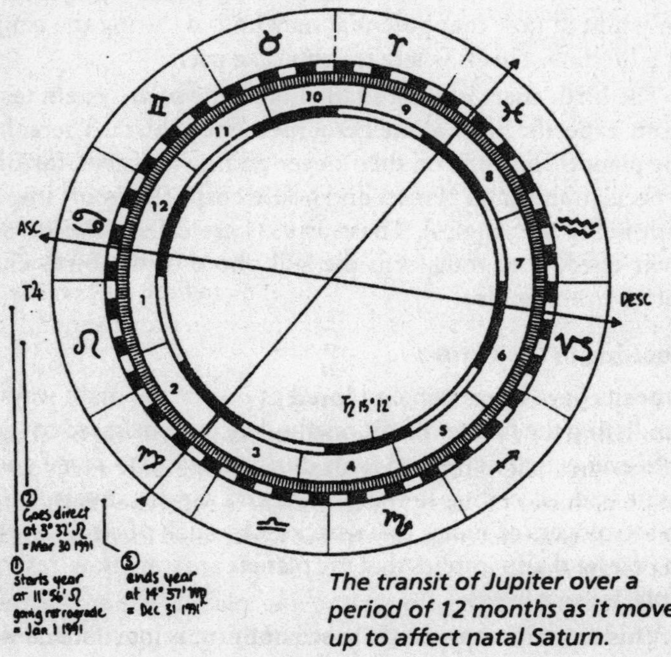

The transit of Jupiter over a period of 12 months as it moves up to affect natal Saturn.

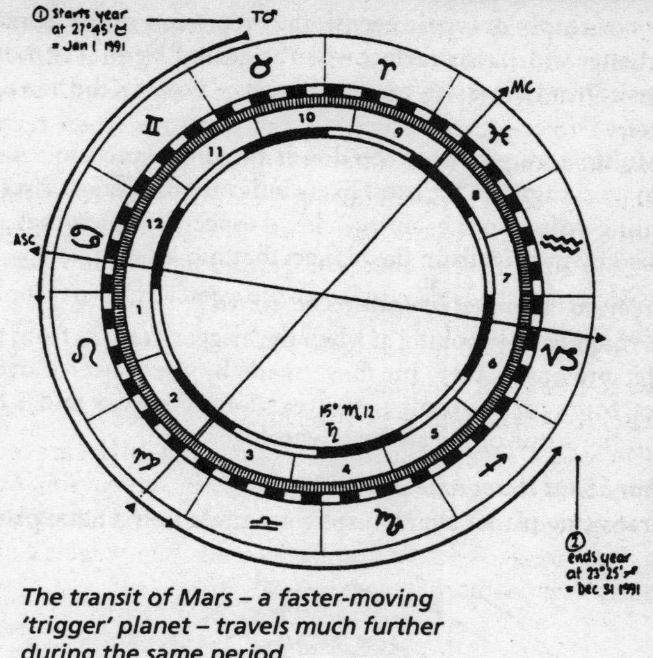

The transit of Mars – a faster-moving 'trigger' planet – travels much further during the same period.

How long do transits last?

Transits from the inner planets to natal planets or Angles are short lived, varying from about three hours for the Moon, to a day to several weeks for Venus and Mars. Transits from the outer planets last much longer: despite the tight orb allowance, Jupiter and Saturn can hover over a natal planet for up to one year, while Uranus, Neptune and Pluto may linger for 18 months or more.

Are all transits equally important?

No. Transits from the faster-moving planets are too brief to be of any great significance on their own. The only exception is when a cluster of faster-moving planets combine on the same day to form a network of aspects which also focus on a natal planet or Angle.

Transits from the slower-moving planets are much more important. Although on their own they may not coincide with any noticeably dramatic events, they represent undercurrents of change which may surface when 'triggered' by one (or more) transits from the faster-moving planets – notably, the Sun and Mars.

Multiple transits from the slower-moving planets to a natal planet or Angle are the most likely indicators of major crises or turning points in the subject's life – especially when they are joined by transits from the planets that move faster.

Can events signified by transits be 'timed'?

Yes, roughly – by looking at when the 'trigger' transits from the faster-moving planets hit those made by the slower-moving ones. More precise timing involves a lot more work and is beyond the scope of the amateur astrologer.

What about retrograde planets?

A transiting planet which turns retrograde over a natal planet

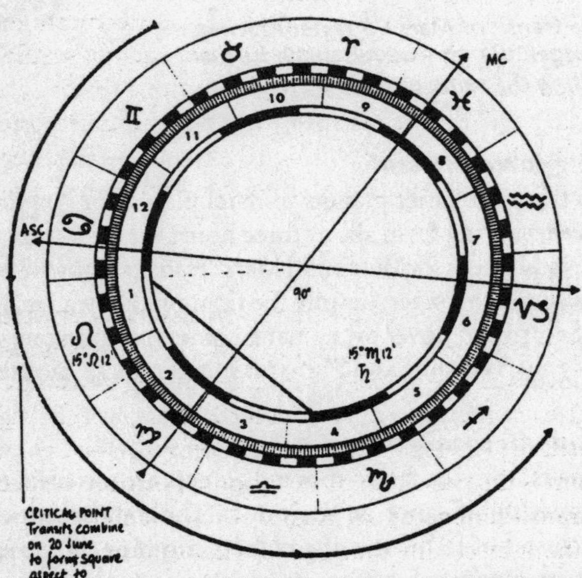

When the transits are combined, you can see that transiting Mars conjuncts transiting Jupiter at the same time as both planets square natal Saturn.

or Angle will usually aspect it three times – once as is passes over, once as it goes back, and once as it moves forward again.

This can be a particularly challenging time, especially with the conjunction and opposition. But if any serious difficulties arise, there are also more opportunities to resolve them.

How do transits affect planets in aspect?

Transits between planets which aspect one another in the birth chart are especially important, since they pick up on issues inherent in the subject's personality. As a rule, the natal aspect defines the essential character, while the transit offers a different slant on it.

The only exception is when the transit is the same as the natal aspect – an indication that the transiting planet has 'returned' to its position in the birth chart and is reactivating natal aspects. This is often a time of reappraisal.

Are all transits equally important?

Newcomers to transits are best advised to concentrate on the major aspects – conjunction, opposition, square, sextile and trine. Even so, sudden changes or disruptions which seem to occur independently of any major transit aspects can often be traced back to the so-called 'minor' aspects. As you become more experienced, you can turn to these for more information.

Signs and Houses

A transiting planet acts like a 'trigger' on natal planets, activating their energies according to the signs, house positions and aspects involved. The guidelines for interpreting transits by sign and house are the same as for the birth chart, but the sign of the transiting planet is of only secondary importance. Far more significant is the transiting planet's house position – especially if it is transiting one of the Angles – since it shows in which area of the subject's life the need for change is likely to arise.

The Scope of Transits

Transits must be interpreted with an understanding of what they can and cannot do. Astrologers have found that even when a complex of astrological factors points to a major 'event' around a certain date, it is extremely risky to predict how that event will manifest itself.

It may, for example, be felt on a psychological level – perhaps as a slow build-up of pressure or a gradual change in awareness. On the other hand it might be experienced through relationships, or as a sudden happening which occurs out of the blue. Usually, it is a combination of all three, but for those new to transits, it is much safer to concentrate on the timing of the event and the subject's own response.

Midpoints

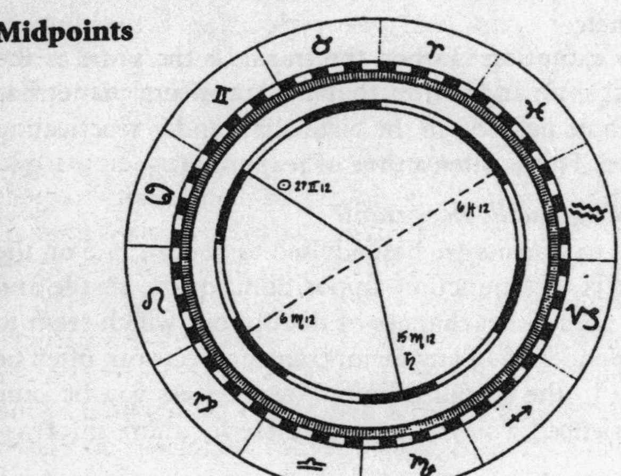

Many astrologers argue that it is a mistake to concentrate solely on transits to the natal planets and Angles. They believe there are other subtle points in the birth chart which can give more information about the nature, timing, and possible outcome of transits. These are known as the *midpoints*.

As the term suggests, a midpoint is the exact degree and minute halfway between two natal planets (or a planet and an Angle). Midpoints exist between all the planets and Angles in a birth chart, thereby linking planetary factors which at first sight may appear to be totally unconnected.

There are two midpoints for every planetary pairing – one on the shorter arc (distance) between the two, and one on the longer arc. Both are thought to be highly sensitive to transits, as they symbolize points where the energies of the two natal planets merge.

Midpoint interpretation is one of the more advanced areas of astrology and is beyond the scope of this course. Even so, it is a must for all serious students.

Transit Cycles

When a transiting planet makes a conjunction to a natal planet, it begins a cycle which will only be completed when it returns to the same point. For example, if transiting Saturn conjuncts natal Mercury, it will make every conceivable aspect to Mercury over the course of its 29-year cycle before it conjuncts it again. During the same period transiting Mercury will make an identical pattern of aspects to natal Saturn – except that it will do so about 29 times!

This creates a permanent and subtle link between the two planets – a link which applies equally to planets not in aspect in the birth chart. Each transit aspect marks a new stage of development in the relationship between the two planetary energies, as follows:

Conjunction – The first stirring of a new process – sometimes accompanied by a sudden burst of energy – depending on the nature of the planets involved. The energy represented by the transiting planet often overwhelms the natal planet, so that at this stage of the cycle it is not always clear what is going on.

Separating Sextile – What happened at the Conjunction becomes clearer. A helpful time to make adjustments for the next stage.

Separating Square – The first real test. Opportunities are limited, and decisions made a the Conjunction are challenged. If this time is dealt with successfully, it should pay dividends at the Opposition; if not, the consequences will have to be faced later on.

Separating Trine – A time of relative ease, or for revising plans if the previous Square led to major changes. It may also be a time when things are taken for granted, leading to a false sense of security. This is a good time to pay heed to the writing on the wall!

Opposition – If decisions have worked out well, this is time when prizes can be claimed! If previous decisions and actions were inappropriate, this can be a very difficult time. On the other hand, it offers the chance to sweep past errors away to one side and start all over again.

Applying Trine – This may mark a 'second harvest' when things appear to go well and changes are easily made, or it may act in a similar way to the Separating Sextile if new activity was begun at the Opposition. Whatever the circumstances involved, there could be a tendency to rest on one's laurels.

Applying Square – Often brings a sudden demand to adapt to new situations, even if there were no apparent difficulties before. There is a need to let go or to radically change old structures and attitudes. Resistance to change at this stage can lead to collapse at the next Conjunction, but it can also act like a Separating Square – especially if a new cycle was begun at the Opposition.

Applying Sextile – The final preparation which makes way for the next cycle and hopefully a brand-new burst of energy. Alternatively, it may act like the Separating Trine.

Second Conjunction – Represents the beginning of a new cycle, but can also mark the same kind of changes as the Opposition, particularly if there is a strong reluctance to face up to change.

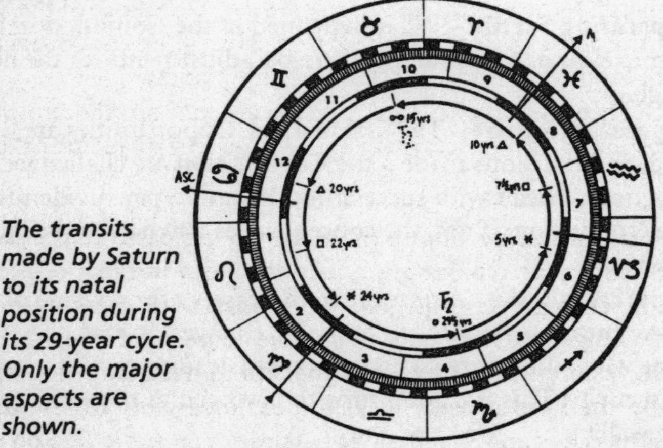

The transits made by Saturn to its natal position during its 29-year cycle. Only the major aspects are shown.

Transits – The Inner Planets

Transits are aspects between planets on the move and sensitive points in the birth chart which remain fixed. At first sight they may seem complicated, but it is worth remembering that they are derived from exactly the same principles as those governing natal chart interpretation.

As with natal aspects, the old distinction between 'good' and 'bad' transits has largely been dropped, since the way a transit unfolds depends entirely on how the individual copes with the flow of energies symbolized by the particular planets involved.

The first rule of transit interpretation is to decide at the outset if the planets involved are compatible. For example, Mars-Pluto contacts are never easy, whereas Venus and Jupiter hardly ever combine stressfully. You must also decide which transit aspects to work with. Most astrologers concentrate on the harder ones – conjunction, opposition, square, semi-square and sesquiquadrate – as these seem to be much more indicative of change.

Softer aspects represent the kind of circumstances in which a person is not pressurized into changing, and often nothing happens as a result! Even so, it is wise not just to cast them aside without trying them out, and they should always be used when they connect with hard aspects from other transiting planets. Of the inner planet transits described, those of the Sun are the most important – but only when they are combined with long-term transits from the outer planets.

Of the other three, Venus' transits are perhaps the most interesting, since they can have a major bearing on relationships.

Transits of the Sun

The transits of the Sun to the natal planets occur at the same time each year. On one level, they show our internal response to the changing seasons, like a personal clock marking individual high and low spots during the course of the year.

For example, the transits of the Sun to natal Saturn – especially the hard aspects – are almost invariably times when vitality is low and a faint air of pessimism creeps in. We do not

To the Sun: Of the Sun's transits, the most important is its return to its natal position around a person's birthday. Known as the Solar Return, a chart set up for this moment gives a foretaste of what is likely to be in store over the next 12 months.

To the Moon: Highlights personal, domestic and emotional issues, as well as focusing on unconscious habits, or matters connected with the past. Problems arise only if there are negative emotions that need to be dealt with. The conjunction acts like a New Moon, paving the way for changes; the opposition corresponds to the Full Moon – a time of possible inner tension and conflict.

To Mercury: Stimulates an exchange of ideas; good for travel and business arrangements, communications, and paperwork.

To Venus: Sociable occasions and a time to enjoy other people's company; sometimes signifies the beginning of a new love affair; good for financial dealings, although it can also indicate extravagance.

To Mars: Emphasizes initiative and motivation; in the mood to do battle; increased physical energy; maybe a tendency to be too pushy.

To Jupiter: An optimistic, expansive time, good for studying; with hard aspects, opportunities may be wasted due to over-confidence.

To Saturn: Brings one's duties and responsibilities to the fore; good for tidying up any loose ends, or planning new ventures; energy levels tend to be low, so there is a tendency to feel dispirited.

To Uranus: A sudden impulse to do something different and break away from rigid routines; a rebellious spirit which can create friction with people in authority; ideas may not go according to plan with the hard aspects, causing a build-up of frustration.

To Neptune: Increased sensitivity and compassion, but possible confusion and unwillingness to face facts; a bad time to confront.

To Pluto: Powerful external forces may appear to obstruct one's path, but this only reflects a need to look within and make changes where necessary; dealings with others will be intense.

need an astrologer to tell us that there are certain times of the year when we feel more subdued than others.

On their own, the Sun's transits are not thought to be long enough to signify major events or changes. The Sun simply accentuates issues connected with the house and planet it transits.

However, when the Sun joins a lingering transit from one or more outer planets to a natal point, its arrival frequently coincides with a decisive turn of events. In fact, many astrologers have found that without the Sun to act as a trigger, even long-term transits can pass by without any significant events occurring.

The Sun's transits last two to three days at the very most. Like the Moon, the Sun never goes retrograde.

Transits of Venus

Venus is a 'passive' planet, representing our ability to attract what is desired – mainly love, but also money, power, or simply a good time. Little effort is required to enjoy the fruits of this planet's transits, which are usually associated with agreeable events. Since many of them pass without too much fuss, most astrologers pay no more than passing attention to transiting Venus.

Aspects of Love

All the same, it would be rash to dismiss Venus transits entirely. While it is true that they are too brief to indicate major new love affairs – or even significant changes to existing ones – relationships can nevertheless 'take off' or alter course during a Venus transit. Indeed, some of the hard aspects – notably those to Mars, Saturn and Pluto – sometimes trigger short-lived crises in a relationship which may appear to blow over quickly, but in actual fact reflect unconscious energies deeply buried in the psyche. If the causes are not confronted at the time, they may reemerge later on with even greater force.

Venus transits last for two to three days, unless Venus turns retrograde over a natal planet, in which case it can stay there for up to three weeks.

To the Sun: A perfect day for partying, looking one's radiant best, and for falling in love, though the latter cannot be guaranteed; not good for work with a challenging routine.

To the Moon: An affectionate, romantic mood prevails, coupled with a general feeling of well-being; all the same, minor conflicts may arise if one is emotionally too demanding.

To Mercury: A light-hearted time, perfect for indulging romantic tastes; good for rubber-stamping business deals, but not for sorting out serious differences of opinion.

To Venus: Possibly a new love affair, but only if other factors support it; good for co-operative ventures; a danger of going on a spending spree; normally a lazy time.

To Mars: Definitely a time when passions are easily aroused; intense sexual feelings; a new attraction is likely to be impulsive, so it is not a good time to embark on a stable relationship; disagreements with lovers; good for artistic endeavours.

To Jupiter: Traditionally, the conjunction is held to be good for weddings; generally speaking, relationships will be harmonious, although the urge to relax coupled with a complete lack of self-discipline may possibly lead to over-indulgence.

To Saturn: Duty takes precedence over pleasure; a good time to tighten one's belt financially; dissatisfaction with others; possible break-ups in love; feelings of loneliness.

To Uranus: Surprise happenings; in the mood to experiment; a new love now would be exciting but unstable; sudden financial gains or losses.

To Neptune: Heightened romantic yearnings can lead to unrealistic expectations; good for work which requires a touch of inspiration; poor for practical matters.

To Pluto: Intense and possibly stressful feelings in love and relationships; hidden resentments are likely to come to the surface; inner compulsion may lead to a new infatuation.

Transits of the Moon

The Moon's transits are so brief (two to three hours) that they usually amount to little more than a fleeting mood, which as often as not passes by unnoticed.

Unless the Moon ties in with other transiting factors, its transits tend not to be taken too seriously by modern astrologers.

The main exception to this is when a New or Full Moon falls

To the Sun: A fresh burst of vitality; minor irritations with others; traditionally, the conjunction is an unfavourable time for surgery.

To the Moon: A chart drawn up for the conjunction (Lunar Return) can be used to predict emotional responses over the following month.

To Mercury: Thinking is affected by moods; good for expressing feelings, but not for rational decisions under hard aspect.

To Venus: A day for socializing, entertaining at home, or spending money freely; a temptation to over-indulge in food and drink.

To Mars: May attract quarrels through irritability, or hasty actions; good for bold initiatives, but care is needed to avoid accidents.

To Jupiter: A benevolent, confident mood; tolerant of others; can also trigger exaggerated reactions; a danger of over-confidence.

To Saturn: Feelings of being weighted down by domestic duties; a difficult time to resolve emotional problems; pessimistic attitudes.

To Uranus: Reacting rashly, seemingly out of character; poor concentration; impatient; hidden tensions spring to the surface.

To Neptune: Heightened sensitivity; strange, dreamy moods; easily discouraged; confused feelings may create misunderstandings.

To Pluto: Powerful emotional responses to others which express deeply buried feelings; possible confrontations on the domestic front.

on a sensitive natal point, in which case the 'effects' – according to the planets and Houses involved – are quite likely to last for anything up to a month.

Transits of Mercury

Operating principally in the realm of ideas, Mercury transits stimulate all forms of mental activity. As it breezes through the houses, the aspects it makes to the natal planets focus on routine and day-to-day dealings.

Mercury transits are thought to be lightweight unless they

To the Sun: A day for knowing and speaking one's mind; a need to be on the move; possibly a tendency to be self-opinionated.
To the Moon: Responsive to other people's feelings; emotions tend to cloud judgement; possible stress under hard aspect.
To Mercury: Mentally alert; good for studying and putting ideas across; idle chatter; new acquaintances; opinions may be challenged.
To Venue: Stimulates a spirit of compromise; good for clearing the air in relationships; also favourable for business deals.
To Mars: Increased mental stamina makes this a good time for getting plans off the ground; a lack of tact may provoke needless arguments.
To Jupiter: Good for taking a fresh look at old ideas, and preparing an overall plan of action, but not for work needing detailed analysis.
To Saturn: A day for serious concentrated thinking, negative attitudes may colour outlook; generally uncommunicative.
To Uranus: Mental processes are speeded up; good for sudden insights and original ideas, but trying to rush things may lead to exhaustion.
To Neptune: Assists artistic inspiration, but woolly-mindedness may confuse matters; not an easy time to be direct or honest.
To Pluto: Good for research and putting ideas across persuasively; wilfulness or a sharp tongue may spark off conflicts.

are linked to the more substantial transits of the outer planets; their contribution is usually to clarity the issues at stake. They last about two days, unless Mercury is retrograde, when they may last up to 11 days.

Transits – The Outer Planets

To get the most out of transits, it is important to interpret them in the context of what has already happened in the subject's life. This may appear obvious, but it is often forgotten, and can result in vague – or worse, totally inaccurate – predictions.

A helpful way of establishing what future trends are likely to hold in store is to refer an imminent major transit from an outer planet to previous transits involving the same transiting and natal planet. For example, a conjunction of transiting Saturn to the natal Sun should be interpreted in the light of what happened over the previous 14 or so years – when Saturn opposed, trined and then squared the Sun. By looking at each transit as part of a cycle, you can assess how the subject has dealt with this energy in the past and get a good idea of how he or she is likely to respond to it this time around.

This method is particularly useful for the transits of the outer planets – most notably, Jupiter, Saturn and Uranus, since their cycles seem to correspond closely with the critical stages of our development from childhood through to maturity. The inner planets complete their cycles too quickly to coincide with anything more than subtle or minor issues, while Neptune and Pluto only ever complete part of their cycles during the average lifetime.

Transits of Mars

Mars brings energy and drive to the houses and planets in transits – sometimes in uncontrollable doses. Still uncharitably referred to as 'the Lesser Malefic', this planet has earned a reputation for being the planetary equivalent of dynamite.

Without doubt, some people experience the transits of Mars as particularly trying periods – usually because they find it hard to deal with the sudden fluctuations in energy levels. If they

To the Sun: A good transit for any activity requiring high levels of physical energy; can be uncompromising towards others, stirring up opposition to plans; frustration may spark off explosive bursts of anger.
To the Moon: Tempers are likely to be on a short fuse, especially in close relationships; intense emotional reactions may cause minor disagreements to be over-dramatized; a good time to air grievances.
To Mercury: Great mental energy provides the enthusiasm to promote ideas; a tendency to react to even the most constructive criticism as a personal affront; a poor time for subtle negotiations.
To Venus: Heightens sensuality and the sex drive; a new love affair under this transit will probably be extremely physical, if short-lived; a good time to find creative ways to express feelings.
To Mars: Surplus energy heeds a healthy outlet to avoid hasty actions; a need to prove one's effectiveness may result in unusually forceful or overbearing behaviour; a good time to 'get things done'.
To Jupiter: Good for making 'fortunate' decisions, partly because belief in oneself is high; the energy to cope with almost anything; resistance to any restrictions; rushing headlong into conflicts.
To Saturn: A limiting, restricting time when it is difficult to let off steam; depleted energies; efforts appear to be blocked by circumstances beyond control; temporary feelings of impotence.
To Uranus: Expect the unexpected; a spirit of rebellion may suddenly surface, disrupting normal life or prompting escape from obligations.
To Neptune: Feeling listless and easily depressed; muddle-headed aims may cause self-doubt; a poor time to draw up new plans; try to avoid diffusing energies; good for solitude and inspiration!
To Pluto: Increased self-confidence and physical stamina; good for making constructive changes, but the need to win may be too intense.
To the Descendant: Tension between personal goals and the need for others' support can lead to stormy relationships.
To the MC: A time to be recognized for one's achievements, although any impulse to 'go it alone' is likely to meet with resistance.
To the IC: Pressures of home life may have an effect on work; quarrels are likely if differences are not settled calmly.

are not confident in themselves, they may unconsciously seek to prove their strength through aggressive and disruptive behaviour.

But it is not true that Mars transits always end up in explosive conflicts or accidents. Many people take them in their stride, barely noticing the difference apart from a sensation of stepping up a gear or two in vitality and stamina. They can be productive times, when hard work produces positive results.

Another thing to remember about the transits of Mars is that they are short compared with those of the other outer planets – just four days when Mars is direct; up to several weeks when it goes retrograde. Consequently, on their own they seldom amount to much.

But in common with the Sun, when the transits of Mars join forces with those of the slower-moving planets, they seem to act as a kind of 'trigger'. The arrival of Mars on the scene often 'sets off' an event corresponding to the nature of the other planetary transits involved.

Transits of Jupiter

Benevolent Jupiter, true to his larger than life mythology, has, by tradition, a somewhat inflated reputation in astrology. Known as 'the Greater Benific' (Venus being the Lesser), this planet was thought to be the direct opposite of Saturn – bringing hope, good fortune and success to anyone lucky enough to be under its generous 'influence'.

Although Jupiter is one of the 'pleasure' planets, its transits are 'pleasure' planets, its transits are no longer seen to be a firm guarantee of prosperity. It is not that Jupiterian energy is inherently difficult – in fact, quite the opposite. It is precisely because everything seems to be going our way during Jupiter's transits that they can turn out to be so disappointing.

Symbolizing the urge to expand and widen our boundaries, Jupiter transits often coincide with genuine opportunities for growth – usually according to the House and planet involved. The downside is that this planet does not always know when to stop.

To the Sun: Can bring a ray of sunlight into one's life, especially if it coincides with other difficult transits; traditionally good for health; advisable to avoid sitting back and trusting entirely to luck.

To the Moon: A pervasive mood of emotional well-being; good for property investment or moving home; with the hard aspects, a danger of being too demanding of others; a possible gain in weight.

To Mercury: A wealth of ideas and opportunities which require careful attention if anything is to come of them; good for business deals and settling legal matters; beware of over-confidence and sharp practices.

To Venus: Enhances popularity and the urge to indulge in just about everything pleasurable; favourable for a new romance, though under hard aspect, too carefree an attitude may lead to conflicts.

To Mars: An ebullient time, perfect for improving one's physical condition; the energy to achieve aims, especially in career; a good time to settle disputes; a lack of moderation may upset superiors.

To Jupiter: The conjunction marks the start of a 12-year cycle bringing opportunities for growth which must be seized, not wasted.

To Saturn: The principles of expansion and restriction join forces; either an unsettled time when dissatisfaction urges a break from old commitments, or a time to achieve through patience and hard work.

To Uranus: Sudden benefits or changes in direction; the urge to become more independent; a good time to review one's beliefs.

To Neptune: The possibility of a dream coming true; a bubble of idealism is likely to burst out of misplaced optimism; not a time for practical ventures, so care is needed in finances and relationships.

To Pluto: Good for taking the lead and organizing things one's own way; the urge to change one's circumstances drastically; a danger of squandering potential success by using unscrupulous means.

To the Ascendant: A positive time for enlarging social contacts and position; a liking for self-indulgence may come across as arrogance.

To the Descendant: Increases opportunities through partnership of all kinds; possible clashes in outlook; favourable for legal actions.

To the MC: Traditionally an auspicious time for advancing one's professional standing; can also lead to nothing through complacency.

To the IC: The focus is on improving the quality of home life; good for building a solid base from which to launch oneself into the world.

Unless transiting Saturn is also close at hand, Jupiter's blind optimism can easily over-step the mark, arousing the kind of hopes that have no foundations in reality. Jupiter transits can end in shattered dreams just as much as in golden opportunities. The truth is that some effort is required to cash in on them; Jupiter's gift is to signpost the way generously – not to hand things out on a plate.

Jupiter transits last from about two weeks up to six months if it goes retrograde.

Transits of Saturn

In the astrology of our forebears, Saturn was known as the 'Greater Malefic'. Roughly speaking, this meant that on a scale of one to ten, this planet scored maximum points for its ability to bring misfortune into a subject's life.

Despite the fact that modern astrologers no longer take this old, simplistic view, few of them look forward to Saturn's transits with glee.

The reason is that this planet invariably plays the role of examiner in our lives; its transits through the houses – especially the sensitive natal points – frequently coincide with times when our attitudes and actions (as symbolized by the relevant planets and houses) are tested to the core, often with painful results.

The Teacher Within

Even if these tests of strength appear to be forced on us by external events or other people's actions, it is important to remember that Saturn represents 'the teacher within'. Restricting or burdensome circumstances often come about through our reluctance to see that we may have outgrown the people, places and ambitions which seem to mean so much to us. But it is our inability to let go that leads to losses and difficulties – not the transits themselves. Indeed, it is perfectly possible to experience positive results under a Saturn transit – it is just that any success is usually hard-earned.

Saturn's transits can last for about a month, or for the best part of a year if it goes retrograde over a natal point.

To the Sun: Either a time to reap the rewards of past endeavours, or to accept and sort out failures; life will be a struggle even if successful; low vitality; an end to burdensome relationships.
To the Moon: Emotional balance undermined by feelings of loneliness and of not being up to scratch; good for reassessing past deeds and seeing oneself in a more realistic light; emotional separations.
To Mercury: Serious, possibly gloomy thoughts; good for activities requiring mental endurance; a danger of being too single-minded and narrowing one's options; obstacles to ideas; lack of confidence.
To Venus: Inhibitions or a sense of reality may pervade relationships to test them; feeling unloved; seeking emotional stability.
To Mars: Events appear to conspire to test one's strength and ability to endure setbacks; a time to keep one's head down and work steadily and hard; important to find constructive outlets for pent-up energies.
To Jupiter: Patience and caution will be rewarded with opportunities for sustainable progress; a time to adjust expectations to reality; a need to shake free from restrictions and have more time to oneself.
To Saturn: Saturn's transits to its natal position represent periods of self-examination; attitudes and achievements are tested; often a time to (reluctantly) let go of unrewarding parts of one's life.
To Uranus: A desire for change battles against the instinct to hang on, creating inner tension; an urge to break free from rigid routines.
To Neptune: An unnerving time of uncertainty, pessimism and self-questioning moods; dissatisfaction with the drearier realities of life; a good time to decide how to set about realizing one's dreams.
To Pluto: A feeling of being hemmed in by circumstances; a need to live within restricted means; clinging on to old ways, or the end of a chapter and a time to start aiming for more control of one's life.
To the Ascendant: A time to review one's obligations and role in life; relentless demands to get things done; frustrated by others.
To the Descendant: Relationships can become more stable and sober, or so restrictive that they break down; new responsibilities.
To the MC: Great tenacity needed to persevere with aims; new commitments test one's ability to deal with responsibility.
To the IC: Possibly weighted down by domestic and family obligations; a good time to find a secure base and put down roots.

Transits – The Slower-Moving Planets

There are occasions – admittedly few – when major events or turning points in our lives do not appear to be backed up by any significant transits, or when major transits do not seem to reflect what is happening in our lives. There are several reasons why this should be so, the most common being human error. For newcomers to astrology, it is all too easy to overlook some of the less obvious indicators, just as it is tempting to put too much emphasis on the major ones. So remember, when plotting or interpreting transits:

- Those of the slower-moving planets – especially Uranus, Neptune and Pluto – can last up to 18 months. During this time, nothing remarkable may happen unless other transiting planets become involved.
- If the transits on a day when something important happened to you do not seem to reflect the event, check that you have not forgotten the minor aspects – especially the semi-square (45°) and the sesquiquadrate (135°) – and double-check the positions of the inner planets.

Transits of Uranus

There are good grounds for arguing that Uranus is the joker in the astrological pack. The only safe prediction to be made about a transit from this planet is that the outcome will be unpredictable!

Often referred to as the planet of the 'higher mind', Uranus represents the potential within us to break away from our early conditioning and become independent-minded individuals. For most of us, this urge has to contend with our varying needs for stability and predictability. It makes for an uncomfortable arrangement, because while one part of us wants to rebel against set patterns in our lives, another always prefers to settle for the devil it knows.

Need for Change

More often than not, the conformist within us wins out – but by clinging to old habits and views, we may neglect the Uranian

To The Sun: A sudden impulse to change course and improve one's circumstances; considerable unrest and inner tension; either striving for greater freedom, or unexpected setbacks which restrict liberty.

To the Moon: A time of emotional turmoil, possibly because of unsettling changes on the home front; a need to become more independent – often at the expense of personal or family ties.

To Mercury: Great mental excitability; a time to break free from old ideas and develop an original line in thinking; exhaustion through a tendency to rush things; others may challenge opinions.

To Venus: A conflict between the need for love and greater freedom; a new love affair now is likely to be impulsive, unusual and unstable; existing close relationships may require greater flexibility.

To Mars: Energy levels are extremely high and potentially explosive; a need to find a goal which demands extraordinary effort; a tendency to blast one's way through obstacles; spoiling for a fight.

To Jupiter: A fortunate turn of events, or sudden recognition; missed or wasted opportunities; a good time to broaden horizons through travel or education; one's outlook on life may be severely tested.

To Saturn: Great tension resulting from a conflict between the urge to rebel and the instinct to conform; unexpected upheavals in job or personal relationships; resistance to change may prove restrictive.

To Uranus: The major transits tie in with critical stages in life; the square at 21 (breaking away from adolescence) and the opposition at about 42 (the mid-life crisis) are especially significant.

To Neptune: A time when radical ideas may inspire a vision of a new order or slide into vague idealism; a desire to escape empty routine.

To Pluto: A period of traumatic or rapid changes – possibly through social upheaval which has an indirect effect on one's circumstances.

To the Ascendant: Sudden and often disruptive events which overturn the status quo; an unconscious urge to break away from commitments.

To the Descendant: Personal relationships may become tense or need to be redefined; sudden new contacts; expected legal conflicts.

To the MC: An irresistible urge to free oneself from suffocating obligations; fortunate changes for the better, or sudden upsets.

To the IC: Unforeseen changes within the home – including a sudden move of house; events that force a new level of self-awareness.

side of our personality. If we are resistant to change, a transit from this planet is likely to jolt us out of our sleepy ways and force us to acknowledge that, according to the natal planet and house under transit, we are in danger of becoming living fossils.

Uranian transits – notably the hard aspects – are rarely dull, frequently disruptive and sometimes painful. But it is helpful to remember that they are only made difficult by our reluctance to face the truth about ourselves or our fear of taking risks. Uranus' great gift is to free us from our past so that we can become more truly ourselves.

Transits of Neptune

For most of us, a transit from Neptune often coincides with a time of considerable confusion. Neptune's trick is to show us that nothing is what it appears to be, so that the issues connected with a natal planet or House under transit no longer unfold in their customary way. Invariably, the source of this confusion lies within ourselves, even though it may seem at times as if other people are conspiring to undermine our position.

A Neptune transit often begins with a creeping dissatisfaction with everyday life, followed by a longing to experience something out of the ordinary. Sometimes this results in a blind rush to escape whatever ties us down and chase a heartfelt dream – although in fact we are merely fleeing from problems of our own making. At other times, we may actually take on new commitments in an unconscious or a misguided attempt to give our lives more meaning.

It is because Neptune operates on such a deep, feeling level that the effects of its transits can only truly be assessed long after they have passed. Even if we fall victim to our own illusions and go off the rails, there is more to Neptune transits than the disappointments that so often seem to accompany them.

On the positive side, Neptune makes us aware that there is more to life than meets the eye. By loosening our grip on mere reality, it helps us become more sensitive to the less tangible influences around us.

To the Sun: Stimulates the imagination; good for creative inspiration, but poor for making intentions clearly known; a risk of becoming involved in unrealistic or dishonest schemes.
To the Moon: Heightens sensitivity to surroundings and the need to help people in trouble; overwhelmed by strange, irrational feelings; exploitable as a result of being too receptive to others' wishes.
To Mercury: Opens the mind to subtle, new influences which can also be confusing; favourable for developing intuition; a temptation to bend the truth stresses the importance of being honest and direct.
To Venus: Intensifies one's sense of beauty and romantic yearnings; a dreamlike infatuation which ends in disappointment; the need to infuse ideals and hopes with a strong measure of practicality.
To Mars: Lack of drive and initiative, or circumstances that seem to conspire against one's best efforts; a crisis of confidence that helps one to accept failure and redirect energies realistically.
To Jupiter: The stirring of unfulfilled dreams; new spiritual insights; a desire to escape from humdrum existence; a danger of living in a cloud of optimism and over-reaching oneself.
To Saturn: Frequent swings of mood, or feelings of dissatisfaction with one's lot; a time to reassess spiritual and material needs and tailor one's life accordingly; a fear of letting go of the 'old order'.
To Uranus: Changing states of consciousness which affect most people through issues that embrace the whole of society, if not the world!
To Neptune: The square occurs during the 'mid-life crisis', the trine at 55 and the opposition at about 84; they involve facing up to one's deeper desires by letting go of, or chasing, unrealized dreams.
To Pluto: A generational influence, producing a ground swell of profound dissatisfaction with 'establishment' values.
To the Ascendant: Increases sensitivity; obscures one's grasp of 'self'; a danger of becoming a victim of one's circumstances.
To the Descendant: A tendency to lean or be leant on by others; misunderstandings in close relationships; a betrayal of trust.
To the MC: Uncertain about direction in life; devotion to a cause; feeling unfulfilled in career, a deep need for spiritual nourishment.
To the IC: Confusing feelings of inadequacy may affect sense of purpose; a time to withdraw and sort out one's true needs and aims.

Transits of Pluto

What Mars and Saturn were to the ancients, Pluto has become to modern astrologers – the dark hand of fate. But while this may well be the case in mundane astrology (world events),

Pluto's transits in a birth chart are by no means a guaranteed omen of doom and destruction.

Although in the years since its relatively recent discovery, Pluto has come to be associated with drastic upheaval, the other

To the Sun: A time of sudden, though not easy, progress; seeking to become more influential and effective; a risk of overestimating one's strengths; a need to face one's less pleasant personality traits.

To the Moon: Powerful emotional outbursts, usually triggered by deep-seated insecurities; obsessive behaviour often connected with childhood; good for bringing subconscious feelings to the surface.

To Mercury: Intensifies powers of observation and the ability to uncover the truth; a danger of being drawn to fanatical views; or opposed for one's own; nervous exhaustion through mental effort.

To Venus: Emphasizes sexual drive and the need for love; a love affair begun under this transit is likely to be compulsive and highly sexual; difficulties point to a need to transform attitudes to love.

To Mars: A period of extraordinary energy; increases the will to overcome through sheer effort, thought the urge to win at all costs can lead to ruthless behaviour or create violent opposition.

To Jupiter: Increases the desire to achieve and improve oneself; possible public influence; a rebirth of optimism or spiritual faith; conflicts with authority; inflated self-importance; traumatic losses.

To Saturn: A stressful time because Saturn resists change whereas Pluto makes it inevitable; the end of an old order and the chance to relinquish what is no longer essential to one's self-development.

To Uranus: Stimulates the zeal to change and break away from old conventions; often coincides with a period of upsets, intolerance and fanaticism; trying to achieve aims by disruptive or forceful means.

To Neptune: An inner transformation of beliefs and values which only becomes clear much later. The effects are generational.

To Pluto: Only the sextile and square are possible in a lifetime; may correspond to issues and changes affecting an entire generation.

To the Ascendant: A tendency to be too heavy-handed and wilful in dealings with others; a dramatic change in circumstances.

To the Descendant: Intimate relationships may be subject to great pressures; people who strongly influence one's view of life.

To the MC: Dramatically alters one's direction in life; either a gain in authority and influence, or a calamitous fall from power.

To the IC: A period of inner transformation; breaking with the past; upheavals within the family or on the domestic front.

side to this planet is that it only destroys what is decaying or useless to clear the way for positive change and reconstruction. This may sound like cold comfort for anyone anticipating a 'hard' Pluto transit, but Plutonian change *can* happen without the world falling around our shoulders.

Deep Powers

Many astrologers believe it is impossible to know what to expect from a Pluto transit. Part of the problem is that Pluto seems to represent energies buried deep in the psyche – so deep, in fact, that the effects of its transits may not materialize for years.

Far from signifying catastrophic change, a Pluto transit can just as easily mark the beginning of a slow process of psychological growth which only becomes clear much later – perhaps when another planet transits the same part of the birth chart. All the same, there are times when Pluto transits coincide with events that cast us into the depths of despair – a kind of psychological death that enables us to be reborn with renewed strength.

Day-for-Year Progressions

Although widely used in astrology, transits are only one among a host of predictive techniques that have evolved over the years. Another method which is every bit as popular in natal astrology is a system commonly referred to as *day-for-year progressions.*

The principle on which this system works is – as the name implies – that every day after your date of birth is equivalent to one year of your life. So if, for example, you were born at 17.48 GMT on 25 April 1970, the positions of the planets and Angles at exactly the same time the following day (26 April) would correspond to your first birthday – 25 April 1971.

Continuing the conversion, the positions of the planets and Angles on 27 April would correspond to your second birthday, their positions on the 28 April would correspond to your third birthday, and so on.

Charts drawn up using this 'day-for-year' method are known

as *progressed* charts, and are said to herald issues or events for the years in question.

In other words, if your birthday is 25 April 1990 and you want to see what your twentieth year is likely to hold in store, you draw up a chart showing the planets' exact positions on 15 March (20 days from your birthday – corresponding to 25 April 2010), then look at how these positions compare with each other and with those in your own birth chart.

Interpreting Progressions

How do progressions differ from transits in interpretation?

The traditional view is to see them as indicators of inner psychological growth and change, while transits relate more to external events and conditions we meet in the world around us. A growing number of astrologers refute this, however, arguing that as far as interpretation goes, there is no clear distinction between the two systems. They look at transits *and* progressions before drawing any conclusions, though as always in astrology, there is no substitute for personal experience.

What are the advantages of using progressions?

Progressions are strong where transits are weak – namely, with the inner planets and the Angles. As far as transits are concerned, these move too quickly to have more than a fleeting significance, and the emphasis is always on the slow-moving planets.

With progressions, the focus switches to the inner planets and Angles because on a day-for-year basis the rate at which these move, or 'progress', is much slower – slow enough, in fact, for them to make significant aspects to planets and Angles in the birth chart.

Another advantage of progressions is that you can – preferably with the help of a computer and the appropriate astrological software – progress the entire birth chart, so that from year to year the planets, Angles *and* house cusps inch their way forward (unless, of course, a planet is retrograde).

Astrologers who do this claim that it can provide an extremely detailed map of approaching trends in a subject's life, although this method should never be used on its own, without reference to the birth chart.

How long do progressions last?

The generally accepted view is that a progression lasts as long as it takes the progressed planet to pass 1° either side of a natal planet or Angle.

However, the energies symbolized by the progressed and natal planets will be at their most intense when the aspect is exact.

With the inner planets, the progressed Sun takes just over two years to move over a natal point, Mercury and Venus an average of about a year, and Mars about three years. Only the Moon, which travels 12–14° over a progressed year, covers any significant ground, and its aspects last a correspondingly shorter time – usually no more than a couple of months.

Are the outer planets used in progressions?

Over a 'progressed' lifespan of, say, 75 years, the outer planets will not move a great deal – after all, this period is equivalent to only 75 'real' days. During this time, Jupiter would need a full head of steam (when it is not 'slowed down' by a bout of retrograde motion), to progress as far as 17°. And from Saturn to Pluto, the planetary momentum never for a moment rises above a snail's place.

Clearly, there is little point looking at progressions from the slow-moving planets to the natal planets and Angles, as in the vast majority of cases the outer planet will already be aspecting that point in the birth chart. The one exception is when the aspect from the outer planet is applying and is within a close enough orb to become exact during the subject's lifetime. This point is usually marked by some memorable event or a critical stage of development for the subject in keeping with the planetary energies involved.

Can events actually be timed by progressions?

Yes, over the period of a year it is possible to predict major events, but generally only if the progressions involve the Angles and the Sun. It also requires experience – beginners are best advised to consider only the general outlook of a progressed year.

THE DAY-FOR-YEAR PRINCIPLE

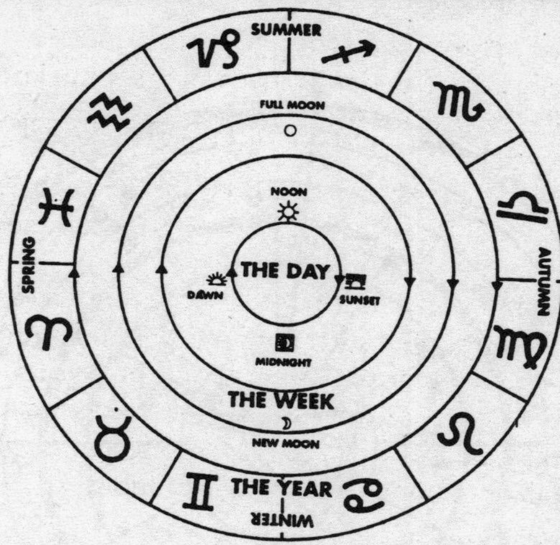

Whereas transits track the actual movements of the planets as they circle the zodiac, day-for-year progressions correspond to purely symbolic planetary movements. It may seem strange that the Sun or any other planet's position on the twentieth day after your birth has any bearing on conditions surrounding your twentieth year. But quite apart from the fact that the day-for-year method of progressing the birth chart produces highly accurate results, there are good astrological grounds for taking seemingly different time scales – such as a day and a year – treating them as one.

In the course of a day, the Earth rotates once on its axis, and in so doing completes one full circuit of the zodiac. Over a period of a year, the Sun (as seen from Earth) also circles the zodiac once. Moreover, if you were to plot a chart for each day after you were born, using exactly the same data for your time and place of birth, you would find that after 365 days, your Ascendant, MC and House cusp would have progressed through every degree of the zodiac to end up in exactly the same position as they were in your birth chart.

So while day-for-year progressions work on a symbolic time scale, there is still a clear link – based on the Earth's movement relative to the Sun – between a day and a year. Hence their adoption as the most popular method of progressing a birth chart.

A SAMPLE PROGRESSED CHART

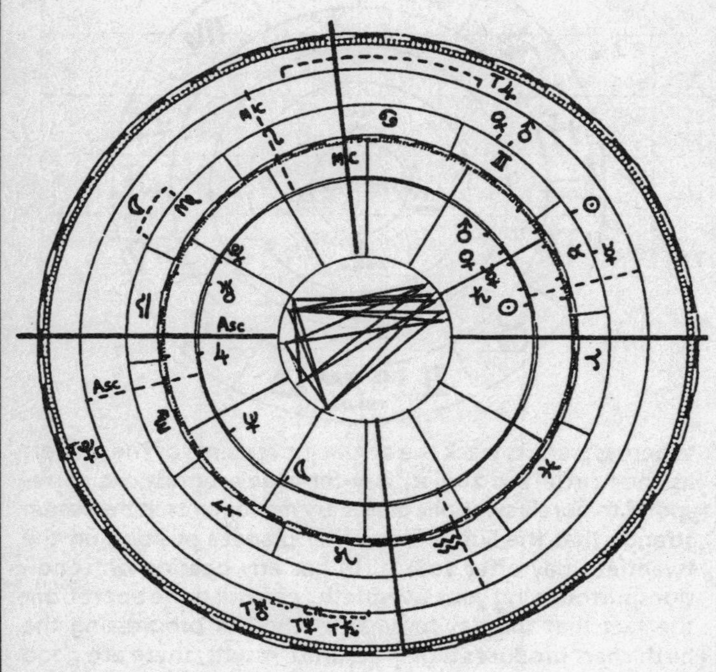

PERPETUAL NOON DATE

Name: SAMPLE X

House System: EQUAL

AGE: 20	Day	Month	Year
Noon positions on:	15	5	1970
Correspond to:	28	1	1990

POSITIONS OF PROGRESSED PLANETS

☉ : 24 ♉ 14	♀ : 21 ♊ 27
☽ : 16 ♍ 48	♂ : 18 ♊ 9
☿ : 14 ♉ 50 R	ASC 7 ♏ 42 MC 19 ♌ 36

THE PROGRESSED MOON OVER ONE YEAR

MONTH	Position	Aspects to Natal Planets/Angles	Aspects to Prog Planets/Angles
28th JAN	♍ 16° 48'		
28th FEB	17° 48'	□ ♂	
28th MAR	18° 49'		
28th APR	19° 49'		

PROGRESSIONS OF SUN, MERCURY, VENUS, MARS, ASC & MC		
YEAR	Aspects to Natal Planets/Angles	Aspects to Progressed Planets/Angles
1990	☉△♇	☉△♇ ☿☌♄
1991	☉△♇ ☽✱♆ ☽✱MC ♀△Asc ☽☌♅	☉△♇ ☽✱♆ ☿☌♄ ☽☌♅
1992	☉△♇ MC□☿ ♀△Asc ☽☌Asc	☿☌♄ ☽✱MC ☽△♀ ♀□♇ ☽△♂
1993	☉☌♀ ☽☍☉ ♀□♇ ☽☌Asc ♀☍☽ MC□☿	☿☌♄ ☽☌♃ ♀□♇
1994	☉☌♀ Asc☍♄ ♀☍☽ MC✱Asc	☿☌♄

28th MAY	20° 50'	□♀	
28th JUN	21° 50'		△☿
28th JULY	22° 51'		
28th AUG	23° 52'	△☉ ☌♇	
28th SEPT	24° 53'	☌♇	☌♇
28th OCT	25° 54'		☌♇
28th NOV	26° 55'		□☽ △♀
28th DEC	27° 56'		
28th JAN	28° 57'		

Copying this layout will enable you to keep all your progression information neatly organized.

In the top box, fill in the data for the progressed year in question, including the subject's Perpetual Noon/Midnight Date.

In the box below it, enter the positions of the progressed planets and Angles from your Ephemeris for the appropriate Progressed Date. You do not need to enter the positions of the slower planets.

Next draw up the progressed chart. The natal planets and Angles go on the inner wheel. Outside them go the progressed planets and Angles. The outermost ring can then be used to plot the transits for the year, as shown here.

In the progressed Moon box, enter the Moon's average monthly motion and the aspects it makes to natal and other progressed points over the year – starting from the Perpetual Noon/Midnight Date.

Repeat for the remaining planets and Angles. As these are slower, you can fill in their progressions over the next five years.

How important are the signs and houses in progressions?

Very – just as for transits, except that the sign of a progressed planet or Angle is given more prominence in progressions. This is especially true when a progressed planet or Angle changes sign, as this is believed to represent a new phase of personal experience or growth.

For example, if you have a Cancer Ascendant, the Moon will be your lifetime ruling planet. But when your Ascendant progresses into Leo (the timing of which depends entirely on the degree of your natal Ascendant) the Sun takes on a powerful significance; although it will always be secondary to the Moon, you may start to approach life with a renewed sense of vitality.

The house cusps are also important. Aspects between the progressed planets and the natal cusps, and from the progressed cusps to the natal planets are thought to highlight the affairs of that House, making them more noticeable than normal. However, this is really a matter for a professional astrologer.

Aspects and Progressions

It is all too easy to look at progressions (or transits) for a year and get carried away by a particularly sparkling aspect – for example, a conjunction between the Ascendant and Venus. Equally, there may be a temptation to wallow in despair if progressed Mars on the natal MC also forms a menacing square to natal Pluto. The fact is, though, that aspects involving progressions should never be interpreted on their own, or without first considering the natal condition of the planets involved.

A 'favourable' progressed aspect between the Ascendant and Venus is far less likely to promise a happy time if natal Venus is part of a testing T-square involving Saturn and Pluto. Similarly, a progressed Mars square to Pluto will most probably be softened if natal Mars is well aspected.

Individual Interpretations

But even these guidelines cannot be taken at face value, for just as different people respond to the same things in different ways, so the 'effects' of planetary aspects (whether in progressions, transits or in the birth chart) can never be the same for everyone – not even those born within a few minutes of one another.

When astrologers interpret progressions accurately, it is not because they have some mystical insight into how they work; it is because they observe one of astrology's golden rules – that any 'predictions' must be based not only on what is shown in the birth chart, but on the way each of us goes about handling our planetary energies.

In day-for-year progressions, the Midheaven, Ascendant and their opposite points appear to play more or less the same part as the Sun and Mars do in transits; they are the triggers which activate other planetary energies.

As far as interpretation goes, there seems to be no difference in meaning between aspects made by progressed Angles to natal or progressed planets, and those made by progressed planets to natal Angles. In fact, it is quite possible for aspects between both sets of Angles and planets to happen simultaneously – for example, for progressed Mars to oppose the natal MC, while the progressed MC trines natal Mars.

No Difference

Some astrologers also believe that there is little to distinguish between the Angles themselves. So while we may have grown used to thinking of the MC in terms of our position in the world, and the Ascendant more as a mirror of our immediate environment, we should not cling to these distinctions too tightly – at least not when interpreting progressions!

One word of caution: progressing the angles only works if your birth time is accurate. Four minutes can make the difference of one degree, which in the day-for-year time scale is the equivalent of a year. So if the birth time is unknown or uncertain, the progressed Angles can only be of limited value.

Astrologers cannot agree on how relevant the Signs and Houses are when it comes to interpreting the aspects in progressions. It seems there is no cut and dried answer – indeed, many of the conflicting standpoints each have something to recommend them!

ASPECTS BETWEEN PROGRESSED ANGLES AND PLANETS

SUN – Hard: Loss of position or status; struggling to achieve goals; a need for privacy; conflict between domestic and professional life.
SUN – Soft: Public recognition; growing prestige, sometimes on account of partner's achievements; gain through land or property.

MOON – Hard: Adverse publicity; loss of popularity; dashed hopes; upsetting changes on the home front; lowered vitality.
MOON – Soft: An increased need for security; strong links with women; in a man's chart, marriage (usually if Venus is also active).

MERCURY – Hard: Unhappy changes of residence; domestic squabbles; fraudulent activities; notoriety through slander or libel.
MERCURY – Soft: Increased opportunities to travel; communicating to a wider public; academic achievements; successful commercial ventures.

VENUS – Hard: Misdirected feelings, attracting the 'wrong' sort of lover; loss of creature comforts; financial extravagance.
VENUS – Soft: Greater popularity; new friendships; romance, and in a man's chart, marriage; also divorce if this restores 'harmony'.

MARS – Hard: Accidents resulting from hasty actions; strife at home; loss of or damage to home; setbacks through upsetting others.
MARS – Soft: Successful endeavours; marriage in a woman's chart (if Venus is also active); preparing the ground for future actions.

JUPITER – Hard: Loss of face through poor judgment or taking unsound advice; financial troubles through over-expansion; legal problems.
JUPITER – Soft: Helpful contacts from 'people in high places'; greater prosperity and popularity; an engagement, marriage or birth.

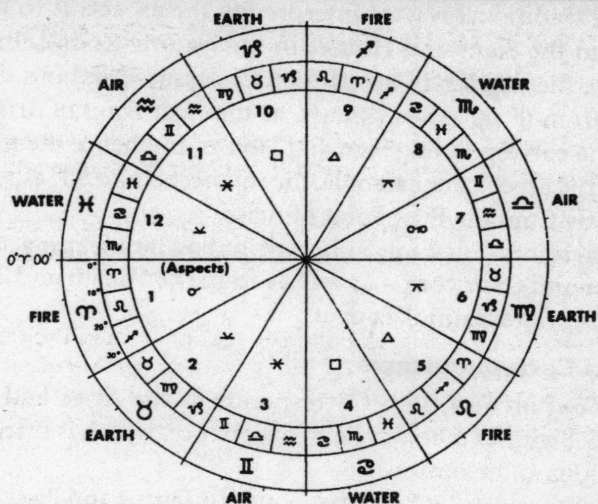

SATURN – Hard: Setbacks from lack of discipline or staying power; illness of, or separation from, loved ones; missed opportunities.
SATURN – Soft: Hard work with slow but steady progress; mettle-testing commitments; greater domestic security or social reputation.

URANUS – Hard: Sudden upsets, including separations or divorce; reacting against change, or rebelling against established patterns.
URANUS – Soft: Setting up new ventures; new contacts; greater independence; a sudden end to troubles; rapid progress; parenthood.

NEPTUNE – Hard: A shattered dream; involved in a scandal, or dishonest practices; failure through vague aims or impracticality.
NEPTUNE – Soft: Realizing a long-cherished dream; catching the popular imagination; willingly making a sacrifice for an ideal.

PLUTO – Hard: A ruthless attitude to others (or vice versa); damage to home; financial upheavals; power struggles; loss of a loved one.
PLUTO – Soft: Determination to succeed pays off; beginning a new direction in life; improved finances; increased influence in public.

One traditional way of interpreting the aspects is to relate them to the Signs and Houses in the Natural Zodiac. In this system, the degrees of an aspect are measured in both directions from 0° 00' Aries (known as the *First Point of Aries)* to find the corresponding Sign and House, and hence the meaning of the aspect. For example, the square, being a 90° aspect, is 90° away from the First Point of Aries.

It therefore lines up with, and draws its meaning from, Cancer and Capricorn – as well as from the Fourth and Tenth Houses of the Natural Zodiac.

Aspect Correspondences

The Conjunction (0°): Corresponds to the Aries and First House. Signifies a new cycle of experience, which is often unconscious at the outset.

The Semi-sextile (30°): Corresponds to Taurus and Pisces, and to the Second and Twelfth Houses. Signifies the potential to expand or integrate energies, bringing greater stability to the subject's life.

The Sextile (60°): Corresponds to Gemini and Aquarius, and to the Third and Eleventh Houses. Signifies harmony in surroundings and social contacts; a mind at ease with itself.

The Square (90°): Corresponds to Cancer and Capricorn, and to the Fourth and Tenth Houses. Signifies conflict between sudden changes in the subject's professional (conscious) and personal (unconscious) life.

The Trine (120°): Corresponds to Leo and Sagittarius, and to the Fifth and Ninth Houses. Denotes easy opportunities for growth and gain on all levels – sometimes too easy!

The Inconjunction (150°): Corresponds to Virgo and Scorpio, and to the Sixth and Eighth Houses. Signifies a need for the subject to face up to and overhaul areas of life in need of improvement.

The Opposition (180°): Corresponds to Libra and the Seventh House. Signifies conflict or union, depending on how the two opposing energies can be merged.

The Semi-square (45°) and Sesquiquadrate (135°): Correspond respectively to Taurus and Aquarius, and Leo and

Scorpio. Although they don't fit neatly into the House system, together they form a Grand Cross at 15° of the Fixed signs – which perhaps explains why they are said to represent sudden and unexpected change.

Progressions and the Decanates

Although progressions involving the Angles are important, there are other, more subtle influences connected with the progressed Ascendant and Midheaven which can give clues to developments and changes in the subject's life. One such influence is that of the *Decanates* – a system whereby each sign is divided into three parts of 10° each. Within each sign, the First Decanate is the sign's purest expression, the Second has a flavour of the next sign from the same Element, and the Third has a flavour of the last sign from the same Element.

For example, with the Fire sign Aries, 0°-10° belongs to Aries itself, 10°-20° belongs to Leo, and 20°-30° to Sagittarius; with the next Fire sign, Leo, the First Decanate is ruled by Leo, the Second by Sagittarius and the Third by Aries. And so it goes, through the signs and Elements.

When an Angle progresses from one sign to another, it often coincides with a big change in direction; when it changes Decanates, the shift in emphasis is less marked. All the same, the use of Decanates in progressions can shed considerable light on the quality of experiences we are likely to draw to ourselves.

The Meaning of the Decanates

Aries (Aries): Plenty of energy and opportunities to make changes, get ahead in life and realize goals.

Aries (Leo): A sense of being rejuvenated, coupled with new experiences that deepen one's feelings.

Aries (Sagittarius): An awakening spirit of exploration may lead to travel or further studies.

Taurus (Taurus): A time to get practical affairs in order; stubbornness may make it hard to change.

Taurus (Virgo): A need to sharpen critical talents and also to re-evaluate oneself in a more objective light.

Taurus (Capricorn): A time of stirring ambitions; new commitments, and maybe public recognition.
Gemini (Gemini): Increased restlessness and curiosity as the mind speeds up; hunger for knowledge.
Gemini (Libra): Emphasizes the need to see and experience life from as many sides as possible.
Gemini (Aquarius): A period of mental stability, and a chance to focus deeply on one area of life.
Cancer (Cancer): May put the spotlight on domestic issues; opens up a whole new world of feelings.
Cancer (Scorpio): Traditionally thought to denote a time of loss and sorrow; releases buried feelings.
Cancer (Pisces): Increased sensitivity to surroundings needs to be offset by periods alone.
Leo (Leo): Awakens the urge to give emotionally; a time of greater vitality and *joie de vivre.*
Leo (Sagittarius): Opportunities to expand on all levels; a good time for developing intuition.
Leo (Aries): Stimulates a spirit of enterprise; a risk of being thwarted through being too assertive.
Virgo (Virgo): Not a time for 'making it' in the world; keeping one's head low and working hard.
Virgo (Capricorn): Much better for stirring one's ambitions; honour or gain through perseverance.
Virgo (Taurus): Tempers Virgo's more critical side; opportunities to improve financial position.
Libra (Libra): A strong need for peace and harmony; partner(s) may be especially influential now.
Libra (Aquarius): Learning to be more decisive; contacts who awaken one's humanitarian instincts.
Libra (Gemini): A more active mind seeks travel, a better social life or creative expression.
Scorpio (Scorpio): A greater determination to succeed; new and intense feelings and experiences.
Scorpio (Pisces): A need to guard against the less than honest; seeing the sad side of life.
Scorpio (Cancer): Domestic upheavals; over-sensitive to others; strange romantic attractions.

Sagittarius (Sagittarius): Foreign travel or living abroad; a spiritual quest, or spirit of rebellion.
Sagittarius (Aries): Greater independence of mind; suffering through being over-wilful and impulsive.
Sagittarius (Leo): A phase of falling in love rather too easily; over-dramatising emotions.
Capricorn (Capricorn): A chance to leave one's mark on society – through merit or mere social climbing.
Capricorn (Taurus): The single-minded pursuit of fixed goals can lead to financial gain.
Capricorn (Virgo): A suitable period to sow for the future; a danger of becoming too self-obsessed.
Aquarius (Aquarius): Either swept off one's feet by new ideas and friends, or sticking to old views.
Aquarius (Gemini): An excitable, erratic mentality; living in one's head; seeking a marriage of minds.
Aquarius (Libra): A more balanced state of mind; a binding commitment; a sharpened sense of justice.
Pisces (Pisces): A need to develop stronger resolve in dealings with others; heightened awareness.
Pisces (Cancer): Learning self-reliance; hypersensitivity to surroundings; clinging to the past.
Pisces (Scorpio): A danger of becoming ensnared by negative feelings; a need for self control.

Progressions of Sun and the Planets

As with transits, it takes time to learn how to use progressions. Part of the problem is that there are so many different shades of meaning attached to each planetary combination that it is very hard to establish on which level to pitch your 'forecast'.

The answer, to begin with at least, is not even to try. The first step is to discover how the subject responds to the energy patterns indicated by the planets and their signs, houses and aspects in the birth chart. With a progression involving the Sun and Saturn, for example, some people may have experiences that reflect the gloomier or more selfish side of this aspect. Others, however, may find events have a sunnier twist to them

– perhaps as they gain some reward or recognition for their efforts.

Whatever the outcome, progressions do not hold the key; they merely point to the nature of the 'event'. Another reason for not relying on progressions (or transits) to 'predict' what will happen is that the full effects of a progressed aspect will not necessarily be obvious straight away. Even though a major event or change of direction is on the cards, it may take months or years for it to materialize.

As a guideline, it is safe to say that progressions involving the Angles and the Sun are more powerful indicators of major events than those of the other planets, the exception being those progressions of the chart ruler.

Progressions of the Sun

Whether you are looking at progressions, transits, or an ordinary birth chart, never forget that the Sun is the focal point of all the other planetary energies. Astrologically, the Sun mirrors its function in the solar system: it is fundamental to our existence – so much so, in fact, that it is hard to define what its function is!

One way of looking at the Sun is as our essential 'life force', pushing us to discover our true purpose. While it may not tell us specifically about our mission in life (which is for each of us to choose), it can nevertheless show how we set about looking for it – or not, as the case might be!

Core Issues

Along with those of the Angles, the Sun's progressions are thought to be the most important, for they raise issues that affect us to our very core. But how we cope with these issues cannot be gauged simply from the progressed aspects and planets involved; as always, the answer lies in the Sun's placement in the birth chart by sign, house and aspect.

There will be years when neither the progressed nor the natal Sun are involved in any progressions. This does not mean that life will be uneventful – there are always the transits to consider – but it does suggest that changes or developments during these 'fallow' periods might not affect us radically. It is important, too, to check the Sun's progressions into a new sign or house, as these will bring new issues to the surface.

To the Sun: These happen at roughly the same age for everyone – the semi-sextile is at 30, the semi-square at 46 and the sextile at 61. It is impossible to say what 'effects' might be expected without detailed reference to the Sun's placement in the birth chart.

To the Moon: Most astrologers only consider progressions of the Sun to the natal Moon, which represent a process of inner change which gradually turns outwards. But also important are the progressed New Moon, which marks a time for change through personal initiative, and the progressed Full Moon, which implies changes through confrontation and breaking with the past.

To Mercury: The conjunction from the progressed Sun to Mercury (or vice versa) is the most significant aspect, as it occurs early in life (early 20s at the latest). It often coincides with changes or events connected with experiences at school or in further education.

To Venus: The conjunction is traditionally linked with marriage, or failing that, with increased popularity and rosier prospects. Of the hard aspects, only the semi-square and square are possible; they may coincide with disappointment in love or friendship, and money worries.

To Mars: All these aspects are associated with turbulent times, since the will to achieve is heightened. A tendency to over-reach oneself may lead to accidents. In a woman's chart there may be marriage. Hard aspects often correspond to domestic break-up – even divorce.

To Jupiter: Traditionally, the conjunction marks public honour and general good fortune, though modern astrologers place the emphasis on striving for success. Possibly marriage in a woman's chart. Even the hard aspects can be helpful, though over-confidence may lead to loss.

To Saturn: A character-forming progression: it invariably brings greater responsibility which either furthers ambitions or is seen as an unwanted burden. The soft aspects are good for investments or career promotion. Hard aspects often coincide with a fall from grace.

To Uranus: Behaviour becomes erratic, old ways of life seem stifling and there is a need to be 'more oneself'. The hard aspects can be especially stressful, representing sudden reversals and separations.

To Neptune: A longing for spiritual enlightenment; dissatisfaction with present circumstances; experiences that point out character faults; a sacrifice made in order to gain one's heart's desire.

To Pluto: A powerful progression linked with events that bring about a major change of direction in life – often accompanied by a feeling of inevitability. Discovering and following one's true vocation. The hard aspects can symbolize organized opposition to one's schemes.

Progressions of the Moon

As a rule, progressions from the planets to the natal Moon are more important than progressions of the Moon itself, as the Moon progresses so rapidly. But aspects from the progressed Moon to a natal or progressed outer planet are worth watching, since these can last up to six months.

Where the progressed Moon really comes into its own is when it joins progressions from the other progressed planets to the planets or Angles in the birth chart. Under these conditions the Moon can act very much like a trigger, setting off a chain of events which reflect the nature of the planets involved.

To the Moon: The Moon completes a full cycle every 28 years; the progressions to its natal position depend on its natal aspects.

To Mercury: A lightweight combination; may focus on day-to-day issues at the office or at home; an emphasis on travel; adverse publicity.

To Venus: Denotes the path of least resistance; does not promise much on its own, as there is no drive to succeed; an emotional attraction.

To Mars: Highlights restlessness; an urge to travel; tempers can run high; feelings blown out of proportion may create discord all round.

To Jupiter: New social contacts; a change of residence; sometimes events during this time have an almost fated quality.

To Saturn: Brings stability to lunar affairs; attractions to older people; feelings of loneliness brought on by inhibited emotions.

To Uranus: Unusual encounters or experiences trigger changes; emotional crises; marriage in a man's chart; estrangements.

To Neptune: Heightened emotions; increasingly sympathetic; helping the less fortunate; over-idealising friendships; escape from reality.

To Pluto: People or events that spark off fundamental changes; an awakening of intense emotions; mass popularity – or unpopularity.

Progressions of Mercury

Operating as it does in the realm of the mind, the effects of Mercury tend to be less visible than those of other planets. But just because its progressions may not be immediately obvious does not mean they should be ignored. In fact, progressions to or from Mercury often coincide with specific developments – such as travel, a change of residence, or the start of a commercial venture – which affect not only our state of mind, but the way we choose to live our lives in the future.

To Mercury: More concerned with mental development than outside events, unless the natal aspects of Mercury suggest otherwise.

To Venus: Not a serious planetary combination in progressions; may highlight social life, or financial affairs of friends and partners.

To Mars: Sharpens the mind, bringing an added measure of common sense to all affairs; impatience may lead to ill-considered actions.

To Jupiter: Chances to expand the mind through travel or study; hard aspects may warn of dishonest practices; libel or legal troubles.

To Saturn: Dealing with feelings of not being mentally up to scratch; confidence undermined through a gloomy outlook; ambitious ideas.

To Uranus: An acute state of mental excitement; increasingly outspoken – and probably less popular; strained family relations.

To Neptune: Inspires the imagination; new ideas lead to a broadening of horizons, or mental confusion results in self-deception.

To Pluto: An inquisitive mind; a perfect time to embark on any work involving in-depth research; consumed by self-destructive notions.

Progressions of Mars

When Mars becomes active by progression, whichever part of our lives is stirred by its arrival certainly won't be dull – and may never be the same again! Traditionally, Mars was seen as an 'evil' influence, and even the soft aspects were given a lukewarm reception by astrologers. But although the energies symbolized by Mars can easily be disruptive if we fail to channel them constructively, when handled wisely, they can also give us the strength of will to move mountains.

To Mars: Only the semi-sextile and semi-square are possible in an average lifespan, and their meaning is not clear.

To Jupiter: An increase in drive and initiative can bring gains – especially good for expanding the business; marriage in a woman's chart; losses through lack of restraint; ill-judged risks.

To Saturn: Something of an endurance test – with both hard and soft aspects, progress is slow, issues that demand courage, or which call on one to prove oneself; a time to focus on the bare necessities.

To Uranus: Unexpected opportunities for 'overnight' success; often an exciting, adventurous time highlighting the need to be resourceful in the face of unforeseen circumstances; rash behaviour and accidents.

To Neptune: Favourable for artistic inspiration; the hard aspects often bring out escapist tendencies; attractions to peculiar – even deceptive – people or beliefs.

To Pluto: Total resolve in all actions, which may come across to others as ruthless determination; situations in which negative emotions such as anger or fanaticism have to be confronted.

Progressions of Venus

Although Venus is traditionally the goddess of love, progressions involving this planet do not necessarily mean wedding bells. While it is fair to say that when other progressions or transits bear them out, Venus progressions may well coincide with marriage or a major new love affair. This is because Venus itself embodies the principle of balance and harmony – a condition we most commonly experience when in love.

When this sense of inner well-being is completely absent from a relationship, we might just as easily expect progressions involving Venus to redress the balance – even if initially this means a painful break-up.

To Venus: Without other progressions or transits to point the way, this progression is thought to be more or less insignificant.

To Mars: Emotionally impulsive and prone to 'love at first sight' encounters; a danger that the heart may rule the heard; if reason prevails, a more balanced attitude to relationships is on the cards.

To Jupiter: Prosperity, comfort and emotional fulfilment are the 'positive' benefits of this progression, although it is equally possible to fritter away opportunities and then end up with nothing.

To Saturn: Often coincides with a strong, permanent relationship – sometimes with someone older; good for investment, but can also indicate financial hardship; leant on by friends and loved ones.

To Uranus: Unexpected financial benefits – or losses; sudden friendships or love affairs; breakdowns in relationships and upheavals on the home front, forcing one to become more independent.

To Neptune: Greater emotional sensitivity to others; idealized feelings of love can lead to romantic infatuation – and possible deception; a risk of falling for 'get-rich-quick' schemes.

To Pluto: An intense, all-consuming affair fraught with obstacles; emotional upsets which dramatically alter sense of values; learning to love unconditionally; discovering hidden talents.

Is Prediction Possible?

Is it possible to make truly accurate predictions using transits and progressions? For the amateur astrologer, the answer must be no – although the predictive techniques used by specialists in the field can produce amazingly accurate results, they are way beyond the scope of this course. Even those astrologers who do attempt to gaze into the future tread warily, if only because it would be irresponsible to interfere with a client's free will. But assessing responses to future trends is a different matter altogether, for here the astrologer can show a person exactly how to maximize their strengths and minimize their weaknesses in the interests of leading a more fulfilling life.

Seeing for Yourself

To this end, once you have mastered the basics of transits and progressions, the next – and most fascinating – step is to back-track through your own chart and see how their combinations worked for you by measuring them against real-life events. Remember, what you are looking for are general patterns and trends which develop themes already established in the birth chart.

Transits and progressions do not 'produce' events, nor do they bring about radical personality changes; their symbolic function is simply to activate planetary energies – for better or for worse, according to how we handle those energies as and when they combine in the birth chart.

Synastry and Composite Charts

Where personal relationships are concerned, the birth chart alone is of limited value. It may show what we seek in the world, and how we set about finding it, but it cannot reveal the flip side of the coin, in other words, what the world seeks in us. Astrology's solution to this dilemma is both simple and effective. By comparing the charts of the people involved in a process called *Synastry*, it becomes possible to build up a picture of the unique qualities of their relationship – for better or for worse.

There are several techniques for comparing the astrology between two (or more) people, one of which – the *composite chart* – involves merging the separate birth charts into one (ideally, with the aid of a computer). Happily, the most commonly used method of synastry is much less complicated. You simply draw up the two birth charts in the usual way, then look at the aspects formed between their respective planets and Angles.

In theory, any two charts can be compared – between friends, business partners, parent and child, teacher and pupil, or even boss and company! Not surprisingly, though, the greatest demand for synastry tends to come from would-be lovers, or people in long-term relationships.

How to Use Synastry

Synastry is a symbolic language which shows how people 'talk' to each other on many different levels – some of them conscious, some of them not. It can pinpoint areas of mutual attraction or tension, and suggest ways of resolving problems, but it cannot reveal whether a relationship is 'meant to be', or even how long it will last; that rests on how much the two people involved want the relationship to work!

The theory is that an abundance of hard aspects in synastry may create too many blocks for the relationship to survive, while a proliferation of soft aspects implies harmony and mutual understanding. However, this guideline should not be followed rigidly.

There are many examples of couples with supposedly disastrous synastry who manage to pull through against all apparent odds. Similarly, a host of gentle aspects is no guarantee of a strong or lasting relationship; it can just as easily suggest a relationship that will disintegrate at the first sign of trouble, or run out of steam as soon as the initial flurry of passion is exhausted.

Bearing these limitations in mind, the best way for a beginner to approach chart comparison is to employ the same step-by-step procedure as that used for interpreting an ordinary birth chart.

STEP 1: Before making any comparisons, start by assessing the main focal points of each chart. In particular, look at the signs, sign rulers and any planets (as well as the aspects to them) that fall in the Seventh and Eighth Houses of each chart. Although either House can be considered in total isolation, both have a major bearing on what sort of relationships we seek.

STEP 2: Using the blank aspect grid given in Drawing up a Birth Chart (p. 20), fill in all the aspects between the two charts. Beginners should concentrate on the major aspects, and use the standard orbs.

In the process make a note of the balance of Elements and Qualities between the charts. These show at a very basic level what each of us tends to look for in another – usually to compensate for what is actually missing in ourselves.

This is especially true when one or both charts shows a relative emphasis or lack of one or more Elements or Qualities.

STEP 3: Next, look at the Angles and see where they fall in each other's charts. It is safe to say that no relationship will get very far without planetary contacts from one person's planets to the other's Angles, and this applies to both the Ascendcant-Descendant and the MC-IC axis.

Aspects between the Ascendant rulers are important, as they throw light on the nature of the couple's attraction. Contacts between their Angles – for example, when the Ascendant of one conjuncts the Ascendant or MC of the other – are also significant, as these reflect similarities of outlook on life.

STEP 4: Compare the signs and House positions of the so-called personal planets – the Sun, Moon, Mercury, Venus and Mars. These represent the basic thrust of the relationship, and show how and in what area the feelings, emotions and mental attitudes of one party affect and influence those of the other.

While Mercury is said to be 'neutral', strong aspects between the 'male' planets (the Sun and Mars) and 'female' planets (the Moon and Venus) are the clearest indicators of sexual attraction. For an affair of the heart to get off the ground, there must be some form of contact between the male and female planets – whether the aspects are hard or soft.

STEP 5: Finally, repeat the same process for the outer planets –

Jupiter to Pluto. Aspects between these are not critical unless their position in one or other of the charts is especially powerful (for example, on, or ruling, the Ascendant). Even so, they should not be ignored, since they can throw light on issues which arise as a result of age differences.

Aspects from the outer to the personal planets must always be considered in synastry. They symbolize deep and powerful emotional responses within the relationship which at times may be almost compulsive. In fact, the way these energies are handled will, to a large extent, determine whether the relationship stands or falls by the wayside.

The next two parts of this section provide a detailed interpretation guide to help you put the theories and techniques of synastry into practice.

Care in Interpretation

As in birth chart interpretation, you have to tread cautiously when following the 'rules' governing synastry – the comparison of two charts. By tradition, for example, the most highly prized sign of compatibility was when a man's Sun aspected a women's Moon – preferably by conjunction. If the women's Sun also happened to touch the man's Moon, this was held to be the perfect union.

The danger of following this principle to the letter, though, can be seen by looking at the pairing of a Sun-Leo, Moon-Scorpio man with a Sun-Scorpio, Moon-Leo woman. Even if these planets do not actually form squares to each other natally, or between the two charts, they are still square by sign – and so, being Fixed signs, they constitute a highly formidable combination.

It might be that the combined energies of the planets blend naturally. But equally, they could signify a high level of competition and emotional tension within the relationship. Beyond the perfectly reasonable observation that this particular mixture is the planetary equivalent of dynamite, there is little more that can be said without referring back to the couple's birth charts to see what each of them is looking to contribute to the relationship.

In synastry, the Sun is a vitally important agent in the 'glue' of a relationship. But that does not mean one partner's Sun has to be compatible with the other's for the relationship to hold together. Admittedly it helps if the two Suns make soft aspects to one another, or failing that, fall in mutually sympathetic signs. But if they don't, it is by no means the end of the world.

Just as important are the aspects made between the couple's Suns and their other planets. As the bringer of light, the Sun of one person energizes the planets it aspects in the other's chart, and it is these aspects which give the relationship its sense of purpose. Without strong solar contacts, neither partner is likely to have a lasting effect on the other one, and the two will probably drift apart.

In most cases, a smattering of hard aspects (preferably involving both Suns, to keep the balance even) is just what is needed to give a stimulating, dynamic twist to the relationship. On the other hand, too many will create friction which in time may become intolerable.

By contrast, a relationship with mostly soft solar aspects will have a sense of ease and spontaneity, but may also lack direction. Even though the attraction is likely to be a strong one, there may not be enough tension to make it binding. A healthy spread of hard and soft aspects means that there is incentive to change and grow with each experience – and to do so with confidence.

Sun Contacts

To the Sun: The conjunction can either bring harmony, or the kind of friction that comes through being too similar. Soft aspects blend most easily, although they may lack the dynamic tension of a square, or the balanced viewpoint of an opposition.

To the Moon: A traditional indicator of a strong physical attraction, as well as friendship – especially with the conjunction. With the hard aspects, the initial pull is likely to fade if the Sun becomes too overbearing, while the Moon may be seen as indecisive and moody.

To Mercury: A stimulating mental rapport with many interests in common. Differences of opinion implied by the hard aspects need not become a problem providing each is prepared to hear the other out.

To Venus: An excellent sigh of sexual attraction, especially if the woman's Sun contacts the man's Venus. Of the hard aspects, only the square and inconjunction indicate possible tension in affections.

To Mars: Action-packed and volatile, this is not for the faint-hearted. The hard aspects in particular need outlets to vent anger. Often a strong pull when the man's Sun contacts the woman's Mars.

To Jupiter: All aspects point to opportunities to learn from one another. There is mutual support with the soft aspects, whereas more effort is needed to tolerate differences with the hard aspects.

To Saturn: Sombre Saturn can quickly deflate the Sun's confidence, and both sides may have to swallow some painful truths. With patience the Sun can energize Saturn and learn self-discipline in return.

To Uranus: A sudden, magnetic attraction which is likely to be short-lived if the novelty proves too much. A mixture offering the chance to open up to new ideas on relating; never likely to be dull.

To Neptune: The Sun is beguiled and nurtured by Neptune, the spell breaking only when reality forces both sides to face up to more worldly matters. A risk of falling into saviour-victim roles.

To Pluto: Pluto can either raise the Sun's level of awareness, or indulge in power games. Change on a deep level is probable with this contact, although it is likely to be resisted if the pace is forced.

To the Ascendant-Descendant: A combination that is likely to have a powerful impact. Even though this is one of the traditional signs of compatibility, each can end up blaming the other for joint failures!

To the MC-IC: The Sun often identifies strongly with issues concerning the other person's MC-IC axis, although it might just as easily be tempted to hog the limelight.

Moon Contacts

The Moon represents our emotional response to (and expectations of) life at a very basic level. Our 'gut' feeling when we first meet someone, or the type of person we instinctively feel drawn to, reveals a great deal about our own lunar energy. But the astrological reasons as to why a particular relationship seems to 'make' people behave the way they do only become clear when we compare the positions and aspects of the Moons in the couple's charts.

Light and Dark

It is worth bearing in mind that psychologically the Moon in a relationship has both a light and a dark side. And since it also tends to reflect the nature of any planets which it aspects in the other person's chart, there are times when it is hard to know who is triggering which reaction in whom! As a rule, soft aspects from one person's Moon to the other's speak of a strong emotional bond, based on intuitive understanding and an urge to protect and support one another. But soft aspects can also encourage one or both parties to indulge in compulsive habits (usually connected with unconscious behaviour patterns from the past) which may prove hard to break.

Hard aspects point to areas in the relationship where feelings of inhibition or rejection are likely to surface. The intense feelings involved mean that there is no soft option: these issues will eventually have to be faced and resolved one way or another.

To the Moon: Contacts between Moons are like tuning into an emotional frequency. The soft aspects – and also the conjunction – show that the signals between both sides are being received loud and clear; with such mutual sensitivity, it is second nature to adjust to one another's moods. Although there are distinct signs of 'interference' with the opposition, there is usually enough give and take in the relationship to outweigh the differences. The squares are extremely difficult to handle because something is felt to be missing at a deep level and neither side ever feels truly 'at home' with the other.

To Mercury: There is usually an instinctive understanding, plus an ability to air and work out any grievances, with these two planets. The hard aspects denote more tension and less objectivity.

To Venus: All these aspects are extremely positive, bringing a soothing hand to soften any friction elsewhere. With the square, the attraction may be compulsive but feelings will be no less genuine.

To Mars: Highly strung and hot blooded – a relationship where the crockery is likely to fly. Sexual energy is high, but it may not be enough to offset the explosive conflicts of the hard aspects.

To Jupiter: These two planets feel good together, offering mutual support and protection. However, this combination also needs space – especially with the hard aspects – to avoid exaggerating differences.

To Saturn: Often an indicator of emotional barriers. Saturn may cause the Moon to close up and feel unwanted, while the Moon may be too intuitive for Saturn. Emotional stability is prized above all else.

To Uranus: An electric, unusual combination which may prove too highly charged after the initial attraction wears thin. The 'on-off' quality means that nothing is predictable – even the outcome!

To Neptune: Seeking an out-of-the-ordinary relationship, couples with this contact are as likely to lose their way through making unrealistic demands on each other as they are to fulfil their dream!

To Pluto: Symbolizes a journey into unchartered waters which is likely to dredge up deeply buried emotions. This contact offers much but there is also a danger of possessiveness and emotional blackmail.

To the Ascendant-Descendant: Traditionally a sign of strong physical attraction, but the emotional bond is also powerful. Often this contact stirs strong feelings of 'deja vu', even with the square.

To the MC-IC: The Moon is usually tremendously supportive of the MC-IC partner, relating instinctively to (and often blending in with) his or her deepest feelings. The square points to family interference.

Mercury Contact

While the other personal planets are traditionally regarded as symbolising classically 'male' or 'female' energies in synastry, Mercury is often described as a 'neutral' or nonsexual planet. But this is misleading, for the Messenger of the Gods is certainly no eunuch when it comes to romantic or sexual encounters! Often he makes his presence felt from the moment Cupid's arrow strikes its target. He is 'responsible', among other things, for the oily charms of the seducer, and it is he who is absent when we open our mouths only to be lost for words.

Mercury contacts in synastry reveal whether we are likely to have a good mental rapport with our partner, the kind of mutual interests we enjoy, and whether or not we share the same sense of humour – one of the greatest aphrodisiacs of all. Easy contacts may also symbolize an unspoken understanding – almost as if, to quote one astrologer, 'we naturally learn to speak each other's language'.

Even if we are not tuned into each other intuitively, positive Mercury contacts show that a relationship is unlikely to break down due to poor communications! – and as long as couples talk, there is always a chance that problems can be sorted out. Difficult aspects from one Mercury to another often show themselves more clearly once the physical side of the relationship has settled down. It is at this stage that people often discover if there is something to build on.

To Mercury: Soft aspects and the conjunction are particularly important in synastry, as they show mental compatibility and the likelihood of shared interests outside the bedroom! The opposition gives objectivity and an ability to appreciate the different ways in which one another's minds work; the square and inconjunction may indulge in cutting remarks, and can also prove difficult when it comes to everyday decisions or listening to each other's viewpoint.

To Venus: This pairing shows a natural urge to express affections and be sensitive to one another's feelings. There may be a tendency to suppress grievances, though less so with the hard aspects.

To Mars: Sparks are likely to fly, as Mercury and Mars both enjoy locking antlers mentally or letting off steam. With the hard aspects, early passionate disagreements may stop a relationship flowering.

To Jupiter: A strong indication of mental compatibility. Even when they don't see eye to eye, they complement one another – Mercury is good with details, Jupiter likes to orchestrate the overall picture.

To Saturn: Saturn can block Mercury's flow, although this may be just what is needed when Mercury goes into overdrive. Better for business than love, as Saturn may strip away any romantic illusions!

To Uranus: Mentally this is a bit like being connected to a live wire. Both planets stimulate each other to question and challenge accepted beliefs. Likely to be exciting, but with the hard aspects there is a habit of taking the opposite view just for the sake of it.

To Neptune: Rational Mercury is easily overwhelmed by Neptune's formless, and often unreachable, world. Communication may be almost telepathic and the exchange of ideas inspired. But just as often there is impracticality, confusion or downright lying.

To Pluto: At their best, Pluto and Mercury combine to unearth what makes a relationship tick. With the hard aspects, old prejudices and patterns of thinking have to be faced. It is important that both sides learn to accept the other's views in the process.

To the Ascendant-Descendant: This combination stresses the importance of a marriage of minds. Sometimes a couple may think as one, but they may also be drawn to the kind of healthy disagreements that stimulate debate – although with the square, they may easily become too analytical for their own good.

To the MC-IC: An extremely positive combination in business. In love, life is likely to be stimulating – and with the square, maybe even controversial. Other factors will show if the difference in opinions is serious enough to have a major effect on the relationship.

The Signs and the Houses

In the excitement of comparing planetary aspects between two charts to see whether or not they are compatible, it is all too easy to overlook other important synastry factors – especially the signs and houses. For example, an enticing trine between a man's Mars in Aries and a woman's Venus in Leo is not just different in substance from the same trine in Taurus and Virgo. There would also be a subtle change of emphasis if the signs were reversed – with his Mars in Leo and her Venus in Aries. Similarly, the balance of sexual and emotional energy would shift if his Venus were in Aries and her Mars in Leo. It may not weaken the attraction, but it would be interesting to speculate as to who wore the trousers in the relationship!

The same careful consideration must be given to precisely where one person's planets fall in the other's chart. For example, Venus in the partner's Second House will not have the same 'effect' as when it falls in the Fifth. The first denotes a shared interest in the good and beautiful things in life; the second will really fire up the couple's sexual chemistry!

On the other hand, if a Venus-Pluto square happens to fall between the partner's Second and Fifth Houses, the affairs of both houses will be brought into play. In this case, the relationship might have to deal with issues of possessiveness on both a material and romantic level.

Venus Contacts

Venus represents the principle of attraction, and also its opposite – repulsion! Its main function in the birth chart is to sort out our likes from our dislikes at every level – a process we tend to feel most acutely when we are attracted to someone else. But although Venus may show us where our heart's desire lies, it does not produce any tangible results on its own. Being passive by nature, Venus in synastry needs to contact one of the would-be partner's 'active' planets for the attraction to lead anywhere.

Aspects from Venus to the partner's Sun, Mars and Angles were traditionally thought to offer the best odds on an attraction developing into something more substantial than a mere fluttering of hearts. Nowadays, astrologers consider the outer planets to be powerful magnets, too.

Mutual Satisfaction

Soft aspects from Venus to a partner's planets or Angles show that the couple enjoy each other's company, and share similar tastes and values. If Mars is involved in the synastry, there is also a strong probability that the couple will be sexually compatible. A surfeit of hard aspects to Venus is commonly found in love affairs that have an 'eyes met across the table' quality about them. The attraction is usually compulsive, pushing one (if not both) partners to behave destructively, though on the positive side, relationships as intense as these can in some cases lead to a deeper level of self-awareness.

To Venus: Couples with a conjunction or soft aspects tend to find each other's company soothing. Those with hard aspects may not share the same values, but are still likely to find each other appealing. The differences signified by hard Venus aspects rarely become serious unless other factors also point in this direction.

To Mars: Mars arouses Venus' desires. Contacts here indicate tremendous magnetic attraction and show how a relationship functions physically. With soft aspects, the physical and emotional side of the relationship will be well balanced. With hard aspects, the sexual atmosphere may be steamier – perhaps compulsively so at times.

To Jupiter: All these contacts promise great warmth and affection, although with the conjunction and soft aspects there is a tendency to accept things as they are. The hard aspects put backbone into the relationship in a way that is mutually beneficial.

To Saturn: The classic 'going steady' relationship – cool and reliable. Feelings are genuine but largely inhibited. Hard aspects often hint at 'bad timing'; the attraction is there but somehow the relationship never gets off the ground. This combination can also show great commitment, but not necessarily for the right reasons.

To Uranus: Zappy Uranus can wreak havoc with Venus' sense of values – often in a thrilling way. This planetary pairing brings a spirit of exploration to a relationship, and any attempt to settle into a cosy routine is likely to end in tears. The unexpected ups and downs – particularly with the hard aspects – may be too much for some.

To Neptune: These highly idealistic contacts point to a search for the 'beautiful' partner which as often as not ends in shattered dreams – especially with the hard aspects. A planetary duet which often starts with a romantic fanfare, only to find the harsher truths of the affair disappointing. Can inspire tremendous feelings of love.

To Pluto: There is nothing lightweight about these contacts. Venus and Pluto are both adept at playing power games in love, and a relationship with this pairing often has a compulsive love–hate or manipulative side to it. With the hard aspects, the compulsion is often unconscious and only becomes clear after the couple have parted.

To the Ascendant-Descendant: Traditionally one of the best signs of compatibility. Both sides are affectionate and want to give what the other needs. With the square, Venus offers the other half a break from life's toils, though both draw strength from just being together.

To the MC-IC: Often prominent in the charts of people who look good together in public. With Venus on the partner's IC, the emphasis is likely to be more on enjoying each other's company in private.

Mars Contacts

Mars represents quite the opposite energy to Venus. On a psychological level is shows our need to be our 'own person', whereas Venus symbolizes our desire to link arms with someone else. In synastry the balance between these two forces is critical in deciding whether the relationship is likely to be harmonious or unstable.

Balancing Act

When Mars is prominent in synastry, the chances are that one or both sides will be more concerned with looking after their own interests than supporting the other. On the other hand, few or no aspects to Mars suggests a lack of impetus to become involved at all – even if other synastry contacts indicate a strong attraction!

Soft aspects from Mars to the partner's chart imply that the couple are temperamentally well suited and have compatible sex drives – especially if Venus and Jupiter are in the picture. With the possible exception of aspects to Saturn or Neptune, both sides should gain individually from being together.

Hard aspects – and with Mars, this includes the conjunction – do not mean that the relationship is doomed to failure, but it is vital that the energies of Mars are not suppressed, otherwise the pressures may become intolerable. Often sexual energy is extremely high, providing an outlet for bottled-up feelings. However, there is also a danger that passions may run out of control, or simply be 'out of synch'.

To Mars: The impulsive energies of Mars can prove quite a handful when they combine in synastry. The hard aspects often point to tempestuous emotions and a spirit of confrontation. Sexual energy is high, but there is often a lack of tenderness. With the soft aspects – and to a lesser extent the conjunction – passions continue to be easily stirred, but with more consideration for the other party.

To Jupiter: Releases great physical energy, although there is a meeting of minds as well. Jupiter has faith in Mars' ambitions, while Mars can make Jupiter more dynamic and active, as well as finding outlets for their combined energies. Sexually, this is a compatible blend – particularly with the conjunction and soft aspects.

To Saturn: The direct opposite to Mars-Jupiter, bringing feelings of frustration and a sense that both hot and cold taps are running at the same time! Saturn thinks Mars is self-centred, while Mars finds Saturn harsh and obstructive. The truth is that with all the aspects, both sides must give plenty of room to breathe if there is to be any chance of a lasting relationship.

To Uranus: This combination often occurs between two people seeking (consciously or not) to break away from previous relationship patterns. The attraction is usually immediate, extremely physical and off-beat. A once-in-a-lifetime affair that may not last, but has a lasting effect, opening the door to a new way of relating.

To Neptune: These are difficult energies to work with. Mars

JUPITER CONTACTS

To Jupiter: Even if the aspects are hard, these contacts usually signify that both sides are likely to broaden the other's mind.

To Saturn: Despite symbolising opposite principles of growth and limitation, these planets combine well and balance each other out.

To Uranus: Hard aspects make Jupiter over-reach himself, though soft aspects and the conjunction often indicate a telepathic link.

To Neptune: Denotes great sensitivity. Good for sharing one another's spiritual goals, but poor for day-to-day practical matters!

To Pluto: Relationships with this pairing often have a deep level of understanding; the hard aspects may point to a lack of co-operation.

To the Angles: Whatever the outcome, these aspects suggest that the relationship offers a valuable opportunity for mutual growth.

gets befogged by Neptune's other-worldliness, while Neptune finds it hard to appreciate the Mars 'go out and prove yourself' approach. The combined effect is rather like a hall of mirrors in which the relationship become distorted through a total lack of mutual understanding.

To Pluto: This combination frequently starts off as an unconscious power struggle in which Pluto seeks to dominate Mars, who in turn tries to get Pluto to show his cards. Both sides have to prove themselves right – though less compulsively with the soft aspects. At times the relationship may resemble a battlefield, in which case the powerful sexual attraction may not be strong enough to sustain it.

To the Ascendant-Descendant: These aspects tend to magnify other factors in the chart. The effect on the relationship depends on whether the couple see themselves primarily as a team or (especially with the square) as individuals. Probably best in a working relationship where disagreements can be kept under tight rein!

To the MC-IC: Mars can help the MC-IC partner make it in

SATURN CONTACTS

To Saturn: Shows how both parties deal with the other's inhibitions and insecurities, and what kind of ambitions they share.

To Uranus: Usually indicates tension through Uranus being too rebellious and Saturn too restrictive for each other's liking.

To Neptune: Slippery Neptune is too elusive for Saturn, who can be too rigid for Neptune; the conjunction may help dreams become reality.

To Pluto: Although Saturn might feel threatened by Pluto, and Pluto distanced by Saturn, this pair can survive great hardship.

To the Angles: Saturn can either be a restrictive influence or bring a much-needed sense of structure and stability to the partner's life.

the world or be fiercely competitive. Similarly, home may be a stimulating environment, or a cauldron of arguments and accusations! This combination demands a spirit of compromise to be of mutual benefit.

Contacts Between the Slower Planets

In synastry, aspects between Jupiter, Saturn and the outer planets are less significant than aspects from these slower-moving bodies to the 'personal' planets.

In the case of Uranus, Neptune and Pluto this is not surprising: they travel around the zodiac so slowly that most couples either have them in the same sign, or in the sign next door. Only if there is a big age gap will they make substantially different aspects from those in the birth chart.

Yet although aspects between the slower-moving planets may have little to say about how a relationship gets off the ground, they can reveal a great deal about what keeps it together or pulls it apart. Contacts between Jupiter and the partner's outer planets, for example, raise a relationship's expectations. There is an optimistic, fun-loving streak which keeps things on an even keel, although hard aspects can also bring out Jupiter's extravagant side.

Saturn, by contrast, restricts or inhibits any planet it contacts, and can unfortunately kill all the romance and spontaneity. Yet Saturn also has the power to bring a relationship down to earth and teach some important lessons about living together – the kind of lessons that most of us need to learn from time to time!

Outer Planet Contacts to the Angles

Uranus: This planet tends to disrupt any attempt to settle into a conventional relationship; an unstable influence with the square.

Neptune: Can indicate an inspired, spiritual bond, or an affair which loses itself in a web of illusion, false hopes and deception!

Pluto: Deep, fascinating and intense, Pluto usually acts on an unconscious level as an agent of transformation or destruction.

Three Case Studies

As in most areas of astrology, chart comparisons often yield what appears to be confusing or contradictory data – for example, when the Moon in one chart trines Uranus in the other, while the Moon in the second chart squares Uranus in the first. Traditional astrology gives quite different meanings to these two aspects. The modern approach is to suggest that both partners are looking for emotional excitement and freedom in a relationship, but that one will be more at ease with the notion than the other. Either way, such a relationship is unlikely to be stable in the conventional sense, although in some ways this is precisely what both partners want.

If the Moon square Uranus were a Moon square Saturn instead, the result would be entirely different. In all probability, the Moon-Uranus trine would fail to generate the same magnetic intensity; the Moon-Saturn square would have a depressing effect – perhaps so much as to prevent a relationship from starting in the first place!

In the light of examples like this, it is important not to lose sight of one of astrology's golden rules; that the nature of the planets involved always takes precedence over the type of aspect. You can see this, too, in the sample chart comparisons below, which illustrate some of the very different planetary energies that can bring people together – or drive them apart.

The 'Uranus' Couple: Alan & Helen

Background

Five years ago, when they became next door neighbours, Alan and Helen were so immersed in their careers that neither of them imagined they would ever find anyone to share their lives. But they had not allowed for the Uranus factor in their synastry. What began as a casual affair suddenly took off when Helen became pregnant. Two 'unexpected' children later, Helen and Alan live together as common-law husband and wife and still manage to run separate businesses.

Mentally

At first sight, the mental chemistry in Alan and Helen's synastry appears unstable: her Mercury-Jupiter opposition makes a powerful square to his Jupiter-Uranus conjunction, suggesting a rather volatile, argument-prone relationship. But in synastry, this kind of planetary combination only creates problems if the partners are pulling in different directions.

In both Alan and Helen's charts, Uranus falls in the Seventh House. This suggests that they are both looking for independent-minded partners who will in turn give them room to follow their own interests.

Moreover, with his sun conjunct her Mercury, and her Mercury square his Ascendant, the channels of communication between them are clearly open. They draw strength from the fact that others see their unconventional lifestyle as eccentric, although the combined effect of all the squares to their Jupiters means that they must both make a conscious effort to adjust to the day-to-day routine of running two businesses and raising a family!

Emotionally

By far the strongest feature in Alan and Helen's 'emotional' synastry is the Uranian need for space and freedom in their relationship. The 'Grand Trine' between his Mercury and her Moon and Uranus shows that there is an intuitive understanding between them as to when to be close and when to give one

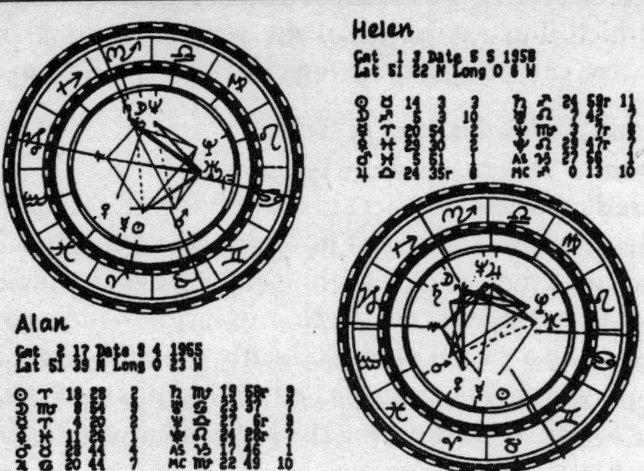

another room to breathe, as well as the ability to discuss their feelings openly.

Perhaps this is just as well, since Alan's Moon opposes Helen's Sun, as well as squaring her Uranus and trining her Mars – an unsteady alliance which might be more manageable if it centred on Helen's Moon instead. As it is, this planetary mixture perfectly describes Helen's preference to 'wear the trousers' emotionally; she is the more dynamic – and, as it happens, unreliable – force in the relationship, whereas Alan, with his Scorpio Moon, plays a more receptive and soothing role. In the beginning this balance between 'male' and 'female' roles did not go down too well with Alan's 'macho' Aries Sun, but the two of them struck a deal which effectively gave him free rein as long as he toed the line at home!

Physically

Despite the sexual chemistry between them – shown by the wide conjunction of his Venus and her Mars, and by the sextile from his Mars to her Venus, the physical intensity of this planetary embrace is dampened a little by the prevalence of dreamy Pisces! In the bedroom, the romantic, feminine sides of Helen's Piscean Venus and Mars dovetail quite neatly with Alan's robust Sun-Aries and Mars-Taurus. All the same, she has never shared his appetite for lengthy and regular bouts of love-making; she is more interested in the fantasies of sex than in the act itself.

This difference is still the source of the odd emotional power struggle (his Mars squares her Pluto), but it is not serious enough to undermine the overall balance of their relationship.

The 'Neptune' Couple: George & Louise

Background

George and Louise were instantly drawn to each other when they first met, although true to the strong Neptune presence in their synastry, it took them a while to get round to doing anything about it! For a while they seemed like the 'dream couple', and were so wrapped up in one another that to their friends, they appeared far removed from the ordinary world. Yet within two years, hope had turned to disillusionment. With more than a hint of bitterness, Louise eventually left George for another man.

Mentally

Initially, George and Louise believed they had a great deal to offer each other. The trine between their Jupiters – also linked by trine to both their Neptunes – shows much common ground in their outlook on life, with a capacity for inspiring one another with their ideals.

But in time, other qualities began to surface. Louise's Sun forms the fourth 'arm' of George's Fixed T-Square. Opposing his Third House Mercury-Saturn conjunction, her lively way with words appeared all the more bubbly when set against George's rather slow, deliberate way of expressing himself. With her Twelfth House Sun reflecting his Neptune on the Ascendant (which is also involved in the aspect pattern), they gradually began to erode each other's confidence and self-respect.

Eventually, these planetary energies became locked into a total lack of understanding on both sides. When the quarrelsome, destructive side of the inconjunctions from her Mars, Uranus and Pluto to his Mercury began to dominate the relationship, the underlying differences of opinion quickly became too much for them to bear.

Emotionally

To begin with, Louise was totally beguiled by George's elusive Neptunian personality, which seemed to combine a rare

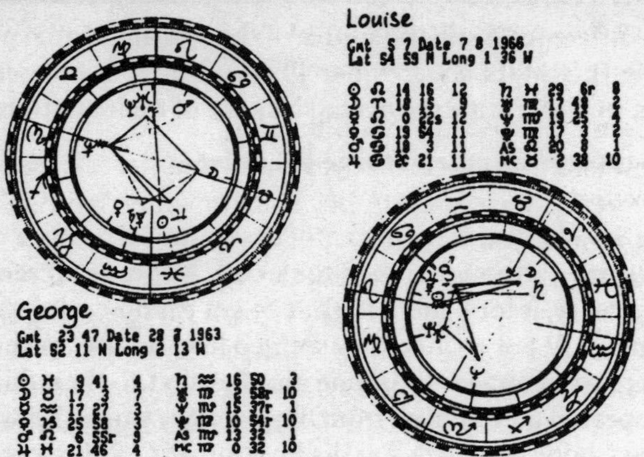

mixture of emotional depth and extreme sensitivity. Her Sun square his Neptune-Ascendant and Moon-Descendant axis is a spell-binding but unrealistic – sometimes even deceptive – combination in synastry.

In Louise, George found someone he could instinctively protect and nourish (his Moon sextiles her Venus-Mars-Jupiter stellium in Cancer). She, as a Sun-Leo, was happy to be adored, and responded well to his need for a strong commitment.

But while his Saturn on her Descendant gave the relationship an air of emotional stability, it was not enough for George. It also proved too restrictive for Louise. With the trine from her Uranus to George's Moon mirroring her own natal inconjunction between these planets, Louise eventually felt a need to break out of the rut – to stop being suffocated by her lovers' needs, and to find out what she really wanted from a relationship.

Physically

With a Venus-Mars-Jupiter conjunction, Louise was never short of admirers. But because it fell in moody Cancer, few had been able to make sense of the way she blew 'hot and cold' sexually – few, that is, until she met George. The sextile from his Moon, together with the wide trine from Neptune and the opposition from his Venus to her Cancer stellium, reflected George's sensitivity to her rather wayward moods. Louise in turn was deeply grateful for his gentle and considerate ways. Only when the relationship began to fail did the critical side of his

Mercury-Saturn inconjunction to her Cancer planets kill the tenderness and passion between them.

The 'Venus' Couple: Matthew & Anna

Matthew and Anna met three years ago. Despite their ten-year age difference, they felt that they had known each other 'since the beginning of time'.

Of the three couples analysed, they show the most obvious signs of 'romantic' compatibility – with both his Venus and Ascendant conjuncting her Sun-Descendant. Indeed, the strong Venusian component in their synastry goes a long way towards explaining why they virtually fell into each other's arms the first time they met, and have been inseparable ever since.

Mentally

While a prominent Venus in synastry usually denotes a powerful attraction, it does not necessarily reflect the quality of that attraction. A closer look at Matthew and Anna's charts shows that the real strength of their relationship lies in the extraordinary level of mental compatibility.

Generally, there is a fine balance of aspects between their respective 'mind' planets – Mercury, Jupiter and Uranus. But more significantly, Matthew and Anna both have Mercury conjunct Uranus – one in sensitive, intuitive Cancer, the other in practical, analytical Virgo.

Even though these conjunctions do not aspect one another, they are in mutually sympathetic signs – indicating a constant source of mental stimulation. Both are also in sextile to the other partner's Jupiter – a remarkable combination which gives Matthew and Anna an almost 'telepathic' ability to tune in to what the other one is thinking, as well as a willingness to talk over problems rather than let them build up.

Emotionally

Despite their restless mental energy, both Matthew (Moon in Capricorn) and Anna (Sun in Leo) look for stability in their close relationships. Even so, the emotional cross-currents running between their charts are anything but stable!

Apart from having Moons in inconjunct signs, Matthew's

Sun squares Anna's Moon, which suggests an almost permanent state of heightened tension between them. In Mutable signs, the effect is rather like an endless game of hide and seek – fun when both are in the mood, but hardly relaxing otherwise. His Saturn in square to her Sun can also be woundingly cold and critical at the wrong times.

Yet in spite of these problems the emotional bond between them is extremely powerful. The double conjunction between their respective Suns and Venuses, as well as Matthew's Venus conjunct Anna's Descendant, shows that they are never likely to lose sight of the special love they feel for one another – even in their most miserable moments. A match made in heaven!

Physically

An irresistible physical attraction was the spark that set this relationship alight. This is hardly surprising considering that Matthew's Gemini Sun sits tantalisingly between Anna's Venus-Mars conjunction, while her Sun falls close to his Ascendant, and her Venus sextiles his Pluto. The Gemini emphasis does not immediately call to mind steamy passion, but it is versatile. An adventurous trine from his Mars to her Uranus makes them both strongly aware of the dangers of falling into an unimaginative routine.

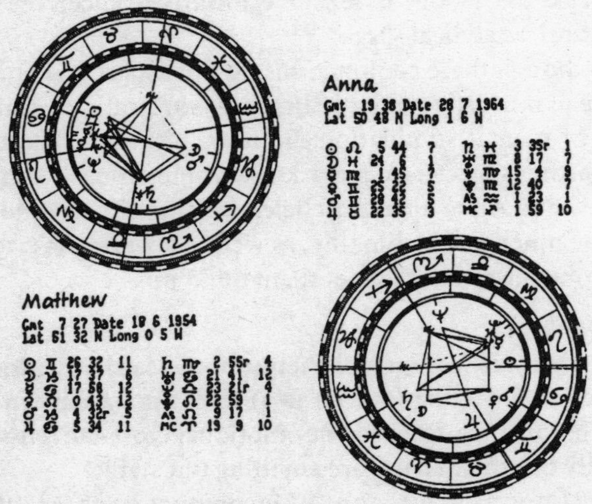

CHINESE ASTROLOGY

The Chinese Calendar

For many of the Chinese, astrology is not merely a pastime; it is a revered part of their way of life. Horoscopes of new-born children are cast as a matter of course, and many marriages are only contracted if the local astrologer is satisfied that the horoscopes of both parties are compatible.

According to tradition, a young man would offer a prospective father-in-law a card with his name on one side and on the other, the 'four pillars' (the time, day, month, and year) of his birth as a formal proposal of marriage. If these blended with those of his intended fiancée, well and good. If not, the young man's hopes were dashed – unless of course, there happened to be a sister whose horoscope was compatible!

In ancient China, lists of stars and even maps of the heavens had been carefully compiled long before anything of their kind had appeared in the western world. But centuries later, when China first became an empire, anyone discovered practising astrology was liable to be condemned to death for treason – not because astrology was considered a black art, but because it held the sacred key to Heaven's secrets, fit for the Emperor's ears only.

Court Astrologers

In the second century BC, the Grand Astrologer held one of the highest ministerial posts at court. Dozens of astrologers were employed to keep track of the motions of the planets, the paths of the Moon and Sun, and variations in the appearance of the stars. All their observations were meticulously recorded (a treasure trove for astronomers today), and any deviations from their normal courses were noted and analysed.

But it was the coming of Buddhism which brought astrology to a wider public. Although it was an offence to study the heavens, the astute

wandering monks soon discovered that there was enough astrological data in the complex Chinese calendar, which was freely available to all. And when the casting of horoscopes proved to be a valuable source of income for those early Buddhist missionaries, the 'Chinese horoscope' assumed a form that was to remain unchanged for more than a thousand years.

Although, officially, astrology is frowned upon in modern mainland China, the majority of people are still curious to know their guiding animal sign according to the ancient Chinese calendar.

In western astrology, a person's 'birth sign' is based on the month of birth; the Chinese, however, take the year of birth as the crucial factor when assessing general characteristics. When first encountering Chinese astrology, it is easy to be sceptical of a system which seems to declare that all people born in a certain year are doomed to failure or guaranteed success. But the strongest case in favour of Chinese astrology is precisely the way it recognizes year-types. Nearly every teacher discovers sooner or later that each yearly intake of children has its own characteristic personality.

The Chinese Calendar

The Chinese and many other eastern nations have a calendar of twelve years, each ordinary year being a 'month' of a Great Year of twelve earthly years. Today, the twelve years are popularly known by familiar names: Rat, Ox, Tiger, Hare, Dragon, Snake, Horse, Sheep, Monkey, Rooster, Dog and Pig. Popular legend relates that the Buddha called all the animals to him, but only these twelve turned up, and the Lord Buddha named the twelve years in the order of their arrival.

The first mention of the twelve animals did not appear until the eighth and ninth centuries, a time

THE ANIMALS

Which animal of the Chinese zodiac are you? Discover your sign by consulting the charts.

Rat	Ox	Tiger
31 Jan 1900 – 18 Feb 1901	19 Feb 1901 – 7 Feb 1902	8 Feb 1902 – 28 Jan 1903
18 Feb 1912 – 5 Feb 1913	6 Feb 1913 – 25 Jan 1914	26 Jan 1914 – 13 Feb 1915
5 Feb 1924 – 24 Jan 1925	25 Jan 1925 – 12 Feb 1926	13 Feb 1926 – 1 Feb 1927
24 Jan 1936 – 10 Feb 1937	11 Feb 1937 – 30 Jan 1938	31 Jan 1938 – 18 Feb 1939
10 Feb 1948 – 28 Jan 1949	29 Jan 1949 – 16 Feb 1950	17 Feb 1950 – 5 Feb 1951
28 Jan 1960 – 14 Feb 1961	15 Feb 1961 – 4 Feb 1962	5 Feb 1962 – 24 Jan 1963
15 Feb 1972 – 2 Feb 1973	3 Feb 1973 – 22 Jan 1974	23 Jan 1974 – 10 Feb 1975
2 Feb 1984 – 19 Feb 1985	20 Feb 1985 – 8 Feb 1986	9 Feb 1986 – 28 Jan 1987
19 Feb 1996 – 6 Feb 1997	7 Feb 1997 – 27 Jan 1998	28 Jan 1998 – 15 Feb 1999

Hare	Dragon	Snake
29 Jan 1903 – 15 Feb 1904	16 Feb 1904 – 3 Feb 1905	4 Feb 1905 – 24 Jan 1906
14 Feb 1915 – 2 Feb 1916	3 Feb 1916 – 22 Jan 1917	23 Jan 1917 – 10 Feb 1918
2 Feb 1927 – 22 Jan 1928	23 Jan 1928 – 9 Feb 1929	10 Feb 1929 – 29 Jan 1930
19 Feb 1939 – 7 Feb 1940	8 Feb 1940 – 26 Jan 1941	27 Jan 1941 – 14 Feb 1942
6 Feb 1951 – 26 Jan 1952	27 Jan 1952 – 13 Feb 1953	14 Feb 1953 – 2 Feb 1954
25 Jan 1963 – 12 Feb 1964	13 Feb 1964 – 1 Feb 1965	2 Feb 1965 – 20 Jan 1966
11 Feb 1975 – 30 Jan 1976	31 Jan 1976 – 17 Feb 1977	18 Feb 1977 – 6 Feb 1978
29 Jan 1987 – 16 Feb 1988	17 Feb 1988 – 5 Feb 1989	6 Feb 1989 – 26 Jan 1990
16 Feb 1999 – 4 Feb 2000		

Horse	Sheep	Monkey
25 Jan 1906 – 12 Feb 1907	13 Feb 1907 – 1 Feb 1908	2 Feb 1908 – 21 Jan 1909
11 Feb 1918 – 31 Jan 1919	1 Feb 1919 – 19 Feb 1920	20 Feb 1920 – 7 Feb 1921
30 Jan 1930 – 16 Feb 1931	17 Feb 1931 – 5 Feb 1932	6 Feb 1932 – 25 Jan 1933
15 Feb 1942 – 4 Feb 1943	5 Feb 1943 – 24 Jan 1944	25 Jan 1944 – 12 Feb 1945
3 Feb 1954 – 23 Jan 1955	24 Jan 1955 – 11 Feb 1956	12 Feb 1956 – 30 Jan 1957
21 Jan 1966 – 8 Feb 1967	9 Feb 1967 – 29 Jan 1968	30 Jan 1968 – 16 Feb 1969
7 Feb 1978 – 27 Jan 1979	28 Jan 1979 – 15 Feb 1980	16 Feb 1980 – 4 Feb 1981
27 Jan 1990 – 14 Feb 1991	15 Feb 1991 – 3 Feb 1992	4 Feb 1992 – 22 Jan 1993

Rooster	Dog	Pig
22 Jan 1909 – 9 Feb 1910	10 Feb 1910 – 29 Jan 1911	30 Jan 1911 – 17 Feb 1912
8 Feb 1921 – 27 Jan 1922	28 Jan 1922 – 15 Feb 1923	16 Feb 1923 – 4 Feb 1924
26 Jan 1933 – 13 Feb 1934	14 Feb 1934 – 3 Feb 1935	4 Feb 1935 – 23 Jan 1936
13 Feb 1945 – 1 Feb 1946	2 Feb 1946 – 21 Jan 1947	22 Jan 1947 – 9 Feb 1948
31 Jan 1957 – 17 Feb 1958	18 Feb 1958 – 7 Feb 1959	8 Feb 1959 – 27 Jan 1960
17 Feb 1969 – 5 Feb 1970	6 Feb 1970 – 26 Jan 1971	27 Jan 1971 – 14 Feb 1972
5 Feb 1981 – 24 Jan 1982	25 Jan 1982 – 12 Feb 1983	13 Feb 1983 – 1 Feb 1984
23 Jan 1993 – 9 Feb 1994	10 Feb 1994 – 30 Jan 1995	31 Jan 1995 – 18 Feb 1996

when Buddhism was flourishing in China. Yet Chinese astrologers were writing about the Great Year of twelve earthly years a thousand years before then, using strange mystical Chinese characters called 'the twelve branches' instead of the now familiar animal names.

When Buddhist astrologers brought their science to a wider audience, they tried to make the subject more understandable, and hit on the happy notion of substituting the animal names for the twelve branches. The idea caught on at once, and the use of these twelve animal names spread speedily through Asia, from Japan in the East, through Mongolia, and as far as Turkey in the West.

The principles of astrology were already well-established. Now an animal name was chosen according to how well it portrayed the characteristics of each of the twelve years. Hundreds of years of constant observation had revealed, for instance, that the fifth year of the cycle was usually marked by exceptional rains and flooding (fine if you lived in an area which was desperate for water, but unfortunate for those whose harvests were engulfed by raging torrents). For this reason, the dragon, symbol not just of rains and floods, but also of gains and losses in fortune, was chosen as the fifth emblem.

Mysteriously, the animal types for each year also appear to mould the personal characteristics of those born during them, as well as that year's course of events. So you might well expect people born in Tiger years to be proud and valiant, while also noting that the world was plunged into a disastrous war during the Tiger year 1914.

Compatibility

Chinese horoscopes also reveal the compatibility of people born under one animal sign with those of another, with some surprising stable-mates. The Snake and the Hare are said to be a supremely happy couple. The Rat and the Ox, a year apart, can make an ideal couple; but the Ox and the Tiger, also a year apart, would be forever at loggerheads.

In later sections, we shall look at the characteristics of each sign; the personalities of people born under their influence and how this will affect their relationships with others, beginning with the first sign of the Chinese zodiac – the Rat.

The Rat

5 Feb 1924 – 24 Jan 1925
24 Jan 1936 – 10 Feb 1937
10 Feb 1948 – 28 Jan 1949
28 Jan 1960 – 14 Feb 1961
15 Feb 1972 – 2 Feb 1973
2 Feb 1984 – 19 Feb 1985
19 Feb 1996 – 6 Feb 1997

The Rat has an honoured place in Chinese astrology, being the first of the 12 animals in the Chinese zodaic. Before the adoption of the popular animal names, the Chinese symbol for the first sign was the character for an infant, indicating the beginning of a new cycle through rebirth. The Rat is also used to represent midnight on Chinese clocks, indicating the birth of a new day; and it is likely that Buddhist monks in ancient times, deciding which animals should represent the 12 divisions, chose the Rat because midnight is the time when rats are at their busiest.

Some Chinese believe that rats make good watchdogs since their shrill squeaking warns the household of the surprise presence of an intruder. And should a rather fat rat pay an unexpected visit, this is a sign of great prosperity to come.

The Rat Personality

Being a Rat is actually far from contemptible, especially since the Chinese word for rat can also mean mouse, vole, hamster, or any other loveable rodent. Indeed, for the Rat personality, the keyword is 'charm'.

Since the Rat is the first sign in the Chinese zodiac, it is not surprising that the characteristics of the Rat type are leadership, stimulation and a love of novelty. Rats are excellent innovators, and are good with new ideas, but not so proficient at following them through. They like to leave practical matters to their more technically inclined friends.

Problem-solvers

Rats have an uncanny knack of being able to see through to the knot of a problem, and can produce solutions.

The Rat hour is midnight, and this seems to be the time when the Rat's mind is most active. Often, just when the family is preparing for bed, the Rat member of the household suddenly surfaces with a new idea, and sleep is impossible until the whole notion has been thrashed out. But the enthusiasm does not always last until morning.

The Rat's disdain of practical detail extends to a contempt for financial matters, in which he or she is frustratingly erratic. Important aspects of economy, such as keeping accounts and records up-to-date, are often neglected. Indeed, Rat-types may be reduced to scrimping, having to save and cut corners in lean times; but as soon as money appears, they lose restraint, forget all they have learnt, and go on spending sprees.

Agile Minds

Rat-types are generally clever and quick-witted. Their ability to deal with abstract concepts means that they are often good with figures. They also make excellent conversationalists, one fault perhaps being that they are a little too apt to name-drop, or even place-drop. 'I've not tasted anything as good since the time I went ballooning with Tom Cruise in Kathmandu', is the kind of casual remark that the Rat likes to let slip occasionally.

The Rat Year

Since the Rat year is the first in the cycle of 12, Chinese astrologers have always declared that it is the ideal time to begin work on public projects which, of course, involve people born under every sign. Just as the New Year brings fresh hopes, resolutions and renewed confidence, so a Rat year gives everyone additional opportunity to start afresh. Rat years are never the remarkable ones; just as the Rat hour is the midnight hour when most people are sleeping. But it may be that apparently insignificant events during Rat years are the seeds of later world-shattering events.

A New Start

Unless your sign is one of the few which actually conflict with the Rat, choose the Rat year for beginning a long-term commitment involving yourself and other members of your family, or perhaps a business. A change of house or premises, a move to a new location and family emigration are all matters that find favour in Rat years. But for matters which concern only you, or perhaps you and your partner (such as beginning a new career, or marriage), choose a year which is suited to your personality.

Rat Relationships

With another Rat

Rats make good companions with each other. But long-term commitment, whether in business or romance, will need a lot of help from other people.

With the Ox

The Rat's converse is the reliable Ox; but it is unlikely that the Rat will make this advisable choice of partner. The Ox is too dependable and staid for the inventive Rat.

With the Tiger

This will prove a happy relationship if the Rat is prepared to be subordinate. The Tiger can bring the security – financial or physical – which the Rat often needs.

With the Hare

The Rat is likely to be exasperated by the Hare's very different interests. At first, it may be merely minor matters which cause conflict, but later on opinions may clash.

With the Dragon

The Rat finds the Dragon's exuberant personality magically attractive, while the Dragon recognizes the effectiveness of the Rat's stimulating and creative ideas.

With the Snake

The Snake provides intellectual stimulation for the mentally active Rat. So it will be a happy enough relationship, provided that neither participant expects practical results!

With the Horse

The Rat and Horse have a grudging respect for each other, but it rarely becomes a mutual attraction, and the initial suspicion and distrust lingers.

With the Sheep

Outsiders may wonder what these two people see in each other. They are both so wrapped up in their own worlds that it is hard for them to communicate.

With the Monkey

The Rat is likely to be very happy with the technically able Monkey. Each recognizes the other's gifts and talents, and they soon develop an understanding.

With the Rooster

Both Rat and Rooster are highly individual personalities. Sometimes, when they agree, each thinks the other is wonderful! But, when they differ, the relationship suffers.

With the Dog

In home life, the Rat will be the organizer, with the Dog partner faithfully putting the plans into action. In business, the same kind of relationship applies.

With the Pig

This is an odd relationship, with its plus and minus points. There is often immediate romantic attraction, but many differences of interest that threaten.

The Year of the Rat

Whatever your animal sign, study the list below to find out how you will fare in a Rat year.

The Rat – This is the ideal time for the Rat to begin any new project. It is necessary to take care, however, that momentum is maintained.

The Ox – It is best to use this year to begin short-term, rather than long-term projects. Plan to finish them by the end of the year.

The Tiger – This is a good year for the Tiger, whether for

beginning or continuing projects. Romance, finance and health are sound.

The Hare – This year can bring its share of problems. Do not worry if there are setbacks; matters will eventually be resolved.

The Dragon – Overall, this will be an excellent year for the Dragon. Make the most of the opportunities while they are available.

The Snake – There should be good progress this year; but for important changes, it would be better to wait until next year.

The Horse – This is not the ideal period to strike out in a new direction. A great deal of effort is needed to maintain progress.

The Sheep – There could be disappointments this year; so it is better not to launch into an experimental phase.

The Monkey – An excellent time to put ideas into practice. Business should be a great success; love, the basis of a permanent relationship.

The Rooster – Too many possible directions ahead make it difficult to choose. This is not the ideal time to decide: keep your options open.

The Dog – This is a favourable year, especially for matters connected with the home or family. In business, act now, too.

The Pig – It should be a fair year, but if possible leave important decisions until next year: there are too many distracting changes ahead.

How the Hour of Birth Affects the Rat Personality

Rat hour (11pm-1am) Good fortune, resourcefulness, caution and charm. The heart should not rule.

Ox hour (1am-3am) Positive and negative aspects of creativity are combined in this independent personality, as is financial success.

Tiger hour (3am-5am) Wide travel, a good marriage and an inheritance; weak family ties.

Hare hour (5am-7am) Much success in love; but marriage, even with children, could be less rewarding. Avoid any risks to health.

Dragon hour (7am-9am) You do better with short-term financial dealings and transactions.

Snake hour (9am-11am) Your intelligent and enquiring mind is fundamental to your way of life. Keep your family in mind.
Horse hour (11am-1pm) A successful marriage requires hard work as it may not be a love match.
Sheep hour (1pm-3pm) Initially, love may be thwarted, but do not lose heart as a contented family life will be your reward.
Monkey hour (3pm-5pm) Many opportunities present themselves to this clever, skilful personality.
Rooster hour (5pm-7pm) You will have to work extremely hard to achieve the fame you desire, even risking your private life.
Dog hour (7pm-9pm) Travel and marriage can bring reward. You will acquire property; but avoid risk.
Pig hour (9pm-11pm) Family matters may come in the way of success. If you have to travel far or move house, take care.

The Ox

24 Jan 1925 – 12 Feb 1926
11 Feb 1937 – 30 Jan 1938
29 Jan 1949 – 16 Feb 1950
15 Feb 1961 – 4 Feb 1962
3 Feb 1973 – 22 Jan 1974
20 Feb 1985 – 8 Feb 1986
7 Feb 1997 – 27 Jan 1998

The Ox is the only sign in the Chinese zodiac which is the same as its Western equivalent. But this is no more than a coincidence – while Taurus represents the month of April, the Ox is the name given to the second year in the Great Cycle of 12 years. Although it is the second sign, oddly enough the Ox has a special position of importance in the Chinese calendar, for it is always shown on the first page of the Chinese yearly almanac. The position of the Ox, and the mode of dress of the man leading the animal, all drawn according to precise astronomical rules, are believed to be indicators of the weather and the harvest for the particular year in question.

The picture is a reminder of an ancient ceremony when the Emperor himself, at the beginning of Spring, would take his whole court to a field and plough the nation's first three furrows. Although China no longer has an emperor, in Thailand, which still uses the Chinese calendar, this significant ritual has been restored. As in former times, after the ceremonial ploughing, the beautifully groomed sacred oxen are presented with samples of different grains, as it is believed that the animal's choice is a guide to which crops should be planted in the coming season.

The Ox Personality

The Ox personality has all the strength and power that would be expected of this sturdy beast of burden. Yet while most people would be flattered to be thought of as trustworthy and thorough, Ox types are usually irritated by this description. They would much prefer to be thought of as adventurous and unpredictable; for them, being reliable and dependable sounds too much like being boring. But they are hardly dull: famous Ox types include Margaret Thatcher, Hitler, and J. S. Bach who all in their individual ways reveal the essential trait of the Ox: a stubborn drive to pursue the chosen course of action, and to ensure that it is cornpleted.

The Ox is the companion sign to the Rat in the House of Creativity; while the Rat is considered to be the innovator, the Ox is the finisher. That is not to say that the Ox does not have a creative side, but as Ox types are wary of anything untried and unproven, many of their excellent ideas remain untested.

The down-to-earth Ox prefers facts and figures to fancy notions. In times of uncertainity, other people will see the rather predictable qualities of the Ox as a steadying influence – at these times Ox-types can rise to positions of authority; but when conditions are more stable, the Ox is likely to be passed over.

Unromantic Types

In personal relationships, Ox types may seem to others to be unromantic, partly because their approach to love is more physical than spiritual, but basically because they keep their emotions to themselves. In any case, they prefer the affection of a few trusted friends to casual contact with many acquaintances.

The Ox Year

The Chinese astrologers of old discovered that there were certain favourable years which always seemed to usher in a period of stability. Although there may have been little of interest to record in the history books for those years, the absence of wars, climatic disasters, dynastic upheavals, or other impediments, meant that plans for any existing projects could get underway without hindrance. As a consequence, when those distant sages were compiling animal names to be titles for the years, they chose the Ox to symbolize the constancy and steadiness which was the principal feature of the second year in the 12-year astrological cycle.

Develop Your Ideas

During the year of the Ox, it is best to keep to the established routine. While it is not generally advisable to embark on new projects, this is an excellent time to develop those that might have been begun the year before.

It is a less favourable period to begin new projects, unless they can be completed before the year's end. By the same token, it is a good year for marriage, but less promising for an engagement.

Ox Relationships

With the Rat

The Rat and the Ox are astrological partners; the Ox often patiently finishes what the Rat begins and leaves. A happy partnership whether it is in business or romance.

With another Ox

A happy partnership; they will be totally loyal to each other, perhaps leading a very close-knit, private existence. The two types are so closely in harmony that they often think alike.

With the Tiger

An immovable Ox meeting an irresistible Tiger makes an unlikely partnership and creates its own problems. There may be fireworks, but this could lead to a lively relationship.

With the Hare

This relationship works better as a friendship than as a romance; in the latter case there is bound to be jealousy, since the Ox values loyalty, and the Hare prizes its freedom.

With the Dragon

The Ox may be won over by the charisma of the Dragon, but the two are so distinctly different that they need their own space. If both follow their seperate interests they will stick together.

With the Snake

A strange relationship, but this is one of the best for the Ox. The two partners are very different, and yet each benefits from the other's special qualities in all kinds of ways.

With the Horse

Although these two personalities think that they have much in common, it is the subtle differences which cause rifts in this relationship. Some confrontation is possible here.

With the Sheep

There has to be deep love and understanding for the relationship to survive; deep-seated differences are difficult to dislodge, while family quarrels often threaten happiness.

With the Monkey

This partnership is more of a friendship than a romance, and is probably the result of a shared interest, since each partner has complementary skills which the other admires.

With the Rooster

Two entirely different personalities, both going their separate ways, and yet both happily matched. A very successful partnership – life promises to be full of surprises.

With the Dog

If these two are happy with their partnership, then well and good. But the Ox and the Dog personalities usually find it difficult to make their relationship work due to suspicion and insincerity.

With the Pig

Although romance and adventure may be lacking in this partnership, there is no shortage of love, as a happy home and a contented family will eventually prove.

The Year of the Ox

Study the chart below to find out how each Chinese zodiac character is likely to fare during the Ox year.

The Rat – This is an excellent time to develop any projects that were begun last year. But beware of embarking on fresh ventures.

The Ox – This is your own year; use it to your advantage. An excellent time for reaping in the rewards of all your labours.

The Tiger – Beware of delays and obstacles. You may be frustrated in your plans, especially for travel. There are greater benefits at home.

The Hare – Though not a particularly memorable year – unless you decide to marry – this is generally a happy and progressive period.

The Dragon – Do not be discouraged if everything does not go your way this year. Try to avoid any risky ventures. Next year will be better.

The Snake – This year brings its successes and rewards, particularly to the student. It is an advantageous period: make the most of it.

The Horse – For those content to progress slowly and steadily, the year will prove satisfactory; but it would be unwise to try to force the pace.

The Sheep – The fewer the expectations, the less the disappointment. This year brings its share of obstacles in business and in relationships.

The Monkey – This is a period of immobility which may not be a bad thing. It is a good time to review matters which have been neglected.

The Rooster – Try to organize your present position, and do not get caught in a demanding situation, as there is a promise of exciting change.

The Dog – Watch your financial position this year, and do not let your plans be too ambitious as there are likely to be some setbacks.

The Pig – An ideal time for family concerns. Take any opportunities which present themselves, as next year holds less promise.

How the Hour of Birth Affects the Ox Personality

Rat hour (11pm-1am) You have perseverance, creativity and good organisational and business skills.

Ox hour (1am-3am) Reliability and endurance are emphasized, as is property investment. However, romance may bring disappointments.

Tiger hour (3am-5am) Happiness will be doubled with the right partner. Wealth from abroad.

Hare hour (5am-7am) Excellent health, great personal happiness and good fortune in love may be accompanied by a secret sadness.

Dragon hour (7am-9am) Good luck and happiness will arrive after some initial tribulation.

Snake hour (9am-11am) Your intelligence could make you an excellent teacher. Do not rely on manual skills for money.

Horse hour (11am-1pm) A good marriage in which romance does not play a strong part is possible.

Sheep hour (1pm-3pm) Children and family feature prominently in your happiness, but be careful with your financial investments.

Monkey hour (3pm-5pm) Your wealth will derive from manual dexterity. Do not travel for profit.

Rooster hour (5pm-7pm) Possible fame, or a career in the public eye. Romance and marriage may not always bring happiness.

Dog hour (7pm-9pm) Possible problems with an inheritance. Foreign travel is highly likely.

Pig hour (9pm-11pm) You will have a long and happy life with many children. Refuse offers of work or marriage abroad.

The Tiger

13 Feb 1926 – 1 Feb 1927
31 Jan 1938 – 18 Feb 1939
17 Feb 1950 – 5 Feb 1951
5 Feb 1962 – 24 Jan 1963
23 Jan 1974 – 10 Feb 1975
9 Feb 1986 – 28 Jan 1987
28 Jan 1998 – 15 Feb 1999

The third animal in the Chinese zodiac, the Tiger symbolizes bravery, ferocity and strength. The Chinese once believed that the tiger's image had the power to frighten away the evil demons of disease and corruption, so an effigy was usually displayed on the posts of magistrates' houses to protect them against moral and bodily harm. Young boys were also given tiger masks to wear, in the belief that they would absorb the tiger's valour as part of their characters.

Yet there is a darker side to the tiger's symbolism. The tiger is said to devour the souls of the dead, while the ghost of anyone killed by a tiger becomes its slave until it has led the animal on to the track of another victim.

Partly because of the tiger's luxuriant fur, and partly because only the rich and leisured classes could assemble the resources for a tiger hunt, the tiger also became the symbol of royalty, wealth and power.

In Chinese astrology, the Tiger's symbolism is full of perplexing contrasts. The ancient sages gave the name 'Tiger' to the western part of the heavens, to complement the Dragon who ruled the eastern side. In this respect the Dragon and the Tiger represent the dual forces of *yin* and *yang*, but, surprisingly, it is the Tiger which is the symbol of the softer, recessive *yin* influence.

The Tiger Personality

The Tiger has a powerfully magnetic personality which immediately demands attention. In a crowd, the Tiger will easily be found in the middle of a group of eager admirers. Tiger personalities exude a kind of brilliant assertiveness which demands respect, although this is sometimes given grudgingly, for this display of supreme self-confidence can be alienating to others.

The Tiger's mere presence can intimidate the less confident all too easily. Tiger personalities should therefore try to avoid making enemies, and remember that their success may breed jealousy, or they may lose out socially. Yet beneath the Tiger's tough veneer is a warm and caring personality which can feel the cold chill of loneliness.

Assertive Leaders

Because of the Tiger's symbolic association with the more aggressive, or masculine side of human nature, the Chinese do not take easily to women born in the year of the Tiger. 'Never bring a Tigress into the house' runs one old Chinese proverb. But Tiger women are excellent in business, make natural leaders, and can rise to the top of their careers – that is, unless they meet with other Tigers on the way who will present them with a challenge.

Tiger Careers

In careers generally, the uniformed services – with the possible exception of nursing and the caring professions – are especially suited to the Tiger personality. Any situation which brings the Tiger into contact with other people, particularly as a guide or director, will utilize the Tiger's natural gifts of leadership.

The Tiger Year

The Year of the Tiger ushers in a period of upheaval and dramatic change: it was in 1914, a Tiger year, that the First World War erupted. Even when humanity is at peace with itself, there may be other impending dangers: the weather itself may become tyrannical, bringing devastation through typhoons and gales of exceptional ferocity. In brief, it is a time to be well prepared for the unexpected.

Riding the Storm

The powerful forces at work can, however, be harnessed for good. It is the Tiger's own year, and Tigers can ride the storm. But those who ride the Tiger, as the Chinese say, may find it hard to dismount. Those embarking on any risky enterprise in the year of the Tiger should be sure that they have the resources to finish.

If your animal sign is one which has the promise of a favourable year, now is the time to risk going where you have never been before – the year will bring success for the adventurous. But for every winner there must be losers; if this is not going to be your year, then you are going to need to take every precaution regarding your finances, personal relationships, health – indeed, every aspect of your life. One thing is sure in the year of the Tiger: its unpredictability.

Tiger Relationships

With the Rat
Tigers and Rats can make a strong team where leadership matters. For a long-term relationship, whether in romance or business, the partnership is strong.

With the Ox
'One Ox can conquer two Tigers' runs an old Chinese saying, the Ox being the only one of the animals of the Chinese zodiac able to resist the Tiger.

With another Tiger
Two of a kind usually go together, but between Tigers there is usually too much competition for this relationship to work amicably all the time. Occasional sparks will fly.

With the Hare
An off couple, but a mutually devoted partnership. It will be difficult to come between these two, the Tiger being fiercely protective of the Hare partner.

With the Dragon
A formidable partnership between two people who can take on the world together. However, the Tiger must be prepared to defer to the Dragon.

With the Snake
There is some distrust between these two. In business, every detail has to be scrutinized. In romance, sexual attraction is most important.

With the Horse
This is a partnership of like minds and interests without the conflict of mutual competition. A good solid partnership which promises to last a while.

With the Sheep
The interests of these two partners are so diametrically opposed that it is difficult to see what brought them together as they are so different.

With the Monkey
Love must be very strong to keep these two together! In business, there will be a constant clash of ideals; in romance, the two find it hard to settle together.

With the Rooster
This partnership will have a difficult time. The Tiger is likely to tire of the Rooster's need to be the centre of attention, and the feeling may be reciprocated.

With the Dog
The Tiger personality will always be pleased to have the Dog as a companion; a happy and prosperous relationship in business or romance.

With the Pig
The Tiger has far too dominant a personality for the Pig to be truly happy. Perhaps the Tiger should be more careful with the sensitive Pig.

The Year of the Tiger

Whatever your animal sign, study the list below to find out how you will fare in a Tiger year.

The Rat – This promises to be an exciting year, with substantial changes in your life. It is worth putting up with the upheaval to gain benefit later.

The Ox – The only animal to get the better of the Tiger, the shrewd Ox will reap considerable benefits from this period of change. A fruitful year.

The Tiger – A time to strike out and be adventurous. The more daring will succeed; calculated risks will pay off handsomely. Decisive action brings rewards.

The Hare – A good year for initiating plans which are meant to come to fruition next year: an ideal time, therefore, to get engaged or begin saving.

The Dragon – An excellent year: finances are sound, health good, romantic and social life spectacular. You may meet someone famous.

The Snake – This may be a hazardous year. Take particular care regarding your finances, property and health, and watch your personal relationships.

The Horse – A very profitable period, and one which will leave you with many happy memories. A good year for making any momentous changes.

The Sheep – Despite the upheaval all around, the changes brought by this year affect the Sheep only minimally, or not at all.

The Monkey – This is not a secure year. It is important to be careful in all matters, whether financial or social, and avoid taking any kind of risk.

The Rooster – Avoid being over-ambitious during this very uncertain period. The greatest dangers come from over-confidence.

The Dog – An excellent year for all matters to do with the home, property, career and social life. Projects involving partnerships will be satisfactory.

The Pig – this year brings its hazards, unfortunately. The constant changes and upsets are likely to have a discouraging effect though this will not last.

How the Hour of Birth Affects the Tiger Personality

Rat hour (11pm-1pm) Fortune lies in personal happiness rather than public success.

Ox hour (1am-3am) Inner conflict and changing attitudes are a stumbling block. Too many matters vie for attention.

Tiger hour (3am-5am) The positive sides of the personality – drive and leadership – thrive.

Hare hour (5am-7am) A robust constitution and sound health are assured. Children will be loving and bring great happiness.

Dragon hour (7am-9am) Luck and good fortune are likely, with some unexpected wealth.

Snake hour (9am-11am) There is a chance of personal fame and public success, but beware of illegal transactions.

Horse hour (11am-1pm) A successful marriage will bring wealth through inheritance.

Sheep hour (1pm-3pm) Happiness hinges on romantic life, which may be unsettled. Health is good, but finances problematic.

Monkey hour (3pm-5pm) Manufacture and craft bring rewards through hard effort.

Rooster hour (5pm-7pm) Gifted and intelligent, you are likely to aim for a place in the public eye, but happiness may be sacrificed.

Dog hour (7pm-9pm) Property, travel and commerce may all bring wealth. Marriage is firmly based.

Pig hour (9pm-11pm) Health and long life are assured, but children and family life may require careful attention.

The Hare

14 Feb 1915 – 2 Feb 1916
2 Feb 1927 – 22 Jan 1928
19 Feb 1939 – 7 Feb 1940
6 Feb 1951 – 26 Jan 1952
25 Jan 1963 – 12 Feb 1964
11 Feb 1975 – 30 Jan 1976
29 Jan 1987 – 16 Feb 1988
16 Feb 1999 – 4 Feb 2000

The fourth sign of the Chinese animal zodiac is the Hare or Rabbit – the Chinese word can mean either.

The Buddhist monks of old had a special reason for adopting the Hare as the fourth animal. The fourth Chinese month is the one which includes the Spring Equinox (21 March) and in folklore all over the world the hare is associated with this season. According to the Chinese clock, the Hare hour is dawn, when rabbits and hares are at their most active.

The Hare is the emblem of self-sacrifice. The story is told that when the animals brought their gifts to the Buddha, the Hare had nothing to offer but his own body. He threw himself on to a fire, but only after carefully combing his fur to remove any insects that would have died through this action. As a reward for his selflessness, the Buddha transferred the Hare to the Moon, there he can still be seen to this day, at his cauldron, distilling the elixir of life.

The Hare Personality

The association of the Hare with the celestial pharmacy and the supreme quality of self-sacrifice extends to those born in the year of the Hare. Hare types are primarily concerned with the welfare of others and are drawn to the medical profession, particularly paediatrics and nursing. Their natural inclination to tend the less fortunate may lead them to charitable work, and if they are not involved in the care or teaching of children, they will probably work with animals.

Healers and Dipomats

Hare types often have natural healing gifts, but this may not be restricted to tending the sick: their diplomatic natures make them good mediators, arbitrators or counsellors. Some practical Hares put their knowledge of chemistry to use in the preparation of dyes or cosmetics.

The clear-sightedness of the Hare symbolizes the Hare type's foresight and perspicuity. People born in the year of the Hare are adept in sensing deceit and falsehood and are good judges of character.

Although Hare types like to go along with the crowd, they still value their own independence. They instinctively know how to become the focus of attention by being on the edge of a group, rather than be obscured by it. Friends are important;

Hare types like to socialize, pay visits and enjoy a good gossip. When alone, the Hare is fond of reading and has a refined taste in literature. The Hare is very house-proud and dislikes any kind of clutter and disorder.

Quiet Determination

The Hare is the *yin* counterpart of the Tiger: whereas the Tiger conquers by aggression, the Hare can overthrow enemies by diplomacy. Although Hare types may go out of their way to avoid confrontation, they can nevertheless succeed in achieving their ends eventually through quiet determination. Yet they can be very brave and defensive when faced with real danger.

The Hare Year

The year of the Hare is the counter-balance to the aggressive Tiger year. Provided that the Tiger's warlike influences are not too powerful to be appeased (as they were, unfortunately, in 1915 and 1939), the Hare year should be a time of peace and conciliation. The Hare year promises greater co-operation between nations, and the development of commercial activities and travel.

Politically, it is not a time for great change, but a time for consolidation and strengthening of the present position. At home, success will be achieved through tact and diplomacy rather than taking too forceful an approach.

Medical Discoveries

The Hare as celestial pharmacist points to new discoveries in the field of medicine, and any matters which concern the prolongation of life or improvements in the quality of social welfare are always highlighted in this year. The negative side is that people who, for health reasons, begin taking medication this year must avoid becoming totally dependent on it.

This year is also an ideal time for romance, beginning families and raising children.

Hare Relationships

With the Rat

It is in the nature of the Rat type to lead, and in this partnership it will be very much a case of the Hare following in the Rat's footsteps; this may lead to resentment.

With the Ox

There are no problems with this couple; the Hare will derive considerable support from the Ox partner. This is an enduring relationship, though predictable at times.

With the Tiger

Although these two partners have different natures, they get along together extremely well as long as each plays his or her complementary role in the relationship.

With the Hare

Hare types get on well together but the relationship is not an exciting one. An ideal match for the home- and family-loving couple, but poor for a business partnership.

With the Dragon

This type of partnership is much better for a whirlwind romance than any long-term relationship. The Hare is seldom hurt, but manages to upset the Dragon's plans.

With the Snake

When the hare meets the Snake, according to an old proverb, there is great happiness. With the Hare's concern for welfare and the Snake's practical sense, this is an ideal match.

With the Horse

There seems to be little common ground for these two, but if the Horse is the male partner, the relationship is workable and could muddle along.

With the Sheep

A very harmonious rapport exists between Sheep and Hare. Love life is both passionate and romantic. Shared interests make this an ideal partnership for lovers or just friends.

With the Monkey

This partnership could bring unhappiness for the Hare, who, trying to make this relationship work, may put more effort into it than the Monkey deserves.

With the Rooster

The Rooster can hold a fatal attraction for the Hare, but the feelings may not be entirely reciprocated. There is often a lack of deep understanding between these two.

With the Dog

A few domestic crises are not enough to spoil an almost ideal partnership. Both partners need the supportive influence of the other, so don't let pettiness intrude.

With the Pig

For family and home life an ideal relationship, with continuing health, a blissful domestic atmosphere and the joys of many children and grandchildren.

The Year of the Hare

Whatever your animal sign, study the list below to find out how you will fare in a Hare year.

The Rat – This is not one of the Rat's best years. Rather than attempting too much the Rat should be content with average progress.

The Ox – The Ox should be highly satisfied with the way things turn out this year, as matters proceed smoothly.

The Tiger – After a year of exciting change, the Tiger personality may well find that the coming months are dull in comparison.

The Hare – An ideal time for putting oneself forward and succeeding either in business or romance. An excellent year ahead.

The Dragon – Finances take a setback this year. Be careful with any risky undertakings. Personal relationships may take a knock.

The Snake – The Snake personality will find this to be a happy year of quiet satisfaction and personal achievement.

The Horse – This is a fallow year, which should be used for building up reserves for the busier times which lie ahead.

The Sheep – Those planning marriage or those romantically involved can expect this year to be a stimulating time.

The Monkey – This is not one of the Monkey's better years. Ensure that all dealings are absolutely above board.

The Rooster – A dangerous year, both financially and romantically – but forewarned is forearmed. Avoid any reckless speculation.

The Dog – This is a reasonably happy year. Family matters are highlighted and there may be the chance of a move to a new home.

The Pig – This is an excellent year. All matters to do with health, children, family and home life are positively aspected.

How the Hour of Birth Affects the Hare Personality

Rat hour (11pm-1am) Material rewards are strong, especially for handicrafts. Watch your marriage.

Ox hour (1am-3am) Investment may prove successful, but be cautious with property. A suitable marriage supersedes romance.

Tiger hour (3am-5am) Select one goal and avoid complications. Travel and marriage are rewarding.

Hare hour (5am-7am) Contentment and kindness are enhanced; love and personal satisfaction with life are also favourable.

Dragon hour (7am-9am) The right partner will boost business prospects and financial stability.

Snake hour (9am-11am) The legal profession or an academic following are possible. Financial prosperity and stability are assured.

Horse hour (11am-1pm) Upsets in marriage and family are likely. Travel may bring wealth.

Sheep hour (1pm-3pm) A happy home life with plenty of children, good health and prosperity are all strong possibilities.

Monkey hour (3pm-5pm) Care for others may mean family is neglected. The surgeon's skills are indicated.

Rooster hour (5pm-7pm) Over-ambition is a problem, although success will come eventually. Good health and long life are likely.

Dog hour (7pm-9pm) Problems over possession of property are possible; avoid speculation.

Pig hour (9pm-11pm) Happiness is achieved through the

family more than wealth and material assets, but your domestic bliss is enviable.

The Dragon

16 Feb 1904 – 3 Feb 1905
3 Feb 1916 – 22 Jan 1917
23 Jan 1928 – 9 Feb 1929
8 Feb 1940 – 26 Jan 1941
27 Jan 1952 – 13 Feb 1953
13 Feb 1964 – 1 Feb 1965
31 Jan 1976 – 17 Feb 1977
17 Feb 1988 – 5 Feb 1989

The Chinese have always especially venerated the Dragon. As the only mythical animal among the 12 signs in the Chinese zodiac, this exotic and exuberant creature signifies Heaven's authority. As a result, dragons have long been associated in China with nobility, material power and success.

Imperial insignia often employed dragon imagery, particularly during the Manchu dynasty (1644-1912). The lavish dragons embroidered on the Emperor's court dress had five claws, while those of lesser princes had four. The nobility, meanwhile, had to be content with only three claws!

Traditionally, the Chinese dragon was also linked with the gentle fertilising rains of spring. The rainy season was always heralded by the appearance of the Green Dragon constellation – one of the five great constellations into which Chinese astronomers divided the heavens. Thus the dragon came to symbolize rains and floods, and was believed to live in deep pools and rivers.

As one of the four benevolent spiritual animals (the others are the unicorn, the phoenix and the tortoise), the astrological Dragon is far removed from the fire-breathing monster of western legend. On the contrary, this noble creature is considered by the Chinese to be their paramount symbol of luck and good fortune – qualities which are reflected in the characteristics of the sign.

The Dragon Personality

As a symbol of royalty and authority, the Dragon is exuberant, brash, and full of self-confidence. Those born in this year rarely need to be reassured that they are destined to play a leading role in life. Seldom bound by the constraints of convention, they like to be in the forefront of fashion and are far more likely to be found setting trends than they are following them.

Creative Thinking

Dragons can be relied on to have a creative and imaginative approach to work. They often use their acute perceptive powers in an unorthodox way to solve difficult or complex problems.

Needing praise, Dragons are not inclined to hide their light under a bushel. They are likely to be drawn to careers in the public eye, such as the stage, or other fields where their achievements can be seen and rewarded in an obvious way.

Fresh Pastures

Dragons are drawn to anything out of the ordinary. This may include a fascination with occult or supernatural subjects.

Always seeking variety, the Dragon's perpetual interest in exciting and novel ventures can, however, be a serious failing. This sign is often tempted to leave matters unfinished in order to set off on some new and more exciting scheme. Dragons generally leave the more pedestrian aspects of any project to someone else.

Money Luck

Dragons are reputed to have a tremendous business sense; unfortunately, their undoubted flair for making money is offset by their equally gifted talents for spending it. The Dragon's luck is particularly at risk when this sign comes into contact with the Hare, long regarded as an ill omen for Dragon personalities.

The Dragon Year

Changes and upheaval are predicted for the volatile Dragon year. Such instability will be evident on a broad scale, embracing the world of nature as well as human affairs. The weather will be notable for unexpected storms and floods. Artistic and occult interests will also come to the fore and flourish at this time.

Politically, it is not an ideal period for democratic policies. People will tend to be drawn more strongly than usual to charismatic personalities. As a result, both monarchies and dictatorships are likely to become popular with their – for the moment – loyal bands of followers.

Who Dares Wins

There are likely to be spectacular gains and losses, particularly in business and finance. Extravagant and risky plans are best inaugurated during the Dragon year, which favours the imaginative and adventurous, rather than the careful, the well planned and the practical.

It follows that businesses which can meet the demand for excitement and spectacle will prosper; but the boom is destined to be short-lived. Those who prefer a more staid and old-fashioned approach may find the current period a lean one, but they will reap their rewards later.

Dragon Relationships

With the Rat

The Rat and Dragon have many common interests, leading to a harmonious personal relationship. This could imply either a prosperous business partnership, or a successful marriage.

With the Ox

These two have a totally different approach to life. Though there may be an instant attraction, conflicts of interest call for every effort to be made to guarantee lasting happiness.

With the Tiger

Highly charged signs, they have enormous respect for each other's gifts. This combination makes for an excellent business relationship or a passionate romantic partnership.

With the Horse

A sound combination. The Horse gives the bold, brash Dragon steadying, but encouraging support, while the Dragon supplies the trusty Horse partner with excitement and stimulation.

With the Sheep

Not one of the ideal partnerships. The gentle, sensitive Sheep may be distrustful of the Dragon's motives, while the Dragon can find the Sheep's introvert nature somewhat inhibiting.

With the Monkey

This is an extraordinary combination, each acting as a catalyst for the other. Business prospects are formidable, while a deep understanding of the other's needs favours a sparkling romance.

With another Dragon

Dragons together make for a lively duo, sharing the same interests and taking part in the same madcap schemes. This is a great pairing, notable for its sense of fun, both in business and in love.

With the Hare

These two very different personalities find it hard to appreciate each other's view, leading to misunderstanding rather than confrontation. They are likely to drift apart after a time.

With the Snake

A good partnership, one having the broad ideas, the other the ability to fill in the details. Particularly harmonious in romance, especially if the Dragon is male and the Snake is female.

With the Rooster

Not an ideal match, since both are fiercely individual. There is a lack of understanding of mutual differences, and resentment borne out of jealousy where there are similarities.

With the Dog

The Dragon and the Dog have a totally different attitude to life. But if they can learn to respect one another's individuality, they could complement each other and live together in harmony.

With the Pig

In this relationship, the Dragon will always get the upper hand

and take advantage of the Pig. But although obliged to suffer in silence, the Pig will nevertheless remain loyal and faithful.

The Year Of The Dragon

Whatever your animal sign, study the list below to find out how you will fare in a Dragon year.

The Rat – Great excitement is in store for the Rat. Travel to far-off places is promised, and finances are more secure. Good news for the romantically inclined.

The Ox – Matters may move too fast for the Ox personality. Despite slow progress, trust to your instinct and play safe; this is a risky time.

The Tiger – An excellent year financially and romantically for the Tiger. There is public recognition for your achievements, too.

The Hare – Matters do not turn out as well as you had anticipated this year. Take care over health and watch out for some unexpected changes.

The Dragon – A wonderful year, full of achievement and successes. But try to curb your enthusiasm, and make sure you keep something in reserve.

The Snake – A very good year ahead, when many personal ambitions may be realized. Study trends carefully, and prepare for future successes.

The Horse – A very stimulating year, bringing great opportunities; ideal for business and social ambitions and for the romantically inclined.

The Sheep – Not a good year for the Sheep. You must avoid getting irritated over trifles. The minor mishaps are only temporary, so be patient.

The Monkey – All kinds of crafty schemes can come to fruition, but make sure that they are completed before the end of the year, or they may lead to disaster.

The Rooster – Some opportunities for social climbing, and public recognition. Finances may be less sure and romance may bring disappointments.

The Dog – Take great care over matters concerning the home. Not an ideal time to move house; it is much better to save rather than spend.

The Pig – There may be some problems with the family; make sure that differences of opinion are sorted out. Do not lavish money on relatives.

How the Hour of Birth Affects the Dragon Personality

Rat hour (11pm-1am) Happiness lies in not striving for material success. Take care with health.

Ox hour (1am-3am) Fortune is linked to land and estate. Use your intelligence and avoid speculation or all could be lost.

Tiger hour (3am-5am) Travel and living abroad are recommended. Short romances, secure marriage.

Hare hour (5am-7am) More than one marriage, but intellectual and travel achievements foreseen. Avoid risks to health.

Dragon hour (7am-9am) You have great flair and will be fortunate. Risk of carelessness.

Snake hour (9am-11am) Drawn to mystery and philosophy. Fame and fortune possible, especially in connection with the law.

Horse hour (11am-1pm) You need to avoid becoming stale and plan ahead. Romance may be rocky.

Sheep hour (1pm-3pm) Beware of unreliable partners. Children bring happiness in later life and health is good.

Monkey hour (3pm-5pm) Avoid confrontations, bad company and risk-taking.

Rooster hour (5pm-7pm) Fame and fortune can be found on the stage but domestic life is less favoured. Health must be watched.

Dog hour (7pm-9pm) Avoid property speculation. A happy marriage and travel foreseen.

Pig hour (9pm-1pm) Extra-marital affairs a possibility, so take care with the upbringing of any children involved.

The Snake

4 Feb 1905 – 24 Jan 1906
23 Jan 1917 – 10 Feb 1918
10 Feb 1929 – 29 Jan 1930
27 Jan 1941 – 14 Feb 1942
14 Feb 1953 – 2 Feb 1954
2 Feb 1965 – 20 Jan 1966
18 Feb 1977 – 6 Feb 1978
6 Feb 1989 – 26 Jan 1990

Throughout the world, the snake has long been regarded with awe and respect – and quite justifiably, too. Walls and doors present no barrier to them, while to make an enemy of one could well turn out to be fatal.

Not surprisingly, this powerful and mysterious creature became an object of worship among many ancient cultures, and even today snake temples still exist in India and Malaysia. Western mythology, meanwhile, has long associated the snake with the Underworld – which perhaps accounts for our instinctive fascination and dread at the sight of one in the hands of a snake charmer.

In Chinese astrology the Snake is the complement to the Dragon, both signs forming the House of Mystery. But while the Dragon represents the extrovert magician, brash and gaudy, the subtle Snake symbolizes the hidden aspects of mystery and occult knowledge.

Like the Dragon, the Snake is a sign of good fortune for the Chinese, who believe it to be the guardian of buried treasure. Some are even reluctant to kill snakes which enter the house, no matter how dangerous, since there is a chance they might bring wealth with them.

In the Chinese calendar the Snake month is the first month of summer, approximating to May-June – a time when these creatures can frequently be spotted basking in the sun.

The Snake Personality

Few animal names in the Chinese zodiac are complementary, so there is no need to feel offended if your discover that you are a Snake – particularly since this creature is said to symbolize wisdom and cleverness. Even so, it has to be said that the Snake is very adept at giving the impression of being profoundly knowledgeable, simply by keeping mysteriously silent.

Understated elegance is a keynote of the Snake's style. Extravagant gestures are no match for the subtlety of the Snake, who is capable of quietly upstaging any celebrity. These people can advance in society, not through wealth and position, but by instinctively knowing where to be and when.

Snakes can often affect a high moral stance, while at the same time taking more than a passing interest in other people's failings in this department. Yet deep down the Snake individual is a sensual creature, often feeling caught between what is desirable, and what is ethical.

Snakes are also fond of gossip, and when life is dull they are not above scandal-mongering or collecting odd snippets of information which can later be put to some creative use. For this reason, Snake-types tend to make excellent intelligence agents or detectives. They also have a built-in capacity for directing their investigative abilities into academic or scientific research.

Safe Investments

Financially, Snakes are usually sound money managers, inclined to save carefully and avoid risky – though tempting – high-yield investments. Their natural inclination to guard or hoard their money often tempts the career-oriented Snake into banking or accountancy.

The Snake Year

Since snakes are closely in tune with the earth, and usually make their home there, the Chinese believe them to be particularly sensitive to the onset of earthquakes. As a consequence, the Snake year is said to be one in which earthquakes are more than usually severe – witness the disastrous events in China and Armenia which preceded the San Francisco earthquake in the Snake year of 1989.

Such catastrophes are likely to be matched by policital upheavals. Coups, conspiracies and the ballot box are the means by which governments are overthrown, for it is a time of internal revolution rather than war. Similarly, in business, the dangers are not from takeover bids by outside companies, but through intrigue and insider dealing.

Yet the Snake year is also a period when the needs of the environment are highlighted. There is greater awareness of the value of the earth's resources, and 'green' issues come to the fore.

Generally speaking, it is not such a favourable time to embark on any new ventures or risky projects. The year is best taken up with initial planning, research and feasibility studies; caution is the key to survival.

Snake Relationships

With the Rat

The Snake is very much the dominant partner in this relationship. In the longer term, however, there is a chance that it may find the Rat's complacency rather irritating.

With the Ox

Whether in romance or business, this is likely to develop into a strong and lasting partnership. The Snake may well find the Ox highly supportive at critical times.

With the Tiger

Not the ideal match. Two strongly individual personalities clash, and even though there may be great initial passion, it is likely to fade away after a time.

With the Hare

According to an ancient Chinese proverb, when the Snake meets the Hare, there is true happiness. This is a particularly auspicious partnership for the romantically inclined.

With the Dragon

An interesting and successful partnership, whether it concerns romance or business. The long-term prospects for staying together are among the best of all the signs.

With another Snake

Very much a mutual admiration society. This pairing is ideal for romance, but a business partnership could end through a lack of objective thinking.

With the Horse

With two such different characters, there are likely to be many misunderstandings. Each must learn to respect the other's views if the pairing is to succeed.

With the Sheep

Romantically, a very happy and successful relationship. Each partner is likely to be full of appreciation for the other's fundamentally caring and considerate nature.

With the Monkey

Such a partnership could well go through testing times. Both signs should learn to be open with each other, and should try not to distrust the other's motives.

With the Rooster

Although they are hardly ever at oods, the attraction between these two is so strong that it is likely to carry their partnership through even the most stormy patches.

With the Dog

The Dog, sadly, will be the loser in this relationship. The individualistic Snake is likely to go its own way and may well be the cause of a separation later on in life.

With the Pig

Probably, these two became partners more through circumstance than choice. Not the ideal relationship, but both will strive to make the best of it.

The Year of the Snake

Whatever your animal sign, study the chart below to find out how you will fare in a Snake year.

The Rat – This is not a good year for the Rat. But whatever the setbacks, good will result – often in a surprising way.

The Ox – An excellent year for the Ox personality. Routine gives way to welcome change and brings exciting prospects.

The Tiger – This year all kinds of unexpected hindrances, such as bureaucratic or legal tangles, impede the Tiger's progress.

The Hare – A year of extremely satisfying progress for the Hare. Both business and romance have a satisfactory outcome.

The Dragon – Matters begun last year come to a satisfactory conclusion. Finances may be reduced slightly, but will be more secure.

The Snake – An ideal time for the Snake to strike. Both in career and relationships, there should be positive results.

The Horse – Moderate success might be found this year. It is neither good nor bad; the usual benefits, the usual problems.

The Sheep – Those sheep who favour the quiet life and are realistic in their ambitions will find this a happy and successful year.

The Monkey – A time when the Monkey's schemes and plots may come to grief. It is advisable to play matters very carefully.

The Rooster – A satisfactory time. Many problems from the past will be smoothed out, making the way ahead much clearer.

The Dog – Problems will rear their heads, and it is best to be prepared for unexpected delays. Do not push ahead too vigorously.

The Pig – A disappointing year, especially where the family is concerned. It is advisable not to consider ambitious plans.

How the Hour of Birth Affects the Snake Personality

Rat hour (11pm-1am) Obstacles in the path to happiness. Do not neglect health for sake of career.

Ox hour (1am-3am) Love of the unusual and an ability to follow things to a conclusion. Romance may bring heartaches.

Tiger hour (3am-5am) An adventurous life, with much travel in pursuit of wealth. Romance comes late.

Hare hour (5am-7am) Romance plays a large part in life, with many involvements. Career may well be in the arts field.

Dragon hour (7am-9am) An interest in the supernatural and an off-beat career. Charisma.

Snake hour (9am-11am) Intellect and astuteness emphasized. Wealth comes through education and commerce. Family contentment.

Horse hour (11am-1pm) Successful marriage and financial stability. New interests every ten years.

Sheep hour (1pm-3pm) A long-lasting happy marriage and children bring contentment. Wealth less important. Cultured tastes.

Monkey hour (3pm-5pm) Career may involve working with the hands. Obstacles to financial success.

Rooster hour (5pm-7pm) Fame and fortune on the stage or in the public eye. But health could be adversely affected.

Dog hour (7pm-9pm) Life proceeds smoothly, but with disappointments. Moderate financial success.

Pig hour (9pm-11pm) Children and family the main interest, but conflicts often provoke discord. Good health assured.

The Horse

25 Jan 1906 – 12 Feb 1907
11 Feb 1918 – 31 Jan 1919
30 Jan 1930 – 16 Feb 1931
15 Feb 1942 – 4 Feb 1943
3 Feb 1954 – 23 Jan 1955
21 Jan 1966 – 8 Feb 1967
7 Feb 1978 – 27 Jan 1979
27 Jan 1990 – 14 Feb 1991

From exquisite green-glazed T-ang tomb sculptures to delicate watercolours brushed on rice paper, the Horse – symbol of wealth and success – has long been a popular subject in Chinese art. White horses, in particular, are esteemed because of their associations with nobility, while the mythical Dragon-horse is considered to be the embodiment of prosperity and luck.

To ancient peoples the almost supernatural energy and speed of the horse linked this noble animal with the sky gods and the passage of the Sun through the heavens. For the Chinese astrologers of old, the Horse symbolized the yang forces of nature (in other words, the active, masculine attributes). Since Great Yang was also the astrological name for the Sun, it is not surprising that the noon hour – when the Sun is at its highest – became known as the hour of the Horse, and that the Chinese month with the longest day became the Horse month.

The Horse Personality

Just as the horse is a friend to mankind, so the Horse-type has all the qualities that people look for in an ideal companion, being helpful, dependable, and entirely trustworthy.

Highly sociable, Horse personalities are always good conversationalists, always ready to discuss the latest news or current issues. Horse people often hold firm views on controversial matters, although they may seem unoriginal in their opinions. This could be due to their fear of showing the kind of independence which might end up putting them out on a limb socially.

The Horse Career

The Horse personality will be drawn towards careers which involve close contact with other people, but this type's natural competitiveness and ambition mean that working life will never be without the cut and thrust of a daily challenge.

The Horse also represents talent and precocity. Indeed, it is even said that the famous tied-back hairstyle worn by the Mandarins – the Imperial officials who advanced within the state structure through talent rather than accident of birth – represented a horse tail; not, as westerners call it, a 'pigtail'.

The influence of the Horse is positive and energising. Although ambitious, Horse personalities take great pleasure when their success is of benefit to others.

A Masculine Sign

The Horse symbolizes interests and attributes traditionally considered to be predominantly masculine. Its female counterpart is the Sheep, the next animal in the Chinese zodiac. Together these signs form the House of Gender and, according to Chinese astrology, both men and women born in this year have strong feelings about sexual roles.

This masculine emphasis leads many Chinese to be wary of girls born in the Horse year, as they are believed to make bossy wives. Boys, on the other hand, are welcomed, since they are thought to bring their parents honour.

There is a general wariness of all those born in the years of the Fire-Horse (1906, 1966); these are said to produce both tyrants and revolutionaries.

The Horse Year

The Horse year is a powerful one, bringing sweeping changes in its wake. Yet despite this upheaval, the changes, great though they may be, should not have come entirely as a surprise; they are the inevitable result of development and expansion.

It is important to remember that people who try to impede the course of progress are likely to be swept aside during this exciting and challenging period. Those who are prepared to forge ahead with imagination and vision are the ones most likely to succeed in the Horse year.

To Risk or not to Risk?

For those involved in business or commerce, this year will be fiercely competitive; there are fortunes to be made –and lost. If your sign is one which is favoured by the Horse, you are likely to be one of the victors and can afford to take risks; if, however, your sign conflicts with that of the Horse, your best advice is to be more careful – wait patiently and see what emerges.

Discontent will surface on the political level, with outbreaks of rioting and civil disobedience rather than outright revolution. Be prepared to see incidences of widespread drought.

Horse Relationships

With the Rat

Interests, outlook on life and opinions are so opposed here that confrontations are likely. Sexual chemistry would have to be very strong for this partnership to work.

With the Ox

Some mutual antipathy and distrust stands in the way of these signs creating a really deep relationship. Partners tend to see each other as rivals rather than companions.

With the Tiger

A splendid choice! Both partners contribute something special towards their mutual happiness and can give each other plenty of support.

With the Hare

There is little understanding between these two partners. They may stick by each other out of a sense of duty, rather than as a result of any great heart-felt affection.

With the Dragon

A wild time is in store for these two! This is a highly ambitious combination, with both partners determined to work hard and play hard. Romance and business are well starred.

With the Snake

This is an average kind of relationship, including both good points and bad points. The partners are very different in nature, but are able to agree to differ.

With another Horse

A partnership that ought to work, but quite often does not. These two seem to be made for each other, yet the magic may be missing. Children can cement the union.

With the Sheep

This is an excellent combination based on true love and lasting understanding, bringing contentment and joy. If the Horse partner is male, so much the better.

With the Monkey

A highly successful and supportive partnership, for business, romance, or both. There is a strong, instinctive attraction and deep affection between these signs.

With the Rooster

These two individuals are so keen on their own personal status that they rarely get to see the other person's point of view. This combination will make for a rough ride.

With the Dog

A strong relationship, built on trust, loyalty – and love. This is a sharing, caring and reliable partnership, able to deal cheerfully with any difficulties that occur on the way.

With the Pig

This is a practical rather than romantic partnership. Both are unlikely to agonize over their occasional differences; life is too short to bother with such trivialities.

The Year of the Horse

Whatever your animal sign, study the list below to find out how you will fare in a Horse year.

The Rat – This is not the ideal year for you, so feel your way carefully and do not make your plans too ambitious just yet.

The Ox – Although this is a year of frustrating setbacks, the delays are only temporary; be prepared to take the rough with the smooth.

The Tiger – An excellent year. If you have any big projects in mind, get them under way now – the opportunity may be lost if you delay.

The Hare – There is likely to be some unhappiness this year. Try to avoid risky projects and beware of relying too heavily on acquaintances.

The Dragon – Some well defined and promising results are indicated for this year, with successes coming in an unexpected quarter.

The Snake – A number of your best-laid plans do not materialize. You would be wise to save more ambitious projects until next year.

The Horse – This is your year. It should mark a turning point in your career. Initiative, daring and decision are the keynotes.

The Sheep – Some success this year with exciting future plans. Romance is starred for women, but men must wait until next year.

The Monkey – Although you may not have completely achieved

your ambition, this year sees you advancing a long way towards doing so.

The Rooster – Do not be too disappointed if last year's promises are not fulfilled. Be patient; success is just around the corner.

The Dog – An excellent year – particularly if you are thinking of those close to you, since they will be able to share in your success.

The Pig – A moderately successful year. If you are planning a long and potentially difficult journey, this would be a good time to go.

How the Hour of Birth Affects the Horse Personality

Rat hour (11pm-1am) Strong opinions can lead to problems with relationships. Finances are good.

Ox hour (1am-3am) The use of land in the country brings secure rewards. Romance is not your first priority. Avoid speculation.

Tiger hour (3am-5am) Success with concerns of distribution and travel. A good marriage is likely.

Hare hour (5am-7am) Health is emphasized and perhaps thought of as a career. Romance may be unhappy but children bring joy.

Dragon hour (7am-9am) Good fortune may encourage gambling. Hard work will bring happiness.

Snake hour (9am-11am) A practical career is likely, perhaps based outdoors. Family and romance are problematic.

Horse hour (11am-1pm) You will be faithful to your true love. Stick to well-established business concerns.

Sheep hour (1pm-3pm) Domestic harmony leads to success in business and to capable children. Avoid speculation.

Monkey hour (3pm-5pm) Use your abilities to bring wealth. You may be loath to settle down.

Rooster hour (5pm-7pm) A career on the stage is possible but business also promises success. Romance may bring disillusion.

Dog hour (7pm-9pm) Property and inheritance are well starred. You may marry and live abroad.

Pig hour (9pm-11pm) A solid and well-ordered, domestic background is indicated. Finances are secure and health is sound.

The Sheep

13 Feb 1907 – 1 Feb 1908
1 Feb 1909 – 19 Feb 1920
17 Feb 1931 – 5 Feb 1932
5 Feb 1943 – 24 Jan 1944
24 Jan 1955 – 11 Feb 1956
9 Feb 1967 – 29 Jan 1968
28 Jan 1979 – 15 Feb 1980
15 Feb 1991 – 3 Feb 1992

The eighth sign of the zodiac, the Sheep, is seen as the provider in ancient Chinese legend. One tale recounts how five celestial visitors, clad in garments of five colours, came to the city of Canton (Guangzhou) in southern China, riding on five rams. Each animal held in its mouth one of the five grains – wheat, corn, barley, millet and rice – necessary for the nourishment of humanity. Once the rams touched the earth, they were turned to stone – and can still be seen in Canton to this day.

The Chinese word for 'sheep' also means 'goat' or 'ram', but it is better to refer to the eighth sign as the Sheep, since this is more suggestive of the feminine, caring qualities of the sign – traits not immediately conjured up by the word 'ram'.

Referring to the Sheep as the Ram could also lead to confusion with the Western astrological sign of Aries. The similarity of names is only a coincidence, since the Sheep month falls between the signs of Cancer and Leo in Western astrology.

The Sheep Personality

The Sheep is the complementary sign to the Horse, and together they form the House of Gender. While the Horse represents the traditionally masculine traits, the Sheep highlights the more gentle and compliant feminine characteristics which can be found in men just as much as they may be lacking in women.

There is also a psychological parallel between the two signs. Horse types tend to be extrovert, while their Sheep counterparts are likely to be rather introverted by comparison.

Artistic Leanings

The Sheep, contentedly grazing on green pastures, symbolizes a peaceful, pastoral existence. It is therefore not surprising that the Sheep personality is associated with those arts that call for quiet contemplation, such as classical music, poetry and line drawing. But while Sheep types may excel in artistic fields, their special gifts lie in interpretation rather than creation. They may have formidable skills and enviable gifts, but their technique often surpasses their originality.

Both Horse and Sheep people love the company of others. Despite the Sheep's rather inward-looking personality, these individuals will possess a very strong urge to belong.

Although Sheep are followers rather than leaders, they certainly do not like to be directed. Even when guidance is obviously needed, the most well-meaning friendly advice is often taken as interference and may be resisted as such.

Sheep types prefer to belong to a group where decisions are made on a democratic basis. But this desire for committee or communal decision-making often disguises a sense of insecurity in the individual concerned.

The World's Peacemakers

Despite their placid natures, Sheep generally do their best to cope with the confrontations of everyday life, smoothing out difficulties here and defusing arguments there. Sheep types are the peacemakers of the world, and so are ideally suited to careers which involve arbitration, public relations, diplomacy or the law.

The Sheep Year

The Year of the Sheep brings a welcome period of reconciliation. It is a time when long-standing differences can be resolved, resentments forgotten, and traditional enmities put to one side – albeit temporarily.

If not actually an uneventful year, it is perhaps the one which holds the fewest surprises; the successes and achievements of the Sheep Year are likely to be the fruits of many years' exertion. Nor will the year's setbacks be unexpected; the wise will have prepared themselves for harder times, while the less fortunate will have only their own negligence to blame for what they lack.

No Changes

In the world at large, both in business and on the political scene, it is a time to avoid making sweeping changes. Certainly it would be unwise to try to disturb the established order, and any planned large-scale projects should be postponed for the time being.

On the other hand, the year of the Sheep is an excellent time for all matters traditionally associated with women's interests and well-being – in other words, the more caring, protective activities and professions.

Sheep Relationships

With the Rat

Differences in attitudes can make this a difficult relationship, although coolness is more likely than confrontation. Trying to understand the other's viewpoint would improve matters.

With the Ox

Not the best of matches, whatever outsiders may think. Viewpoints are not the same, and differences over details can lead to quarrels. Stubbornness on both sides can be a failing.

With the Tiger

If the compliant Sheep is happy to be dominated by the Tiger, then the relationship will work. But the independently minded Sheep is going to be in for a rough time.

With the Hare
Likely to be a very happy relationship, although to friends, their cosy partnership may seem to lack excitement. Life runs smoothly and experiences are shared.

With the Dragon
The Dragon's careless attitudes can be a constant source of worry for the caring Sheep. The value of this partnership must be given some hard and careful consideration.

With the Snake
Here is someone who can bring glamour into the Sheep's life. The Snake will provide colour and the Sheep stability, making for a balanced partnership.

With the Horse
In marriage or business, the ideal partnership. Both sides are able to contribute to their mutual well-being in their own ways, each providing the other with stimulation.

With another Sheep
Sadly a dull relationship. Although it works satisfactorily, daily routine may dig a rut from which it is hard to escape. Both must remind themselves that life has more to offer.

With the Monkey
If this partnership lasts, it is only because the Sheep is content to make allowances for the Monkey's shortcomings. Others may shake their heads.

With the Rooster
A sound partnership, in marriage or in business, for it combines the steady reliability of the Sheep's caring qualities with the Rooster's drive. These two should travel a long way.

With the Dog
If these two remain together, it is only because they recognize their differences and shortcomings, and put up with them. There may be unhappiness borne with fortitude.

With the Pig
An ideal relationship for starting a home and building a large

family. There is co-operation, and domestic bliss. In business, may be too traditional.

The Year of the Sheep

Whatever your animal sign study the chart below to find out how you will fare in a Sheep year.

The Rat – Patience is needed this year, since matters proceed too slowly for the ambitious Rat. But take heart – at least the problems of last year are resolved.

The Ox – There are obstacles and difficulties ahead, but the Ox is able to cope. Though finance may be sound, romance is in the air. Avoid jealousy.

The Tiger – There are some benefits this year, even though they may not be immediately apparent. Life may lack the excitement of confrontation and competition.

The Hare – An excellent year. If romance is in mind, then prospects are ideal. There is happiness at home and at work, and career prospects improve enormously.

The Dragon – Be prepared for snags and hold-ups. Though delays are inevitable, the end result will justify the extra care taken. Watch finances carefully.

The Snake – A great improvement on last year, with progress being made at last. Romantic prospects improve, while artistic pursuits bring rewards.

The Horse – The most favourable signs this year are for those contemplating marriage – but only if you have already found your partner. A year of good health.

The Sheep – All matters concerning the Sheep's personal welfare and well-being are highlighted this year. Be clear about immediate goals; success is imminent.

The Monkey – Some difficulties and personal entanglements stand in the way. Keep romance and social life completely separate from business.

The Rooster – There are many rewards to be had this year, particularly for the career woman. Men will be pleased with their successes with the opposite sex.

The Dog – Some problems with family and social life are likely, and career prospects may be temporarily thwarted. Old and trusted friends are the best.

The Pig – There is great happiness at home. Your personal successes will be matched by those of your loved ones. A wish brings considerable satisfaction.

How the Hour of Birth Affects the Sheep Personality

Rat hour (11pm-1am) Marry sensibly, and happiness will be assured. Try not to strive after fame.

Ox hour (1am-3am) An adverse situation may affect both romance and career; but a legal matter will have a fortunate outcome.

Tiger hour (3am-5am) A career involving travel could damage personal life but bring wealth.

Hare hour (5am-7am) Health positively aspected. Possibly a career in medicine. Career may leave little time for family.

Dragon hour (7am-9am) Fortune comes and goes, affecting the family. Use common sense.

Snake hour (9am-11am) More success from using the brain rather than the hands. A career in education is likely.

Horse hour (11am-1pm) A well-ordered person, able to see both sides. Ideal as an arbitrator.

Sheep hour (1pm-3pm) the positive aspects of the Sheep's character – diplomacy, artistic ability and tenderness – are highlighted.

Monkey hour (3pm-5pm) Likely to succeed best with someone of complementary opinions.

Rooster hour (5pm-7am) An artistic career favourably signed. Expect setbacks in domestic and romantic life. Guard against stress.

Dog hour (7pm-9pm) Financial security and domestic stability with a reliable partner.

Pig hour (9pm-11pm) Possibly a career involving children, such as education or paediatrics. Domestic happiness features positively.

The Monkey

2 Feb 1908 – 21 Jan 1909
20 Feb 1920 – 7 Feb 1921
6 Feb 1932 – 25 Jan 1933
25 Jan 1944 – 12 Feb 1945
12 Feb 1956 – 30 Jan 1957
30 Jan 1968 – 16 Feb 1969
16 Feb 1980 – 4 Feb 1981
4 Feb 1992 – 22 Jan 1993

While on the one hand monkeys are admired for their agility and intelligence, they are just as often associated with mischief, misbehaviour and trickery. It is this very mixture of skill, cunning and impudence which characterizes the Monkey personality in the Chinese zodiac; the unpredictable combination has earned this cheeky animal a special place in the Chinese heart.

According to an age-old legend, the Monkey-King accompanied one of the first Chinese monks to India and back with a precious cargo of Buddhist scriptures. Despite his unruly behaviour, the Monkey proved to be such an invaluable companion on this long and perilous journey that he was rewarded with a place in heaven.

In Chinese astrology, the Monkey is the ninth sign of the zodiac, forming the *yang* (masculine) division of the House of Career with the *yin* (Feminine) sign of the Rooster. The Monkey is very often associated with traditionally male-oriented occupations such as technology, science, and all kinds of invention.

The Monkey Personality

Monkey-types have a habit of causing havoc, and sometimes also hurt, to those around them by failing to appreciate the serious consequences of their actions. 'I never meant to do it,' said with the air of someone pleading their innocence, is a typical Monkey response.

Clearly they make stimulating, if exasperating, companions. Chinese stable owners often have a pet monkey to keep the horses amused, and these unlikely stable-mates often become quite attached to one another. In human terms too, Horse and Monkey people often strike up lifelong friendships.

Monkey Trouble

Monkey-types tend to exhibit a wider than usual range of personality traits, which will vary according to the company they keep. Sometimes these people are gentle and caring, while at other times they may display tendencies bordering on the aggressive and surly. This unpredictability is very much a feature of the Monkey personality.

Many of the Monkey's troubles arise from basic feelings of insecurity and being misunderstood. Unfortunately this is not helped by their over-confidence in other matters and dislike of authority, both of which can get in the way of serious self-analysis.

Quick off the Mark

The Monkey's cunning usually shows itself through technical dexterity. These nimble-fingered individuals often have the precise manual skills of the watchmaker, surgeon – or forger.

Some Monkey types have an impressive flair for words and ideas, coupled with the ability to argue skilfully and confound logic. Thus the Monkey personality may also be spotted behind the persuasive lawyer, the stalling politician – or even the clever confidence trickster.

Monkey personalities work well on short-term projects since they can tackle problems as they crop up. Not surprisingly, they tend to come to grief in the kind of circumstances which call for careful advance planning.

The Monkey Year

As might be expected, the year of the Monkey brings plenty of surprises. It can be a year of frustrations tempered by unexpected delights; the only predictable aspect is its complete uncertainty.

You are best advised not to rely on anything, since even the most dependable of institutions may decide to alter course. The careful will hedge their bets on every side this year, and for investors the key-word is diversification. Those with romantic aspirations should not hold on too tightly; this is a good year for letting go.

New Technology

The Monkey year will be full of the kind of newsworthy events beloved of headline-writers, but although it may appear as if plenty is happening on the world stage, in reality very little will be of lasting significance. The news may be spectacular and bizarre, but happenings which seem momentous at the time will dissolve into the dim mists of history as soon as some new topic emerges to take the spotlight.

The Monkey's influence will be marked, however, by the introduction of ingenious new technological inventions in all kinds of fields. These will bring lasting benefits for everyone.

Monkey Relationships

With the Rat

A happy partnership. Although the two signs have very different ideas, their views complement rather than clash. This leads to mutual encouragement.

With the Ox

There is not a great deal of understanding between these two, unless the Ox can overlook the Monkey's shortcomings and the Monkey tolerates the Ox's dissent.

With the Tiger

These two may be drawn to each other physically, but there is little in common on a spiritual level. Tempers are likely to fray easily.

With the Hare

If this partnership is to survive, it is no use one trying to pretend that the other was their second best choice. Both must face up to the present situation, and give and take.

With the Dragon

A highly stimulating partnership, whether in business or romance, and one of which outsiders must beware. These two act as a catalyst on each other – for good or ill.

With the Snake

The Snake's clever and careful analysis of the situation can hold this difficult partnership together. Attitudes differ but there may be compensations.

With the Horse

Traditionally, one of the most successful of relationships. It works best on a companionship level – regarding each other as brother and sister, rather than lovers.

With the Sheep

This is an average kind of partnership with its share of difficulties and compensations. Many happy experiences and a few differences, but very little animosity.

With another Monkey

An agreeable pairing, but not ideal. Monkeys need a more sober influence. It could be a short-lived relationship – but a merry one.

With the Rooster

These two create a flamboyant couple. They are likely to make a great success of their lives together, since both have the mettle to survive the odd stormy passage.

With the Dog

A sensible choice for the Monkey. They may not always see eye to eye, for the Dog has a far more practical approach to life. Yet this steadying influence is vital.

With the Pig

Not the ideal choice of partner for either the adventurous Monkey or the comfort-loving Pig. The relationship can survive if the bonds are not too tight.

The Year of the Monkey

Whatever your animal sign, study the list below to find out how you will fare in a Monkey year

The Rat – An excellent year, when the Rat's creative ingenuity and inventiveness come to the fore. A good time for rethinking and putting plans into action.

The Ox – Quite a reasonable period. Changes may not be

welcome at first, but they will eventually prove to be for the better. Try to move with the times.

The Tiger – Some difficulties ahead. Avoid getting involved in legal matters. Remember that force will not achieve anything while commonsense will.

The Hare – The year has its share of problems. The difficulties are with things, rather than people. Be prepared for hold-ups due to technical failures.

The Dragon – An exciting time ahead. Use the positive trends to achieve personal ambitions, particularly in a career. The artistic Dragon will have success.

The Snake – Practice is more important than theory this year. Try out your ideas before committing yourself deeply. Be prepared for petty obstacles.

The Horse – A satisfactory year generally, with personal relationships highlighted. You will make new friends, and treasured old friends will return.

The Sheep – A reasonable year. Progress may not be as rapid or as smooth as you would like. You are not likely to be disappointed with the outcome.

The Monkey – This is your year, so make the best of it. Everything goes in your direction, so take advantage of the trends which lead to success.

The Rooster – The year will see you poised on the threshold of a new life. Now is the time to lay the foundations for that important step forward.

The Dog – Positive trends this year make up for some of the disappointments and missed opportunities of the past. Career prospects are greatly improved.

The Pig – Be prepared for disappointments. In business, be careful where you put your money. In romance, do not be misled by flattery or promises.

How the Hour of Birth Affects the Monkey Personality

Rat hour (11pm-1am) Fortunate aspects. Business success and contentment in love.

Ox hour (1am-3am) Stable finances rather than wealth. Intellectual ability, artistic skill and physical prowess are emphasized.

Tiger hour (3am-5am) A spirit of adventure may lead to serious problems, but a happy home life.

Hare hour (5am-7am) Minor health problems and perhaps a career in healing. Romance, marriage and family bring happiness.

Dragon hour (7am-9am) Wealth through technical innovation. Beware of romantic involvements.

Snake hour (9am-11am) An ability to explain complex technical matters clearly. Romance and family life present few problems.

Horse hour (11am-1pm) Personal happiness is linked to a successful marriage. Possible health worries.

Sheep hour (1pm-3pm) A happy marriage and children bring joy, but many obstacles need to be overcome on the way.

Monkey hour (3pm-5pm) Technical skills, physical agility and an enquiring mind are emphasized.

Rooster hour (5pm-7pm) You need to work with an understanding helper. There will be difficulty finding a compatible marriage partner.

Dog hour (7pm-9pm) Few financial worries and an comfortable home. Wealth from property deals.

Pig hour (9pm-11pm) Family life is important. Avoid fretting over children's security; you can help by good example. Health is sound.

The Rooster

22 Jan 1909 – 9 Feb 1910
8 Feb 1921 – 27 Jan 1922
26 Jan 1933 – 13 Feb 1934
13 Feb 1945 – 1 Feb 1946
31 Jan 1957 – 17 Feb 1958
17 Feb 1969 – 5 Feb 1970
5 Feb 1981 – 24 Jan 1982
23 Jan 1993 –9 Feb 1994

Although the Chinese, like most of us, associate the Rooster with the first light of dawn, some perverse logic was at work when the monks of old chose the Rooster to symbolize the tenth sign. This makes the Rooster hour, or more precisely double hour, sunset – from 5pm to 7pm.

The very first Chinese astrologers were more rational. Long before the animal names were invented, the ancient sages used the sign of a wine bottle to represent the sunset hour – perhaps with the suggestion of a welcome drink after a day's work in mind!

In the Chinese lunar calendar the Rooster month includes the Autumn equinox, since it always begins with the New Moon immmediately before 21 September. Thus the Rooster joins the Rat (winter), Hare (spring) and Horse (summer) in heralding a new quarter of the year, as well as symbolising the division of the day into midnight, sunrise, noon and sunset.

The Rooster Personality

From a very early age, people born in the year of the Rooster know that life has to be lived to the full – that every moment is valuable. Instinctively, they feel that to succeed, one must be at one's best, look one's best, and give one's best the whole time. Bearing this in mind, it is hardly surprising to find that one of the Rooster's outstanding personality traits is self-confidence. Unfortunately, this is often combined with a perfectionism and obsessive attention to detail which others find intensely irritating.

Rooster types have artistic flair and a great sense of style – not just in their appearance, but in the way they project themselves. Sometimes, though, this comes across as behaviour which strikes the outside observer as futile or extravagant.

The Rooster Career

The Rooster – despite being a male bird – is the *yin* or feminine sign in the House of Career, its male counterpart being the Monkey.

Females born in a Rooster year tend to have strong career motivation, with the potential to rise to the top of their chosen profession. This is very likely to be one in which a powerful presence is vital, such as the theatre, television presentation, publishing, or any field connected with women's interests, such as fashion or cosmetics.

Fight and Compete

The feminine qualities of this sign, however, do not seem to be so marked in males born in Rooster years. Instead they tend to display the Rooster's more competitive and aggressive characteristics, and may be inclined towards a military or other uniformed career where they can exert their authority.

Curb the Critical

Rooster types of both sexes must avoid unintentionally making enemies – perhaps by moderating their readiness to provide objective criticism, which is always well intentioned, but seldom appreciated. They should also curb their unbounded enthusiasm for new projects, and be careful not to take on more than they can manage – a tip which applies to their social life as well as in business.

The Rooster Year

The Year of the Rooster is a time when individuals begin to be aware of – and expect others to recognize – their own unique qualities.

It may be a troubled period when groups begin to organize themselves into active forces, and minorities – not necessarily oppressed ones – begin agitating for their rights. National unrest, strikes and confrontation within the community affect one country then another, and there are sporadic outbursts of discontent worldwide.

Yet while the year may herald setbacks for some industries, other areas are seen to prosper. This applies particularly to consumer goods for immediate personal use, such as clothing, cosmetics, and jewellery.

Keeping Fit

There is an emphasis in the Rooster Year on personal fitness, and those whose work is connected with sporting or physical activity stand to make money.

The prospects are also fortunate for the catering and hotel trades, especially where the manufacture and sale of beverages is concerned; this is a good year for brewers and wine merchants.

In general, personal style is important in a Rooster Year. It is a time to be, and to avoid relying too much on others.

Rooster Relationships

With the Rat

This can be an abrasive relationship: here are individual personalities with their own views, neither wanting to give way. It works sometimes, but fireworks are likely.

With the Ox

These two characters are different in so many ways that they actually complement each other. Both can recognize the other's special talents and so respect them.

With the Tiger

There is too much competition between these two for such a relationship to work. Each must realize that the other is a person, not just an accessory.

With the Hare

If the Hare partner is prepared to accept a secondary role, then there is a chance of success. Both will have to work hard at keeping this partnership together.

With the Dragon

These two flamboyant characters are likely to have a short but passionate fling – then stay friends for life. Their life-long partners, however, are to be found elsewhere.

With the Snake

These two are destined for happiness in romance, or success in business. They combine flair, ambition and practicality. And love is never far away.

With the Horse

Not one of the best partnerships – there is some mutual distrust and a lack of depth. If they can survive long separations, the understanding may mature with time.

With the Sheep
An unusual relationship which often proves to be a long and happy one. Though their attitudes are different, both can be supportive in their own ways.

With the Monkey
A good partnership: both are determined to live life to the full, and gain every advantage from working and being together. Both full of vitality.

With another Rooster
There is too much competition between these two to create a happy partnership. If they could stop fault-finding and let the other get on, life would be smoother all round.

With the Dog
This partnership works better when the two people concerned are of mature years. If the relationship is formed too early, or too quickly, it is not likely to last.

With the Pig
Like any other couple, these two may go through the occasional bad patch. But generally, theirs is a happy and contented relationship.

The Year of the Rooster

Whatever your animal sign, study the list below to find out how you will fare in a Rooster year

The Rat – There are bound to be some setbacks this year. Be prepared for confrontations with those in authority, particularly at work. Watch finances.

The Ox – Health may prove a problem, but otherwise this should be an excellent year. At work, you have the chance of promotion. Romance beckons.

The Tiger – Not one of your best years. Difficult patches lie ahead, and personal relationships tend to be shaky. Choose your friends carefully.

The Hare – Some sadness is likely to enter your life this year. You may need a close friend to support you through an emotional upset. Better times coming.

The Dragon – If things go a little wrong you are not one to

care, and the way things are going, why should you? As you know, there are good times ahead.

The Snake – Excellent prospects. Whether in career or romance, all the trends are going in your direction, so you should make the most of every opportunity.

The Horse – There are times this year when you will take a cynical view of events. Instinctively, you take the wisest course and stay in the background.

The Sheep – A very satisfactory year, with unexpected advancement and challenges which you will take up successfully – much to your own astonishment.

The Monkey – A year of intense activity, with opportunities to push ahead. Make long term plans, as the next few years will be highly formative.

The Rooster – This year you will gain the rewards of your past efforts. Recognition for your work will bring satisfaction. Romantic prospects are fine.

The Dog – A moderately successful year, with its share of good and bad. It is unlikely to match up to last year; regard it as a breathing space.

The Pig – Some success in store, with your personal standing enhanced. There will be chances for you to improve your position; it is up to you to take them.

How the Hour of Birth Affects the Rooster Personality

Rat hour (11pm-1am) Although talented and competitive, beware of trying to reach unrealistic goals.

Ox hour (1am-3am) Tenacity and persistence lead to success – no goal is too distant to achieve. Avoid romantic idealism.

Tiger hour (3am-5am) Commerce and travel are the avenues to wealth. Contentment in marriage.

Hare hour (5am-7am) The romantic side of marriage may disappoint, but children bring joy. Personal rewards from social service.

Dragon hour (7am-9am) Finances fluctuate – never risk all in speculation. Happiness in romance.

Snake hour (9am-11am) Good aspects for the journalist or dramatist; less favourable for the practical worker. Romance disappoints.

Horse hour (11am-1pm) Wealth through marriage, but personal happiness may suffer.

Sheep hour (1pm-3pm) Heart rules head, but fame takes second place to personal happiness. Marriage and children bring much joy.

Monkey hour (3pm-5pm) An agile mind and an ability to see things through. Family problems.

Rooster hour (5pm-7pm) Determination, flair and judgment emphasized. Wealth likely, but romance may pose problems.

Dog hour (7pm-9pm) Marriage and travel favourably aspected. Look for a supportive partner.

Pig hour (9pm-11pm) Successful marriage and a happy family life. Only likely to achieve moderate financial independence.

The Dog

10 Feb 1910 – 29 Jan 1911
28 Jan 1922 – 15 Feb 1923
14 Feb 1934 – 3 Feb 1935
2 Feb 1946 – 21 Jan 1947
18 Feb 1958 – 7 Feb 1959
6 Feb 1970 – 26 Jan 1971
25 Jan 1982 – 26 Jan 1983
10 Feb 1994 – 30 Jan 1995

Dogs have faithfully stood guard over Chinese families for thousands of years, although their introduction into the household as a companion only came about quite recently.

For many westerners, the most alarming thing about the Chinese attitude to dogs is that they are regarded as acceptable items of food. In the ancient book of Rites, the Chinese scriptures even go so far as to name the months and seasons when dog-meat should be eaten or avoided.

In China the colour of the household's dog is of great importance. The birth of a black dog with white ears is a sign that its owner will be rich and famous; a white dog with a yellow head brings prosperity; a yellow dog with a white tail foretells a high position for the family; and a white dog with a black head ensures riches and fortune.

Astrologically the Dog and the Pig together form the House of Family, and in the Chinese calendar the Dog month is the last month of Autumn, approximating, in the western calendar, to October-November. The hour of the Dog lasts from 7pm to 9pm.

The Dog Personality

The Dog represents friendship and loyalty, and anyone who has a friend born in the year of the Dog is fortunate indeed. The typical characteristics of the Dog personality are a broad but sometimes risqué sense of humour, coupled with a strong sense of honesty, honour and loyalty.

Not surprisingly, Dog types tend to be popular and often rise to prominence within their community. Yet although they may have a large circle of friends, most will be people they have known for a long time; while Dog types make surface friendships easily, they tend to be rather mistrustful at the outset and may put up barriers against newcomers.

While they are happy to join in the fun and socialize, Dogs are wary of anybody who tries to invade their privacy. The sanctity of the home is central to the Dog's personal philosophy, and while Dog types may take a pride in their abode, they seldom wish to put it on display.

The Old Routine

Dog personalities do not care for change. They like things to stay as they always have been, and will bear great inconvenience rather than alter the established routine. When they are obliged to bow to the inevitable, they do not do so gracefully.

The Dog-type's loyalty is enormously strong, and generally speaking it is foolhardy in the extreme to talk ill of their friends or family. This loyalty can have its drawbacks, however, for when the Dog's trust is misplaced, no amount of warning will dislodge their faith in a trusted friend, even when it is obvious that something is amiss.

The curious blend of the two types of personality – the private indoor and public outdoor – can lead to misunderstandings, especially at home, if the partner cannot appreciate the Dog's need to be part of the throng outside. But as long as Dog-types are allowed their freedom to roam, they will always return to the home they are prepared to defend with their last breath.

The Dog Year

The Dog represents protection, defence, and the structure of the family home. So the Dog year brings an opportunity to review the fabric of one's home, and to see what repairs might be needed.

Those for whom the Dog year is favourable (such as Horse, Tiger and other Dog types) may find this a good year in which to move house, or perhaps to have improvements made. Those for whom the Dog year is less sympathetic (the Ox, Dragon, and Sheep) should not delay in attending to essential renovation, or in checking that their home's structure is wind and waterproof.

Resist and Defend

In business matters, companies will close ranks against outsiders, and take-over bids are likely to be frustrated. High-risk ventures should be avoided.

On the world scene the Dog year symbolizes a period of defence and resistance – a time when it would be futile for one nation to attempt to overrun another. Politically, therefore, it is an ideal time for nations to review their defence policies.

In matters of romance, marriages made in the Dog year are said to be happy ones, whatever the partners' Chinese zodiac signs happen to be.

Dog Relationships

With the Rat

These two unlikely companions may not have a designer-made

partnership, but both have sufficient sense and self-confidence to make this a good working relationship.

With the Ox

Not the ideal match. The two are so set and determined in their ways that conflicts often arise. If only they could be more flexible in their approach towards each other.

With the Tiger

An exciting partnership. There are many shared interests which make this a satisfactory and stimulating relationship, whether in business or romance.

With the Hare

In romance, the attraction is mainly physical; in business, it may simply be a matter of short-term contingency. Even so, the relationship often works well.

With the Dragon

There are many conflicts of interest and a major lack of understanding between these two. There has to be some other underlying force to keep them together.

With the Snake

If these two can respect the other's principles, even though they do not share them, this partnership can survive. But it is a curious conflict of personalities.

With the Horse

A very stimulating relationship, and one which is ideal for a couple who want to combine a romantic liaison with a business partnership. Highly successful in all ways.

With the Sheep

There is some lack of understanding here, since one partner always has to give in to the other; the more obliging of them may come to doubt that the sacrifice is worth it.

With the Monkey

A very sympathetic relationship exists here. The two are both highly active, and whether in business or home-making they should succeed very well.

With the Rooster

It is not possible to succeed every time. If they meet on the rebound from a break-up, then it may be a stepping-stone to something more permanent.

With another Dog

Not all same-sign relationships work, but this one does, and very well. Normally such similarities of personality are less than ideal, but these two are not worried.

With the Pig

A cozy arrangement; a relationship ideal for the home-maker who can look forward to a large and happy family. A business partnership prospers.

The Year of the Dog

Whatever your animal sign, study the list below to find out how you will fare in a Dog year.

The Rat – Do-it-yourselfers and artists will benefit from a constructive influence. Tread carefully with financial ventures. Avoid legal wrangles.

The Ox – There are many obstacles ahead, but the Ox is usually able to forge its way forward. Avoid land deals. Romance is a more favourable prospect.

The Tiger – An excellent year, with the promise of long-distance travel. Those involved in sport will be successful. Family problems are likely.

The Hare – The year progresses steadily, with few setbacks and little change. Business and financial prospects are only fair. Romance brings surprises.

The Dragon – Avoid speculation, or making rash decisions. It will be hard to resist temptation; think of the consequences beforehand.

The Snake – Be prepared for some disappointments, keep a tight rein on finances, and avoid being drawn into lawsuits. Concentrate on house and family.

The Horse – A wonderful year. Use the time to its best advantage. In sport, business or romance, be ready to push yourself forward. There are many rewards.

The Sheep – A reasonable year, but better for men than women.

Pay attention to matters at home, and attend to details in your business dealings.

The Monkey – The year promises considerable career success; you can realize some of your ambitions. You may not reach the top, but you will be on your way.

The Rooster – A mixed year, with moments of elation and big disappointments. Be prepared for whatever arrives, and take the good with the bad.

The Dog – This is your year, so plan ahead in order to make the best of each situation as it arises. You can succeed in whatever you set your mind to.

The Pig – A successful year, and the start of a happy period which will bring ample opportunities. Any large-scale plans should be put into operation now.

How the Hour of Birth Affects the Dog Personality

Rat hour (11pm-1am) Adaptable and practical. Despite some restlessness, domestic life is happy.

Ox hour (1am-3am) After some insecurity, a happy home will be found. Fortune and fame arrive after an unexpected incident.

Tiger hour (3am-5am) Travel, romance and good fortune are well aspected. A good marriage.

Hare hour (5am-7am) Success through a career dealing with movable assets and an interest in medical care.

Dragon hour (7am-9am) Possibly speedy profits from speculation but beware of losing everything.

Snake hour (9am-11am) A career requiring quick thinking and intelligence. Domestic matters are not the first consideration.

Horse hour (11am-1pm) Defensive, with set opinions. Protective of the family or other social group.

Sheep hour (1pm-3pm) A home-loving person who puts family ahead of career. Wealth may be elusive but happiness is assured.

Monkey hour (3pm-5pm) A career in crafts, particularly furnishing. Happiness at home and in romance.

Rooster hour (5pm-7pm) Domestic disputes may cause obstacles on the road to success. But fortune, fame and wealth are all within reach.

Dog hour (7pm-9pm) Trust, loyalty and protectiveness are emphasized. No shortage of love.

Pig hour (9pm-11pm) A contented life. Romance blossoms and marriage and career may be combined.

The Pig

30 Jan 1911 – 17 Feb 1912
16 Feb 1923 – 4 Feb 1924
4 Feb 1935 – 23 Jan 1936
22 Jan 1947 – 9 Feb 1948
8 Feb 1959 – 27 Feb 1960
27 Jan 1971 – 14 Feb 1972
13 Feb 1983 – 1 Feb 1984
31 Jan 1995 – 18 Feb 1996

In China, unlike the West, the symbolism surrounding the pig is most agreeable. The Chinese characters for 'pig' and 'roof' together mean 'home', and in ancient China no family home was complete without its pig. Add the symbol for 'man' and the character means 'furniture', for in China men are supposed to busy themselves around the home attending to fixtures and fittings.

When combined with the sign for 'girl', the character means 'marriage', since a man should not be alone under the same roof with a girl unless he is married to her.

The sign of the Pig, the last of the 12 animals of the Chinese zodiac, belongs with the Dog to the House of Family. The Buddhist monks of old chose the Pig to represent the last double-hour of the day, from 9pm to 11pm, because the comfort-loving pig symbolized the time when the family are tucked up in their beds after the day's work. In the Chinese calendar, the Pig month is the first of winter, from November to December.

The Pig Personality

Of all signs of the Chinese zodiac, the Pig is the most lovable. This affable personality makes the most congenial of companions, and since comfort and contentment are essential to the Pig's way of life, Pigs make also the happiest of home-makers. Typically, their concern is always for their family.

Although Pig-types like to surround themselves with luxury whenever they can, they do not care for anything too contrived, preferring whatever comes naturally. Consequently, the Pig-type's home is a warm and welcoming place, where the accent is on softness rather than style.

Perhaps surprisingly, though, they are slow to recognize artificiality in other people, since they like to take everything and everybody at face value. It is very rare to find a Pig-type who is greedy or self-centred; in fact, they generally care for other people's comforts as much as they do for their own.

Finishing and Perfecting

Many Pig-types are drawn towards the caring professions, such as medicine or social services. They are not aggressively ambitious in their careers, preferring to look for a position which will give them satisfaction and security. Yet because they usually manage to find their ideal role, they invariably become recognized as the cream of their profession and rise gracefully to the top.

Pigs who are drawn towards a more commercial life tend to be cooperative rather than competitive. Therefore, they also make good trouble-shooters, and their skills may well be called upon to sort out problems at managerial level – though more often with regard to personnel than technical matters.

Easy-going

Sadly, the Pig is often a poor judge of character, and among a large and widely varied circle of friends and acquaintances there will always be those who will be all too ready take advantage of this sign's kind and easy-going nature. Even so, the Pig is generally too soft-hearted to bear a grudge, and matters are usually forgiven before long.

The Pig Year

Being the last of the 12 years of the cycle, the Year of the Pig is a time of completion, when matters are drawn to a close. Therefore, the year of the Pig is not usually a good time to embark on new ventures, especially those of a long-term nature.

Any plans which should have reached completion must now be treated with urgency. If they are left hanging over into the following year – the start of a new cycle – there is the danger they may not be completed at all.

Family Planning

The one aspect of life in which foundations can safely be laid in a Pig Year is the family. Since the sign of the Pig is associated with large and happy families, one which is started in a Pig year is sure to be contented and fruitful. However, those with romantic aspirations who are not yet ready to marry should take care in their relationships – there is a risk of matters going farther than anyone intended.

In world politics, it is an ideal time for drawing up peace treaties and for the withdrawal of occupying forces. In business, successful fields are likely to be those connected with the leisure industry; elsewhere, commercial activity may be slow.

Pig Relationships

With the Rat

An unusual couple – one is a starter, while the other is a finisher. If only they could find a way to work jointly at the same thing, their life together would be more smooth.

With the Ox

This partnership has all the makings of a stable relationship. Though their existence may appear dull and plodding to outsiders, family life remains happy and contented.

With the Tiger

Storm clouds brood over this partnership. The two have less in common than they imagine, and their views are apt to conflict. Understanding needed from both sides.

With the Hare

A supremely happy partnership, ideal for those keen on children and family life. Later years will bring prosperity, plus the prospect of many grandchildren.

With the Dragon

An uneasy relationship, beset by financial problems, upheavals, and mutual mistrust. The fault is, alas, not always on both sides – the Pig is much more likely to be the loser.

With the Snake

The Snake and the Pig are opposites in the Chinese zodiac, and as a result their attitudes are largely incompatible. Problems need to be aired, instead of hidden, so they can be resolved.

With the Horse

In most respects quite a stable, easy-going relationship – neither wildly passionate nor impossibly shaky. Village social life would suit this couple very well.

With the Sheep

As far as marriage and family are concerned, this is the ideal relationship. But as a business partnership there is not enough stimulus to make it a worthwhile venture.

With the Monkey

The staid, conservative Pig is not the ideal match for the impatient and innovative Monkey. A need for understanding on both sides if the relationship is to survive.

With the Rooster

Whether in marriage or business – and especially when the two are combined – this is a very good working partnership. Both are able to contribute their own special gifts.

With the Dog

One of the most satisfactory and stable of all partnerships. Romantic attachments are strong, ensuring a very happy family atmosphere, success and prosperity.

With another Pig

A pairing which ensures a happy family atmosphere. But

although home life may be comfortable, an outside stimulus is needed for there to be prosperity.

The Year of the Pig

Whatever your animal sign, study the list below to find out how you will fare in a Pig year.

The Rat – An uncomfortable time for anyone concerned with innovation. Use the year to get old projects out of the way ready for a fresh start next year.

The Ox – Although there may be few changes this year, it is generally a very satisfactory time when longstanding ambitions can be realized at last.

The Tiger – Ambitions may be thwarted this year if attention to detail is neglected. Be prepared for disappointments and have alternative plans ready.

The Hare – An excellent year. Family, romance, career, personal ambitions – all these are favourably aspected and can lead to success in many fields.

The Dragon – Not one of the Dragon's best years. Avoid new projects and heavy romantic relationships. Try to let the year pass as uneventfully as possible.

The Snake – A year of conflict and upheaval. Be prepared for expenditure on matters close to the home. Do not neglect insurance.

The Horse – Some of the past year's difficulties begin to clear up. The year sees an end to some problem which has been a persistent obstacle.

The Sheep – Matters are turning in your favour at last. As the year progresses, more opportunities present themselves. Get new projects underway.

The Monkey – The situation is never very good this year. There are many false starts and obstacles, but the adverse conditions are only temporary.

The Rooster – The position is much improved this year. Personal advancement and recognition are possible. Family relationships are much smoother.

The Dog – A very satisfying year. There will be considerable personal gain, matters at home are improved, and career prospects are much better.

The Pig – This is the Pig's own year; an ideal time for bringing long-established plans and ambitions to fruition. Public recognition for voluntary services.

How the Hour of Birth Affects the Pig Personality

Rat hour (11pm-1am) Career and home may go together. Happiness, wealth and business success.

Ox hour (1am-3am) More practicality than romance at home. A career involving children is likely. Wealth only comes from hard work.

Tiger hour (3am-5am) Career and domestic responsibilities may conflict. Wealth late in life.

Hare hour (5am-7am) Good prospects for academic success and personal achievement. A rewarding family life. Possibly many children.

Dragon hour (7am-9am) An instinct for business. Romance will hold many lessons to be learned.

Snake hour (9am-11am) Many obstacles on the road to success. Wealth from property. Romance and family fare adequately.

Horse hour (11am-1pm) Setbacks early in marriage. Support from a colleague brings eventual happiness.

Sheep hour (1pm-3pm) A career in teaching likely. A rich and fulfilling home life, with shared family interests. Good health.

Monkey hour (3pm-5pm) Put technical expertise to work. A relaxed lifestyle.

Rooster hour (5pm-7pm) Decide whether to put career or family first. There may be wealth or contentment – but not both.

Dog hour (7pm-9pm) Great self-sufficiency. Romantic notions give way to practicalities.

Pig hour (9pm-11pm) Adept at bringing business projects to completion. Children and family provide a source of contentment.

The Five Elements

The 12 animals of the Chinese zodiac are probably the aspect of Chinese astrology that westerners are most familiar with. But for professional Chinese soothsayers, they are merely the foundations on which a precise assessment a persons prospects in life can be built.

A complete Chinese horoscope takes into account not just the year of birth, but the month, day and time. These four factors are called the *Four Pillars* by Chinese astrologers, since they are the supports on which all their further calculations are based.

Chinese people have a very practical approach to astrology; they are not usually content with horoscopes which are merely character readings. They want to know whether they will be

HOW TO FIND YOUR OWN ELEMENT

You can find your own personality Element very simply. First take your year of birth according to the Chinese calendar. This is the same as the ordinary western year if you were born between March through to December. Otherwise you need to consult a Chinese calendar as, according to the Chinese way of fixing dates, your birth year may need adjusting. For example, someone born before 23 January 1974 has an adjusted birth year of 1973. (A calendar appears on page 196 showing the animal years starting with the years 1900-1901). See also pages 306-313.

Now take the last figure of your (adjusted) birth year, and find your own Element from the list below. For example, if you were born in 1968, the last figure is 8 and your personality Element is Earth.

Years ending in 4 or 5: Wood
Years ending in 6 or 7: Fire
Years ending in 8 or 9: Earth
Years ending in 0 or 1: Metal
Years ending in 2 or 3: Water.

Now you can combine your Element with your Chinese zodiac sign to find your character type.

rich, which periods of life will be best for them, and even what kind of business they should follow. This is precisely the information a Chinese horoscope conveys. In this section you can find out more about the fascinating subject of Chinese astrology, and learn what destiny has in store for you according to the ancient art of *Ming Shu* – the Reckoning of Fate.

Follow the simple step-by-step instructions in this course, and you will soon master the straightforward procedure for drawing up a Chinese horoscope for yourself or your friends. But first, you need to know more about the basic principles of Chinese astrology. This part of the course deals with one of its most important aspects – the principle of the Five Chinese Elements.

The Five Elements

At the heart of all Chinese thought is the concept of the Five Elements – Wood, Fire, Earth, Metal and Water – which are considered to rule all events and activity in the universe.

Despite their names, the Elements are not thought of as ingredients from which things are made; rather, they are a convenient means of describing the way things happen. When the Elements are in perfect balance, total harmony is achieved. A Chinese physician might diagnose someone's illness as being due to a lack or surfeit of one of the Elements, or a stock broker might blame the uncertain fortunes of the market on a change on the Elements.

The Five Planets

The names of the Five Elements correspond to those of the five planets known to ancient Chinese astrologers. The Wood planet is Jupiter, the Fire planet Mars, the Earth planet Saturn, the Metal planet Venus and the Water planet Mercury.

The Chinese considered the five planets to have particular influences on both nature and human affairs. Thus, the Wood planet embodies the creative or generative element, and symbolizes the beginning of any action. It is associated with growth and development, but also the consumption of resources.

Slow-moving Saturn, the Earth planet, shows stability and strength, but also indicates obstinacy and difficulties. The shining white Metal planet, Venus, reveals ambition and aggressiveness, while the swift-moving Water planet, Mercury, indicates flexibility, communication and all forms of travel.

In some respects the symbolism of the Five Elements is close to that of the corresponding planets in western astrology, especially Mars (Fire), Mercury (Water) and Saturn (Earth). But there are major differences. For example, the Metal planet, Venus, is regarded by Chinese astrologers as a masculine, aggressive planet, while Jupiter (Wood) stands for gentle, feminine qualities.

The Five Elements also have many other associations peculiar to them, such as colour, season and direction. So Wood is associated with the green of growing plants and represents Spring – the 'morning' of the year – as well as East, the direction in which the sun rises.

Order of the Elements

The 'natural' order of the Five Elements – Wood, Fire, Earth, Metal, Water, then back to Wood again – is called the *productive order,* because each Element in the series produces the next. So Wood burns, producing Fire; Fire leaves Earth behind as ash; the Earth is mined to produce Metal; when Metal melts it flows like Water; growing plants need Water, and so back to Wood.

But when each alternate Element in the series is chosen, the *destructive order* appears. Wood (growing plants) extracts nourishment from the Earth; Earth muddies Water; Water quenches Fire; Fire melts Metal; Metal chops Wood.

Harmony and Adversity

If the Elements representing two circumstances or two people are next to each other in the productive order, then the result will be harmonious and successful. But if they fall within the destructive order, this may signal problems. In this case, something representing the intervening Element needs to be introduced in order to restore balance and harmony. For example, if two people are going through a trying period in their relationship – whether it is business or personal – and their respective Elements are Wood and Metal (Metal chops Wood), they would do well to enlist the help of a third person whose Element is Water, to act as a mediator in difficult situations.

The Twelve Wood Types

Combine your animal sign with your Element to reveal the deeper aspects of your character

The Wood Rat

5 Feb 1924 – 24 Jan 1925
2 Feb 1984 – 19 Feb 1985

The most creative Rat type. Artistic, caring and romantic. Best work is done at night. Wood Rats love country life.

The Wood Ox

25 Jan 1925 – 12 Feb 1926
20 Feb 1985 – 8 Feb 1986

An excellent type, combining imagination with practicality. Confident and resolute. Able to work single-handedly.

The Wood Tiger

26 Jan 1914 – 13 Feb 1915
23 Jan 1974 – 10 Feb 1975

Intense and passionate, the most ardent and romantic of the Tiger types. Artistic leanings need to be encouraged.

The Wood Hare

14 Feb 1915 – 2 Feb 1916
11 Feb 1975 – 30 Jan 1976

Affectionate and considerate; an almost saintly personality at times. Happiest when helping others, especially children.

The Wood Dragon

16 Feb 1904 – 3 Feb 1905
13 Feb 1964 – 1 Feb 1965

Can be a great creative artist. Bold and unconventional, with flair and vision, but may lack practicality. A great lover.

The Wood Snake

4 Feb 1905 – 24 Jan 1906
2 Feb 1965 – 20 Jan 1966

Mysterious and enigmatic, loving intrigue and anything intricate. Can be merciless in romance – a heart-breaker.

The Wood Horse

3 Feb 1954 – 23 Jan 1955

A country-loving romantic, always active and very practical. Hates the city life – happiest working on the land. Thoughtful and caring in love.

The Wood Sheep

24 Jan 1955 – 11 Feb 1956

Quiet and contemplative. Likes gentle, artistic pursuits involving nature and wildlife. Highly considerate in love and will want many children.

The Wood Monkey

25 Jan 1944 – 12 Feb 1945

Highly creative and inventive. Fascinated by intricate things but rather enjoys embellishing facts. Attentive in love, but needs to be dominated at times.

The Wood Rooster

13 Feb 1945 – 1 Feb 1946

Vital and creative, adding zest to any humdrum situation. But can be tediously meticulous, making demands on friends. In love, passionate and headstrong.

The Wood Dog

14 Feb 1934 – 3 Feb 1935

10 Feb 1994 – 30 Jan 1995

Practical and active – DIY and gardening may feature strongly. The Wood Dog may roam, but will always return home.

The Wood Pig

4 Feb 1935 – 23 Jan 1936

31 Jan 1995 – 18 Feb 1996

Caring and home-loving. All efforts are directed towards improving the environment, particularly for the family.

The Twelve Fire Types

Combine your animal sign with your Element to reveal the deeper aspects of your character.

The Fire Rat

24 Jan 1936 – 10 Feb 1937

19 Feb 1996 – 6 Feb 1997

Creativity and intellectual ability are combined. Witty, but may take offence easily. Often unsettled and excitable.

The Fire Ox
11 Feb 1937 – 30 Jan 1938
7 Feb 1997 – 27 Jan 1998
The most quick-witted of the Ox types, combining intellectual and physical strength. In romance, easily aroused.

The Fire Tiger
13 Feb 1926 – 1 Feb 1927
9 Feb 1986 – 28 Jan 1987
Dazzling and charming – a magnetic personality. Not open to criticism, and dislikes advice. Passionate in love.

The Fire Hare
2 Feb 1927 – 22 Jan 1928
29 Jan 1987 – 16 Feb 1988
Bright and enthusiastic. Can follow a demanding and exacting career, possibly in medicine. May marry twice.

The Fire Dragon
3 Feb 1916 – 22 Jan 1971
31 Jan 1976 – 17 Feb 1977
Exotic and stimulating – an exuberant personality. Must be careful.

The Fire Snake
23 Jan 1917 – 10 Feb 1918
18 Feb 1977 – 6 Feb 1978
Admires quality, and has impeccable taste. Often the power behind a successful person. In romance, secretive.

The Fire Horse
25 Jan 1906 – 12 Feb 1907
21 Jan 1966 – 8 Feb 1967
The most dreaded combination – often revolutionaries. Stern disciplinarians as parents.

The Fire Sheep
13 Feb 1907 – 1 Feb 1908
9 Feb 1967 – 29 Jan 1968

Persuasive yet persistent. The best combination of diplomacy, patience, and resolution. Good teachers.

The Fire Monkey
12 Feb 1956 – 30 Jan 1957
Gifted yet perverse with an inclination to mischief. Often unintentionally troublesome and accident-prone. Fond of debate. Unpredictable in love.

The Fire Rooster
31 Jan 1957 – 17 Feb 1958
Highly excitable – must avoid being burnt out intellectually. Fashion-conscious and popular. Personal life has its problems. Romance not always successful.

The Fire Dog
2 Feb 1946 – 21 Jan 1947
Intelligent and active – not afraid of work. Home-loving, but not one to stay at home. Protective and occasionally aggressive. Can be demanding in love.

The Fire Pig
22 Jan 1947 – 9 Feb 1948
A great entertainer. As the home is the centre of activity, success is assured if personal life and career overlap. In love, ardent and amusing.

The Twelve Earth Types

Combine your animal sign with your Element to reveal the deeper aspects of your character

The Earth Rat
10 Feb 1948 – 28 Jan 1949
The most practical of the Rat types, this resourceful personality is well able to put ideas into reality. Conservative in taste and very generous.

The Earth Ox
29 Jan 1949 – 16 Feb 1950
Practical and down-to-earth. Reliable and persevering, but stubborn too. Good business sense. In love, often naive and sometimes misunderstood.

The Earth Tiger
31 Jan 1938 – 18 Feb 1939
Dependable but occasionally impetuous. Shows good leadership and sound judgment. In love, loyal but jealous and possessive.

The Earth Hare
19 Feb 1939 – 7 Feb 1940
16 Feb 1999 – 4 Feb 2000
Thrifty and cautious – dislikes change and making sudden decisions. Needs the security of a long-term relationship.

The Earth Dragon
23 Jan 1928 – 9 Feb 1929
17 Feb 1988 – 5 Fe 1989
Flamboyant and extrovert but practical. In business could make a fortune. Imaginative and romantic, yet reliable.

The Earth Snake
10 Feb 1929 – 29 Jan 1930
6 Feb 1989 – 29 Jan 1990
Thorough and meticulous, dislikes disorder. Can infuriate others with their precision. In romance, can seem unfeeling.

The Earth Horse
11 Feb 1918 – 31 Jan 1919
7 Feb 1978 – 27 Jan 1979
Impetuous when young but matures quickly to become conservative in outlook. May want to dominate in love.

The Earth Sheep
1 Feb 1919 – 19 Feb 1920
28 Jan 1979 –15 Feb 1980
Sociable and friendly – likes clubs and societies. May have an artistic streak. Can be too frank in romance.

The Earth Monkey
2 Feb 1908 – 21 Jan 1909
30 Jan 1968 – 16 Feb 1969
A sense of mischief is balanced by common sense. Good at organising large-scale projects. Needs a few lessons in love.

The Earth Rooster

22 Jan 1909 – 9 Feb 1910

17 Feb 1969 – 5 Feb 1970

Sensible, but has theatrical flair. Good organizer and careful financial manager. Usually caring in love.

The Earth Dog

18 Feb 1958 – 7 Feb 1959

Authoritative, but must avoid being dictatorial. May prefer to work with things rather than people. A romantic side only rarely reveals itself.

The Earth Pig

8 Feb 1959 – 27 Jan 1960

A creature of comfort. Rarely satisfied with anything but the best, but has occasional lapses of taste. In romance, goes to great lengths to impress.

The Twelve Metal Types

Combine your animal sign with your Element to reveal the deeper aspects of your character.

The Metal Rat

31 Jan 1900 – 18 Feb 1901

28 Jan 1960 – 14 Feb 1961

Highly competitive; can be aggressive and ruthless at work. May be cold and calculating in relationship.

The Metal Ox

19 Feb 1901 – 7 Feb 1902

15 Feb 1961 – 4 Feb 1962

Has determination and drive. Highly dependable, but may be tricky to deal with. In love, can be extremely jealous.

The Metal Tiger

17 Feb 1950 – 5 Feb 1951

Personal success is important to this sign. Not afraid of competition or opposition. In love, may be domineering and show a lack of understanding.

The Metal Hare

6 Feb 1951 – 26 Jan 1952

Very protective, often goes on the defensive in aid of the less fortunate. May over-estimate abilities and take needless risks. Possessive in love.

The Metal Dragon

8 Feb 1940 – 26 Jan 1941

May be rich or poor. Too optimistic and tends to take unnecessary risks. With more practicality could be a business success. Can be jealous in love.

The Metal Snake

27 Jan 1941 – 14 Feb 1942

Ambitious and successful. Skilled financial manager but sees everyone as a potential rival. Can be cool and aloof. Needs intellectual companion.

The Metal Horse

30 Jan 1930 – 16 Feb 1931
27 Jan 1990 – 14 Feb 1991

Sound business sense. Will do well travelling. Can deal with rivals face-to-face. May not see love as essential in marriage.

The Metal Sheep

17 Feb 1931 – 5 Feb 1932
15 Feb 1991 – 3 Feb 1992

A sound business sense leads to financial stability. Should avoid large-scale enterprises. May be demanding in love.

The Metal Monkey

20 Feb 1920 –7 Feb 1921
16 Feb 1980 – 4 Feb 1981

All the makings of a financial wizard when talents are put to use. Articulate and witty. In love, may be jealous.

The Metal Rooster

8 Feb 1921 – 27 Jan 1922
5 Feb 1981 – 24 Jan 1982

A highly competitive business sense but can be abrasive in personal dealings. In love, may annoy partner with moodiness.

The Metal Dog

10 Feb 1910 – 29 Jan 1911
6 Feb 1970 – 26 Jan 1971

Easily put on the defensive. Slow to make new friends but loyal to established ones. In love, fidelity is important.

The Metal Pig

30 Jan 1911 – 17 Feb 1912
27 Jan 1971 – 14 Feb 1972
Has a keen eye for property bargains and moves house often while climbing the career ladder. May marry late in life.

The Twelve Water Types

Combine your animal sign with your Element to reveal the deeper aspects of your character.

The Water Rat

18 Feb 1912 – 5 Feb 1913
15 Feb 1972 – 2 Feb 1973
Charming personality with a well-modulated voice. Likes travelling. A diplomat. In love, will prefer a strong personality.

The Water Ox

6 Feb 1913 – 25 Jan 1914
3 Feb 1973 – 22 Jan 1974
Calm and refined. Practical and nature-loving. Often excels at school. Can be both cynical and suspicious in love.

The Water Tiger

8 Feb 1902 – 28 Jan 1903
5 Feb 1962 – 24 Jan 1963
Ambitious, combines physical presence with persuasiveness. A success in business. May not be faithful in love.

The Water Hare

29 Jan 1903 – 15 Feb 1904
25 Jan 1963 – 12 Feb 1964
Highly imaginative and often a dreamer. May follow a career in painting or the arts. In love, romantic and caring.

The Water Dragon

27 Jan 1952 – 13 Feb 1953
Loves mysterious challenges; fond of occult matters. May dabble in spiritualism or secret societies. An avid reader. In love, seeks a kindred spirit.

The Water Snake

14 Feb 1953 – 2 Feb 1954

Introspective and mystical, loves the abstract. May seek a career in law or physics. Dresses fastidiously. In love, the mind is of utmost importance.

The Water Horse

15 Feb 1942 – 4 Feb 1943

A great conversationalist who is destined to travel. Often needs a stimulating environment. Prospective partners should realize they may never settle.

The Water Sheep

5 Feb 1943 – 24 Jan 1944

Gifted, combines creativity with the need to communicate. But a natural modesty can hinder career. May keep a diary of intimate secrets.

The Water Monkey

6 Feb 1932 – 25 Jan 1933

4 Feb 1992 – 22 Jan 1993

Travel is a vital part of this agitated person's life style. Career prospects continually change. Restless in romance.

The Water Rooster

26 Jan 1933 – 13 Feb 1934

23 Jan 1993 – 9 Feb 1994

Personal ambition is balanced by the need for happy relationships. Loves art and music. In love, understanding.

The Water Dog

28 Jan 1922 – 15 Feb 1923

25 Jan 1982 – 12 Feb 1983

Self-assured, not demanding security, may prefer a nomadic life style. Expresses feelings readily. Needs loyalty in love.

The Water Pig

16 Feb 1923 – 4 Feb 1924

13 Feb 1983 – 1 Feb 1984

Caring, fond of children. May be involved in charity work. Happiness more important than money. In love, affectionate.

The Fourth Calendar

The ingenious Chinese have invented several ways to express any date using four calendars simultaneously – one of which forms the foundation for Chinese astrological calculations.

These days, the western calendar tends to be employed for business use, while the Chinese lunar calendar is used to fix festivals and holidays such as the Chinese New Year. In addition, there is a ritual agricultural calendar that divides the astronomical year exactly into 24 periods.

The fourth calendar – one of the oldest in the world – is the 'Stems and Branches' system of calculating years, months, days (and even hours) which forms the basis of the *Ming Shu* horoscope. The ten 'Stems' were originally the names of the old 10-day Chinese 'week'; the 12 Branches are more familiar by their popular modern names – the 12 animals of the Chinese zodiac.

Stems and Branches

When the 10 Stems and 12 Branches are jointly applied to any date, they offer 60 possible Stem-and-Branch combinations. For example, 1984 – the Year of the Rat – was the First Branch Year (the Rat is the first animal in the Chinese zodiac). It was also a First Stem year, making the following year – 1985 – a Second Stem, Second Branch year. Ten years on, 1994 was also a First Stem year, but since there are two more Branches than Stems, it actually was a First Stem, Eleventh Branch year. In the same way, 1996 was a Third Stem, First Branch year, and so on until the year 2044, when the Stems and Branches coincide once again.

One way of using the Stem-and Branch calendar is to discover which are your lucky and unlucky days according to the ancient Chinese astrological method described earlier. Once you can do this, you are a step nearer to setting up your own Chinese horoscope which will be outlined below.

Finding Your Lucky/Unlucky Days

Just as there are 60 years in the ancient Stem-Branch calendar, so there are 60 possible Stem-Branch days before the cycle

TABLE 1 – CODE NUMBER FOR THE MONTH

Month	Jan	Feb	Mar	Apr	May	Jun	Jul	Aug	Sept	Oct	Nov	Dec
Code	0	31	59	30	0	31	1	32	3	33	4	34

TABLE 2 – CODE NUMBER FOR THE YEAR

Year	1901	1902	1903	1904	1905	1906	1907	1908	1909	1910	1911	1912
Code	15	20	25	30	36	41	46	51	57	2	7	12
Year	1913	1914	1915	1916	1917	1918	1919	1920	1921	1922	1923	1924
Code	18	23	28	33	39	44	49	54	0	5	10	15
Year	1925	1926	1927	1928	1929	1930	1931	1932	1933	1934	1935	1936
Code	21	26	31	36	42	47	52	57	3	8	13	18
Year	1937	1938	1939	1940	1941	1942	1943	1944	1945	1946	1947	1948
Code	24	29	34	39	45	50	55	0	6	11	16	21
Year	1949	1950	1951	1952	1953	1954	1955	1956	1957	1958	1959	1960
Code	27	32	37	42	48	53	58	3	9	14	19	24
Year	1961	1962	1963	1964	1965	1966	1967	1968	1968	1970	1971	1972
Code	30	35	40	45	51	56	1	6	12	17	22	27
Year	1973	1974	1974	1976	1977	1978	1979	1980	1981	1982	1983	1984
Code	33	38	43	48	59	54	4	9	15	20	25	30
Year	1985	1986	1987	1988	1989	1990	1991	1992	1993	1994	1995	1996
Code	35	41	46	51	57	2	7	12	18	23	28	33
Year	1997	1998	1999	2000								
Code	39	44	49	54								

TABLE 3: ASPECTS

0	see 60				
1	✔	21	▲	41	✔
2	➔✔	22	✔	42	✔
3	✖♥	23	★☎	43	✔
4	◆	24	◆	44	◆
5	✔	25	✔	45	▲
6	▲!	26	➔✔	46	✔
7	☎	27	♥✖	47	★☎
8	◆	28	◆	48	◆
9	✖	29	☎	49	☎
10	✔✔	30	◆▲	50	➔✔✔
11	★✔	31	✔	51	♥✔
12	◆	32	◆	52	◆▲
13	☎	33	✖	53	☎
14	➔✔	34	✔◆	54	!
15	▲♥	35	★✔	55	✔
16	◆✔	36	◆✔	56	◆✔
17	☎	37	☎	57	✖
18	!	38	➔✔	58	✔
19	☎	39	✖♥	59	★☎
20	◆✔	40	◆✔	60 and 0	◆✔♥☎

✔ Generally positive
✖ Obstacles
◆ Finances good
♥ Promises romance
▲ Fair progress
➔ Good for travel
★ Family welfare
! Danger looms
☎ Good for recreation

repeats itself. The easiest way to refer to these days is to give each of them its own 'Cyclical Number' from 1 to 60.

By doing just a few simple calculations on a sheet of paper, as described below, it is possible to find the Cyclical Number for any day of the year.

According to Chinese astrologers, if you find the Cyclical Number for the day of your birth, then compare it with the Cyclical Number for the day on which you have to do something important, you can tell whether or not that day will be auspicious. This is because some Cyclical Numbers are compatible with each other for certain activities, while others are most definitely not.

To find the Cyclical Number for your Date of Birth:

- Take a piece of lined paper. On separate lines, write the letters A to K down the left-hand side.
- Next to A write the date of the month of your birthday. So if you were born on 14 September, put 14. (Note: the Chinese day begins at 11pm; if you were born between 11pm and midnight, take the following day as your birth date).
- Next to B write the code-number for your birth month given in Table 1 (p. 279).
- Next to C write the code-number for your birth year given in Table 2 (p. 279).
- Next to D write 0 unless you were born during a leap-year on or after February 29, in which case write 1.
- Add A + B + C + D.
- If the answer is 61, or more, subtract 60. If the answer is still more than 61 subtract another 60. Write down the result next to E. This is the Cyclical Number for your date of birth.

To find the Cyclical Number for your Chosen Day:

- Next to F write the day of the month of the chosen date.
- Next to G write the code-number of the chosen month.
- Next to H put the code-number of the chosen year.
- Next to I write 0, unless the chosen date falls in a leap-year on or after 29 February, in which case write 1.
- Add F + G + H + I.
- Using the same method as for Step E, keep subtracting 60 until the result is 60 or less. Write the answer next to J. This is the Cyclical Number for your Chosen Day.

To find out if your two Cyclical Numbers are compatible:

- If the figure you wrote at E is odd, subtract J from E. If the figure you wrote at E is even, subtract E from J. (In either case, if the first figure is smaller than the second, add 60 first.)
- Write the answer below J at K. This is your Aspect Number. Now find out how compatible the two dates are by referring to the Aspect Number in Table 3 (opposite).

The Four Pillars

Central to all Chinese horoscopes are the *Four Pillars:* the time, day, month and year of birth according to the Chinese calendar. In Chinese astrology, the Four Pillars are always placed prominently at the head of the horoscope.

Each Pillar is expressed not according to the Chinese calendar but in terms of the ancient Stem and Branch system and they are regarded with reverential awe by the Chinese. In fact, should a young man wish to declare his intentions of marriage, he usually hands his prospective father-in-law a card on which are written the Four Pillars of his birth.

The card can then be given to an astrologer to assess the couple's compatibility.

Converting the Date

Converting a western date of birth into the Four Pillar system is normally a complex process, but the tables and special Chinese lunar calendar included in this section make the job a lot easier. Once you have done it, setting up the rest of the Chinese horoscope is quite straightforward.

Finding the Four Pillars

The following step-by-step sequence describes how to find each of the Four Pillars for the western birth date under consideration. It cannot be completed correctly unless you have read the earlier parts of this section.

Remember before you start that the Chinese day begins at 11pm. If the time of birth is between 11pm and midnight, adjust the birth date accordingly – one day forward – and use this revised date in all further calculations.

It is also important to make an adjustment for *Daylight Saving* if this was in operation at the time of birth. When the birth time is close to midnight, this may balance out the need to adjust the birth date.

Step 1: Start by taking a piece of lined notepaper. At the top write the time and date of birth being considered (if necessary making the adjustments outlined above). If you do not know

TABLE 4: CYCLICAL NUMBER FOR THE TIME OF BIRTH

Stem of the day	Time of birth 11pm to 1am	1am to 3am	3am to 5am	5am to 7am	7am to 9am	9am to 11am	11am to 1pm	1pm to 3pm	3pm to 5pm	5pm to 7pm	7pm to 9pm	9pm to 11pm
1	1	2	3	4	5	6	7	8	9	10	11	12
2	13	14	15	16	17	18	19	20	21	22	23	24
3	25	26	27	28	29	30	31	32	33	34	35	36
4	37	38	39	40	41	42	43	44	45	46	47	48
5	49	50	51	52	53	54	55	56	57	58	59	60
6	1	2	3	4	5	6	7	8	9	10	11	12
7	13	14	15	16	17	18	19	20	21	22	23	24
8	25	26	27	28	29	30	31	32	33	34	35	36
9	37	38	39	40	41	42	43	44	45	46	47	48
0	49	50	51	52	53	54	55	56	57	58	59	60

the time of birth, assume it to be noon. Now write the letters A to I on separate lines down the left hand side of the paper.

Step 2: Find the Cyclical Number for the Day Pillar by following steps A to E on page 283. (You may already have completed these steps in order to find your Lucky/Unlucky Days.) Afterwards, continue with the following new steps:

Step 3: To find the Cyclical Number for the Time Pillar, write down at F the last digit of the number you wrote at E. This is the **Day Stem Number.** Now find the time of birth under consideration in Table 4 (p. 287) and cross-refer to the appropriate Day Stem Number (F) in the left-hand column. Write the number given where both columns cross at G.

Step 4: To find the Cyclical Number for the Year Pillar, start by turning to the appropriate section of the Chinese calendar. The dates of the Chinese New Years, which begin somewhere between mid-January and mid-February, appear in the far left-hand column; their corresponding Cyclical Numbers are given on the far right.

Simply find the New Year which either **precedes** or **falls on** the date of birth which is being considered. Then look at the end of that row for the Cyclical Number. Write this at H.

Step 5: To find the Cyclical Number for the Month Pillar, consult the same row of the calendar as you did for the Year Pillar. Run along it until you find the monthly date which most nearly precedes or falls on the month of birth that you are considering. Below this date is a number. Write this number down on your paper next to I.

Check the Cyclical Numbers for each of the Four Pillars:

The Number for the **day** is at E

The Number for the **time** is at G

The Number for the **year** is at H

The Number for the **month** is at I

You now have all the data for constructing a Chinese horoscope. Keep your notes carefully for the section on how to interpret the Four Pillars.

The Vital Elements

Chinese astrologers interpret horoscopes in terms of the Five Elements – Wood, Fire, Earth, Metal and Water. They believe that a correct balance of them ensures health, happiness and prosperity. No Element is better or worse than any other, but there should not be too many – or too few – occurrences of any one Element in a chart.

The Elements are found from the Stems and Branches of the Four Pillars – the hour, day, month and year of birth according to the Chinese Calendar. Each Stem and each Branch produces an Element, while the combination of a Stem and a Branch together produces a third Stem-and-Branch Element. So for each of the four Pillars there is one Element for the Stem, one for the Branch and another for the combined Stem-and-Branch, making 12 in all.

To save you lots of separate calculations, the Elements for all 60 combinations of Stems and Branches are given in Table 5 (pages 286-287). To work out the position of the Elements, you need the Cyclical Numbers for the Four Pillars, calculated according to the instructions earlier in this section.

STEP 1: Take a sheet of lined notepaper and copy the horoscope chart (p. 288), including the boxes for the element Totals.

STEP 2: First take the horoscope data of the Cyclical Numbers for each of the Four Pillars. Note the Cyclical Numbers for the time, day, month and year of birth – **G, E, I,** and **H** – and write these under the relevant letter on the chart. Now continue with the following new steps.

STEP 3: Turn to Table 5 and find the Cyclical Number for the Time of Birth. Run your eye along the line and write the Stem number by **J** in the Time column; the Branch number by **K**; the Stem Element by **L**; the Branch Element by **M** and the combined Stem-and-Branch Element by **N**.

STEP 4: Do exactly the same with the three Cyclical Numbers for the Day, Month and Year of Birth to complete the chart.

STEP 5: Finally, make a note of the number of times each

Table 5: Elements for each pillar

Cyclical Number	*Stem*	*Branch*	*Stem Element*	*Branch Element*	*Stem-and-Branch Element*
GEIH	J	K	L	M	N
1	1	I	Wood	Water	Metal
2	2	II	Wood	Earth	Metal
3	3	III	Fire	Wood	Fire
4	4	IV	Fire	Wood	Fire
5	5	V	Earth	Earth	Wood
6	6	VI	Earth	Fire	Wood
7	7	VII	Metal	Fire	Earth
8	8	VIII	Metal	Earth	Earth
9	9	IX	Water	Metal	Metal
10	10	X	Water	Metal	Metal
11	1	XI	Wood	Earth	Fire
12	2	XII	Wood	Water	Fire
13	3	I	Fire	Water	Water
14	4	II	Fire	Earth	Water
15	5	III	Earth	Wood	Earth
16	6	IV	Earth	Wood	Earth
17	7	V	Metal	Earth	Metal
18	8	VI	Metal	Fire	Metal
19	9	VII	Water	Fire	Wood
20	10	VIII	Water	Earth	Wood
21	1	IX	Wood	Metal	Water
22	2	X	Wood	Metal	Water
23	3	XI	Fire	Earth	Earth
24	4	XII	Fire	Water	Earth
25	5	I	Earth	Water	Fire
26	6	II	Earth	Earth	Fire
27	7	III	Metal	Wood	Wood
28	8	IV	Metal	Wood	Wood
29	9	V	Water	Earth	Water
30	10	VI	Water	Fire	Water

Cyclical Number	*Stem*	*Branch*	*Stem Element*	*Branch Element*	*Stem-and-Branch Element*
GEIH	J	K	L	M	N
31	1	VII	Wood	Fire	Metal
32	2	VIII	Wood	Earth	Metal
33	3	IX	Fire	Metal	Fire
34	4	X	Fire	Metal	Fire
35	5	XI	Earth	Earth	Wood
36	6	XII	Earth	Water	Wood
37	7	I	Metal	Water	Earth
38	8	II	Metal	Earth	Earth
39	9	III	Water	Wood	Metal
40	10	IV	Water	Wood	Metal
41	1	V	Wood	Earth	Fire
42	2	VI	Wood	Fire	Fire
43	3	VII	Fire	Fire	Water
44	4	VIII	Fire	Earth	Water
45	5	IX	Earth	Metal	Earth
46	6	X	Earth	Metal	Earth
47	7	XI	Metal	Earth	Metal
48	8	XII	Metal	Water	Metal
49	9	I	Water	Water	Wood
50	10	II	Water	Earth	Wood
51	1	III	Wood	Wood	Water
52	2	IV	Wood	Wood	Water
53	3	V	Fire	Earth	Earth
54	4	VI	Fire	Fire	Earth
55	5	VII	Earth	Fire	Fire
56	6	VIII	Earth	Earth	Fire
57	7	IX	Metal	Metal	Wood
58	8	X	Metal	Metal	Wood
59	9	XI	Water	Earth	Water
60	10	XII	Water	Water	Water

Element appears and write each number in the Element Totals box. As a double-check there should be 12 Elements in all.

Interpreting the Elements

The Wood Element represents the creative and caring side of the personality. It is concerned with well-being, as well as love and family matters.

Fire symbolizes intelligence and enthusiasm and is concerned with decision-making, whereas the Element of Earth reveals practicality and reliability. It also signals the ability to pursue a project to its conclusion as well as being a sign of a good physical constitution.

The Element of Metal represents both money and conflicts, showing competitiveness and business acumen. It concerns financial security.

Chinese Horoscope Chart

	Time G	Day E	Month I	Year H
Stem J				
Branch K				
Stem Element L				
Branch Element M				
Stem-and-Branch Element N				

ELEMENT TOTALS

WOOD	FIRE	EARTH	METAL	WATER

Water symbolizes communication, whether in words, writing, or travelling. It may also indicate legal matters.

Since there are five different Elements and the total number of occurrences in the chart is 12, the Elements can never be equally represented. Chinese astrologers consider the horoscope to be harmonious if each Element appears two or three times.

Often one of the Elements will appear more frequently than the others, although the remainder of the chart may be evenly balanced with two or three occurrences of the other four Elements.

But if an Element only appears once or not at all, this means that the person concerned will have to compensate for the qualities of the Element which is lacking. For example, if the Element of Water is poorly represented or absent then there may be difficulty in communicating with others.

However, if a 'dominant' Element occurs next to a missing or poorly represented Element in the productive order – Wood, Fire, Earth, Metal, Water then back to Wood – it can 'produce' the missing Element. For example, if Wood appears four times but Fire is lacking, the extra Wood (caring) produces the missing Fire (enthusiasm).

On the other hand, a dominant Element may 'overpower' a weaker Element if it occurs next to it in the destructive order of the Elements – Wood, Earth, Water, Fire, Metal then back to Wood again. For example, if Wood appears four times but Earth only once, then the powerful Wood (caring) will overpower the weak Earth (practicality).

Destiny, Fame and Fortune

Since the Elements play such a vital role in a Chinese horoscope, this part of the course continues to look at their importance and what it means when certain Elements either dominate the horoscope or are missing from it altogether. For this part you need the Element Totals from earlier in this section.

From there, using the Stem and Branch Numbers for each of the Four Pillars you can work out the significance of the 10 Stems and the 12 Branches. These give indications of destiny, detail aspects of character and the chances of fame and fortune.

Calculate Element Qualities

The basic or *positive* qualities of each Element are described earlier in this section. Chinese astrologers reckon they are best when an Element occurs 2 or 3 times.

But if an Element is *absent*, its positive aspects need to be actively strengthened. The person concerned needs to make a conscious effort to make up for the qualities lacking. For example, if Water is missing from a chart, then it is important to develop writing and communication skills.

When the Element rating is higher than 4, it is too dominant, and its *malign* side may make itself felt. So if Water has a high rating, it is inadvisable to take up a job that involves much travelling.

To find out how the Elements affect a person's character, take the Element Totals box and compare its ratings with Table 6: Element Qualities.

Find Your Destiny

First work out the significance of the Branch numbers. For this you will need data from the horoscope chart featured earlier in this section. Look along the Branch line (K) and note the 4 numbers under G, E, I and H. These range from I to XII as

TABLE 6: ELEMENT QUALITIES

WOOD	**Positive:** creativity; artistry; a caring nature. **Absent:** emphasizes Earth qualities. Denotes lack of originality and aloofness. A high Water rating balances this lack. **Malign:** dreaminess; lustfulness; impracticality.
FIRE	**Positive:** stimulation; vigorous; excitement. **Absent:** reticence, even dullness. A high Wood rating restores energy. **Malign:** unrestrained; extravagant.
EARTH	**Positive:** stability; reliability; perseverance. **Absent:** reveals need to develop determination and self-discipline. A high Fire rating helps re-establish drive. **Malign:** obstinacy; fear of change; obstructiveness.
METAL	**Positive:** ambition, drive, business skills. **Absent:** complacency; feelings of inferiority. A high Earth rating restores the sense of purpose. **Malign:** aggressiveness, meanness, selfishness.
WATER	**Positive:** literacy; eloquence; knowledge-seeking; flexibility. **Absent:** inflexibility; nervous anxiety; weakened constitution. Here it is best for the other Elements to be well-balanced. **Malign:** restlessness; caprice; dissatisfaction.

there are 12 Branches. Then compare your findings with Table 7: Destiny and the Branches, matching each Branch number to the appropriate entry. This gives an overview of the destiny of the person in question.

The 12 Branches are now called by their modern names – the 12 animals of the Chinese zodiac – but the Chinese still know them by their ancient names and symbols. For example, the first Branch – the Rat – is called 'Child' in the old scheme and represents the birth of the day. It signifies new life and opportunities for success.

Fate, Fame and Fortune

Now take a closer look at the significance of the Stems and Branches. First tackle the Branches by drawing a circular chart with 12 divisions like a clockface, but with I at the top in the 12 o'clock position (see the illustration overleaf). On the clockface, draw the positions of the Branches as clock hands. For this you need the 4 Branch numbers from the horoscope chart used in the previous section (line K under G, E, I and H) marking them 'Time', 'Day', 'Month', and 'Year' according to the Pillar they refer to.

If two or more Branches are the same, then that aspect of character or destiny (again see Table 7) is obviously emphasized. If they stand at positions representing 'two-hourly'

TABLE 7: DESTINY AND THE BRANCHES

I (Rat) A Child. New Life and opportunities. Success.
II (Ox) Continuity and strength. Sense of humour.
III (Tiger) Reverence, idealism, respectfulness.
IV (Hare) Self-sacrifice. Fond of children.
V (Dragon) An eclipse. Concern with the occult.
VI (Snake) Thought. A schemer.
VII (Horse) Mid-day. Ambition; may be a revolutionary.
VIII (Sheep) Waiting. Patience; withdrawal from worldly matters.
IX (Monkey) Stretching. Continual development and expansion.
X (Rooster) Wine Bottle. May tend to drink.
XI (Dog) A Weapon. Loyalty and defence.
XII (Pig) Darkness. Privacy; obscurity.

intervals, for example, Branches I and III, this is beneficial and the positive aspects of the Branches are heightened.

It is even better if the Branches stand at 'four-hourly' intervals, at say, III (idealism) and VII (ambition). This represents someone fiercely loyal and ambitious, perhaps a dedicated politician. But if the Branches are opposite each other, as I and VII, or at 'three-hourly' intervals, as II and V, this can sometimes reveal difficulties and obstacles. In the case of I (success) and VII (ambition) this could indicate an overwhelming concern with advancement and promotion.

Fortunate Stems

Now draw a similar chart for the 10 Stems to analyse the chances of fame and fortune. This time divide the clockface into ten divisions (see below).

Take the Stem Numbers for each Pillar from the horoscope chart shown earlier (see line J under G, E, I and H) and draw them as clock hands.

THE PRINCESS OF WALES' BRANCHES AND STEMS

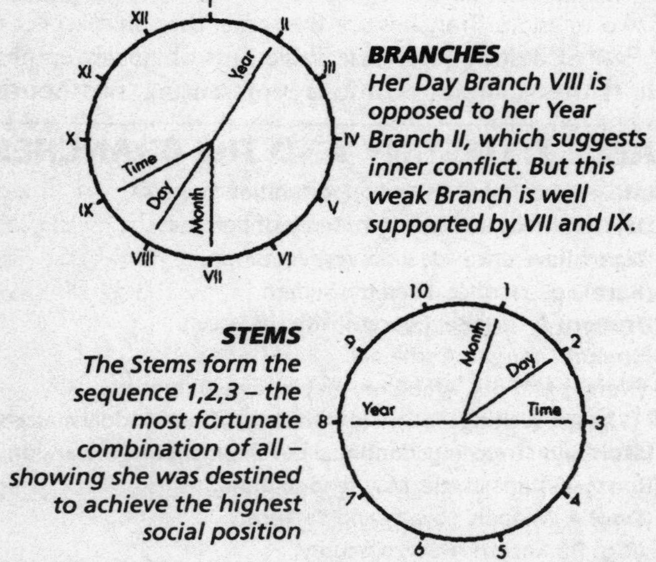

BRANCHES
Her Day Branch VIII is opposed to her Year Branch II, which suggests inner conflict. But this weak Branch is well supported by VII and IX.

STEMS
The Stems form the sequence 1,2,3 – the most fortunate combination of all – showing she was destined to achieve the highest social position

Unlike the Branches, a different rule applies to the Stems, for they are considered to be harmonious when they appear opposite each other on the clockface. So it is beneficial when 1 is opposite 6; 2-7; 3-8; 4-9; 5-10.

A sequence of Stems, such as 1, 2, 3; 2, 4, 6; 3, 6, 9 indicates people destined to achieve a high position. Alternating Stems, for example, 3, 5, 7, or 2, 4, 6, may indicate success in the world of entertainment or sport. When the Stems include several low numbers they often indicate a successful political career.

The Life Cycle Chart

Generally speaking, the western approach to astrology revolves around the analysis of personality types. The Chinese, however, take a much more practical view – they want to know from their astrologers when conditions are favourable to embark on, say, new ventures and when to wait.

This is where the *Life Cycle Chart* comes into its own. It shows the course of life's fortunes at a glance, it reveals the periods in life when successes and failures are most likely to occur and even gives an insight into the form that these events might take.

Step-by-step Guide

All the data needed for constructing a Life Cycle Chart is contained in your filled-out horoscope chart. You will also need a copy of the blank Life Cycle Chart.

Before you begin, it is a good idea to read the explanation of the basic meanings of the Chinese Stages of Life, the Five Forces that determine a person's destiny and the effect the Five Elements have upon them. Then you can follow the step-by-step guide to setting up and interpreting a Chart.

To Construct a Life Cycle Chart

Step 1: Draw a rough copy or take a photocopy of the blank Life Cycle Chart – on page 303.

Step 2: First find the Element associated with the stage in life called the Kuan Tai.

For this, you need to know the Branch of the Month Pillar of

	TIME	DAY	MONTH	YEAR
	G	E	I	H
Stem	J			Y
Branch	K		Z	
Stem Element	L			
Branch Element	M			X
Stem-and-Branch Element	N			

the horoscope, and the Stem of the Year Pillar. Turn to your filled in horoscope chart (p. 288).

Write down the Branch of the Month Pillar (the figure in the horoscope chart at Z in the example above) and the Stem of the Year Pillar (the figure at Y).

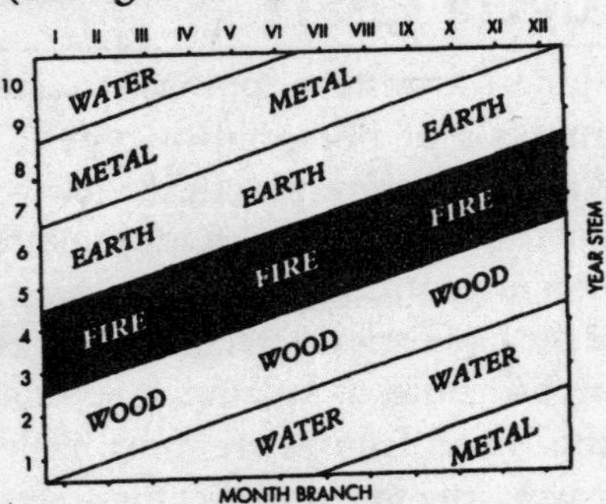

Step 3: To find the Element of Kuan Tai refer to the table above. Take the figure representing the Year Stem (Y) and run your eye across the table until it meets the figure representing the Branch Month (Z). This is the Element of Kuan Tai. Note the Element where it is found. For example, if the figure Y is 3 and figure Z is IX, the Element will be Wood. But if the Kuan Tai happens to fall between two Elements note both of them.

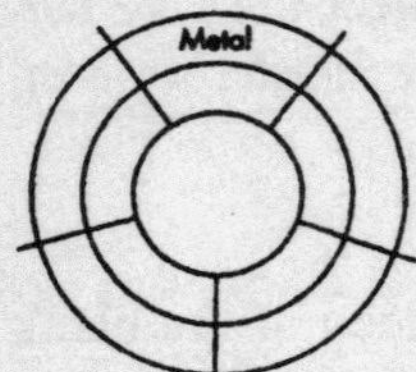

Step 4: Take your blank copy of the Life Cycle Chart and write the name of the Kuan Tai Element in the outer band at the top of the circular disc. If the Kuan Tai falls between two Elements, write both their names neatly side by side in the same space. The example shows exactly where to position the element(s) on the disc.

Step 5: Next write the names of the other four Elements (or three if you have found two elements in Step 3) in the outer

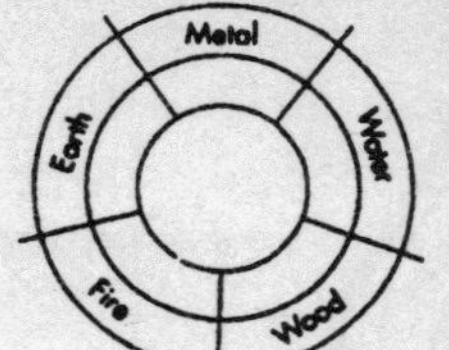

band. Work clockwise and follow their usual productive order – that is Wood, Fire, Earth, Metal and then back to Water again.

So in the example Metal is followed by Water, Wood, Fire then Earth.

Step 6: Next to each Element, write its rating, that is, the number of times it occurs in the Element Totals box.

As a check, the total of the ratings for all the Elements together should add up to 12.

Step 7: Next find the position of the Fate Force. Refer to your horoscope notes earlier in this section. Note the Element of the Branch of the Year (at the letter X in the blank example on the previous page). This is the Element of Fate.

Step 8: Write the word 'Fate' in the inner band on the Life Cycle Chart, placing it under its appropriate Element.

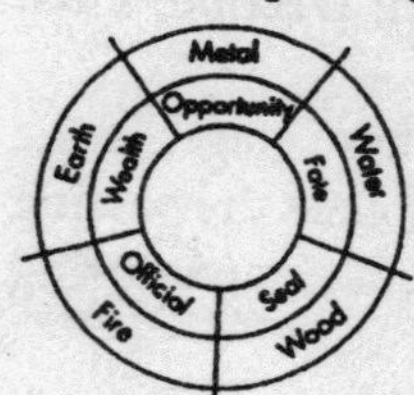

Step 9: Complete the Life Cycle Chart by writing the names of each of the remaining four Forces on the inner band, working round in a clockwise direction.

Step 10: As a double check, use the guide below.

> **If the Fate is in Wood,** then the Seal is in Fire, the Official in Earth, the Wealth in Metal and the Opportunity in Water.
>
> **If the Fate is in Fire,** then the Seal is in Earth, the Official in Metal, the Wealth in Water and the Opportunity in Wood.
>
> **If the Fate is in Earth,** then the Seal is in Metal, the Official in Water, the Wealth in Wood and the Opportunity in Fire.
>
> **If the Fate is in Metal,** then the Seal is in Water, the Official in Wood, the Wealth in Fire and the Opportunity in Earth.
>
> **If the Fate is in Water,** then the Seal is in Wood, the Official in Fire, the Wealth in Earth and the Opportunity in Metal.

How the Life Cycle Chart Works

William Shakespeare wrote of the 'Seven Ages of Man' but Chinese philosophers chose instead to divide the life-span into 12,

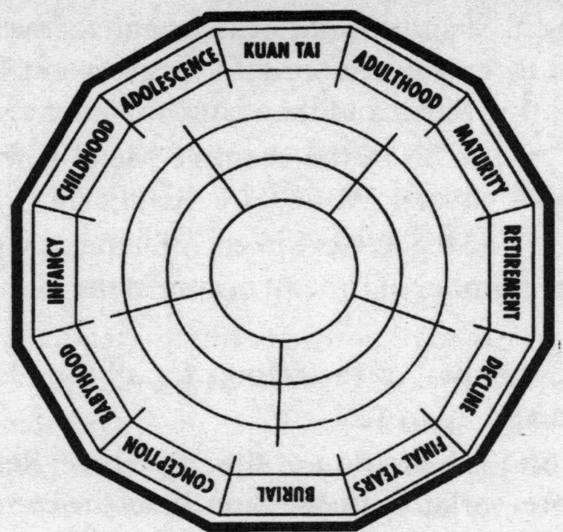

including one stage before conception and another after death. The 12 stages are as follows:

Conception: Babyhood; Infancy; Childhood; Adolescence; *Kuan Tai;* Adulthood; Maturity; Retirement; Decline; Final Years; Burial.

For the Chinese, the most important of these stages is the *Kuan Tai,* meaning Matriculation. This symbolizes the passing from youth into adulthood. For most people it occurs during their early twenties.

The Five Forces

The basic principle behind the Life Cycle Chart is that of the *Five Forces* or Aspects of Destiny. They are called the *Fate,* the *Seal,* the *Official,* the *Wealth* and the *Opportunity.* During a person's life, each of the Five Forces reigns in turn, the Fate followed by the Seal, the Seal by the Official and so on. But the exact time when each Force exerts its influence varies.

The timing of the Fate is the key factor. It may occur during any of the 12 stages of life, for example, during 'Babyhood' or even at the 'Burial'. Basically, the Fate determines a person's destiny and whether success is likely. Chinese astrologers stress, though, that what is done with any gifts bestowed is up to the individual. If the benefits of the Fate are used well, then the Seal, representing home and happiness, will reveal this.

However, someone with no Fate-endowed gifts can certainly

lead a purposeful and happy life – the Seal also shows this.

The Official reveals public recognition of a person's work or talents, promotion to high office or the inheritance of a title.

Wealth is what it says, and indicates when people will be richer or poorer during their lifetimes. Finally, the Opportunity provides a chance to change direction in life.

Forces And The Elements

Just as the Five Forces follow each other through life, so do the Five Elements, in their usual productive order.

The Five Forces usually coincide with the Elements, but occasionally the periods of time ruled by each Force may fall under the influence of a single Element and then merge into another. For example, the Seal period could begin with the influence of Wood falling away, and the continue with the strengthening influence of Fire, the Element that follows.

Element Ratings

While the Element indicates the form the Force is likely to take, its rating shows whether its influence is likely to be powerful, moderate or negligible.

If the element rating is low, then the influence of the complementary Force can be disregarded. On the other hand, a powerful Element rating may have no effect, and be virtually 'wasted' if the Force occurs at an inconvenient time in life. For example, if Wood (creativity) has a high rating and is associated with the Fate, this can indicate a gifted artist. But if the Fate occurs at the time of Burial, then these talents would, unfortunately, never be used.

To Interpret the Life Cycle Chart

To interpret the filled-in chart, consider the Forces in relation to their associated Elements, the ratings of those Elements, and the stages in life when the Forces exert their influence.

The Five Forces

FATE is the key to the Life Cycle. It shows the moment of life when destiny is determined. The greater the rating of its associated Element, the greater the destiny.

SEAL is the 'seal of approval' on life and happiness. A person may be of humble origins and means, yet if the Seal has a high rating, the life will be contented, healthy and happy.

WEALTH shows financial success. At the beginning of life, it reveals an inheritance; at the end of life, it indicates that a bequest will be left. The associated Element shows the likely source.

OPPORTUNITY shows when life can take a new direction. The best period in life for the Opportunity to appear is in early adulthood, after the Kuan Tai. If it appears in childhood, it points to a continuation of family traditions.

OFFICIAL shows public recognition. At the beginning of life, it indicates someone born into a noble family; at the end of life, it shows honours for the subject's work.

The Five Elements

WOOD signifies the family, health, marriage, and creativity. In the professions, it is associated with crops and horticulture. If weak, it denotes ill-health and needs Water to compensate.

FIRE shows matters to do with changes through heat – for example the oven or forge. It also concerns livestock and intellect.

EARTH refers to the land – property, civil engineering, building and so on. At the beginning of life, it indicates the inheritance of property; at the end of life, it shows one who leaves property.

METAL represents both the gold coin and the sword, and so concerns both trade and military activity. It is best for Metal to appear towards the end of life, rather than at the beginning – then it shows wealth which is acquired, rather than lost.

WATER shows communication and travel. People born in foreign countries often have strong Water at the start of life; those likely to emigrate may find a high Water rating in Fate. Water at the end of life is often the sign of a writer.

Step-by-Step Guide

At first, the calculations for drawing up a Chinese horoscope may seem long and complicated. But with practice you should

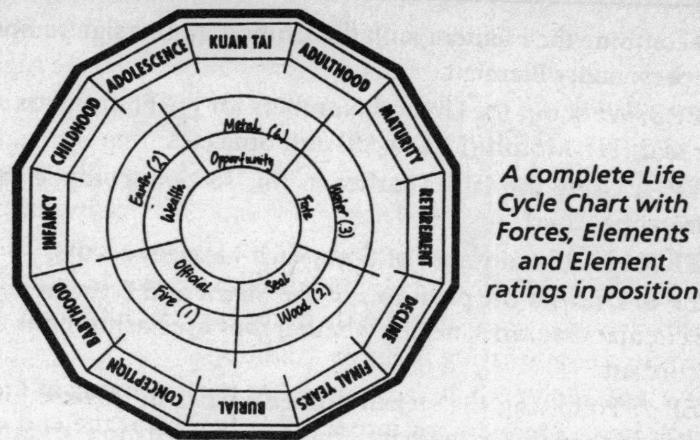

A complete Life Cycle Chart with Forces, Elements and Element ratings in position

be able to convert the date to the Chinese calendar, assemble the basic horoscope data, calculate the Stems, Branches and Elements and even construct a Life Cycle Chart in about 20 minutes.

However, interpreting the horoscope is something that will only come after a number of attempts, for each person's horoscope is virtually unique. Your understanding of the rise and fall of the elements will also increase the more you cast horoscopes. A useful ploy, once you have drawn up horoscopes for friends, is to talk them through the various aspects and take note of their comments to see whether you are on the right track.

On page 303 is a full blank chart for you to copy or photocopy. The instructions below describe how to fill in and interpret the chart step by step, given that you are already familiar with the rest of both this and the Chinese Astrology course.

Completing Your Horoscope

Before you start you will need a notepad and a photocopy or hand-drawn copy of the blank horoscope chart. Then follow these steps:

STEP 1: Begin by heading the chart with the name of the person and then add the western date and time of birth.

STEP 2: Convert the western date of birth to the Chinese date following the method outlined earlier in this section. Now you can combine the Element with the Chinese zodiac sign to find the personality Element.

STEP 3: Work out the Cyclical Numbers for the Four Pillars of the Year (H), Month (I), Day (E) and time (G).

STEP 4: Using the tables earlier in this section, compile the Horoscope Chart.

STEP 5: Note the number of times each Element occurs.

STEP 6: Draw in the positions of the Stems and Branches on the circular diagrams, noting whether they are harmonious or discordant.

STEP 7: Following the steps outlined earlier in this section, construct the Life Cycle Chart. You are now ready to start analysing the horoscope in depth.

Step-by-Step Interpretation

Take the completed horoscope and work through the following steps carefully:

STEP 1: From the sections on the twelve animals of the Chinese Zodiac you will be able to make character assessments based on the year of birth and hour of birth.

STEP 2: Use the sections on the Element-Animal combinations to add more detailed and specific comments.

STEP 3: From the ratings of the Elements in the Horoscope Chart, you should be able to comment on the significance of the proportions of the Elements.

STEP 4: Examine the Stems in the Chart, noting if they form sequences and whether they are significant.

STEP 5: Next look at the Branches, noting if they are harmonious or discordant and whether this is significant.

STEP 6: Finally, turn to the Life Cycle Chart and make a note of the position of the Five Forces, the related Elements and their ratings. Interpret according to the guidelines given earlier.

What Our Sample for 'Dorothy Best' Reveals

From the data given in the sample horoscope, you will see there are no sequences in the Stems. The Branches II:X are

A Sample Horoscope

Name: Dorothy Best
Date of Birth: 3rd February, 1953
Time: Not known: use noon
A: 3
B: (February) 31
C: (1953) 48
D: (Not leap year) 0
E: 3+31 +48 = 82; 82−60 = 22
F: (22, last digit) 2
G: (noon x 2) 19
H: (See 1952 row) 29
I: January 15 50

Year = H = 29
Month = I = 50
Day = E = 22
Time = G = 19

Life Cycle Chart

Y = 9; Z = II
Kuan Tai/Matriculation Element = Metal/Water
Burial = Fire
Fate Element = Year Branch Element = Earth
Position of Fate = Childhood
Elements pertaining to the Five Forces:
Fate/Earth (2); Seal/Metal (1);
Official/Water (5); Wealth/Wood (3);
Opportunity/Fire (1)

harmonious, indicating reliability (II) and success in personal ambitions (X). But X and VII are unfavourable, suggesting difficulties with male competitors, as VII represents masculine attitudes.

The Elements are all present in the chart, indicating a well-balanced personality. The emphasis is on Water, showing much communication and travelling. Wood has a good rating, revealing creative ability. This means that Dorothy has all the necessary qualities for her job as a writer for women's magazines.

Chinese Horoscope Chart		Time G	Day E	Month I	Year H
Stem	J	9	2	10	9(Y)
Branch	K	VII	X	II(Z)	V
Stem Element	L	Water	Wood	Water	Water
Branch Element	M	Fire	Metal	Earth	Wood
Stem-and-Branch Element	N	Wood	Water	Wood	Water

ELEMENT TOTALS

WOOD	FIRE	EARTH	METAL	WATER
3	1	2	1	5

In the Life Cycle Chart, Fate is in early life, in Earth, suggesting that her parents were comfortably off. The Seal, in Metal, is also in early life – the lowest Element rating, suggesting that the period shortly after leaving school was memorable in some way, if not unhappy. She may even have had a broken engagement.

The Official is in Water in early adulthood, with a high rating. This reveals that Dorothy very soon found her niche in life and was recognized for her abilities. Wealth, in retirement, shows that she will be financially secure. Finally, Opportunity is in Burial, showing that she achieves her successes in life largely through her own efforts.

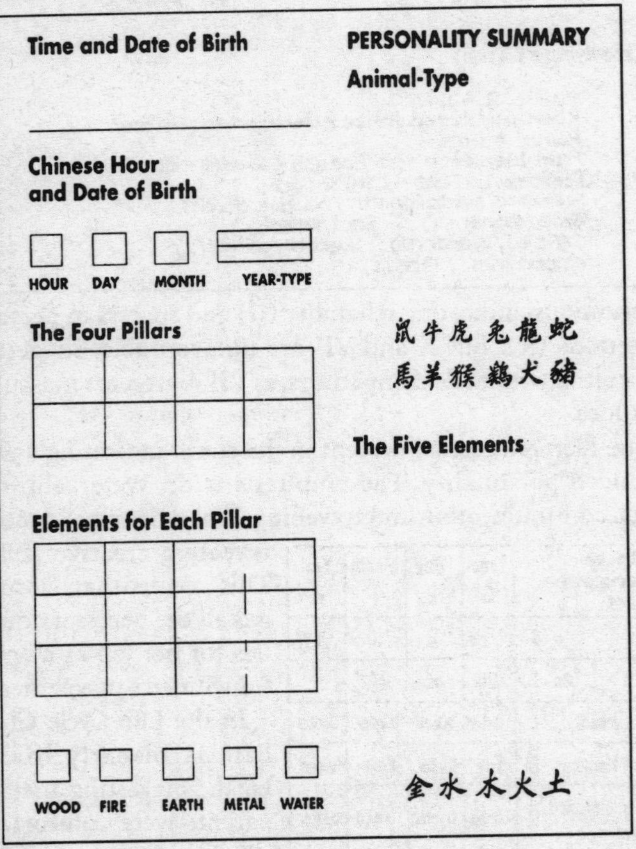

Time and Date of Birth

PERSONALITY SUMMARY

Animal-Type

Chinese Hour and Date of Birth

HOUR	DAY	MONTH	YEAR-TYPE

The Four Pillars

鼠牛虎 兎龍蛇
馬羊猴 鷄犬豬

The Five Elements

Elements for Each Pillar

WOOD	FIRE	EARTH	METAL	WATER

金水 木火土

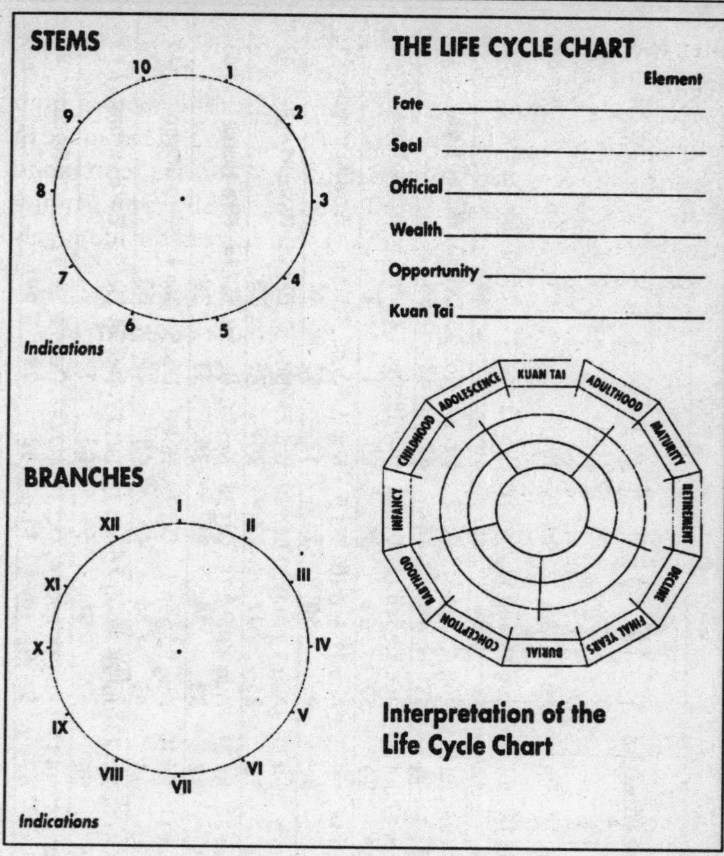
STEMS
10
1
2
3
4
5
6
7
8
9
Indications
BRANCHES
I
II
III
IV
V
VI
VII
VIII
IX
X
XI
XII
Indications
THE LIFE CYCLE CHART
Element
Fate
Seal
Official
Wealth
Opportunity
Kuan Tai
KUAN TAI
ADULTHOOD
MATURITY
RETIREMENT
DECLINE
FINAL YEARS
BURIAL
CONCEPTION
BABYHOOD
INFANCY
CHILDHOOD
ADOLESCENCE
Interpretation of the
Life Cycle Chart

The Chinese Calendar
The Lunar Numbers for the Chinese Months

1st month		*2nd*	*3rd*	*4th*	*5th*	*6th*	*7th*	*8th*	*9th*	*10th*	*11th*	*12th*	*Year Type*	*Year Cyclical Number*
Feb 19 **27**	**1901**	Mar 20 **28**	Apr 19 **29**	May 18 **30**	Jun 16 **31**	Jul 16 **32**	Aug 14 **33**	Sep 13 **34**	Oct 12 **35**	Nov 11 **36**	Dec 11 **37**	Jan 10 **38**	**Metal-Ox**	38
Feb 8 **39**	**1902**	Mar 10 **40**	Apr 8 **41**	May 8 **42**	Jun 6 **43**	Jul 5 **44**	Aug 4 **45**	Sep 2 **46**	Oct 2 **46**	Oct 31 **47**	Nov 30 **48**	Dec 30 **50**	**Water-Tiger**	39
Jan 29 **51**	**1903**	Feb 27 **52**	Mar 29 **53**	Apr 27 **54**	May 27 **55***	Jul 24 **56**	Aug 23 **57**	Sep 21 **58**	Oct 20 **59**	Nov 19 **60**	Dec 19 **1**	Jan 17 **2**	**Water-Hare**	40
Feb 16 **3**	**1904**	Mar 17 **4**	Apr 16 **5**	May 15 **6**	Jun 14 **7**	Jul 13 **8**	Aug 11 **9**	Sep 10 **10**	Oct 9 **11**	Nov 7 **12**	Dec 7 **13**	Jan 6 **14**	**Wood-Dragon**	41
Feb 4 **15**	**1905**	Mar 6 **16**	Apr 5 **17**	May 4 **18**	Jun 3 **19**	Jul 3 **20**	Aug 1 **21**	Aug 30 **22**	Sep 29 **23**	Oct 28 **24**	Nov 27 **25**	Dec 26 **26**	**Wood-Snake**	42
Jan 25 **27**	**1906**	Feb 23 **28**	Mar 25 **29**	Apr 24 **30**	Jun 22 **31**	Jul 21 **32**	Aug 20 **33**	Sep 18 **34**	Oct 18 **35**	Nov 16 **36**	Dec 16 **37**	Jan 14 **38**	**Fire-Horse**	43
Feb 13 **39**	**1907**	Mar 14 **40**	Apr 13 **41**	May 12 **42**	Jun 11 **43**	Jul 10 **44**	Aug 9 **45**	Sep 8 **46**	Oct 7 **47**	Nov 6 **48**	Dec 5 **49**	Jan 4 **50**	**Fire-Sheep**	44
Feb 2 **51**	**1908**	Mar 3 **52**	Apr 1 **53**	Apr 30 **54**	May 30 **55**	Jun 29 **56**	Jul 28 **57**	Aug 27 **58**	Sep 25 **59**	Oct 25 **60**	Nov 24 **1**	Dec 23 **2**	**Earth-Monkey**	45
Jan 22 **3**	**1909**	Feb 20 **4***	Apr 20 **5**	May 19 **6**	Jun 18 **7**	Jul 17 **8**	Aug 16 **9**	Sep 14 **10**	Oct 14 **11**	Nov 13 **12**	Dec 13 **13**	Jan 11 **14**	**Earth-Rooster**	46

Feb 10 **15**	**1910**	Mar 11 **16**	Apr 10 **17**	May 9 **18**	Jun 7 **19**	Jul 7 **20**	Aug 5 **21**	Sep 4 **22**	Oct 3 **23**	Nov 2 **24**	Dec 2 **25**	Jan 1 **26**	**Metal-Dog** 47
Jan 30 **27**	**1911**	Mar 1 **28**	Mar 30 **29**	Apr 29 **30**	May 28 **31**	Jun 26 **32***	Aug 24 **33**	Sep 22 **34**	Oct 22 **35**	Nov 21 **36**	Dec 20 **37**	Jan 19 **38**	**Metal-Pig** 48
Feb 18 **39**	**1912**	Mar 19 **40**	Apr 17 **41**	May 17 **42**	Jun 15 **43**	Jul 14 **44**	Aug 13 **45**	Sep 11 **46**	Oct 10 **47**	Nov 9 **48**	Dec 9 **49**	Jan 7 **50**	**Water-Rat** 49
Feb 6 **51**	**1913**	Mar 8 **52**	Apr 7 **53**	May 6 **54**	Jun 5 **55**	Jul 4 **56**	Aug 2 **57**	Sep 1 **58**	Sep 30 **59**	Oct 29 **60**	Nov 28 **1**	Dec 27 **2**	**Water-Ox** 50
Jan 26 **3**	**1914**	Feb 25 **4**	Mar 27 **5**	Apr 25 **6**	May 25 **7***	Jul 23 **8**	Aug 21 **9**	Sep 20 **10**	Oct 19 **11**	Nov 18 **12**	Dec 17 **13**	Jan 15 **14**	**Wood-Tiger** 51
Feb 14 **15**	**1915**	Mar 16 **16**	Apr 14 **17**	May 14 **18**	Jun 13 **19**	Jul 12 **20**	Aug 11 **21**	Sep 9 **22**	Oct 9 **23**	Nov 7 **24**	Dec 7 **25**	Jan 5 **26**	**Wood-Hare** 52
Feb 3 **27**	**1916**	Mar 4 **28**	Apr 3 **29**	May 2 **30**	Jun 1 **31**	Jun 30 **32**	Jul 30 **33**	Aug 30 **34**	Sep 27 **35**	Oct 27 **36**	Nov 25 **37**	Dec 25 **38**	**Fire-Dragon** 53
Jan 23 **39**	**1917**	Feb 22 **40***	Apr 21 **41**	May 21 **42**	Jun 19 **43**	Jul 19 **44**	Aug 18 **45**	Sep 16 **46**	Oct 16 **47**	Nov 15 **48**	Dec 14 **49**	Jan 13 **50**	**Fire-Snake** 54
Feb 11 **51**	**1918**	Mar 13 **52**	Apr 11 **53**	May 10 **54**	Jun 9 **55**	Jul 8 **56**	Aug 7 **57**	Sep 5 **58**	Oct 5 **59**	Nov 4 **60**	Dec 3 **1**	Jan 2 **2**	**Earth-Horse** 55
Feb 1 **3**	**1919**	Mar 2 **4**	Apr 1 **5**	Apr 30 **6**	May 29 **7**	Jun 28 **8**	Jul 27 **9***	Sep 24 **10**	Oct 24 **11**	Nov 22 **12**	Dec 22 **13**	Jan 21 **14**	**Earth-Sheep** 56
Feb 20 **15**	**1920**	Mar 20 **16**	Apr 19 **17**	May 18 **18**	Jun 16 **19**	Jul 16 **20**	Aug 14 **21**	Sep 12 **22**	Oct 12 **23**	Nov 11 **24**	Dec 10 **25**	Jan 9 **26**	**Metal-Monkey** 57

(*denotes an intercalary month, i.e. the month is 'repeated' in order to bring the calendar into line with the seaons of the year, so accounting for what appears to be an inordinately long month)

The Chinese Calendar

The Lunar Numbers for the Chinese Months

1st month		*2nd*	*3rd*	*4th*	*5th*	*6th*	*7th*	*8th*	*9th*	*10th*	*11th*	*12th*	*Year Type*	*Year Cyclical Number*
Feb 8 **27**	**1921**	Mar 10 **28**	Apr 8 **29**	May 8 **30**	Jun 6 **31**	Jul 5 **32**	Aug 4 **33**	Sep 2 **34**	Oct 1 **35**	Oct 31 **36**	Nov 29 **37**	Dec 29 **38**	**Metal-Rooster**	58
Jan 28 **39**	**1922**	Feb 27 **40**	Mar 28 **41**	Apr 27 **42**	May 27 **43***	Jul 24 **44**	Aug 23 **45**	Sep 21 **46**	Oct 20 **47**	Nov 19 **48**	Dec 18 **49**	Jan 17 **50**	**Water-Dog**	59
Feb 16 **51**	**1923**	Mar 17 **52**	Apr 16 **53**	May 16 **54**	Jun 14 **55**	Jul 14 **56**	Aug 12 **57**	Sep 11 **58**	Oct 10 **59**	Nov 8 **60**	Dec 8 **1**	Jan 6 **2**	**Water-Pig**	60
Feb 5 **3**	**1924**	Mar 6 **4**	Apr 4 **5**	May 4 **6**	Jun 2 **7**	Jul 2 **8**	Aug 1 **9**	Aug 30 **10**	Sep 29 **11**	Oct 28 **12**	Nov 27 **13**	Dec 26 **14**	**Wood-Rat**	1
Jan 25 **15**	**1925**	Feb 23 **16**	Mar 24 **17**	Apr 23 **18**	Jun 21 **19**	Jul 21 **20**	Aug 19 **21**	Sep 18 **22**	Oct 18 **23**	Nov 16 **24**	Dec 16 **25**	Jan 14 **26**	**Wood-Ox**	2
Feb 13 **27**	**1926**	Mar 14 **28**	Apr 12 **29**	May 12 **30**	Jun 10 **31**	Jul 10 **32**	Aug 8 **33**	Sep 7 **34**	Oct 7 **35**	Nov 5 **36**	Dec 5 **37**	Jan 4 **38**	**Fire-Tiger**	3
Feb 2 **39**	**1927**	Mar 4 **40**	Apr 2 **41**	May 1 **42**	May 31 **43**	Jun 29 **44**	Jul 29 **45**	Aug 27 **46**	Sep 26 **47**	Oct 26 **48**	Nov 24 **49**	Dec 24 **50**	**Fire-Rabbit**	4
Jan 23 **51**	**1928**	Feb 21 **52***	Apr 20 **53**	May 19 **54**	Jun 18 **55**	Jul 17 **56**	Aug 15 **57**	Sep 14 **58**	Oct 13 **59**	Nov 12 **60**	Dec 12 **1**	Jan 11 **2**	**Earth-Dragon**	5
Feb 10 **3**	**1929**	Mar 11 **4**	Apr 10 **5**	May 9 **6**	Jun 7 **7**	Jul 7 **8**	Aug 5 **9**	Sep 3 **10**	Oct 3 **11**	Nov 1 **12**	Dec 1 **13**	Dec 31 **14**	**Earth-Snake**	6

Jan 30	**1930**	Feb 28	Mar 30	Apr 29	May 28	Jun 26	Aug 24	Sep 22	Oct 2	Nov 20	Dec 20	Jan 19	**Metal-Horse**	7
15		**16**	**17**	**18**	**19**	**20***	**21**	**22**	**23**	**24**	**25**	**26**		
Feb 17	**1931**	Mar 19	Apr 18	May 17	Jun 16	Jul 15	Aug 14	Sep 12	Oct 11	Nov 10	Dec 9	Jan 8	**Metal-Sheep**	8
27		**28**	**29**	**30**	**31**	**32**	**33**	**34**	**35**	**46**	**37**	**38**		
Feb 6	**1932**	Mar 7	Apr 6	May 6	Jun 4	Jul 4	Aug 2	Sep 1	Sep 30	Oct 29	Nov 28	Dec 27	**Water-Monkey**	9
39		**40**	**41**	**42**	**43**	**44**	**45**	**46**	**47**	**48**	**49**	**50**		
Jan 26	**1933**	Feb 24	Mar 26	Apr 25	May 24	Jul 23	Aug 21	Sep 20	Oct 19	Nov 18	Dec 17	Jan 15	**Water-Rooster**	10
51		**52**	**53**	**54**	**55***	**56**	**57**	**58**	**59**	**60**	**1**	**2**		
Feb 14	**1934**	Mar 15	Apr 14	May 13	Jun 12	Jul 12	Aug 10	Sep 9	Oct 8	Nov 7	Dec 7	Jan 5	**Wood-Dog**	11
3		**4**	**5**	**6**	**7**	**8**	**9**	**10**	**11**	**12**	**13**	**14**		
Feb 4	**1935**	Mar 5	Apr 3	May 3	Jun 1	Jul 1	Jul 30	Aug 29	Sep 28	Oct 27	Nov 26	Dec 26	**Wood-Pig**	12
15		**16**	**17**	**18**	**19**	**20**	**21**	**22**	**23**	**24**	**25**	**26**		
Jan 24	**1936**	Feb 23	Mar 23	May 21	Jun 19	Jul 18	Aug 17	Sep 16	Oct 15	Nov 14	Dec 14	Jan 13	**Fire-Rat**	13
27		**28**	**29***	**30**	**31**	**32**	**33**	**34**	**35**	**36**	**37**	**38**		
Feb 11	**1937**	Mar 13	Apr 11	May 10	Jun 9	Jul 8	Aug 6	Sep 5	Oct 4	Nov 3	Dec 3	Jan 2	**Fire-Ox**	14
39		**40**	**41**	**42**	**43**	**44**	**45**	**46**	**47**	**48**	**49**	**50**		
Jan 31	**1938**	Mar 2	Apr 1	Apr 30	May 29	Jun 28	Jul 27	Sep 24	Oct 23	Nov 22	Dec 22	Jan 20	**Earth-Tiger**	15
51		**52**	**53**	**54**	**55**	**56**	**57***	**58**	**59**	**60**	**1**	**2**		
Feb 19	**1939**	Mar 21	Apr 20	May 19	Jun 17	Jul 17	Aug 15	Sep 13	Oct 13	Nov 11	Dec 11	Jan 9	**Earth-Hare**	16
3		**4**	**5**	**6**	**7**	**8**	**9**	**10**	**11**	**12**	**13**	**14**		
Feb 8	**1940**	Mar 9	Apr 8	May 7	Jun 6	Jul 5	Aug 4	Sep 2	Oct 1	Oct 31	Nov 29	Dec 29	**Metal-Dragon**	17
15		**16**	**17**	**18**	**19**	**20**	**21**	**22**	**23**	**24**	**25**	**26**		

(*denotes an intercalary month, i.e. the month is 'repeated' in order to bring the calendar into line with the seasons of the year, so asccounting for what appears to be an inordinately long month).

The Chinese Calendar

The Lunar Numbers for the Chinese Months

1st month		*2nd*	*3rd*	*4th*	*5th*	*6th*	*7th*	*8th*	*9th*	*10th*	*11th*	*12th*	*Year Type*	*Year Cyclical Number*
Jan 27 **27**	**1941**	Feb 26 **28**	Mar 28 **29**	Apr 26 **30**	May 26 **31**	Jun 25 **32***	Aug 23 **33**	Sep 21 **34**	Oct 20 **35**	Nov 19 **36**	Dec 18 **37**	Jan 17 **38**	**Metal-Snake**	18
Feb 15 **39**	**1942**	Mar 17 **40**	Apr 15 **41**	May 15 **42**	Jun 14 **43**	Jul 13 **44**	Aug 12 **45**	Sep 10 **46**	Oct 10 **47**	Nov 8 **48**	Dec 8 **49**	Jan 6 **50**	**Water-Horse**	19
Feb 5 **51**	**1943**	Mar 6 **52**	Apr 5 **53**	May 4 **54**	Jun 3 **55**	Jul 2 **56**	Aug 1 **57**	Aug 31 **58**	Sep 29 **59**	Oct 29 **60**	Nov 27 **1**	Dec 27 **2**	**Water-Sheep**	20
Jan 25 **3**	**1944**	Feb 24 **4**	Mar 24 **5**	Apr 23 **6**	Jun 21 **7***	Jul 20 **8**	Aug 19 **9**	Sep 17 **10**	Oct 17 **11**	Nov 16 **12**	Dec 15 **13**	Jan 14 **14**	**Wood-Monkey**	21
Feb 13 **15**	**1945**	Mar 14 **16**	Apr 12 **17**	May 12 **18**	Jun 10 **19**	Jul 9 **20**	Aug 8 **21**	Sept 6 **22**	Oct 6 **23**	Nov 5 **24**	Dec 5 **25**	Jan 3 **26**	**Wood-Rooster**	22
Feb 2 **27**	**1946**	Mar 4 **28**	Apr 2 **29**	May 1 **30**	May 31 **31**	Jun 29 **32**	Jul 28 **33**	Aug 27 **34**	Sep 25 **35**	Oct 25 **36**	Nov 24 **37**	Dec 23 **38**	**Fire-Dog**	23
Jan 22 **39**	**1947**	Feb 21 **40***	Apr 21 **41**	May 20 **42**	Jun 19 **43**	Jul 18 **44**	Aug 16 **45**	Sep 15 **46**	Oct 14 **47**	Nov 13 **48**	Dec 12 **49**	Jan 11 **50**	**Fire-Pig**	24
Feb 10 **51**	**1948**	Mar 11 **52**	Apr 9 **53**	May 9 **54**	Jun 7 **55**	Jul 7 **56**	Aug 5 **57**	Sep 3 **58**	Oct 3 **59**	Nov 1 **60**	Dec 1 **1**	Dec 30 **2**	**Earth-Rat**	25
Jan 29 **3**	**1949**	Feb 28 **4**	Mar 29 **5**	Apr 28 **6**	May 28 **7**	Jun 26 **8**	Jul 26 **9***	Sep 22 **10**	Oct 22 **11**	Nov 20 **12**	Dec 20 **13**	Jan 18 **14**	**Earth-Ox**	26
Feb 17 **15**	**1950**	Mar 18 **16**	Apr 17 **17**	May 17 **18**	Jun 15 **19**	Jul 15 **20**	Aug 14 **21**	Sep 21 **22**	Oct 11 **23**	Nov 10 **24**	Dec 9 **25**	Jan 8 **26**	**Metal-Tiger**	27

Feb 6 **27**	**1951**	Mar 8 **28**	Apr 6 **29**	May 6 **30**	Jun 5 **31**	Jul 4 **32**	Aug 3 **33**	Sep 1 **34**	Oct 1 **35**	Oct 30 **36**	Nov 29 **37**	Dec 28 **38**	**Metal-Hare**	28
Jan 27 **39**	**1952**	Feb 25 **40**	Mar 26 **41**	Apr 24 **42**	May 24 **43***	Jul 22 **44**	Aug 20 **45**	Sep 19 **46**	Oct 19 **47**	Nov 17 **48**	Dec 17 **49**	Jan 15 **50**	**Water-Dragon**	29
Feb 14 **51**	**1953**	Mar 15 **52**	Apr 14 **53**	May 13 **54**	Jun 11 **55**	Jul 11 **56**	Aug 9 **57**	Sep 8 **58**	Oct 8 **59**	Nov 7 **60**	Dec 6 **1**	Jan 5 **2**	**Water-Snake**	30
Feb 3 **3**	**1954**	Mar 5 **4**	Apr 4 **5**	May 3 **6**	Jun 1 **7**	Jun 30 **8**	Jul 30 **9**	Aug 28 **10**	Sep 27 **11**	Oct 27 **12**	Nov 25 **13**	Dec 25 **14**	**Wood-Horse**	31
Jan 24 **15**	**1955**	Feb 22 **16**	Mar 24 **17***	May 22 **18**	Jun 20 **19**	Jul 19 **20**	Aug 18 **21**	Sep 16 **22**	Oct 16 **23**	Nov 14 **24**	Dec 14 **25**	Jan 13 **26**	**Wood-Sheep**	32
Feb 12 **27**	**1956**	Mar 12 **28**	Apr 11 **29**	May 10 **30**	Jun 9 **31**	Jul 8 **32**	Aug 6 **33**	Sep 5 **34**	Oct 4 **35**	Nov 3 **36**	Dec 2 **37**	Jan 1 **38**	**Fire-Monkey**	33
Jan 31 **39**	**1957**	Mar 2 **40**	Mar 31 **41**	Apr 30 **42**	May 29 **43**	Jun 28 **44**	Jul 27 **45**	Aug 25 **46***	Oct 23 **47**	Nov 22 **48**	Dec 21 **49**	Jan 20 **50**	**Fire-Rooster**	34
Feb 18 **51**	**1958**	Mar 20 **52**	Apr 19 **53**	May 19 **54**	Jun 17 **55**	Jul 17 **56**	Aug 15 **57**	Sep 13 **58**	Oct 13 **59**	Nov 11 **60**	Dec 11 **1**	Jan 9 **2**	**Earth-Dog**	35
Feb 8 **3**	**1959**	Mar 9 **4**	Apr 8 **5**	May 8 **6**	Jun 6 **7**	Jul 6 **8**	Aug 4 **9**	Sep 3 **10**	Oct 2 **11**	Nov 1 **12**	Dec 1 **13**	Dec 30 **14**	**Earth-Pig**	36
Jan 28 **15**	**1960**	Feb 27 **16**	Mar 27 **17**	Apr 26 **18**	May 25 **19**	Jun 24 **20***	Aug 22 **21**	Sep 21 **22**	Oct 20 **23**	Nov 19 **24**	Dec 18 **25**	Jan 17 **26**	**Metal-Rat**	37
Feb 15 **27**	**1961**	Mar 17 **28**	Apr 15 **29**	May 15 **30**	Jun 13 **31**	Jul 13 **32**	Aug 11 **33**	Sep 10 **34**	Oct 10 **35**	Nov 8 **36**	Dec 9 **37**	Jan 6 **38**	**Metal-Ox**	38

(*denotes an intercalary month, i.e. the month is 'repeated' in order to bring the calendar into line with the seasons of the year, so accounting for what appears to be an inordinately long month)

The Chinese Calendar

The Lunar Numbers for the Chinese Months

1st month		*2nd*	*3rd*	*4th*	*5th*	*6th*	*7th*	*8th*	*9th*	*10th*	*11th*	*12th*	*Year Type*	*Year Cyclical Number*
Feb 15 **27**	**1961**	Mar 17 **28**	Apr 15 **29**	May 15 **30**	Jun 13 **31**	Jul 13 **32**	Aug 11 **33**	Sep 10 **34**	Oct 10 **35**	Nov 8 **36**	Dec 9 **37**	Jan 6 **38**	**Metal-Ox**	38
Feb 5 **39**	**1962**	Mar 6 **40**	Apr 5 **41**	May 4 **42**	Jun 2 **43**	Jul 2 **44**	Jul 31 **45**	Aug 30 **46**	Sep 29 **47**	Oct 28 **48**	Nov 27 **49**	Dec 27 **50**	**Water-Tiger**	39
Jan 25 **51**	**1963**	Feb 24 **52**	Mar 25 **53**	Apr 24 **54**	Jun 21 **55**	Jul 21 **56**	Aug 19 **57**	Sep 18 **58**	Oct 17 **59**	Nov 16 **60**	Dec 16 **1**	Jan 15 **2**	**Water-Hare**	40
Feb 13 **3**	**1964**	Mar 14 **4**	Apr 12 **5**	May 12 **6**	Jun 10 **7***	Jul 9 **8**	Aug 8 **9**	Sept 6 **10**	Oct 6 **11**	Nov 4 **12**	Dec 4 **13**	Jan 3 **14**	**Wood-Dragon**	41
Feb 2 **15**	**1965**	Mar 3 **16**	Apr 2 **17**	May 1 **18**	May 31 **19**	Jun 29 **20**	Jul 28 **21**	Aug 27 **22**	Sep 25 **23**	Oct 24 **24**	Nov 23 **25**	Dec 23 **26**	**Wood-Snake**	42
Jan 21 **27**	**1966**	Feb 20 **28**	Mar 22 **29**	May 20 **30**	Jun 19 **31**	Jul 18 **32**	Aug 16 **33**	Sep 15 **34**	Oct 14 **35**	Nov 12 **36**	Dec 12 **37**	Jan 11 **38**	**Fire-Horse**	43
Feb 9 **39**	**1967**	Mar 11 **40***	Apr 10 **41**	May 9 **42**	Jun 8 **43**	Jul 8 **44**	Aug 6 **45**	Sep 4 **46**	Oct 4 **47**	Nov 2 **48**	Dec 2 **49**	Dec 31 **50**	**Fire-Sheep**	44
Jan 30 **51**	**1968**	Feb 28 **52**	Mar 29 **53**	Apr 27 **54**	May 27 **55**	Jun 26 **56**	Jul 25 **57**	Sep 22 **58**	Oct 22 **59**	Nov 20 **60**	Dec 20 **1**	Jan 18 **2**	**Earth-Monkey**	45
Feb 17 **3**	**1969**	Mar 18 **4**	Apr 17 **5**	May 16 **6**	Jun 15 **7**	Jul 14 **8**	Aug 13 **9***	Sep 12 **10**	Oct 11 **11**	Nov 10 **12**	Dec 9 **13**	Jan 8 **14**	**Earth-Rooster**	46
Feb 6 **15**	**1970**	Mar 8 **16**	Apr 6 **17**	May 5 **18**	Jun 4 **19**	Jul 3 **20**	Aug 2 **21**	Sep 1 **22**	Sep 30 **23**	Oct 30 **24**	Nov 29 **25**	Dec 28 **26**	**Metal-Dog**	47

Jan 27 **27**	**1971**	Feb 25 **28**	Mar 27 **29**	Apr 25 **30**	May 24 **31**	Jul 22 **32**	Aug 21 **33**	Sep 19 **34**	Oct 19 **35**	Nov 18 **36**	Dec 18 **37**	Jan 16 **38**	**Metal-Pig** 48
Feb 15 **39**	**1972**	Mar 15 **40**	Apr 14 **41**	May 13 **42**	Jun 11 **43***	Jul 11 **44**	Aug 9 **45**	Sep 8 **46**	Oct 7 **47**	Nov 6 **48**	Dec 6 **49**	Jan 4 **50**	**Water-Rat** 49
Feb 3 **51**	**1973**	Mar 5 **52**	Apr 3 **53**	May 3 **54**	Jun 1 **55**	Jun 30 **56**	Jul 30 **57**	Aug 28 **58**	Sep 26 **59**	Oct 26 **60**	Nov 25 **1**	Dec 24 **2**	**Water-Ox** 50
Jan 23 **3**	**1974**	Feb 22 **4**	Mar 24 **5**	Apr 22 **6**	Jun 20 **7**	Jul 19 **8**	Aug 18 **9**	Sep 16 **10**	Oct 15 **11**	Nov 14 **12**	Dec 14 **13**	Jan 12 **14**	**Water-Tiger** 51
Feb 11 **15**	**1975**	Mar 13 **16**	Apr 12 **17***	May 11 **18**	Jun 10 **19**	Jul 9 **20**	Aug 7 **21**	Sep 6 **22**	Oct 5 **23**	Nov 3 **24**	Dec 3 **25**	Jan 1 **26**	**Water-Hare** 52
Jan 31 **27**	**1976**	Mar 1 **28**	Mar 31 **29**	Apr 29 **30**	May 29 **31**	Jun 27 **32**	Jul 27 **33**	Aug 25 **34**	Oct 23 **35**	Nov 21 **36**	Dec 21 **37**	Jan 19 **38**	**Water-Dragon** 53
Feb 18 **39**	**1977**	Mar 20 **40**	Apr 18 **41**	May 18 **42**	Jun 17 **43**	Jul 16 **44**	Aug 15 **45**	Sep 13 **46***	Oct 13 **47**	Nov 11 **48**	Dec 11 **49**	Jan 9 **50**	**Fire-Snake** 54
Feb 7 **51**	**1978**	Mar 9 **52**	Apr 7 **53**	May 7 **54**	Jun 6 **55**	Jul 5 **56**	Aug 4 **57**	Sep 2 **58**	Oct 2 **59**	Nov 1 **60**	Nov 30 **1**	Dec 30 **2**	**Earth-Horse** 55
Jan 28 **3**	**1979**	Feb 27 **4**	Mar 28 **5**	Apr 26 **6**	May 26 **7**	Jun 24 **8**	Aug 23 **9**	Sep 21 **10**	Oct 21 **11**	Nov 20 **12**	Dec 19 **13**	Jan 18 **14**	**Earth-Sheep** 56
Feb 16 **15**	**1980**	Mar 17 **16**	Apr 15 **17**	May 14 **18**	Jun 13 **19**	Jul 12 **20***	Aug 11 **21**	Sep 9 **22**	Oct 9 **23**	Nov 8 **24**	Dec 7 **25**	Jan 6 **26**	**Metal-Monkey** 57
Feb 5 **27**	**1981**	Mar 6 **28**	Apr 5 **29**	May 4 **30**	Jun 2 **31**	Jul 2 **32**	Jul 31 **33**	Aug 30 **34**	Sep 29 **35**	Oct 28 **36**	Nov 27 **37**	Dec 27 **38**	**Metal-Rooster** 58

(*denotes an intercalary month, i.e. the month is 'repeated' in order to bring the calendar into line with the seasons of the year, so accounting for what appears to be an inordinately long month)

The Chinese Calendar

The Lunar Numbers for the Chinese Months

1st month		*2nd*	*3rd*	*4th*	*5th*	*6th*	*7th*	*8th*	*9th*	*10th*	*11th*	*12th*	*Year Type*	*Year Cyclical Number*
Jan 25 **39**	**1982**	Feb 24 **40**	Mar 25 **41**	Apr 24 **42***	Jun 21 **43**	Jul 21 **44**	Aug 19 **45**	Sep 17 **46**	Oct 17 **47**	Nov 15 **48**	Dec 15 **49**	Jan 14 **50**	**Water-Dog**	59
Feb 13 **51**	**1983**	Mar 15 **52**	Apr 13 **53**	May 13 **54**	Jun 11 **55**	Jul 10 **56**	Aug 9 **57**	Sep 7 **58**	Oct 6 **59**	Nov 5 **60**	Dec 4 **1**	Jan 3 **2**	**Water-Pig**	60
Feb 2 **3**	**1984**	Mar 3 **4**	Apr 1 **5**	May 1 **6**	May 31 **7**	Jun 29 **8**	Jul 28 **9**	Aug 27 **10**	Sep 25 **11**	Oct 24 **12***	Dec 22 **13**	Jan 21 **14**	**Wood-Rat**	1
Feb 20 **15**	**1985**	Mar 21 **16**	Apr 20 **17**	May 20 **18**	Jun 18 **19**	Jul 18 **20**	Aug 16 **21**	Sep 15 **22**	Oct 14 **23**	Nov 12 **24**	Dec 12 **25**	Jan 10 **26**	**Wood-Ox**	2
Feb 9 **27**	**1986**	Mar 10 **28**	Apr 9 **29**	May 9 **30**	Jun 7 **31**	Jul 7 **32**	Aug 6 **33**	Sep 4 **34**	Oct 4 **35**	Nov 2 **36**	Dec 2 **37**	Dec 31 **38**	**Fire-Tiger**	3
Jan 29 **39**	**1987**	Feb 28 **40**	Mar 29 **41**	Apr 28 **42**	May 27 **43**	Jun 26 **44***	Aug 24 **45**	Sept 23 **46**	Oct 23 **47**	Nov 21 **48**	Dec 21 **49**	Jan 19 **50**	**Fire-Hare**	4
Feb 17 **51**	**1988**	Mar 18 **52**	Apr 16 **53**	May 16 **54**	Jun 14 **55**	Jul 14 **56**	Aug 12 **57**	Set 11 **58**	Oct 11 **59**	Nov 9 **60**	Dec 9 **1**	Jan 8 **2**	**Earth-Dragon**	5
Feb 6 **3**	**1989**	Mar 8 **4**	Apr 6 **5**	May 5 **6**	Jun 4 **7**	Jul 3 **8**	Aug 1 **9**	Aug 31 **10**	Sep 30 **11**	Oct 29 **12**	Nov 28 **13**	Dec 28 **14**	**Earth-Snake**	6
Jan 27 **15**	**1990**	Feb 25 **16**	Mar 27 **17**	Apr 25 **18**	May 24 **19***	Jul 22 **20**	Aug 20 **21**	Sep 19 **22**	Oct 18 **23**	Nov 17 **24**	Dec 17 **25**	Jan 16 **26**	**Metal-Horse**	7

Feb 15 **27**	**1991**	Mar 16 **28**	Apr 15 **29**	May 14 **30**	Jun 12 **31**	Jul 12 **32**	Aug 10 **33**	Sep 8 **34**	Oct 8 **35**	Nov 6 **36**	Dec 6 **37**	Jan 5 **38**	**Metal-Sheep**	8
Feb 4 **39**	**1992**	Mar 4 **40**	Apr 3 **41**	May 3 **42**	Jun 1 **43**	Jun 30 **44**	Jul 30 **45**	Aug 28 **46**	Sep 26 **47**	Oct 26 **48**	Nov 24 **49**	Dec 24 **50**	**Water-Monkey**	9
Jan 23 **51**	**1993**	Feb 21 **52**	Mar 23 **53***	May 21 **54**	Jun 20 **55**	Jul 19 **56**	Aug 18 **57**	Sep 16 **58**	Oct 15 **59**	Nov 14 **60**	Dec 13 **1**	Jan 12 **2**	**Water-Rooster**	10
Feb 10 **3**	**1994**	Mar 12 **4**	Apr 11 **5**	May 11 **6**	Jun 9 **7**	Jul 9 **8**	Aug 7 **9**	Sep 6 **10**	Oct 5 **11**	Nov 3 **12**	Dec 3 **13**	Jan 1 **14**	**Wood-Dog**	11
Jan 31 **15**	**1995**	Mar 1 **16**	Mar 31 **17**	Apr 30 **18**	May 29 **19**	Jun 28 **20**	Jul 27 **21**	Aug 26 **22***	Oct 24 **23**	Nov 22 **24**	Dec 22 **25**	Jan 20 **26**	**Wood-Pig**	12
Feb 19 **27**	**1996**	Mar 19 **28**	Apr 18 **29**	May 17 **30**	Jun 16 **31**	Jul 16 **32**	Aug 14 **33**	Sep 13 **34**	Oct 12 **35**	Nov 11 **36**	Dec 11 **37**	Jan 9 **38**	**Fire-Rat**	13
Feb 7 **39**	**1997**	Mar 9 **40**	Apr 7 **41**	May 78 **42**	Jun 5 **43**	Jul 5 **44**	Aug 3 **45**	Sep 2 **46**	Oct 2 **47**	Oct 31 **48**	Nov 30 **49**	Dec 30 **50**	**Fire-Ox**	14
Jan 28 **51**	**1998**	Feb 27 **52**	Mar 28 **53**	Apr 26 **54**	May 26 **55***	Jul 23 **56**	Aug 22 **57**	Sep 21 **58**	Oct 20 **59**	Nov 19 **60**	Dec 19 **1**	Jan 17 **2**	**Earth-Tiger**	15
Feb 16 **3**	**1999**	Mar 18 **4**	Apr 16 **5**	May 15 **6**	Jun 14 **7**	Jul 13 **8**	Aug 11 **9**	Sep 10 **10**	Oct 9 **11**	Nov 8 **12**	Dec 8 **13**	Jan 7 **14**	**Earth-Hare**	16
Feb 5 **15**	**2000**	Mar 6 **16**	Apr 5 **17**	May 4 **18**	Jun 2 **19**	Jul 2 **20**	Jul 31 **21**	Aug 29 **22**	Sep 28 **23**	Oct 27 **24**	Nov 26 **25**	Dec 26 **26**	**Metal-Dragon**	17

(*denotes an intercalary month, i.e. the month is 'repeated' in order to bring the calendar into line with the seasons of the year, so accounting for what appears to be an inordinately long month)

CARDS

The Pack

Card-reading, or cartomancy as it is known, has been a popular pastime for centuries. Most people associate this practice with Tarot cards, yet ordinary playing cards can be used just as easily.

All forms of card-reading are based on symbolism; the cards are used to represent archetypes, actual people, events or various aspects of life. A full deck of playing cards consists of 52 cards, and there are the same number of weeks in the year. The pack is divided into four suits, just as there are four seasons, four quarters and four elements. The suits are of two colours, red or black, reflecting the essential duality of life itself – male and female, light and dark, positive and negative – and so on.

Preparations

Cards intended for divination should be kept exclusively for this purpose and not used for games. This is because cards, like everything else, pick up influences, becoming imbued with certain invisible yet tangible qualities according to the use to which they are put.

Before reading cards for others, it is best to practise shuffling and laying them out with a list of their individual meanings close to hand. Try a few practice spreads with a specific query in mind and see whether you can find a solution by studying the cards laid out before you.

Shuffling and Cutting

If you are reading for someone else, shuffle the whole pack thoroughly before allowing the enquirer to hand them. This helps to rid the cards of any previous influence and set the mood for a reading.

Next, hand the cards to the questioner to shuffle and cut. Traditionally, they are cut twice towards the reader, using the left hand, then the three heaps are put one on top of the other to form one pile in the centre of the table. It is the reader who lays out and interprets the cards.

General or Particular?

During this initial process it is a good idea for the two parties to establish what is expected from the reading. Does the enquirer want a general reading, or does he or she wish to highlight one particular question?

Some spreads call for the introduction of a significator: a card to represent either the person for whom the reading is being done or the matter under consideration. So the first thing to decide is which suit accords best with the characteristics of the enquirer or the nature of the particular enquiry.

Clubs represent people with rich brown or red hair, a high colour and brown or hazel eyes. An active, energetic personality. Enterprise and fresh activity.

Diamonds represent very pale people with fair or white hair and light blue or grey eyes. Assured, sophisticated types. Money and material possessions; business; status; and security.

Hearts represents light brown or auburn haired people with pinkish complexions and blue, grey or hazel eyes. A friendly, sympathetic nature. Emotional matters; love and marriage; children; and artistic pursuits.

Spades represent sallow-complexioned people with dark brown or black hair and eyes. Powerful or influential people, strong characters. Power or position; conflict; mental activities; law and order; foreign affairs.

Once you have decided on the appropriate suit, choose the relevant court card for the age and sex of the enquirer: a **King** for a mature man; a **Queen** for a mature woman; a **Jack** for a young person of either sex. Or, if selecting an impersonal card, use the Ace of the designated suit.

The Suits

The Clubs Suit

Ace – An unexpected gift, financial windfall or good news concerning money. Gain through a business venture or successful speculation. An important letter or legal document.

Two – Long-term plans could meet with opposition or delay as a result of another's interference. Beware of idle chat or malicious gossip.

Three – Successful marriage, remarriage or a declaration of intent is possible for those who have experienced a long-term relationship.

Four – Fortunes could take a turn for the worse due to another's deceit or treachery, so do not take everything on trust. Keep plans flexible.

Five – A time of change for the better, with the accent on partnership. Business ventures will be financially rewarding; the prospects are equally rosy for marriage plans.

Six – A good omen for those seeking commercial success: established businesses should flourish and new projects obtain necessary financial backing.

Seven – A small gift or money gain; perhaps a debt will be repaid. A new friendship may bring much pleasure. Seek legal advice if signing a contract.

Eight – A time of uncertainty when minor problems could be blown out of all proportion. Avoid get-rich-quick schemes.

Nine – This card warns against obstinacy, as friction could arise if you ignore the wishes of others. However, there is a possibility of monetary or other gain due to an unforeseen business offer or marriage proposal.

Ten – Sudden financial gain, perhaps through a legacy, insurance payment or tax rebate. Travel, probably abroad, could prove surprisingly profitable and may lead to a romantic encounter.

Jack – A clever, enterprising young person who is well disposed towards the questioner. In the case of a female enquirer, probably an admirer or lover; or a good, reliable friend of a male enquirer.

Queen – A warm-hearted, charming, quick-witted and trustworthy woman of middle years; perhaps the wife of a male questioner or a close friend of a female. In either case, she is very supportive and wise.

King – A mature professional man, honest and straightforward in his dealings, who can be of great assistance. Probably a relative of a female enquirer or a colleague.

The Spades Suit

Ace – A card of challenge, signifying the end of one cycle and the start of the next. Underlying tensions or problems, whether at home or work, are about to erupt; this may be distressing but will clear the way ahead.

Two – Change is imminent: this may mean a new home or job, or possibly the end of a relationship. Whatever the case, despite a feeling of loss, the new situation leads to improved circumstances long-term.

Three – Caution and prudence are advised, especially in any form of partnership. In business or emotional life, conflict can arise if you allow a third party to interfere or let outside interests intrude.

Four – Disappointment is the key word. Plans may be delayed or disrupted, promises could be broken and, on the home front, much-needed support may be lacking. Do not worry; there will be fresh opportunities.

Five – Do not despair if things fail to go according to plan; financial or business problems are only temporary and can be resolved in time. All will be well if you have patience, reschedule your programme and persevere.

Six – Progress may seem irritatingly slow, especially if you are hoping to complete a deal. Despite setbacks, plans will come to fruition eventually, with hard work and persistence, so do not give up.

Seven – You may have to cope with an unexpected burden or onerous task. Try to keep a sense of proportion: foolish anxiety over minor issues could cause tension and lead to unnecessary conflicts.

Eight – Difficulties all round; a testing time when close relationships could be under severe strain, business and travel plans go awry or a friend lets you down. Resist harsh words or hasty actions and guard health.

Nine – Physical and mental energy may be at a low ebb due to anxiety, so do not take on extra burdens until this trying period is over. Offset depression by taking stock of assets and make realistic plans and goals for the future.

Ten – Unwelcome news or worry over a loved one adds to an already tricky situation. It may be difficult to summon up enthusiasm, yet this phase will soon be over and the prospect for the future looks considerably rosier.

Jack – An acquaintance or relative of the enquirer who, despite good intentions, may well cause problems. Friendly and witty, this young person may be good company but is also immature, irresponsible and unreliable.

Queen – An independent, capable and efficient woman, possibly a widow or divorcee, who can be ruthlessly ambitious. She makes a strong ally but a formidable foe, and may be too forthright to have many close friends.

King – A successful man of some standing, perhaps a lawyer or other professional, who is in a position to help the enquirer. Influential and authoritative, he will demand respect and his advice is to be trusted.

The Diamonds Suit

Ace – A long-awaited letter or important document will arrive shortly, bringing welcome news. A financial offer or marriage proposal could be made.

Two – A love affair or close friendship should be developing steadily even if attracting the disapproval of others. Business matters should be showing progress.

Three – Partnerships come under scrutiny and tact may be required if disputes are to be avoided. Litigation is possible, though the outcome could be beneficial. The outlook is promising if cooperation can be maintained.

Four – Do not allow harsh words or rash actions to mar a relationship. Despite petty squabbles, matters can be resolved with patience and understanding; perhaps an old friend could help reconcile differences.

Five – News of a birth in the family or a child's achievement will bring much joy. A small financial loss could be offset by an exciting business opportunity; new ventures are especially favoured.

Six – Marital difficulties are a probability and in come instances could lead to divorce or separation. Alternatively, there may be reconciliation.

Seven – There may be minor problems or disputes at work or home due to unkind gossip, petty jealousy or misunderstandings. Yet such upsets are likely to be short-lived and surprise news will lift everyone's spirits.

Eight – Romance and travel seem to be linked in some way, especially for the very young or elderly. Fluctuations of fortune are indicated: either a small financial loss or a windfall or lucky gamble.

Nine – A business deal or fresh undertaking bodes well, as does a change of residence or occupation. For those with initiative, opportunities abound for romance, increasing income or enjoying a super social round.

Ten – A planned journey brings unforeseen benefit; perhaps a job offer, an opportunity to expand business interests or even a chance of new romance. Improved finances could enable the questioner to secure his or her future.

Jack – A personable young friend or relative of the enquirer, probably male, who brings news. This may be unwelcome if the enquirer is female, though not disastrous. Alternatively, a warning to guard against dishonesty.

Queen – This card represents a woman who may pose a threat to a female questioner's love life or who could interfere in a male enquirer's business affairs. In either case, this lady needs careful handling, so tact is advised.

King – An ambitious and influential man who has it in his power to help or hinder the enquirer's interests. Any proposition should therefore be considered very thoroughly.

The Hearts Suit

Ace – A card promising affection and domestic happiness. It could refer to a birth, marriage proposal, new friendship or reunion.

Two – Good fortune, perhaps greater than anticipated. The consolidation of a current partnership or new romantic liaison. All friendships and close personal ties should flourish.

Three – An engagement or news of a wedding. A difficult choice may have to be made; if so, try to defer a decision until you can consider all the possibilities.

Four – A time of change, either of employment or residence, or perhaps both. Marriage or remarriage is a possibility for a mature enquirer.

Five – Not a time to make important decisions or to contemplate dramatic changes in your way of life. The best advice is to take a short break, relax and get your thoughts in order before tackling any business or domestic worries.

Six – Pleasing family news, perhaps of an engagement or a child's achievement. However, others may try to take advantage of your good nature, so avoid taking on too much.

Seven – Keep plans flexible: a friend or colleague could let you down at the last moment or an anticipated event be cancelled without warning. Romance is well starred.

Eight – Social life is highlighted and will bring much pleasure. A journey or outing could lead to a romantic encounter which develops into an enduring relationship.

Nine – Often known as the wish card, this good omen promises success in whatever is closest to the enquirer's heart at the time of the reading. Any existing misunderstandings will soon be resolved.

Ten – A fortunate card promising happiness in love, a fulfilling domestic situation and business success. An opportunity to secure the future may arise unexpectedly; if so, do not hesitate to take it up.

Jack – An amiable, sincere young person, probably a friend of long-standing or near relative of the enquirer. He or she could be instrumental in introducing the enquirer to someone who is to become very important emotionally.

Queen – A warm-hearted, mature woman who has the enquirer's best interests at heart. Kind, affectionate and sensible, she offers sound advice, practical help and comfort.

King – A good-natured man, well-disposed towards the enquirer. Sociable, generous and enthusiastic, he may lack discretion, so is not always a wise judge. Alternatively, an indication that any minor money problems will be short-lived.

Spreads

Some readers always use the same spread when interpreting the cards, while others prefer to use different layouts according to the purpose of the reading. It is also possible to use the same method of laying out the cards each time but to ask the enquirer to shuffle or cut more than once during the course of a reading, or to select further cards and add these to the original spread in order to clarify a particular point.

Because there are so many choices, it is sensible for a beginner to learn several different methods of laying out the cards in order to decide which is most appealing.

The Celestial Circle

Also known as the 'wheel of the year', the celestial circle is a very useful layout for anyone wanting a good indication of the general trends for the next 12 months. After shuffling and cutting, 13 cards are selected; the first 12 are laid out in order like a clock face, beginning at the one o'clock position and moving clockwise. The 13th is placed in the centre of the circle.

This card is interpreted first because its suit signifies the overall flavour of the coming 12 months. For instance, a Club card indicates that the enquirer will be concerned mainly with practical or business matters; a Diamond denotes financial affairs or status; a Heart augurs well for emotional or romantic interests; and a Spade signals a challenging, changeful year ahead.

The other 12 cards, each representing one calendar month, are then read in clockwise sequence. The first card dealt, in the one o'clock position, relates to the month in which the reading takes place, and is indicative of the overriding influence in the enquirer's life at the time. Card two refers to the month immediately following the reading, card three to the month after that, and so on.

The Bohemian Spread

The Bohemian spread is a very simple layout, consisting of only seven cards, and is therefore ideal for answering a specific query but is less suitable for a general reading.

The cards are shuffled and cut in the usual way, then the first seven are laid out in an open pyramid, or inverted 'V', from left to right. They are interpreted according to the positions in which they fall, as follows:

1 The enquirer's home environment and domestic issues: household goods, renovations and removals.
2 Current influences: factors that relate directly to present circumstances, such as hopes or worries.
3 Relationships of all kinds: love, friendship, business or romantic partnerships, rivals or enemies.
4 The enquirer's wishes in the matter under consideration: what he or she hopes or wants to achieve.
5 Unexpected assistance or obstacles that are likely to help or hinder the aim signified by the preceding card.
6 Those events that are likely to affect the enquirer's immediate future, both the possibilities and probabilities.
7 Any helpful influences or fortunate circumstances that the enquirer can use to advantage: lucky opportunities.

Mystic Cross

A significator is required for this spread, and this card should be taken from the pack and looked at before the remaining cards are shuffled and cut. Twelve cards should then be selected and laid face down in a pile on the table. Once this is done, the enquirer is asked to place the significator anywhere he or she likes among the other 12 cards chosen, and the interpreter then lays out all 13 in two rows, one vertical and one horizontal, to form an equal-armed cross.

The vertical row is read from top to bottom and refers to the enquirer's present situation; the horizontal row, read from left to right, relates to influences affecting current events.

If the significator falls in the vertical row, it indicates that the enquirer is in the grip of circumstances beyond his or her control; but should it fall in the horizontal row, he or she has the matter in hand.

The fourth card laid, at the centre of the cross, represents the factor around which the entire situation revolves. This card will, therefore, provide the key to the matter.

The Romany Spread

This simple and popular spread relies on the interpreter's ability to blend the meanings of cards within the same row to convey a single message. It is best used when the questioner has a specific question.

After shuffling and cutting, the questioner deals the 21 cards in three rows of seven running from left to right. Read the rows separately, but with a single theme at the back of your mind.

The Top row refers to past influences and recent events that have contributed to the present situation. **The Middle row** reflects current circumstances, hopes and fears regarding the issue in question. **The Bottom row** denotes the likely outcome.

The Magic Square

For this spread, the questioner should start by selecting a significator from the pack as described earlier. He or she should then shuffle and cut the rest of the cards in the usual way. Place the significator on the table and deal eight cards around it in the order shown. Then deal a ninth card over the significator.

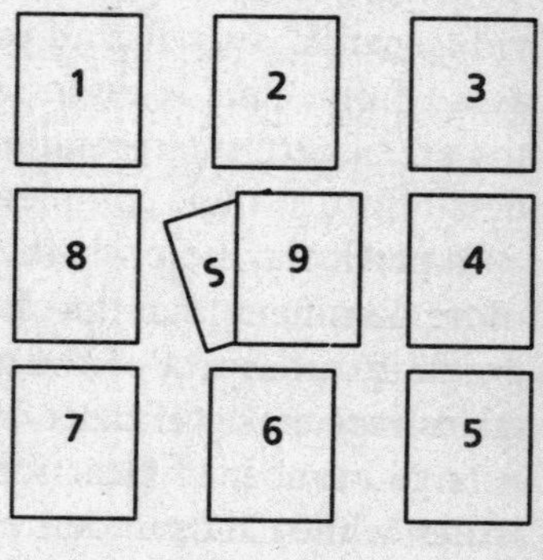

The cards are interpreted according to their positions:

1 The Individual – the state of mind of the questioner.
2 External influences and unexpected factors.
3 Surroundings – friends, family, colleagues and home.
4 Hopes and fears.
5 Alternatives – possible opportunities and challenges.
6 Aspirations and beliefs.

7 Negative factors – those which limit or oppose the questioner.
8 Positive factors – constructive or helpful influences.
9 Potential – initiative and natural abilities.

The rows of cards should be interpreted both horizontally and vertically.

Horizontally, the top row shows the prevailing atmosphere, the middle section conveys the basis of the issue, and the bottom row indicates future possibilities.

Vertically, the first column expresses three aspects of the questioner's character, the centre column denotes important factors which must be considered before any decisions are made, and the final column indicates the opportunities which are possible if the correct decision is made.

The most important card is the one covering the significator. This relates to every other card and indicates the questioner's potential in relation to the message conveyed by the spread as a whole. Do not forget to take account of the significator when interpreting the card's meaning.

As you become more familiar with the meanings of the individual cards, you will find yourself starting to look at a spread as a whole. This is essential for an accurate reading, since the art of card interpretation lies in blending all the relevant details into a single complete picture.

In particular, note whether any suit or group of members is more dominant than the others. Emphasis on a particular suit points to an aspect of the questioner's life which is about to take on special significance or which is uppermost in their mind. A large number of Hearts, for example, highlights emotional issues, while Clubs underline enterprises and activities.

Generally speaking, the higher numbered cards offer the most potential. A predominance of low numbers suggests that the questioner's life is unlikely to change radically in the immediate future. Aces, however, are an exception to this rule. Since they represent the essence of each suit, they tend to mark the end of the current cycle and the start of a new one.

CRYSTAL DIVINATION

The Major Stones

From the earliest times, gems and crystals have played an important part in divination rites. Various properties were attributed to the stones according to their texture, colour and markings. In the Middle Ages, for example, amethyst was used as a protection against drunkenness, while opal was believed to make people invisible.

There are at least two methods of casting crystals to form a pattern for reading. Gypsy divination takes 12 precious and semi-precious stones, plus a rough pebble, known as the 'Significator'. An 18 inch (40.4cm) circle is drawn on the ground, and the questioner takes the 13 stones and throws them inside the circle to be interpreted. If the Significator stone falls outside the circle, the stones must be re-thrown. If this happens a second time, the reading has to wait until the next day.

Another method involves the reader sitting opposite the questioner, with the crystals placed between them on a tray covered in black velvet. A mat, also covered in black velvet, is put in front of the questioner, who chooses nine stones from the tray and places them on the mat.

Although many kinds of crystals can be used, it would be simplest for beginners to start with the 12 major stones listed here. While traditional practices use precious stones, they can be used in their raw 'geological' state. It is also acceptable to substitute stones of lesser value, such as clear quartz for diamond, amber for topaz, rose quartz for ruby, jade for emerald and tourmaline for sapphire, if some are unavailable.

When using the gypsy method of reading, take notice of which stones lie nearest to the Significator stone. If it lies close to a ruby and topaz, for example, you might advise the questioner to be cautious of a stranger. The closer to the centre of the circle a stone is positioned, the more immediately it is believed that the event will occur.

When using the tray, mat and velvet, the first stones selected show the questioner's immediate concerns. Those chosen and then rejected can have some bearing on negative indications.

Agate – Agate is said to give increased vitality and confidence, aiding the wearer with sudden bursts of energy. In a reading, agate can indicate a pleasant surprise for the questioner.

Amethyst – Amethyst is considered to be an aid to spiritual enlightenment, and is also said to be a lucky stone for lovers. In readings, it indicates that something of substantial value may be lost.

Bloodstone – In reading, a bloodstone can indicate physical aches and pains and give a warning to slow down. It is often seen as a sign of stress, and sometimes shows the advent of an unpleasant surprise.

Diamond – The diamond symbolizes strength and bravery. Worn on the left side, it is believed to protect the wearer from enemies. In a reading, is usually indicates a business promotion.

Emerald – Emerald can help the wearer overcome depression and insomnia and improve the memory. In a reading, it can indicate that there is a secret admirer in the questioner's life.

Garnet – Garnet encourages a cheerful disposition, increasing courage and self-esteem. In a reading, it can foreshadow the imminent arrival of a letter of some kind.

Opal – Said to induce daydreaming in the wearer, opal is sometimes held to be unlucky, especially in an engagement ring. In a reading, the opal can indicate a possible death.

Ruby – Ruby is said to increase energy, encourage friendship and aid intuition. It can show that the questioner is too much of a perfectionist. It can also indicate the influence of a stranger.

Sapphire – This stone is said to be lucky for lovers. The bearer of good fortune, sapphire indicates peace and harmony in a reading. It can also mean that a past mistake will catch up with the questioner.

Sardonyx – Semi-precious sardonyx brings happiness to married couples. In a reading, it indicates a wedding, although not necessarily that of the questioner.

Topaz – Topaz helps the wearer overcome insomnia, and brings fidelity in love. In a reading, it advises the questioner to exercise extreme caution.

Turquoise – Turquoise is said to protect the wearer from harm. It can indicate contentment, and usually shows an affirmative answer to the question asked.

The Minor Stones

In addition to the 12 major stones, many lesser stones are also said to have beneficial or prophetic qualities which are useful in divination. The following 12 stones, which are quite cheap to buy in their raw state, should all be included in a beginner's divination kit.

There are several methods of casting the stones to form a pattern for divination. In one of the most common methods, the reader sits opposite the questioner, with the stones and crystals placed between them on a tray covered in black velvet. A mat, also covered in black velvet, is put in front of the questioner, who then chooses nine stones from the tray and places them on the mat.

The first stones chosen show the questioner's immediate concerns. Thus if someone first chooses an aquamarine, it may indicate skepticism about crystal prediction. But if the aquamarine then becomes surrounded by other stones which indicate trouble, it may show that the questioner's usual objectivity has been temporarily lost.

If the questioner chooses the iron pyrite crystal, it may indicate that he or she is being deceived by someone. Look to the surrounding stones for further clues. If red jasper is also found close by, this could mean the questioner is being deceived by an unfaithful jealous lover.

The stones can also indicate abilities of the questioner. For instance if rose quartz – the healer's crystal – is chosen, look to the surrounding stones for indications of the type of healing. Found near an aquamarine, this shows the person would make a good therapist, concentrating on healing the mind. If near an amethyst, it may indicate a purely spiritual healer.

After familiarising yourself thoroughly with the specific properties of each stone, look at the patterns they make. They let them tell you their own stories. Let intuition be your guide and never be afraid to relax and let your mind make its own connections.

Green Jasper indicates that the person is a rejected lover, or is neglected by the family. This can be the true situation, or a reflection of the person's negative feelings at the time.

Iron Pyrite or 'fool's gold' is a glamorous-looking mineral, considered to signify mistrust or deception. In a reading, it may indicate that the questioner is a person of blind faith who rushes headlong into situations, so caution is advised. It can also mean that the person is so trusting as to be gullible about the basic motivations of others.

Beryl indicates that the questioner is experiencing a general increase in his or her intuition and psychic powers.

Aquamarine is the stone of logic, a clear mind, and common sense. It is thought to promote sound thinking, and is good for examinations. In a reading, the appearance of this stone means the questioner doubts the validity of the reading itself.

Pink and Grey Jasper may indicate that an older person – perhaps a parent – is going to affect the life of the questioner. It could also foretell a legacy or an unexpected gift.

Tiger's Eye is worn to promote self-confidence and awareness. In divination, it signals independence. It may be that the person concerned is alone or at a turning point, but it almost always indicates change for the better.

Clear Quartz Crystal is thought to release psychic powers. In divination, it indicates the return of good health, vitality and strength to someone who has been ill, and is a strong positive sign for the future. It may mean that the questioner should take on more responsibility and rely less upon the efforts of others.

Red Jasper, in common with all jaspers, quietens a troubled mind. In a reading, red japser indicates love, deep emotions, jealousy, and passionate feelings.

Tektite, a dull black stone, may signal a period of depression or withdrawal on the part of the questioner, or someone close to him or her.

Jet in a reading reveals unfaithfulness, either that of the questioner or of someone close.

Ladrodorite in a reading shows some link with a country overseas. It may foretell foreign travel for business or pleasure, or the beginning of a relationship with a foreigner.

Rose Quartz is used to stimulate the imagination, restore peace of mind, and promote feelings of love. It is also the healer's crystal. In a reading, it usually indicates that the questioner has healing abilities. If the question posed concerns another person, this stone can mean that the person needs healing.

Crystals and the Houses

This alternative method of divination combines the astrological houses with crystal fortune-telling, but instead of placing them at random on a tray, they are arranged as the questioner chooses on top of a blank zodiac wheel showing houses. The houses are numbered anti-clockwise from one to 12 beginning with the Ascendant. Once the questioner has placed all the stones on the diagram, the reader can interpret the meaning of the crystals in conjunction with the houses on which each is placed.

The Houses

The different sections or houses of the diagram are each concerned with one particular aspect of the questioner's life. Briefly, the First House relates to the questioner; the Second to the financial position; the Third to brothers and sisters or communications; the Fourth to the home; the Fifth to the children or lovers; the Sixth to health, pets or jobs; the Seventh to marriage or business partners; the Eighth to sex or death; the Ninth to long-distance travel or advanced study; the Tenth to career and profession; the Eleventh to friends, groups or hopes and wishes; and the Twelfth to various kinds of imprisonment or confinement, generally psychological rather than physical.

Interpretation

The meaning of each crystal is interpreted in the light of the house on which it has been placed. The combinations of crystal and placement can provide endless fascination and lead us to focus more carefully on all the different aspects of life surrounding us. For example, if the questioner has placed a blue lace agate in the Third House, this would relate to a younger sister, or a person who occupies that role in the questioner's life. If in addition a jade stone is placed next to this one, we can assume that the young woman is also a protective reliable friend.

Again, if a moonstone were to be found near petrified wood in the Seventh House, the reader could advise the questioner to develop a more realistic attitude to some legal or contractual obligation, to stop daydreaming and attend to the matter at hand!

Blue Lace Agate (1) – Although this stone also refers to a specific person, this time it is usually a young girl. Agate crystals are unusually sensitive to the stones surrounding them. It is thus advisable to ascertain from the questioner the identity of the young person indicated, since agates never represent a superficial association.

Jade (2) – In a reading, jade shows protection from one's enemies. It is also said to indicate a true friend.

Coral (3) – Coral is supposed to indicate a turning from foolishness to wisdom. It is also thought to show a safe passage through tempests and floods.

Agate Quartz (4) – This crystal is usually taken to represent a young man in a reading. This can be the person's son or someone who has been befriended.

Moss Agate (5) – This lovely stone is generally regarded as a very good sign when it appears in a reading. It predicts contentment after a stormy period of life.

Petrified Wood (6) – In a reading this is associated with legal papers of some kind. These could be a will or a lawsuit, but could also pertain to the signing of a marriage license, agreement or contract.

Moonstone (7) – This stone signals loyalty and a long life. It is ruled by the Moon and is seen as the sign of a dreamy state in the questioner. It sometimes signifies success in a creative project, usually with an artistic flavour.

Agate with fossils (8) – This striking stone is associated with financial affairs. It indicates more money in the pocket perhaps resulting from change in career or simply through luck. It may predict a win through gambling or a gift of money.

Rutilated Quartz (9) – This crystal has an arresting appearance with what look like bright threads running through it. One of the most artfully contrived of stones, it is generally taken to represent creative ability in a questioner. This may vary from talent great enough to earn a living as an artist to the pleasure derived from creative pursuits of all types.

Crystal Healing

Alternative medical practice holds that illness results from imbalances and negative feelings in the subtle spiritual, emotional and thinking levels. These affect the physical body through the seven *chakras*, or energy centres. Just as colours relate directly to the chakras, and can be used to restore them to harmony, so crystals and gemstones can heal through their colour vibration as well as through the power derived from the innate structure.

Crystalline structures are thought to be capable of both balancing and transforming the subtle chakra energies – a belief borne out by recent research, which shows them to have a marked effect on brain-wave patterns. Thus green jade is linked with the green heart chakra; it can benefit certain physical heart conditions while at the same time balancing the emotions.

Crystal Healing in Action

Crystal healing is also used as an adjunct to other therapies such as massage or acupuncture. Like most forms of alternative therapy, it is seen as being complementary to traditional medical practice.

It is important to remember that there are two energies at work during a crystal healing session – that of the crystal and that of the healer. Although certain crystals are traditionally associated with certain complaints, the final decision must always rest with the healer's own intuition.

The healer will begin by assessing intuitively where the problem lies – perhaps by mentally tuning into the client's auric field, sensing with the hands, or dowsing the body with a crystal pendulum. Once selected, crystals of various types are then placed on, or close to, the relevant parts of the body.

The client may also be advised to carry a particular crystal in a pocket, protected by cloth. In some countries crystals are still ground and given orally, but this can be very dangerous and should never be tried except under expert supervision.

Medical Lore and Gemstones

Just as selecting crystals is largely a matter of 'gut feeling', so healers must rely on their instinct as to how they use them. Each one possesses very different yet powerful energies which can be harmful in the wrong hands. Yet there are no rules – the energies of both crystal and healer are naturally variable, and are subject to intuition.

Crystals need to be cleansed after use since they can pick up psychic residue from the client – often sensed as a dull or even 'sticky' feeling. This is done by placing them under running water or leaving them in a glass bowl with a handful of sea-salt in full sunlight.

Agate heals skin disease and heart problems, while also boosting vitality and confidence. *Energy centre: according to colour.*

Amber benefits the endocrine system, spleen and heart. *Energy centres: navel, solar plexus, crown.*

Amethyst can heal obsessive behaviour (e.g. alcoholism) while benefiting the endocrine and immune systems, pineal and pituitary glands. *Energy centres: brow, crown.*

Aquamarine helps with fluid retention and nervous, kidney, liver, spleen, thyroid problems. *Energy centres: throat, solar plexus.*

Carnelian is helpful for menstrual cramps and nosebleeds. It also benefits blood and tissue regeneration, plus the kidneys, lungs, liver and gall bladder. *Energy centres: navel, solar plexus, heart.*

Diamond benefits the brain, clearing mental blockages and enhancing mental activity. *Energy centres: all.*

Emerald has a tonic effect, boosting the heart, kidneys and liver, as well as the immune and nervous systems. *Energy centre: heart.*

Garnet (red) benefits the entire system. *Energy centres: root, heart.*

Jade can heal eye and female problems. It strengthens the heart, kidneys and immune system and increases fertility. *Energy centre: depends on colours.*

Lapis lazuli is helpful for thyroid problems, the skeletal system and general vitality. *Energy centres: throat, brow.*

Moonstone can heal water retention and female problems while benefiting the lymph glands, stomach, spleen, pancreas and pituitary gland. *Energy centre: heart.*

Obsidian helps heal digestive problems, particularly in the stomach and intestines. *Energy centre: base.*

Quartz crystal acts as balancer, amplifier and stimulator on all levels. *Energy centres: all.*

Rose quartz can heal migraine. It also benefits the kidneys and circulatory system, and can soothe the emotions. *Energy centre: heart.*

Ruby beneficial for depression, circulatory problems and general lack of vitality. *Energy centre: heart.*

Sapphire benefits the heart and kidneys. *Energy centres: throat, brow.*

Tiger eye vitalizes the spleen, pancreas and digestive organs. *Energy centres: navel, solar plexus.*

Topaz can aid tissue regeneration. Helps the liver, gall bladder, spleen, digestive organs and nervous system. *Energy centres: heart, throat, brow.*

Turquoise helps with circulatory and respiratory problems, as well as toning, strengthening and regenerating the whole physical system. *Energy centre: throat.*

Zircon can benefit those with bowel problems or insomnia. Possesses similar properties as diamond and quartz crystal. *Energy centres: all.*

GEOMANCY

The Figures

Geomancy is an old divinatory system based on interpreting random patterns made in or on the earth. It is a very ancient art which probably originated in the deserts of North Africa, whose inhabitants regarded the earth as a living entity that could be consulted for future predictions by those with the skill to interpret the signs.

The method of producing geomantic figures varies from country to country and has changed considerably throughout history, as has its popularity as a method of divination. Yet geomancy may well be an ancestor of the *I Ching*, with which it shares marked similarities, and it remains one of the simplest and most effective means of consulting the hidden forces of nature.

Via – Literally meaning 'way' or 'road', *Via* is fortunate for solo enterprises but not for joint ventures. It denotes method and favours direct action with no deviations from the chosen path. Often, this figure refers to actual travel and is a good omen for those embarking on a journey, whether for business or pleasure. Equally, it could indicate a way through present difficulties.

Populus – In direct contrast to *Via*, this favours group activities and may indicate an important social occasion, a wedding, party or other gathering. It is especially beneficial for humanitarian or charitable undertakings, or community projects. Less well favoured are individual efforts and intimate relationships. The time is not ripe for going it alone or seeking new conquests.

Conjunctio – This figure means 'uniting' or 'joining together', and relates to close ties of all kinds, especially marriage. It cements existing relationships and holds out the promise of new alliances that will prove highly rewarding. On a less romantic level, it may refer to profitable business partnerships or joint ventures.

Carcer – This figure points to delays, hindrances or obstacles to current plans or enterprises – often through a lack of available resources or missed opportunities. More positively, *Carcer* is a fortunate omen for questions relating to birth. This may refer to pregnancy or to the initial, formative stages of a concept.

Acquisitio – Literally meaning acquisition or addition, this figure implies worldly achievement. It may herald monetary gain, business success or anything that can improve the enquirer's status, such as promotion, public acclaim, fame or honour. It is an excellent omen for those seeking financial backing or other favour.

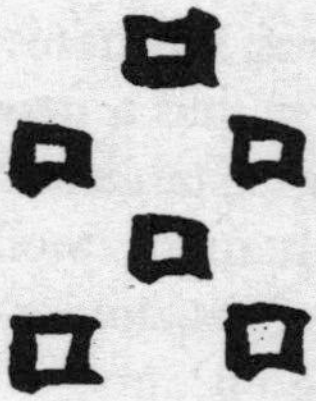

Amissio – Material loss of forecast, perhaps through deceit or trickery. This figure may indicate an unprofitable deal, unwise investment or faulty purchase. Guard prized possessions, too, as there is a chance they could be mislaid or stolen. On a happier note, this figure augurs well for love and romance.

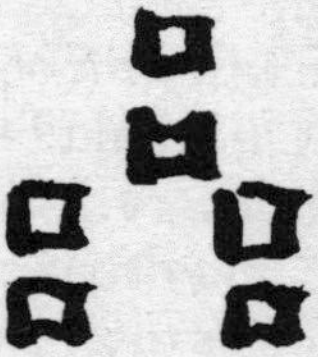

Fortuna Minor – Although this means 'the lesser fortune', it is generally auspicious for any matter about to reach a conclusion. It bodes well for a successful outcome to existing legal proceedings or any undertaking that is in its final stages of completion.

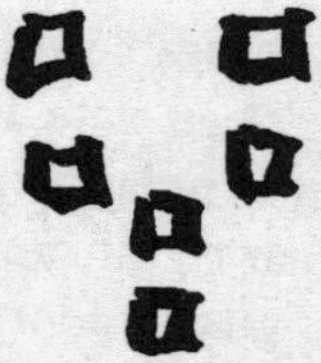

Fortuna Major – Translating literally as 'the greater fortune', this figure relates to worldly ambitions. Its appearance denotes commercial success, increased wealth or status and often coincides with the start of a run of good luck. Long-term projects are especially well starred, so any ongoing project is assured of eventual success.

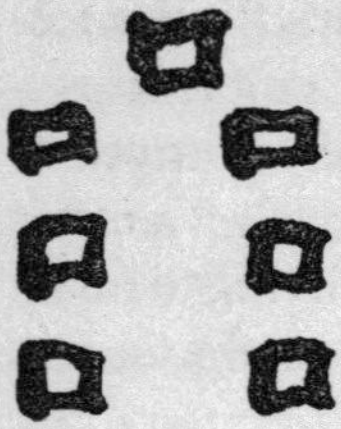

Laetitia – A very auspicious figure denoting joy and happiness. It marks an end to any current doubts or adverse circumstances, so may signal recovery from illness, a favourable legal judgment or unexpected stroke of good luck. There should be cause for celebration, if not immediately, then in the very near future.

Tristitia – *Tristitia* is associated with despair and despondency. Perhaps the enquirer has recently suffered demotion or redundancy, seen plans come to nothing or even lost a loved one. Whatever the cause, there is an aura of unhappiness due to unwanted and unwarranted changes in his or her present circumstances.

Puella – This figure symbolizes the feminine principle and therefore refers to womanly concerns and attributes. It may herald a new romance or, for those already in established relationships, greater harmony. It augurs well for questions concerning partnerships, domestic issues, children's affairs, art and beauty.

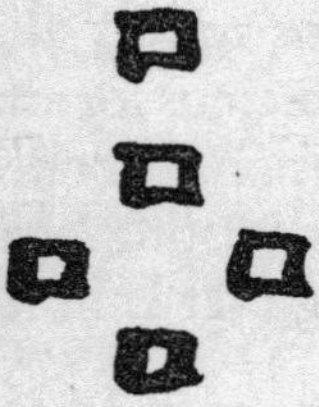

Puer – This is an ambivalent figure relating to decisive action, which may prove wise or foolish depending on circumstances. It would be fortunate in competitive situations, such as sports, examinations, interviews and debates. On a romantic level, *Puer* often refers to a new and exciting love affair.

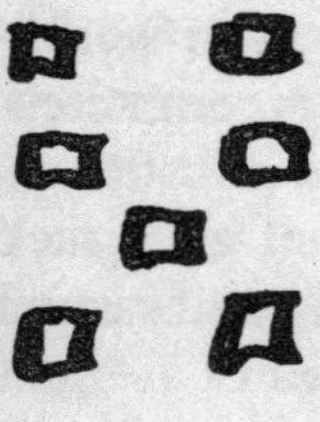

Albus – This figure is generally favourable and is associated with a fresh start or clean slate. It gives the go-ahead to anyone contemplating a new job, residential move or other significant change. Alternatively, *Albus* may signal freedom from past restrictions or obligations that have tied you down.

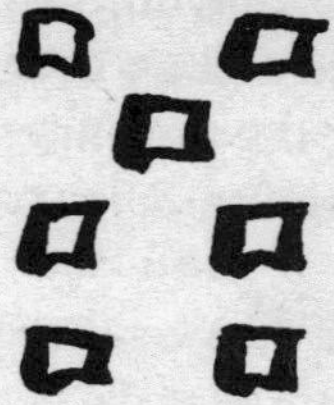

Rubeus – *Rubeus* which means 'red' is associated with fiery passion. It contains a strong warning not to allow emotions or physical desires to breach sensible boundaries. As this figure relates to disgrace, calamity and danger of injury, motivation should be questioned carefully if you are tempted into extremes of speech or action.

Caput Draconis – This figure often indicates that, within days of the reading, an unexpected development will occur which will have significant effects for good or ill, depending on other figures drawn. More usually though, *Caput Draconis* denotes travel, possibly emigration to a foreign country for work.

Cauda Draconis – If you draw this figure, the best advice is to continue along chosen lines even if, as is probable, there are no obvious signs or reward. *Cauda Draconis* is a favourable portent for all matters of the heart. Persistence, selfless devotion and good intent are bound to pay dividends in the longer term.

A Modern Method

Few sand readers exist nowadays, and the most modern form of geomancy relies upon a series of random marks made by pen or pencil upon paper. Before you start, think about the problem or query that is most important to you. Try to formulate this as a simple question capable of being answered by a 'yes' or 'no'. Be as specific as possible and avoid multiple choice queries such as 'Will I change my job or marry Charlie?' Enquiries such as this should be posed as two separate questions.

Once you have formulated your enquiry, write it at the top of a blank sheet of paper. Next, take a pen or pencil and make a series of small dashes across the page, being careful not to count the number of strokes made; they must be random.

You will need four lines of dashes to obtain a geomantic

figure. Each line should be added up separately; an odd number corresponds to one dot of the geomantic figure and an even number corresponds to two dots. For example, the four lines of dashes below will produce the geomantic figure *Fortuna Minor*, shown above.

A fuller reading can be obtained by creating two or three figures and combining their meanings. If eight lines of dashes across the paper produce two identical figures, it is supposed to be a very fortunate sign. Even if the geomantic figure is adverse, this duplication will override its negative implications and signify a positive response to the matter under consideration. When consulting three figures, the second one that is obtained is the principal solution; the others provide more detail.

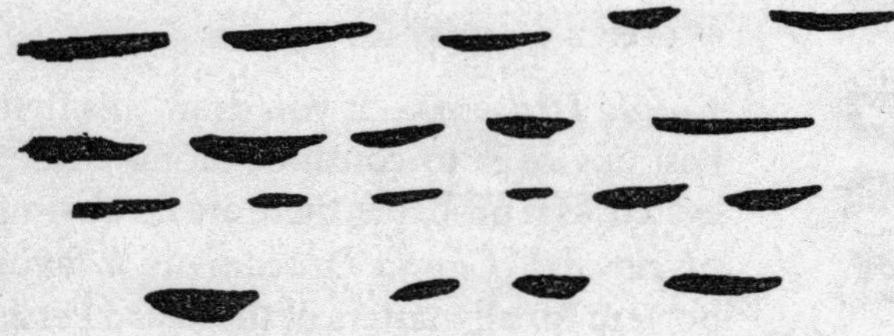

GRAPHOLOGY

Size of Writing

Is your handwriting small and neat, carefully formed and decorative? Or is it exuberantly large and flowing? You will need to look at capital letters, too. Are they very big or almost the same size as the rest of the handwriting?

Broad, Curving Letters

just caught
I am too

Large handwriting is invariably the sign of an extrovert personality. If it is very big, the writer still retains a charming, childlike confidence but may be insensitive to others. Such personalities may think the world revolves around them, but their love of life and all it has to offer makes it easy to forgive them. Clear, large handwriting also denotes realism, and an ability to organize things in a practical way. Large capitals suggest boastfulness.

Small Handwriting

Often associated with intelligence, small writing is usually the sign of an inward-looking type. If it is also very tidy, the writer probably lacks creative imagination, but will be invaluable when it comes to keeping things in order. These people are usually self-controlled, and fond of a regular routine. They make excellent administrators.

Medium-sized Handwriting

A well-balanced personality is suggested by average-sized handwriting. Such individuals work well with others and find it easy to get on with a variety of people. They have a very sensible approach to life, and are able to strike a good balance between work and play.

Spacing

Finally, look at the spacing between words and also between individual letters. Some handwriting is almost like printing, with each individual letter standing on its own. In other examples, the letters crowd together. Much handwriting contains elements of both styles but there is usually a general tendency towards one or the other.

Narrowly-spaced Letters

This style of writing points to rather introverted and cautious individuals who like to look before they leap. In love, they can be prone to jealousy, stemming from an underlying insecurity.

Widely-spaced Words

Good clear spaces between words show an intelligent, independent thinker who will consider problems carefully, and take a balanced view. Such people can be argumentative and critical, but are very good at grasping the basics of a situation.

Closely-spaced Words

Sometimes those with this style of writing have trouble seeing the wood for the trees. They may be specialists in their work but are unlikely to have wide-ranging interests outside it. If the words are actually joined together in some way, this can indicate impatience but also loyalty and the possession of a well-ordered, logical mind.

Widely-spaced Letters

This sort of spacing indicates individuals who are considerate and sensitive to the needs and moods of others. They often need privacy, and time spent alone is important to them. They are generous, broad-minded and usually happy personalities. If the spacing is excessive, this is a sign that they may have difficulty in saying 'no' to the demands of friends or family.

Know, according to the
in your department.
dates on which all

Sir Winston Churchill's neat and regular script indicates good powers of organisation and a logical mind.

Can you tell them I would
will contact them the
in the area.

Uneven lines and the changing angle of the slope show that Linda Lusardi, top model, can be changeable, and that she has a tendency to be impulsive.

The Three Zones

Three zones are used by graphologists to discover how balanced the writer is, how energies are directed and what kind of preoccupations are characteristic. This information can also indicate a suitable career, and attitudes to sex.

A simple way to identify each zone is to rule a line above and below such letters as 's' or 'a' in the handwriting sample. This enables letters such a 'g' or 'y' below the line, or 'h' and 'f' above it, to be picked out.

The Middle Zone

This zone contains all the vowels ('a', 'e', 'i', 'o', 'u') plus the letters 'c', 'm', 'n', 'r', 's', 'v', 'w', and 'x'. Parts of every other letter are, of course, found here, too, but most will usually have stems which extend above or below the line. This does not apply to capitals however.

The middle zone relates to our everyday world, and shows how we deal with it. It reveals how sociable you are, how much practical ability you possess, levels of self-confidence, and your general approach to life.

When the middle zone really stands out, so that the upper and lower letters seem stunted, you are looking at an extremely practical individual. Such a person may lack imagination, but will be good at getting on with work on a day-to-day basis.

If the writing is also rounded, this will indicate someone kind and considerate, who has a full and happy social life. If the writing in the middle zone is very spiky and angular, however, the writer tends to be obstinate and will insist on making a logical decision, ignoring his or her hunches or intuition.

A restricted middle zone is easy to spot, since upper and lower strokes dominate, dwarfing the central letters. Those whose handwriting displays this sign are often unsure of themselves. They may be very gifted, but have trouble in finding a suitable outlet for their talents. They are certainly rather unrealistic, and will find it difficult to budget. When the rest of the writing is clear and well-formed, it signifies an artistic nature.

The Lower Zone

The letters which are stressed in this zone are 'g', 'j', 'p', 'q', 'y', and sometimes 'f', and 'z', depending upon style.

The lower zone is associated with sexuality, working with the hands, and general levels of physical energy. Some graphologists maintain that these letters are also linked to the lower part of the body, and that any sudden changes to handwriting in this zone indicate health problems.

When the lower zone dominates, you are looking at a rather materialistic person. This character also often has highly-developed senses, sees life in a very down-to-earth way and will be unhappy with intellectual arguments. A favourite saying might well be: 'The proof of the pudding is in the eating'. In general, these types have lots of physical energy.

Such personalities are also likely to enjoy food and drink, in addition to physical sports. They are often very sensual lovers, with healthy sex drives. However, if the writing slopes backwards, then you are dealing with a very self-controlled person who may well suffer from guilt about physical pleasure.

A small lower zone shows a distinct lack of interest in physical matters. Such a person may be good at his or her job and be popular with others, but is unlikely to be passionate. These types are not really interested in food, except as a means of keeping alive. They are not good with their hands, and find it hard to relax fully. They may have a lower-than-average sex drive, and find the body distasteful.

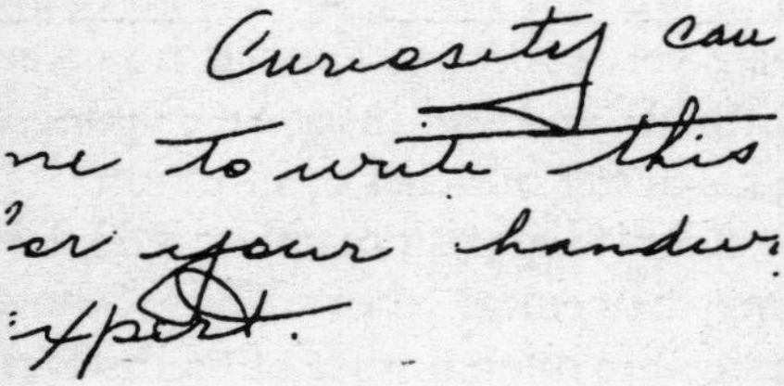

This large, speedily-written script shows John Wayne to have been a man of action, with a great love of life. The lower zones confirm the impression of energy.

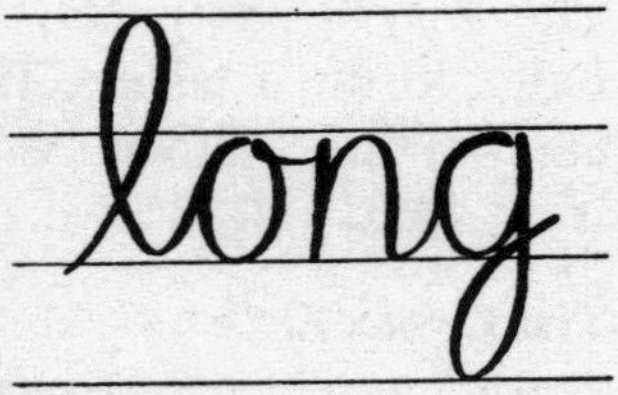

The upper zone relates to the intellect and the imagination; common sense and sociability are reflected in the middle zone; while the lower zone relates to energies, practicality and sex drive.

The Upper Zone

The letters which extend into the upper zone are 'b', 'd', 'f', 'h', 'k', 'l', and 't'. Graphologists also look at where the dots (if any) over the 'i' and 'j' are placed, a complex art in itself.

This is the zone of the imagination, and the realm of ideas. Broadly speaking, if these letters are looped, or decorative in some way, the writer's ideas are coloured by emotion. When they are consistently straight or spiky, the ideas tend towards logic and may even be rather rigid and fixed.

The sign of a thinker, a large upper zone reveals someone who is concerned about the state of the world, and who may be interested in politics, philosophy and other such abstract ideas. If the writing also slopes to the left, this indicates someone with a spiritual outlook or who works selflessly for others.

If the writing slopes to the right, the individual may be more concerned with worldly matters, and perhaps actively working for an environmental group or involved in politics.

Small upper stems reveal someone who is perfectly happy with life as it is. Such people do not build castles in the air.

If the upper strokes are blunt and badly formed, however, life may be ticking along for the writer, but sometimes it all seems rather pointless. Such writing can also reveal a past disappointment which continues to colour present feelings.

Styles of Writing

Angular Handwriting

If there are a lot of angles and vertical strokes, the writer likes to be sure of his or her facts. These types like their lives to be well-organized, and are unsympathetic towards vague, muddled personalities. There could be mathematical, musical, or scientific ability.

Writing which is very rounded reveals someone whose heart rules their head. Feelings count above all, and the writer could be highly intuitive, too.

If there is any uncertainty about how rounded or angular the writing is, take a closer look at the 'a's and the 'o's for further information. A full, broad 'o' and 'a' denote open-mindedness, while narrow ones signal introvert tendencies. When the 'a' is both narrow, and formed with a loop or knot, it suggests sensitivity, while a very angular letter reveals ambition.

If these letters are open at the top it denotes an open, artless tendency – and a trusting personality. But that person is not someone to confide in for he or she will find it almost impossible to keep a secret for long. When 'o' and 'a' are open at the bottom, it reveals a potential liar.

Little inner circles or ovals on both 'o' and 'a' denote secretive tendencies, particularly in emotional relationships. A very square 'a' indicates manual dexterity. But if the 'a' appears 'printed' it reveals artistic leanings.

Two examples of knotted 'a's denoting secrecy. The narrow one shows sensitivity.

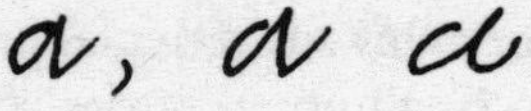

Angular 'a's betray ambition.

Secretive knots in 'o' and 'a'.

The letters of a trusting person.

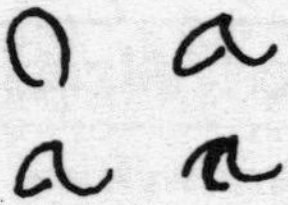

'o's and 'a's open at the bottom may betray a liar.

This square 'A' shows someone who is good with their hands.

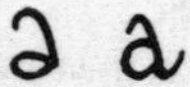

A stylish artistic 'a'.

Envelopes

Handwritten envelopes can reveal some interesting information about the mood and the character of the writer. Most of the clues come from the use of the space on the envelope, rather than the handwriting itself. Remember that unless an address is very familiar, the writer will probably be copying it out carefully. This can make the handwriting seem stilted and lacking in rhythm. You can only take this as a definite personality pointer if the writing inside has exactly the same traits.

However, you can assess the size and direction of the handwriting as usual, looking out for rising, wavy or falling base lines – and also looking to see how legible it is. An illegible, scrawly style suggests thoughtlessness. Other signs will reveal whether this is because someone is in a world of their own, or simply selfish and disorganized. Bearing these points in mind, look carefully at the envelope to see how the address has been written.

An address which is so spread out that it almost fills the entire envelope denotes will-power, extrovert qualities and probably selfishness. This person likes to be noticed and is likely to be a natural leader.

Sometimes you see an address squashed up in the centre of the paper. This denotes someone who feels lonely or misunderstood by the rest of the world.

The Idealist

People who write the address high up are idealistic personalities. You can tell a little about whether their dreams and ideals are a bit battered, or still strong and hopeful, by looking at the base line and the slope of the handwriting itself. If the writing dips down, then the writer could feel that his or her dreams may never be realized. If there is an upward slant, he or she is still optimistic about life.

Those who write the address very low down are generally down-to-earth, and usually concerned with material well-being. If the handwriting is very small, they may be very careful with money or even mean.

Large handwriting combined with this sign indicates a potential big spender who enjoys being generous. A low-down, rather illegible address denotes a muddled thinker who is mainly concerned with day-to-day life, but who may find it hard to take a clear view of a situation.

If the address on the left-hand side of the envelope? If it is, you are probably looking at someone who likes plenty of security. This person is likely to be shy, and may find it difficult to open up with new people.

What heinous or occult
purpose! I look forward

Although some people still write in the copperplate style of old school copybooks, most develop a more individual approach.

If the address is placed to the right, it denotes optimism and a desire to move forward in life. Normally, it also suggests extrovert qualities, an enjoyment of life and a positive attitude towards the future.

This neat, legible writing indicates a logical mind and a preference for tidy surroundings.

Guy Fawkes's style before and after torture shows its crippling effects.

The rounded contours of this writing reveal an emotional nature, and its fullness shows open-mindedness.

Personal Style

Clear, legible handwriting, as you might expect, points to an open, honest personality. This kind of writing belongs to those who like to state their views clearly, who are reliable and make loyal friends or partners. When very plain and simple, clear handwriting reveals self-discipline and considerable practical skills. Such types are logical and realistic.

More complicated characters may also write in an easy-to-read fashion. You can distinguish their handwriting from the more childlike type by looking for these important points:

Does the handwriting follow a particular style, such as Italic or Copperplate? If the letters are clear, but attractively-formed, the writer is likely to be quite sophisticated, and is often a 'visual' type who is highly aware of colours and shapes.

Does the writing adhere strictly to a copybook style, without quirks and personal embellishments? Impersonal handwriting signals an unwillingness to rebel. These individuals may be somewhat submissive. When it is meticulously tidy, evenly spaced and reminds you of the printed word, it denotes someone who finds it hard to be free and spontaneous.

Personal Styles

Personal handwriting is hard to imitate, and easy to recognize as belonging to a particular person. Some, or most, of the letters may deviate from the original copybook style which the person learned at school. The more unusual the style, the more personal it becomes. This denotes originality, or eccentricity.

Confused Handwriting

Illegible handwriting has sometimes been believed to show education and intelligence. After all, how many doctors, lawyers or scientists write clearly?

It is true that handwriting which is difficult to decipher may indicate that the writer's mind is on higher things. He or she may be highly intelligent, but inhabit an imaginary world which can be either primarily creative or intellectual. With a mind full of ideas, dreams and plans, he or she may find it hard to cope with practicalities.

When illegible handwriting slopes forward it suggests impatience; thoughts are coming thick and fast, and the hand simply cannot keep up with the speed. If it slopes back the person may find it difficult to communicate thoughts and feelings to others. Such types may be intensely private individuals.

Finally, do not forget that some kinds of illness, writing with the left hand, and old age can all affect legibility. So do not be too hasty when drawing conclusions from this sign.

Spiky or Rounded?

When analysing handwriting you should also look carefully to see how spiky or rounded it is. Are there a lot of angular, vertical strokes? Or just a few? Even if someone has learned angular Italic handwriting at school, he or she may have developed it considerably in later years.

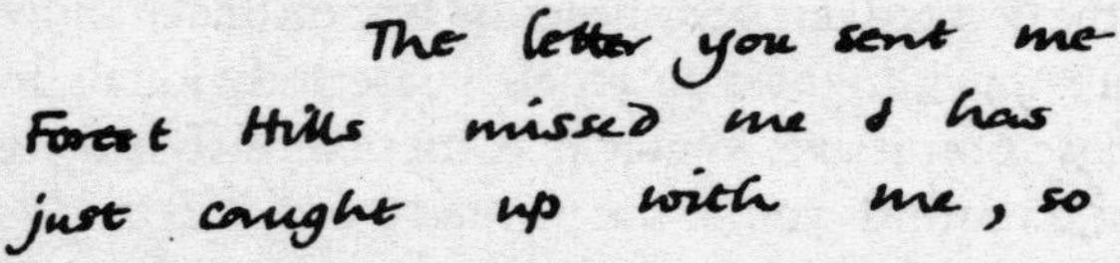

Virginia Wade's writing reveals a well-organized and practical nature. Wide spaces between the words show intelligence and independence of thought, while well-formed descending strokes indicate someone for whom physical activity and sensual comforts are important.

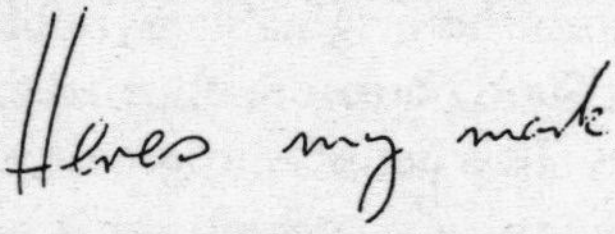

Jimmy Savile's handwriting is large, and slopes forward and upward, showing him to be an extrovert.

Taking a Closer Look

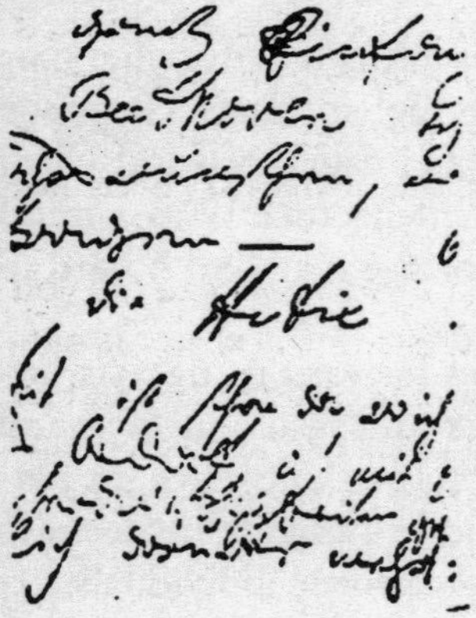

1. Entangled upper and lower zones indicate a very emotional nature. Such great historical characters as Beethoven and Queen Elizabeth I showed this sign, which is often found in the handwriting of people with tremendous energy.

2. The letter 'f' is interesting because it can cross all three zones. A full, open upper loop suggests a flexible outlook and some-

one who is open to new ideas. The larger the loop, the more emotional this person is thought to be. Full lower loops, especially if they are not accompanied by an upper one, signify practicality and balanced physical energy. Someone who does not give the 'f' a tail is inventive and thoughtful.

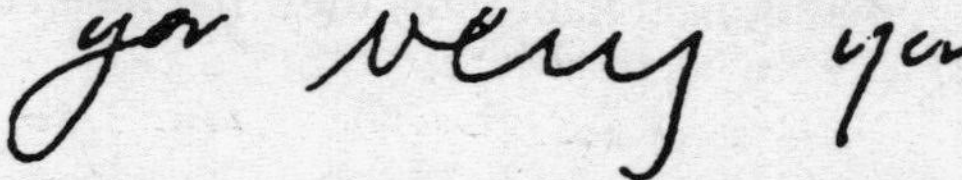

3. A straight down stroke in a 'y' reveals a sensible, yet lively mind; a wide, looped 'y' shows a happy-go-lucky nature; and an unfinished or small, hook-like lower loop can indicate fear of a physical relationship.

Signatures

Once you have opened the letter or card, you can learn more about the writer by looking at his or her signature.

An underlined signature suggests a sense of showmanship and positive and assertive personality. When this underlining is decorative or unusual, the person is likely to be creative.

Look carefully to see if this flourish is actually part of the name or separate from it. Where it joins with the signature, it denotes a fusion between public and private behaviour and self-image. When it is distinctly separate, it suggests that there is a private, hidden part of the personality which is often not revealed to others.

Any imbalance between forename and surname can tell you a lot, too. Where the surname is emphasized, the writer is particularly concerned with his or her social, outer self. A boldly written surname can often be seen on official letters and documents; the private individual – indicated by the forename – is often concealed by a brief initial.

Beginnings and Endings

Handwriting, like the personality itself, is full of small, subtle clues. These enhance the initial analysis by providing clues to those nuances of character which distinguish, say, one extrovert individual from another.

Such signs may vary within one sample of handwriting, and also from one example to another. They are often influenced by mood, the subject of the writing itself, or even the state of the subject's health. So, a number of examples are required by professionals so that they can see how regularly these signs appear. When they appear habitually they may be taken as reliable pointers.

Beginnings

The way a person begins words is a good indication of how he or she initiates projects, starts relationships and operates in the world at large.

Look out for hooks at the beginnings of words. If they are present, how high or low are they? A writer who consistently forms high hooks is likely to have a strong sense of personal identity and self-image. This sign might modify an analysis of small, apparently shy and introverted handwriting. This person may be slow to open up in company, but is certainly not suffering from low self-worth.

Low hooks and initial strokes to letters show an attachment to what is already established. These individuals seek a sense of security. They like to surround themselves with comfort – and depending on other signs – beauty as well. Mentally, they may be quite fixed in their opinions and slow to change.

No initial strokes at all – or very few – suggest a direct kind of person. Such a personality likes to get things done, clarify plans and has little patience with anyone who dithers.

Endings

Being able to complete projects, phases of life and relationships is an important part of the personality. Some people find it hard to let go of the past, while others live more for the moment. First of all, look to see whether the word endings go up or down – if any are present, that is.

Habitual upward flicks, curves or strokes indicate basic optimism – literally, an 'up' personality. The writer may be excited or inspired by his or her present circumstances.

Downward strokes enter the physical zone of handwriting.

They can suggest sensuality, a powerful sense of identity, and sometimes point towards a materialistic, practical nature.

Very plain word endings give little away. This person is probably very reserved and may be slow to reveal inner feelings until they know you very well.

Where the ends of words extend along the line, they usually denote someone with plenty of vitality who knows how to enjoy life. Sometimes these horizontal extensions join one word to another indicating spontaneity and impatience.

Corrections

Retracing and Obliterating

Look out too, for any retraced letters which are the sign of a responsible, self-critical person who may be a perfectionist.

Someone who habitually distorts or obliterates parts of their handwriting is said to be dynamic, passionate and irrational. They may find it hard to take a cool look at their emotions.

T-bars are another fascinating subtle sign, often revealing current states of mind, energy levels and stability or instability.

Basic t-bar analysis begins with a look at how high, low, long or short the t-bar is. A long t-bar denotes enthusiasm, assertiveness and energy. Those who consistently produce this sign are often leaders, may be quick tempered, and are usually determined characters who throw themselves into projects.

T-bars are another fascinating subtle sign

Short, precise bars indicate stability.

Very high t bars enter the spiritual zone

Very low bars show practicality and hesitancy.

A Sign of Stability

Short, carefully constructed t-bars indicate stable, scrupulous individuals. They may find it difficult to express anger and are likely to hate quarrelling. These individuals are precise in their thinking, logical and well-organized at work,

Very high t-bars enter the spiritual, creative zone. Therefore, they suggest someone who aspires to higher things, who seeks inspiration from art, music or literature, and who is an adventurous thinker. The lower the cross, the more practical, down to earth and hesitant the personality is likely to be.

The Alphabet Reveals

After a general look at a person's handwriting has given you an idea of their basic personality, it is time to search for the many more specific clues contained among the various letters.

Each one of us has created – and perhaps is still evolving – a unique style of writing which reflects our own individual personality traits. By carefully examining the way each letter is formed, it is possible to identify many of these traits and assess how they are likely to affect us.

Since it would be an impossible task to analyse the full extent of the variations possible within each letter, this part of the Graphology course lists only the most important indicators. These are described in alphabetical order. Capitals predominate because they tend to be more revealing than the small letters.

The Letter A

While small 'a's have already been described, capitals can be just as revealing. One of the most important clues is the treatment of cross bars.

If placed **low down** on the inverted V, this denotes a well organized, disciplined and – if supported by the rest of the writing – precise individual.

A **high placement** indicates that this person has aspirations and ideals, but could be a little arrogant at times.

A **descending** cross bar may be a sign of unhappiness, particularly if the rest of the writing slopes down the page. However, this may only be temporary.

A **wavy** cross bar is a sign of artistic leanings and imaginative flair. This creativity needs to be expressed verbally, or in the written word if the bar is **rising** – indeed, the writer may well possess talent in this direction.

Circular cross bars indicate an extrovert concerned with promoting their self-image.

An **extended** bar denotes someone who is philosophical about problems.

No cross bar at all suggests hastiness and carelessness.

Adam Ant

One of the early New Wave pop stars, Adam Ant has recently returned to the music scene. The variation in the height of cross bars on both 'A's reveal discipline and ambition. But the cross bar extension on both capitals indicates a philosophical attitude to life.

The Letter B

This letter is formed in the two upper zones, thus providing clues as to a person's mentality and sense of self.

A **wide lower loop** points to naivety, while an **exaggerated upper curve** denotes arrogance. Look, too, for **openings** on the baseline: a large one suggests tendencies towards introspection, while a narrow one is the mark of a lively, sociable character.

Generally, a **narrow shaped** capital 'B' suggests inhibitions, or perhaps even shyness, while **generously curved** 'B's belong to more outgoing, confident types. Watch out for an **angular** formation: it is said to denote a mean streak.

The Letter C

When **angular** or **squared-off**, this letter reveals skill with the hands and possibly some mechanical ability on the part of the writer. If there is an **angle at the base** it is a sign of stubbornness and a memory of slights.

Rounded 'C's – whether capital or small – reveal gentleness, idealism and trust. When decorated with **loops and scrolls** they denote a healthy ego, often coupled with a love of comfort and material success, plus a little vanity thrown in for good measure.

The Letter D

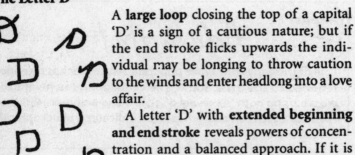

A **large loop** closing the top of a capital 'D' is a sign of a cautious nature; but if the end stroke flicks upwards the individual may be longing to throw caution to the winds and enter headlong into a love affair.

A letter 'D' with **extended beginning and end stroke** reveals powers of concentration and a balanced approach. If it is **open at the top**, this individual could be frivolous, while **open at the bottom** points to a desire to understand life's mysteries. Should the curved part of the letter be completely separate from the upright stroke, there may be some eccentricity in the personality of the writer.

Starting strokes can also be revealing. Watch out for a **long stroke**, indicating argumentative tendencies, or a **short hooked stroke** revealing lack of self confidence – especially if the 'D' is narrow and the handwriting small. Impatience is revealed by a

Salvador Dali, the Spanish surrealist artist, signed his name with a 'D' which is barely recognisable as such, indicating his original approach to both his life and art.

straight starting stroke while a **tall first stroke** rising above the rest of the letter points to a person with initiative.

The Letter E

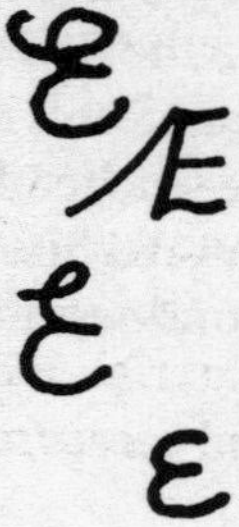

Many people start their capital 'E's with a stroke or hook of some kind. A **large loop** here suggests an impractical person, who may even be poetic or musical. A **long starting stroke** springing from below the baseline denotes a good memory, but also someone who may bear a grudge for years. A **short starting loop** indicates a sense of style, while **Greek 'E's** mark a quick thinker.

The Letter F

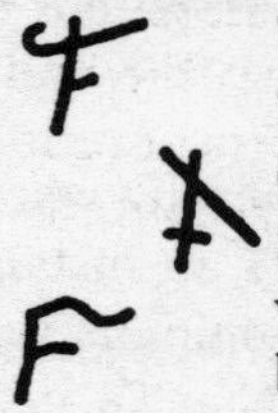

The **top bar** on an 'F' can tell you something about the mentality of the writer. If **sloping upward** it can denote humour, ambition, and a strong-willed individual. Some selfishness is revealed by **downward-sloping top bars** while **wavy top bars** belong to extrovert types.

The Letter G

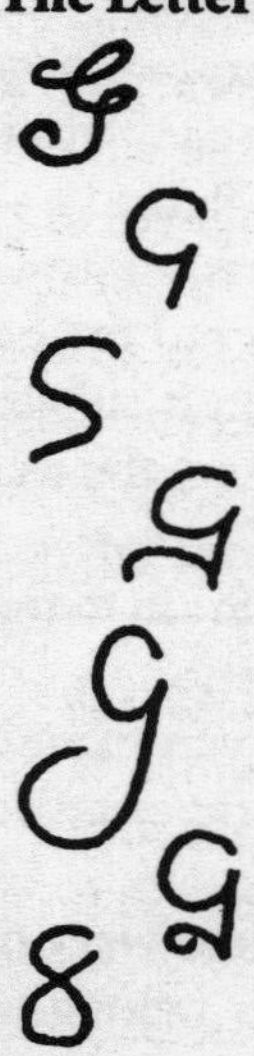

With a 'G' the writer has a choice – they can remain in the top two zones, or extend the letter downwards into the bottom zone.

A **looped beginning** to a capital 'G' suggests someone who has their head in the clouds and tends to ignore practical issues.

'G's with **short, straight down strokes** denote clear-thinking people who can concentrate well on their work. **S-shaped** 'G's denote an inability to cope under pressure, while **arcs and hooks** to the left reveal self-protective tendencies and often a need for material security. Any **large lower loops** on their letter are suggestive of a strong sexual nature, while **Greek 'G's** traditionally indicate taste and cultivation.

The Letter H

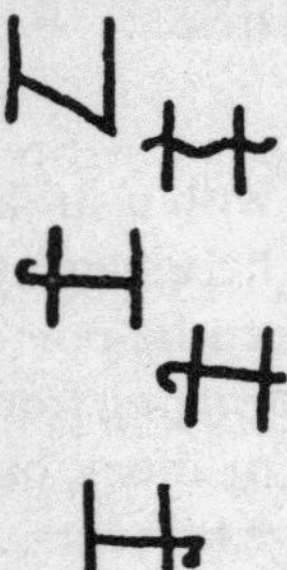

An 'H' **which looks like an 'N'** denotes an open mind, while a **wavy cross bar** reveals a sense of humour. If you spot an **upward-curving hook** on the left of the cross bar then the writer is a practical person, but a **downward hook** in the same position denotes someone who tends to hold back in company. A downward hook **on the right hand side** suggests a fondness for money.

The Letter I

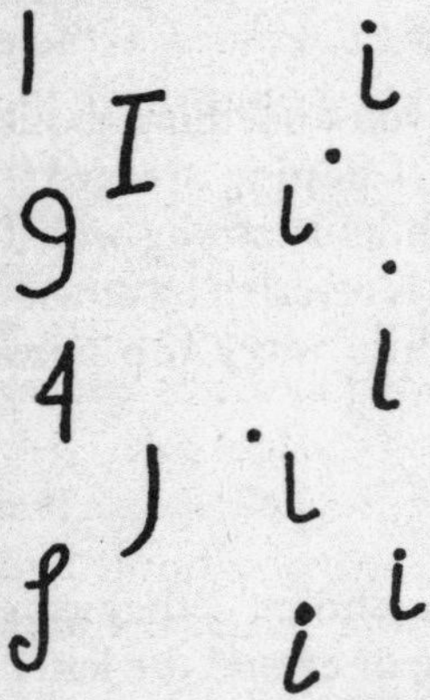

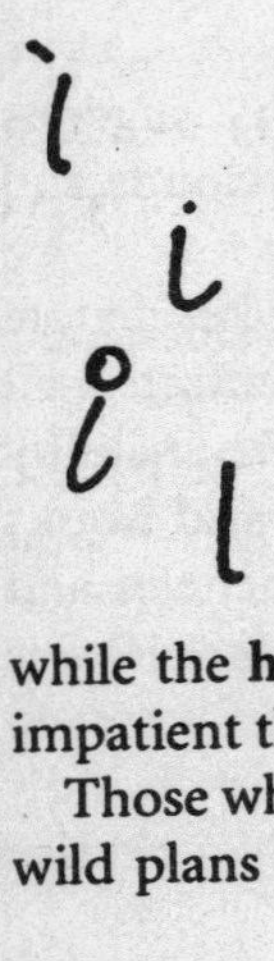

Both capital and small 'I's are fascinating material for the graphologist since this letter is also what we call ourselves, it can hardly fail to be revealing.

The **size** of the 'I' – especially when referring to the self – gives an instant measure of the writer's self-opinion.

Plainly written, clear capital 'I's are a sign of intelligence, while if fenced in by upper and lower **cross strokes** they can indicate a cultured mind. **An upper loop** on this letter suggests a large ego, while an angular one – looking a little like a figure '4' – shows an inability to understand others' motives or character clearly. An end stroke **curved to the left** denotes a thoughtful type, but when it **curves right round** it points to a need to protect the self in some way.

The position of the humble dot in relation to the small letter 'i' can be a mine of information.

A **dot to the right** suggests an observant mind, while the **higher the placement**, the more idealistic but also impatient the writer is likely to be.

Those who dot their 'I's **to the left** are cautious and wary of wild plans or schemes. **Low placed dots** generally belong to more down-to-earth types, while those written with **deliberate pressure** supply evidence of will-power.

Dash-like dots denote energy, stubborn qualities and often high principles. Such types may also be hard on others, especially if the dash-dot **inclines to the left.**

Weak, barely visible dots may occur when someone is not very well or feeling low on energy.

Circular dots reveal a healthy ego, while those who omit to dot their 'I's altogether are – not surprisingly – careless or forgetful.

The Letter J

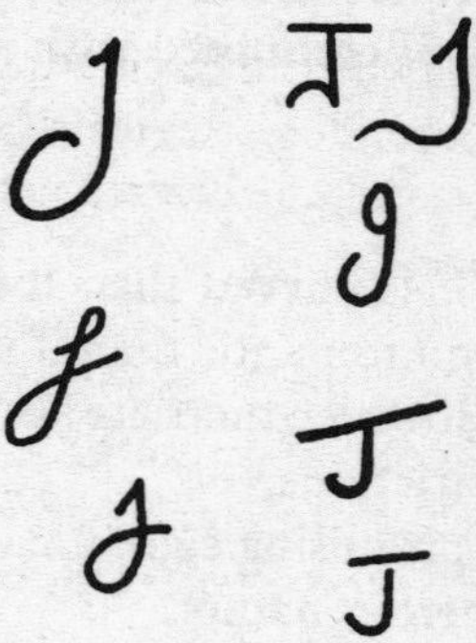

Dots on a small 'j' are often omitted, and are less indicative of carelessness. If there is a dot, however, the meanings are the same as for 'i's.

A capital 'J' may cross all the zones, or remain in the top two. When it descends into the **lower zone**, it indicates a strongly sexual nature in which fantasy probably plays an important role.

Large lower curves and loops on this letter also suggest a love of comfort, and often a fondness for music – particularly when there is a **loop to the left.**

Arcs and hooks to the left reveal the writer's attitude towards material responsibilities: if weakly drawn, they indicate a wish to avoid such entanglements; if heavily emphasized, there is a need to hold on to money and possessions.

Loops in the upper zone suggests a rather head-in-the-clouds type who may well be artistic.

A **large top bar** denotes a changeable mind. If the **top bar is separate** from the rest of the letter, it indicates a clever mind and a person with the ability to analyse other people's behaviour – a graphologist perhaps?

The Letter K

End strokes on the letter K can be highly revealing. **Vertical**

end strokes denote frankness, while those which **descend below the baseline** reveal a self-protective individual who could be on the defensive.

A **short end stroke** which does not extend to the baseline is certainly a sign of ambition.

If the letter is formed of **three separate strokes** it shows good organisational abilities; **two separate halves** reveal an individualistic approach to life.

Look out, too, for a **concave second stroke** like a shallow 'c': this shows leadership qualities, especially if **combined with a tall first stroke.**

The letter L

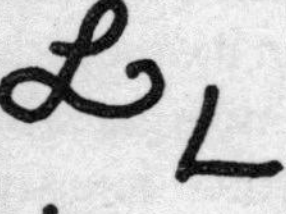

Generally speaking, if an 'L' is **curved** then the writer is more emotional and romantic than if it is very **plain and angular.** However, there are also a number of more subtle variations.

A **large upper loop** is a promising sign, for it reveals someone with a generous nature.

A **very small loop** is said to signify jealousy – and if it is **also hooked,** avarice.

A **large lower loop** extending to the left denotes extrovert qualities, while any **extra decoration** shows a vain streak.

Closed loops on this letter speak of secretiveness, while the more **open and curvaceous** the loop, the more sensitive and imaginative the individual.

The Letter M

Angular 'M's usually reveal mental stability, while the **degree of width** is a clue to the writer's ambition and dynamism.

Curving and **looped** 'M's show a desire to control others and feel that the world around contains no unpleasant surprises.

A **tall first loop** – particularly if part of a signature – shows that the writer has a good opinion of themselves, while a **tall or peaked second loop** is also indicative of pride.

If the **end stroke** extends noticeably to the right, the writer has the ability to see ahead and plan effectively.

Thread-like M's denote indecision and hasty thinking.

The Letter N

Starting and ending strokes are the important things to watch for on a capital 'N'.

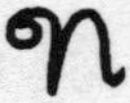

Loopy beginnings suggest modesty and unassertiveness.

A **circle on the first stroke** signifies a jealous nature.

A **descending end stroke** reveals someone who likes to be alone at times. A **hook** here suggests strength of character, while an end stroke which is **shorter than the starting stroke** shows a naturally reserved person.

End strokes **leaning to the left** belong to people who can take care of themselves, but if the strokes are exaggerated it suggests a fear of the future. Any kind of extra pressure here shows a forthright individual who may be too frank for comfort.

Wavy 'N's show a versatile mind, and an ability to get on with people superficially.

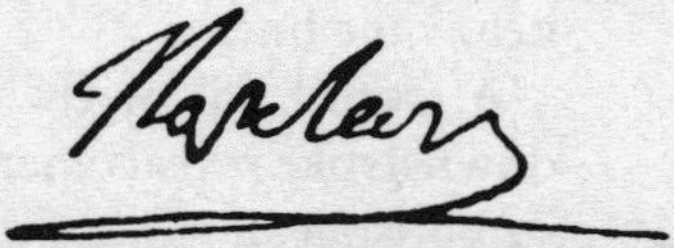

Napoleon's heavy, right-slanting signature shows pride, action and showmanship (note the underline), but also thoughtfulness. The 'p' downstroke suggests sex problems.

The Letter O

Like the number zero, the letter 'O', symbolizes both eternity and nothingness.

Narrow 'O's signify a reserved, cautious person; they may also point to a secretive nature if other handwriting signs verify this. Surprisingly, a **broad, generous** 'O' can suggest similar traits – look for openings and loops to provide further clues.

A **top knot**, is a sign of a secretive nature; an **opening at the bottom**, reveals someone who can not be trusted. An 'O' which is **open at the top** suggests an open but rather naive person.

The Letter P

Capital 'P's show a person's approach to everyday life. See how far a small 'p' drops into the lower zone to learn how the writer feels about sex and their physical nature.

Angular 'P's signal artistic leanings, coupled with drive and ambition if the letter is **upright** or **leaning forward.**

A 'P' formed by **two separate strokes** shows mild eccentricity, a lively nature, and impatience.

A **curled endstroke** denotes a watchful, observant person.

The Letter Q

Judge capital 'Q's as for large 'O's. Similarly, check how far small 'q's – like 'p's – descend below the line.

A small 'q' with a **long straight downstroke** reveals energy, will-power and stubbornness.

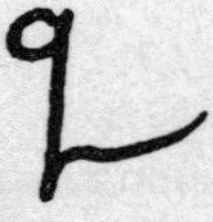

An end stroke which **extends to the right** points to a confident person; one which **flicks upward** denotes an extrovert.

The Letter R

The most important clues in the capital 'R' are contained in the upper loop, the first stroke and the end stroke.

An 'R' formed from **two separate strokes** denotes a logical, decisive mind. When coupled with an **opening at the top**, this indicates communication skills.

A small 'r' written in a **flat, illegible way** hides a potentially disorganized approach to the practicalities of life, while **clear** 'r's signal clear thinking.

The Letter S

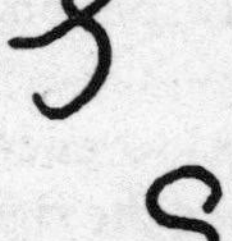

A naturally rounded letter, 'S' often points to a person's creative flow. Decide whether the letter curves freely, or seems to be rather inhibited.

A **rounded** or **looped** capital 'S' signifies an optimistic and expansive nature.

An **inner loop on the baseline** of a small 's' indicates a person who withholds information.

An **open** or **simple** 's' reveals honesty and thought for others.

The Letter T

The cross bar on both small and capital 'T's shows the diversity and application of a person's energy and drive. Where the writer exhibits several kinds of 'T's, look for other clues: a style of writing which suggests overall intelligence reveals versatility and wide vision; poorly formed writing denotes muddled thinking.

When the top bar on a capital 'T' moves **upwards at an angle** it points to freedom and vitality of spirit. If it is **separated** from the stem, this shows an ambitious nature – especially if the stroke **extends upwards to the right.**

A **curvaceous** capital 'T' – the sign of artistic leanings – may reveal selfishness and pride; look for other signs in the writing which might back this up.

Small 't's provide a mine of information.

A **long cross bar** is a sign of enthusiasm; a **short** stroke signals stability, but also inhibition.

Where the cross bar is **written as part of the letter** it points to a quick, practical mind which may be accompanied by a temper.

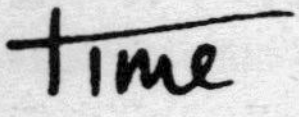

No cross bar suggests a lack of attention to detail; verify this by checking other signs – such as the way 'i's are dotted, and the size and slope of the writing. Either the writer is careless, or has a mind so full of ideas that they simply spill on to the page.

A **descending cross bar** points to low energy but if the bar is **separate and extends to the right**, it shows someone who may have trouble implementing their grand plans and ambitions.

A cross bar that **extends over other letters** shows a protective person who has natural authority. The bar acts as a roof, covering the material and physical zones.

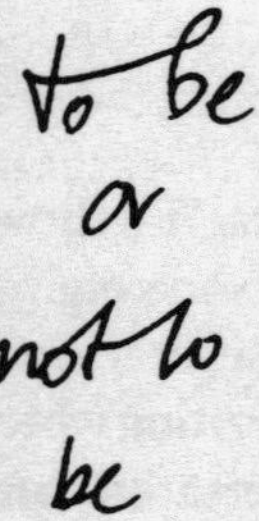

A bar that **links other letters or words** shows an ability to organize ideas into sequence – it is often found in writing of lawyers and chess players. If this sign appears in other words, it shows ambition and mental activity.

Bent cross bars indicate a lack of vitality, or anxiety.

Curvaceous bars point to thoroughness, but also to lack of imagination. Alternatively, they could show erratic energy levels. A number of samples taken at different times will confirm whether the sign is an entrenched part of the character.

The Letters U to Z

On their own, these letters are not particularly significant. Check the direction, the zones occupied, and use of space; also, watch for any hooks, curls or flourishes. These signs can all be used to back up indication signalled by other letters.

Doodle Analysis

From time to time, no doubt, you have come across odd scribblings or doodles on the notepads of colleagues; and most probably, you have dismissed them as the jottings of a bored mind. But, crude as they often are, these patterns and pictures may actually reveal considerable information about the temperament and mood of the person who penned them, for doodles usually come straight from the subconscious.

Picture Language

Doodles, like dreams, involve a form of picture language; and interpreting that language is what doodle analysis is really all about. Among the factors which have to be taken into account when considering doodles, is their position on the page, together with their size.

Doodle very large and in the middle of a piece of paper and this is probably indicative of how important you would like your role in life to be. But doodle in the margin or at the corner of a sheet and this could mark you out as a rather quiet and retiring individual who hates to stand out in a crowd.

Starting Points

Where you start to doodle on the page can also be of relevance. Indeed, doodles that begin to the left of a piece of paper and then develop towards the right are said to be highly significant in the terms of what is going on in the subconscious: whereas those that start to the right and work to the left are thought to be based on logic.

Doodles that have been started at the bottom of a page and which develop upwards are usually the sign of an ambitious personality. More introverted people, however, may well start to doodle at the centre of a piece of paper, working outwards, but then moving inwards again.

Intensity of Ink

You can also tell a great deal about mood from how the intensity of ink or lead varies from day to day. On good days, strokes used will be lighter; but very heavily shaded doodles may signal depression.

A-Z of Doodle Symbolism

Arrows

These are the doodles of the aggressively ambitious.

Boxes

Mostly drawn by men, stacked boxes point to methodical thinkers. Closed, they signify self-centredness and a desire for privacy. When drawn open, however, they may be a reflection of a wish to welcome someone to share your space. Alternatively, they may indicate a desire to escape from a restrictive situation.

Cats

When analysing a doodled cat, you will need to examine the drawing rather carefully. Is the sketch simply playful in nature? Or are there any signs of aggression and spite?

Dots

Masses of dots that form a pattern or picture are usually the doodles of a fragmented personality. They can also indicate an extreme state of anxiety or lack of stability.

Eyes

Usually considered a strongly sexual symbol, the eye doodle may be the sign of a wish to be alluring. But watch for paranoid tendencies, too: for when repeatedly doodled, eyes may indicate that the subject feels he or she is constantly being watched.

Flowers

Most doodled flowers are penned by women and are the sign of a romantic nature, and of the desire to blossom and be fruitful in life.

Guns

Not unexpectedly, doodled guns provide evidence of sublimated aggression.

Houses

Among the most common of all doodles, houses are usually drawn by women and can provide a very clear indication of how the individual feels about her home environment. Look for clues such as whether the front door is open or closed; whether there is smoke coming from the chimney showing a welcoming hearth; or whether the garden is completely fenced in. Unhappy homes are often represented by asymmetrical structures without windows.

Intricate Patterns

Very detailed doodles tend to be drawn by people who are obsessive by nature and who simply will not let go of ambitions or loved ones. They are also likely to be the jottings of highly introverted individuals.

Jets

Airplanes of all kinds are common as doodles among adolescent boys and are said to be evidence of a strong sex drive.

Keys

Doodle a key and it could well be that you are desperately seeking the means to escape from some sort of claustrophobic situation.

Lips

Doodled lips are usually sexual in connotation, pointing to frustrated desire of some kind. They are generally drawn by women.

Mazes

Draw an intricate maze and the chances are that you feel you are in a tight spot. Alternatively, it could be a sign of a need for protection from some threatening element in your life.

Newspaper Headlines

Those who fill in or embellish letters in newspaper headlines are usually thought to be the soldiers in life rather than initiators.

Oceans

Seascapes are typical doodles of those who spend a lot of time indulging their imagination but who rarely put their fantasies into practice.

Portraits

Faces are primarily the doodles of adolescent girls seeking to produce idealized self-portraits. Additionally, they can sometimes represent the mother-figure, seen as a rival for father's affections. Faces in profile, meanwhile, can be a sign of an introverted personality; and comic faces, more often drawn by men, are an indication of a desire to be the centre of attraction.

Question Marks

Not surprisingly, these signify a difficult decision that has to be made, or doubt about one's role in life.

Robots

If you doodle an automation, that may be precisely how you feel: lacking in self-assertion and probably rather bored with your everyday existence.

Signatures

The individual who repeatedly doodles his or her own initials or full name is often someone who has an identity problem. Such doodles are also often drawn by newly-wed women, as if in an attempt to reassure themselves about their new surnames.

Trees

Doodle a tree without leaves or root formation and that may show how you feel inside: isolated and without strong family ties. A tree blowing in the wind may pinpoint instability in a relationship, while a poplar or tall pine tree can sometimes be phallic in significance.

Umbrellas

Drawings of open umbrellas generally signify a desire to extend help to a loved one, or to be protected oneself from unpleasant outside influences.

Vehicles

Doodles of luxury cars usually pinpoint a hankering after the material things in life. A doodled train, however, signifies someone who is more likely to proceed with caution but who is determined to get there in the end.

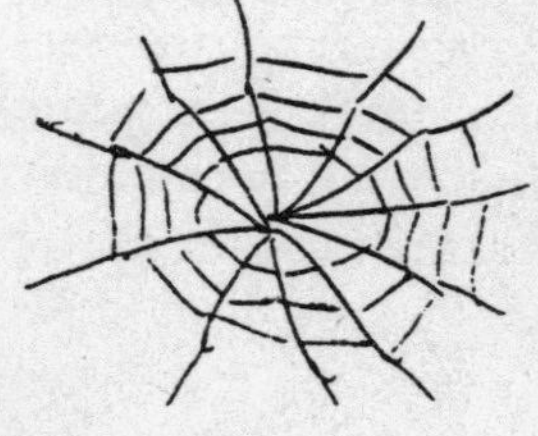

Webs

A doodled cobweb can often symbolize either a sense of being trapped, or the desire to entice someone else into a particular relationship or situation.

X

Repeated star shapes are often drawn by women, and are the sign of the irrepressibly romantic.

Yachts

A doodled sailing boat usually indicates a wish to escape from restricting circumstances.

Zigzags

This sort of pattern, involving a repeated action of pen or pencil, is rather satisfying to draw and so may signal a need for comfort. It can also pinpoint a need to regress to childhood and to withdraw from harsh everyday realities.

I CHING

The Wisdom of Fu Hsi

The *I Ching*, or Book of Changes, is one of the five sacred classics regarded by the Chinese with the same reverence that other nations have for the Bible. It also is probably the oldest method of divination in continuous use. Thousands of years ago, it existed as a simple device to give a 'yes' or 'no' answer to any question asked. But over the centuries, it became a highly organized system, venerated by everyone from the humblest peasant to the Chinese Emperor.

Yet despite its ancient and sacred origins, the I Ching is actually quite simple to use, and is now highly popular all over the world as a method of obtaining guidance in daily life.

Chinese Wisdom

According to legend, about five thousand years ago, the Chinese Emperor Fu Hsi was meditating on the bank of a river when a strange animal, a dragon-horse, climbed from the water. Fu Hsi was intrigued by the curious patterns of lines on its scales, and in a sudden flash of insight conceived the notion of a series of diagrams, which would be sufficient to encompass all knowledge.

To the modern reader, the I Ching may at first appear to be a rather bewildering jumble of disconnected and contradictory utterances. But the reason for this becomes clear once it is realized that it is not meant to be read through as a continuous text. It is actually a list of answers to an oracle, to be consulted for advice on any matter.

Yet although its words may seem enigmatic and tantalising, the I Ching is said by many people who use it to give surprisingly appropriate answers to questions. It will not tell the enquirer exactly what is about to happen, but it will provide advice about how he or she could act in a particular situation.

The Sixty-four Sections & Ten Wings

The book itself has a fairly straightforward structure. There are 64 sections, all of which follow the same pattern. Each section begins with a diagram of six horizontal lines, known as a hexagram, which corresponds to one of the many possible combinations of lines obtained by the coins or yarrow stalks thrown by the person consulting the oracle.

Each line of a hexagram may be broken (representing the Chinese *yin* or feminine principle) or unbroken (representing the Chinese *yang* or masculine principle). There is no obvious order, except that every other hexagram is often the reverse of the one that precedes it.

Hexagram Names

Each hexagram has a name, taken from the first one or two Chinese characters of the text attached to it. After the hexagram is a mystical phrase – the 'main text' -- which might be anything from a couple of words to an entire verse of an ancient song or incantation. In the majority of cases, the main text consists of stock phrases such as 'There will be good fortune'.

These texts are the oldest part of the I Ching, and may represent oracles handed down by word of mouth for thousands of years. Six extra lines follow on from the main text. While the main text applies to the whole hexagram, these six lines apply individually to its six lines.

Ten Wings

Bound together with these 64 texts is another lengthy philosophical commentary, divided into 'Ten Wings'. This is of much later date, and is not part of the original oracle, although it helps to explain its idea.

Consulting the I Ching

The way of consulting the *I Ching* described here is based on the ancient method using yarrow stalks.

You will need a bundle of 49 wood or bamboo splints – matchsticks will do for practice – and a notepad and pencil for marking down the individual lines of the hexagram as it is revealed.

CONSULTING THE I CHING

Today, the most usual method of consulting the I Ching is to throw three coins on to a table, noting whether they fall as heads or tails. Many enthusiasts like to use genuine old Chinese coins, but modern western coins will do just as well. This is done six times, to obtain the six lines of a hexagram. A simple formula based on the correspondence of heads with *yang* and tails with *yin* reveals whether the line is *yang* (unbroken) or *yin* (broken). Alternatively, a serious devotee will take a bundle of yarrow stalks, and go through a laborious process of casting and counting the sticks until the final result is reached. The process is deliberately long and monotonous, because it is believed that it concentrates the mind, producing a state of meditation.

Ask the Oracle

First, decide on the question you wish to put to the oracle. Frame your questions in such a way that they can be answered with a 'yes' or 'no'.

Shuffle the bundle of sticks, thinking hard about your question, and then divide the sticks into seven piles, at random, lining them up from left to right.

Count out the sticks in the first pile by twos; if there is one left over, the bottom line of the hexagram is *yang*, or full (—). If no sticks are left over, the bottom line is *yin*, or broken (— —). Note down the line in the notebook you have set aside.

Repeat the process for all the piles of sticks except the seventh, which is left over, noting down the line each time above the previous one. The resulting hexagram will provide the answer to your question.

Next, consult the table to find the hexagram's number. Once you know the number, you can check the answer to your question.

The text of the 64 hexagrams follows. Although it is brief, the interpretations convey the mysticism of the original.

To find the number of a hexagram, look for its upper three lines, or trigram, along the top line, and its lower trigram along the vertical line at left. Read down and right from these lines to find the number where they meet.

Upper / Lower	☰	☷	☵	☲	☳	☶	☴	☱
☰	1	11	5	14	34	26	9	43
☷	12	2	8	35	16	23	20	45
☵	6	7	29	64	40	4	59	47
☲	13	36	63	30	55	22	37	49
☳	25	24	3	21	51	27	42	17
☶	33	15	39	56	62	52	53	31
☴	44	46	48	50	32	18	57	28
☱	10	19	60	38	54	41	61	58

THE EIGHT TRIGRAMS

☰	**Heaven**	Ch'ien – Creative, positive, masculine Father
☷	**Earth**	K'un – Receptive, negative, feminine, Mother
☵	**Water**	K'an – The Moon, danger, middle son
☲	**Fire**	Li – Lightning, heat, middle daughter
☳	**Thunder**	Chen – Arousing, eldest son
☶	**Mountain**	Ken – Still, obstruction, youngest son
☴	**Wind**	Sun – Penetration, wood, eldest daughter
☱	**Lake**	Tui – Joy, clouds, youngest daughter

The Sixty-Four Hexagrams

These interpretations are based on the original Chinese text.

1. **Action** – Take action: the result will be very favourable. Continue with your plans.

2. **Reaction** – There is no need to force the issue: the desired result will come about.

3. **Germination** – Matters are still in their formative stages: handle them with care.

4. **Growth** – If matters do not succeed at first, by all means make a second attempt.

5. **Watering** – There is great promise for the future. It is to your advantage to cross water.

6. **Dispute** – There will be arguments with former allies. Take the advice of a superior.

7. **Military** – There is opportunity for promotion. Matters improve with determination.

8. **Assistance** – A partnership will bring great success in personal or business life.

9. **Small Containment** – Little comes of great promises. Be thankful for small gains.

10. **Caution** – With caution, you can make a bold move and succeed in the way you wish.

11. **Success** – Bit by bit, you will succeed; but if you are too rash, you will lose out.

12. **Obstacles** – Obstacles ahead mean that you need to be forceful. Do not be too timid.

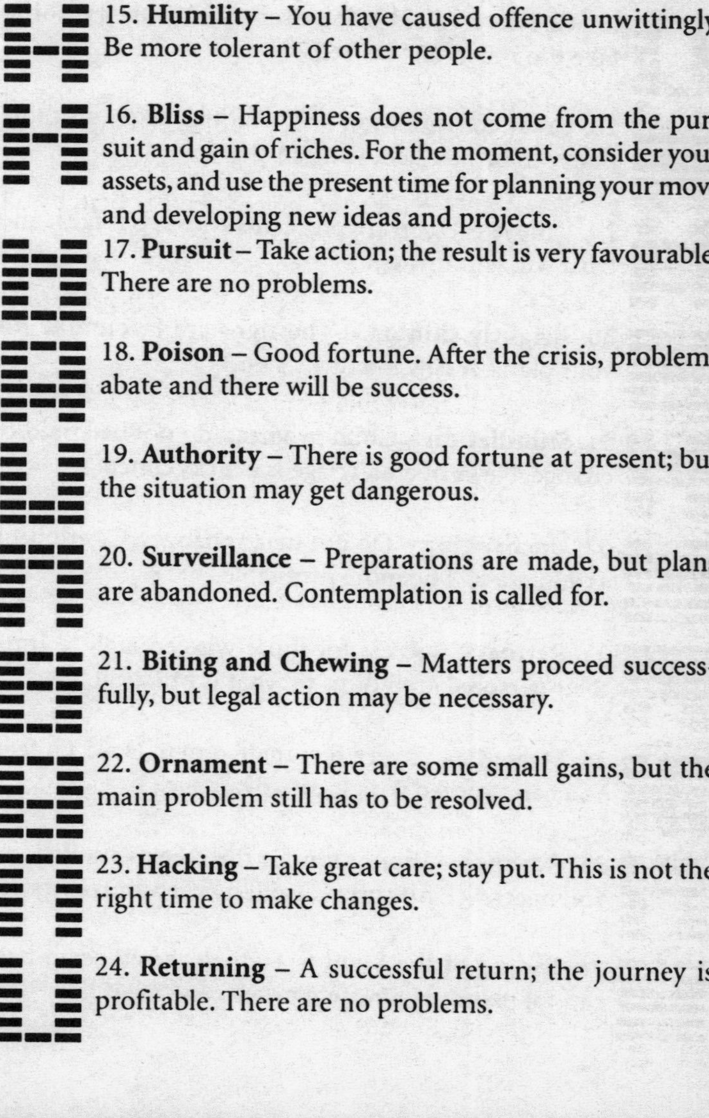

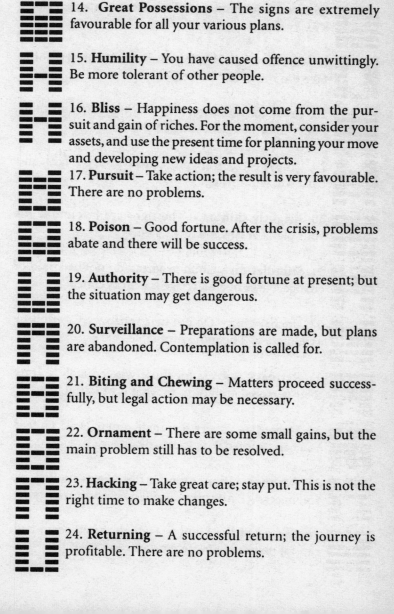

13. **Union of People** – Joining with others will bring success. Crossing water is also favourable.

14. **Great Possessions** – The signs are extremely favourable for all your various plans.

15. **Humility** – You have caused offence unwittingly. Be more tolerant of other people.

16. **Bliss** – Happiness does not come from the pursuit and gain of riches. For the moment, consider your assets, and use the present time for planning your move and developing new ideas and projects.

17. **Pursuit** – Take action; the result is very favourable. There are no problems.

18. **Poison** – Good fortune. After the crisis, problems abate and there will be success.

19. **Authority** – There is good fortune at present; but the situation may get dangerous.

20. **Surveillance** – Preparations are made, but plans are abandoned. Contemplation is called for.

21. **Biting and Chewing** – Matters proceed successfully, but legal action may be necessary.

22. **Ornament** – There are some small gains, but the main problem still has to be resolved.

23. **Hacking** – Take great care; stay put. This is not the right time to make changes.

24. **Returning** – A successful return; the journey is profitable. There are no problems.

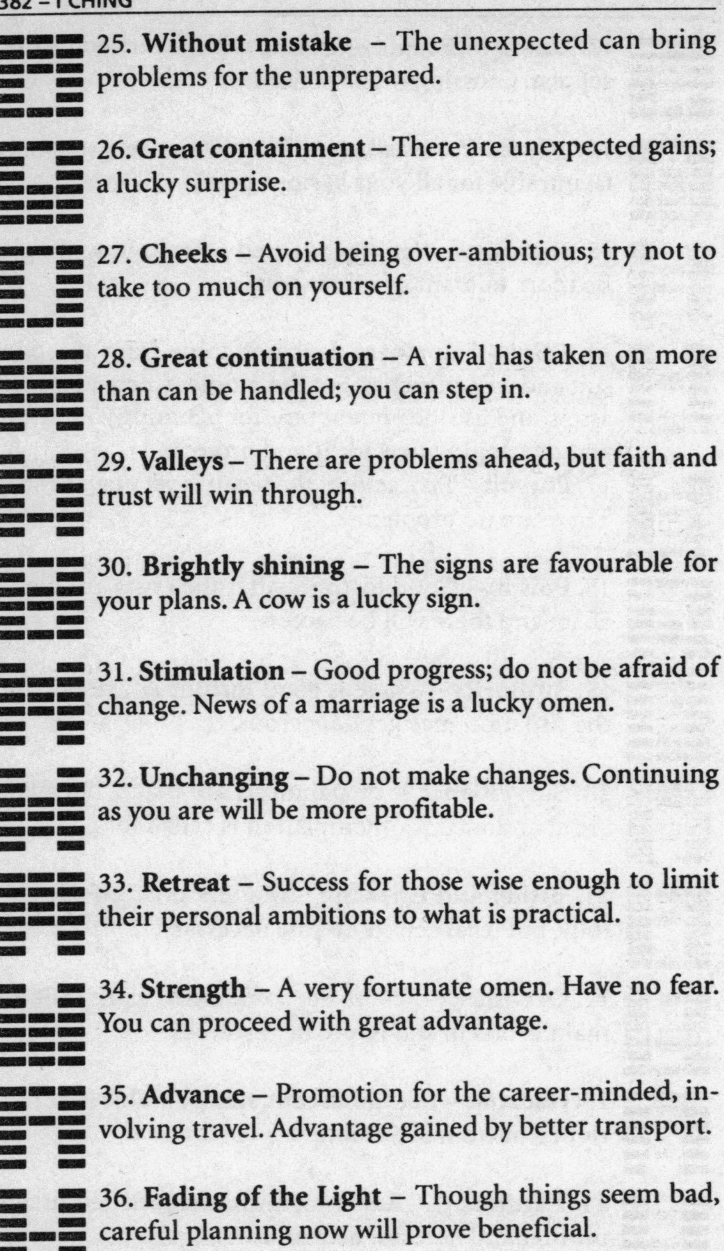

25. **Without mistake** – The unexpected can bring problems for the unprepared.

26. **Great containment** – There are unexpected gains; a lucky surprise.

27. **Cheeks** – Avoid being over-ambitious; try not to take too much on yourself.

28. **Great continuation** – A rival has taken on more than can be handled; you can step in.

29. **Valleys** – There are problems ahead, but faith and trust will win through.

30. **Brightly shining** – The signs are favourable for your plans. A cow is a lucky sign.

31. **Stimulation** – Good progress; do not be afraid of change. News of a marriage is a lucky omen.

32. **Unchanging** – Do not make changes. Continuing as you are will be more profitable.

33. **Retreat** – Success for those wise enough to limit their personal ambitions to what is practical.

34. **Strength** – A very fortunate omen. Have no fear. You can proceed with great advantage.

35. **Advance** – Promotion for the career-minded, involving travel. Advantage gained by better transport.

36. **Fading of the Light** – Though things seem bad, careful planning now will prove beneficial.

37. **Family** – In family matters, it will be wise to allow the woman to make the decision.

38. **Division** – it is beneficial to break off unhelpful relationships. Small deeds bring great rewards.

39. **Stumbling** – The answer lies to the south-west. A meeting with an authority figure brings advantage.

40. **Untangling** – The answer lies in the south-west. Retreat unless there is a pressing need to advance.

41. **Reducing** – It is advisable to cut down on expenditure now. Sacrifice will bring advantages later.

42. **Increase** – Yes, it is all right to go ahead. There will be advantage in crossing over water.

43. **Overflow** – A sudden warning. You must act promptly otherwise you may suffer severe losses.

44. **Meeting** – Beware of becoming trapped in a situation which puts you in a weak position.

45. **Assembling** – Honour and acclaim; a great occasion. Expenditure will be heavy, but justified by results.

46. **Rising** – The answer lies in the south. The signs are extremely favourable for all your plans.

47. **Contraction** – In difficult times trust actions, not words. Success if you remain determined.

48. **The Well** – This hexagram warns of failure and possible misfortune through miscalculation.

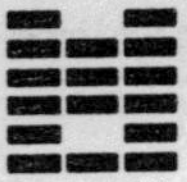

49. **Rotation** – The sixth day brings success. When the troubles have passed you can start again.

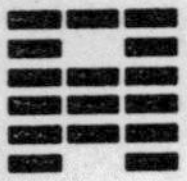

50. **Cauldron** – This hexagram signals great success. You should proceed with advantage.

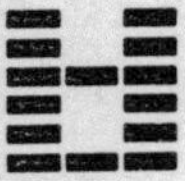

51. **Thunderclaps** – Laughter follows a momentary fright. There should be no damage done.

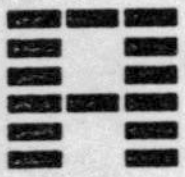

52. **Immobility** – Avoid trouble by keeping out of the way and trying not to be noticed.

53. **Progress** – The marriage of a young girl is a good omen. Proceed with confidence.

54. **The Marrying Maiden** – The marriage of a young lady is a bad omen. Abandon plans.

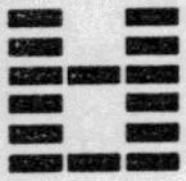

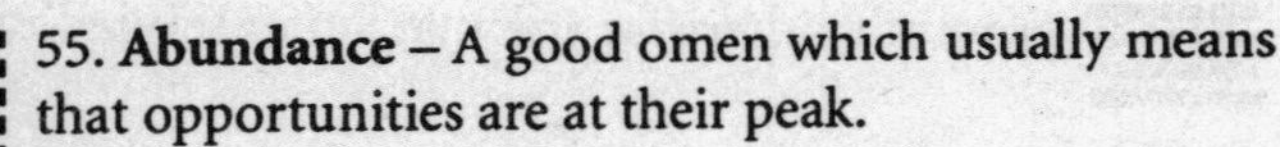

55. **Abundance** – A good omen which usually means that opportunities are at their peak.

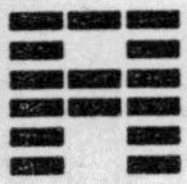

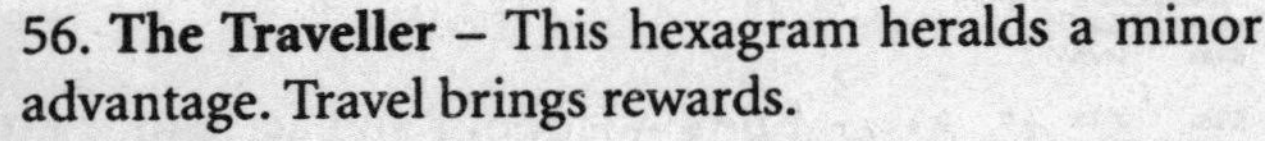

56. **The Traveller** – This hexagram heralds a minor advantage. Travel brings rewards.

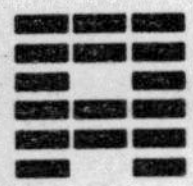

57. **Homage** – This is the time to move up in the world. Seeing a person in authority will help you.

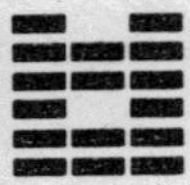

58. **Joy** – This hexagram brings good news. Everything is progressing to your advantage.

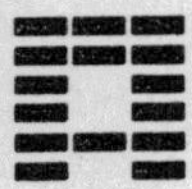

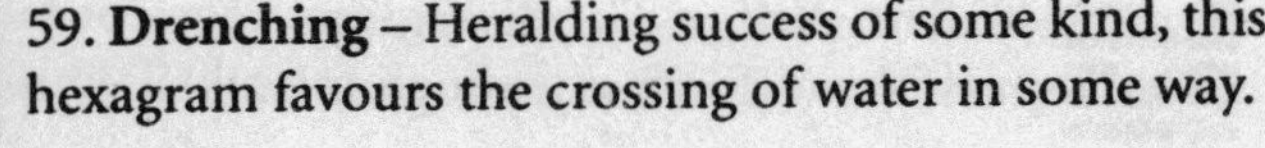

59. **Drenching** – Heralding success of some kind, this hexagram favours the crossing of water in some way.

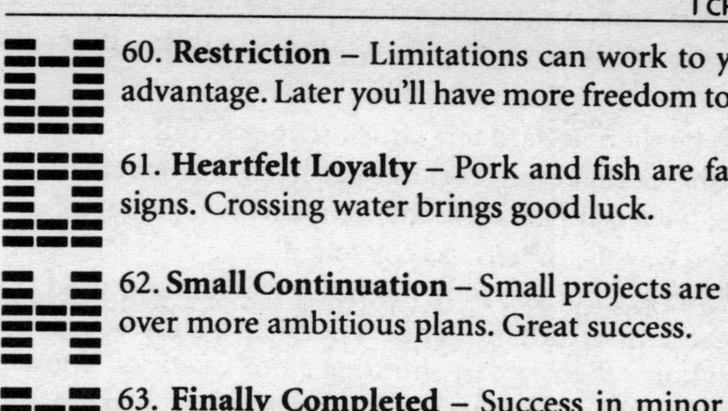

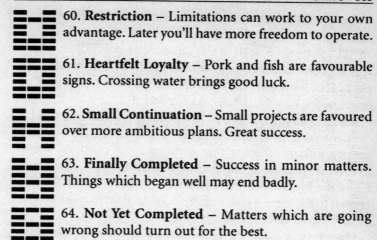

60. **Restriction** – Limitations can work to your own advantage. Later you'll have more freedom to operate.

61. **Heartfelt Loyalty** – Pork and fish are favourable signs. Crossing water brings good luck.

62. **Small Continuation** – Small projects are favoured over more ambitious plans. Great success.

63. **Finally Completed** – Success in minor matters. Things which began well may end badly.

64. **Not Yet Completed** – Matters which are going wrong should turn out for the best.

Interpreting the I Ching

Chinese literature abounds in tales of famous seers who were expert users of the I Ching. Usually, the oracle was consulted on serious matters, such as the course and treatment of an illness (the next of Hexagram 18 hints at this), the success of a hazardous journey (Hexagram 24), or even guidance on marriage (Hexagram 31).

For the most part, however, the hexagram texts were considered symbolic. For example, the odd remark in Hexagram 30 ('A cow is a lucky sign') would mean that the questioner's fortunes would change for the better once a cow, or a picture of one, has been seen unexpectedly.

Sometimes, diviners were tested on their powers by being asked to 'Shoot the Box'. They were presented with a sealed box, and had to divine the contents using I Ching.

One famous sage, Kuan Lu, seems to have specialized in this particular skill, using the I Ching's symbolism to guess such diverse objects as a spider or a pheasant's feather. But he refused to divulge the secrets of his art.

Kuan Lu lived in the third century AD, and it is possible that the text of the I Ching as he knew it was not quite the same as it exists today. There were several variations, as with other classical works, until a monumental copy was carved on stone in 183AD, to be the standard text which scholars could copy.

It is probable that every region once had its own version of the oracle. It even appears that there were wide regional differences in the way the oracle was consulted.

The I Ching is not the only method of divination used by the Chinese. Films from the Far East frequently show someone seeking to know their fate by shuffling a box of sticks. Known as *chim* in Hong Kong, these sticks are extremely popular among Chinese communities the world over. They are, in fact, distantly related to the yarrow stalks of the I Ching, although the method of divination is different.

Usually the client takes a bamboo cylinder containing a bundle of numbered sticks, then shuffles it with a jerking movement until one drops out. The priest or fortune-teller notes the number, and gives his interpretation after referring to a divinatory book.

Another, much simpler, form of oracle is usually used with the chim. Two oyster-shaped pieces of polished wood called *chiao pai* are thrown on to the ground to see whether they land flat or curved side up. Ideally, one lands face up, the other face down.

If this happens three times in succession, it means that the stick which has been chosen has the correct message. But if the chiao pai land with both flat sides up, then the stick is the wrong one, and the bundle has to be shaken again. Two round sides facing up is thought neither good nor bad.

One of the oldest methods of divination in the world, the chiao pai are cast by dedicated Chinese soothsayers to see whether the time is favourable for consulting the I Ching. If they both show flat sides up three times in succession, the yarrow stalks will be put to one side for another occasion.

MAH JONGG

The Organization of the Tiles

Everyone will have seen at some time those intriguing boxes containing white and brown blocks inscribed with Chinese characters. Most people will recognize them as the Chinese game of Mah Jongg, and some will be familiar with the game. Few, however, will realize that the popular pastime is actually the descendant of an honourable system of divination which goes back many centuries. Mah Jongg is, in fact, the Chinese equivalent of the Tarot cards.

Special Symbols

Mah Jongg sets combine all the features of cards, dice and dominoes. Engraved on the tiles are not only numbers, suits and flowers, but other special symbols as well. Originally, every part of China and the Far East had its own regional designs, and it is only within the past half-century that the pieces have become standardized. Mah Jongg sets from the last century show a wide range of patterns and designs, many of which are no longer found today. They give a clue to the strange amalgam of regional variants which have together produced the modern set of Mah Jongg.

Today, however, all Mah Jongg sets, whether the tile or the card type, have the same standard format. The complete set consists of 144 tiles, divided into four identical 'packs' of 34 different tiles. The 34 tiles can be sub-divided into three suits of nine tiles each (Bamboo, Circles and Numbers), four Directions (East, South, West and North), and three Colours (Green, Red and White). There are also eight additional Guardian cards: Plum, Orchid, Chrysanthemum, Bamboo, Fisherman, Woodcutter, Farmer and Scholar. It is usual for the complete set to have a few extra blanks to replace any which get mislaid.

Seasons and Directions

Mah Jongg is full of astronomical and ritual symbolism. The seasons of the year are shown not only by the eight Guardian tiles, but also by the four Direction tiles, East, South, West and North. East and Spring represent the dawn, birth and growth;

South and Summer symbolize midday, good fortune and plenty; West and Autumn are associated with sunset, response, leisure and retirement; while North and Winter symbolize night, emptiness and hardship.

The Chinese hold that there are actually five cardinal points, representing the five elements of Chinese philosophy. East, South, West and North represent the elements Wood, Fire, Metal and Water, and the Centre, from which the other four directions radiate, represents the element Earth. For this reason Mah Jongg also has a tile representing the Centre: it is sometimes called the 'red dragon' by western players. Its symbol, the Chinese character for Centre, shows an arrow striking a target.

Three Suits

The fact that there are three suits is highly significant. Three is regarded as a sacred number, representing the interaction of heaven, humanity and earth. Moreover, the number of tiles in each suit is the magic number nine: three times three. Finally, the number of tiles taken by the person consulting the oracle, is 13, corresponding to the number of lunar months in the year.

Tiles or Cards?

Whether you are fortunate enough to possess a beautifully made antique set of bamboo and ivory, a modern plastic set or one of the many sets of Mah Jongg cards which are currently available, the method of consulting the oracle is the same. The antique sets have a very satisfying feel to them, which helps to create a certain mystical atmosphere, but they are now difficult to find, extremely expensive, and can be difficult to interpret. Much more accessible are Mah Jongg fortune-telling cards that are now widely available, which show the symbolism of each tile pictorially.

The Meanings of the Tiles

Each of the Mah Jongg tiles or cards has its own oracle name. The oracle name suggests its symbolism and a little thought will reveal how this applies to the current situation. Whether the meaning of a tile is favourable or not will usually depend on its position and the tiles which are next to it.

The Mah Jongg Spread

Divination with the Mah Jongg is a straightforward operation. Like its western equivalent, the Tarot, this oracle can either be consulted by you alone or through an expert interpreter.

All 144 tiles or cards of the Mah Jongg set must first be put face down on a table and swirled around. Once they are well mixed up, create a large space or 'lake' in the centre of the spread, pushing the tiles out to the edge of the table. At this point, concentrate hard on the problem or question you wish the oracle to answer and draw 13 tiles into the centre of the space, giving them an extra swirl as you do so.

The Mah Jongg Spread

The 13 tiles need to be divided into five groups within the empty area as follows:

- Push the first three tiles away from you, keeping them face down. These are the *West* tiles.
- Draw the next three towards you. There are the *East* tiles.
- Slide the three *North* tiles to your left.
- Move the final group of three *South* tiles to your right.
- Place the remaining *Centre* tile in the middle of the spread with the four groups of three arranged equidistantly around it.

You may notice that *East* and *West* appear to be reversed. This is because the spread is said to represent a map of the heavens, which in Chinese lore appears as a mirror image of the map of the earth.

Interpreting the Tiles

Turn over the *Centre* tile first. This sometimes gives an immediate response to the question of the moment – particularly if it is the Centre tile of the Honours set (see pages 396-397), in which case you will be sure to reach your objective. Even if the symbolism of this tile is merely close to your own question, it is a sure sign that the Mah Jongg is going to give you a clear response to a question.

Now turn to the *East* row. These tiles apply to you, perhaps revealing facets of your personality which you should develop, or else suggesting aspects of your current situation which need your urgent attention.

The *South* row refers to the immediate outcome of the existing situation. It also can reveal the direction in which events are about to be moving.

Now look at the *West* row. The two outside tiles tell you what obstacles stand in the way of achieving your objectives, and what to guard against. The middle tile shows you the way out of the situation – what you should do, or who could help you.

Finally, the *North* row reveals the outcome in 12 months time, with the third and last tile indicating whether it will be successful, unresolved, or completely different from the present situation.

If, however, you turn up one of the eight Guardian tiles, another tile must be drawn from those around the edge of the table and placed next to the Guardian tile. This indicates that a particular aspect of your fate, as symbolized by the newly drawn tile, is protected by the Guardian tile, regardless of any difficulties. Since each Guardian also represents a season, there is a possibility that the problem will be resolved when the season in question comes around.

The significant difference between Mah Jongg and Tarot is that tiles can be duplicated within the spread (Mah Jongg has four identical 'packs' of Suits, Directions and Colours in addition to the eight Guardian tiles). When this happens, the symbolism of the duplicated tiles is doubly emphasized. Similarly, when a tile appears in more than one direction, it shows that the event foretold by that tile will continue to make its effect felt at a later stage.

The Three Suits

BAMBOO

1 Bamboo PEACOCK Success; A lady of mature years

This tile, the first of the suit tiles, represents personal ambition. If it is in a good position (such as the South), it reveals personal achievement; if badly placed, it indicates over-confidence. Be careful not to confuse this tile with the Bamboo Guardian tile.

2 Bamboos DUCK Fidelity; Partnership

The two Ducks are the sign of a lasting relationship, romance, marriage or business partnership. Usually this portends happiness, but when badly aspected may indicate problems arising in an existing relationship.

3 Bamboos TOAD Healing

The Toad who lives in the Moon, according to Chinese legend, knows how to distil the elixir of life and cure all ills. In questions of health, it is a favourable sign when this tile appears in the middle of the spread. Badly aspected, it means someone is reaching for the Moon or the unattainable.

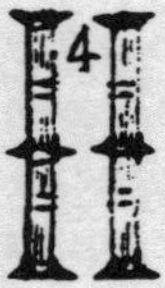

4 Bamboos CARP Longevity; Peace

A long life and a happy one is symbolized by a venerable old man contemplating a Carp in a pool. It suggests peace after a sea of trouble and may reveal recovery after illness and a happy, long life.

5 Bamboos LOTUS Rebirth

The Lotus symbolizes a new birth, either physically as an infant, or metaphysically, as the start of a new life. Life still has much to offer and there is a great deal to look forward to. The opening flower may hint at the passing of grief or realisation of ambition.

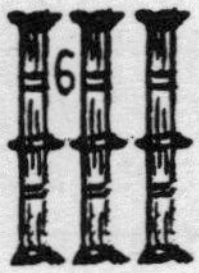

6 Bamboos WATER Correspondence; Travel

Water is the element of communication, whether through word or deed. It may signify travel for pleasure, or business involving more travel, or, when badly aspected, that letters need to be written.

7 Bamboos TORTOISE Thought

No matter how slowly matters seem to be progressing, at least they are moving forwards. The Tortoise lives to a great age and the Chinese associate it with wisdom. Another meaning of the card is therefore 'knowledge' or 'patience'.

8 Bamboos MUSHROOM Eccentricity
The fungus of immortality symbolizes all that is bizarre or unusual. This is a sign of something out of the ordinary. Either the person has unusual talents or the enquirer's life is about to take an unexpected turn.

9 Bamboos WILLOW Compliance
The Willow bends before the storm, but regains its position later. Sometimes matters are best dealt with by waiting for them to reach their own solution. But if badly aspected, the Willow is a warning to attend to problems that have been left untouched.

CIRCLES

1 Circle PEARL Wealth
Chinese Mah Jongg players call this tile 'The Moon at the Bottom of the Sea' – a poetic description of a pearl. It emphasizes the present importance of a sound financial situation. But whether it means that finances will improve, or have to be watched carefully, depends on its position and the tiles which are next to it.

2 Circles PINE A Youth
The Pine represents confidence in youth. It often indicates a young man – a younger brother, a son or a lover, depending on the age and circumstances of the enquirer. Badly aspected, it may mean a rival in love or a dangerous romantic liaison. Another meaning, derived from the fact that pine wood makes both the best ink and the best charcoal, is possible artistic activity.

3 Circles PHOENIX Joy; Virtue
The Phoenix promises future happiness. Its appearance signifies that everything will be in order and matters proceed correctly and legitimately. There will be occasion for rejoicing.

4 Circles JADE Perseverance

Jade only acquires its value when considerable time and effort have been taken to polish the lifeless stone into a perfect object. This tile signifies reward for a job well done and the satisfaction of a lifetime's achievement.

5 Circles DRAGON Good Fortune

The Dragon signifies sudden good fortune, but it can also mean extravagant losses. While it promises wealth, when badly aspected it is a warning against gambling and rash spending.

6 Circles PEACH Feminine Beauty

The Peach is a symbol of femininity and signifies a young girl. It may signify the enquirer herself or a rival in love, a daughter or younger sister. It is important for this tile to be in a strong or favourable position, otherwise it suggests wanton extravagance or vanity. In business matters it refers to the fine arts, particularly painting and drawing.

7 Circles INSECT Industriousness

The tile refers to tasks and activity which may bring no immediate satisfaction, but which, like daily chores, have to be done to make life bearable. It usually characterizes a person who is not afraid of hard work. In some cases, it may refer to nervous anxiety and tension.

8 Circles TIGER A Man in Uniform

This tile signifies strong authority. It may refer to a man older than the enquirer: a father or elder brother, for example. It may also signify conflict with a person in authority. For both male and female enquirers it may suggest a career in uniform.

9 Circles UNICORN The Future

The Chinese Unicorn had the gift of prophesy. This tile shows the need for foresight and forward planning, not for the immediate future, but for the long-term result. Sometimes the Unicorn tile signifies the gift of clairvoyance, or the ability to judge character with uncanny accuracy – to 'see through' people.

NUMBERS

1 一萬

1 Number ENTERING Door

The Chinese numeral for 1 shows a bar placed over a door. This tile represents a door being opened, leading to new opportunities. Only if badly aspected – for example, if it appears in the outside tiles in the West row – does it signify the reverse.

2 二萬

2 Number SWORD Dilemma

The sword is double-edged. A decision has to be made, since one cannot follow two directions at once. Faced with a choice, a course of action must be decided on and followed.

3 三萬

3 Number EARTH Land

A new situation, the countryside, or the purchase of land. This card refers more to the outside of a building that to its interior. It is also often a sign that the enquirer will soon be in unfamiliar surroundings, or making a long journey by land.

4 四萬

4 Number LUTE Music

As well as indicating an interest in music, the Lute also points to increased leisure and social activity. Financial and business matters should not be taken too seriously at present.

5 伍萬

5 Number HOUSE Building

This tile represents the bricks and mortar of a building – such as a home or hospital, depending on the nature of the enquiry. It may be a sign that the enquirer will be spending some time in a hitherto unfamiliar building. The meaning is emphasized when it appears next to 1 Number (Door) or 3 Number (Earth).

6 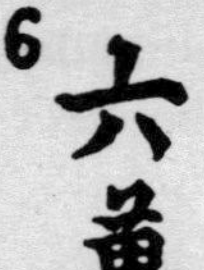

6 Number FIRE Danger

Although this tile can mean intelligence and inspiration, it often warns of danger – especially when it appears next to the 6 Bamboo tile (Water). Look to the adjoining tiles for an indication of the source of the danger. If this tile turns up in the centre of the West row, it means that the solution lies in using one's intelligence.

7 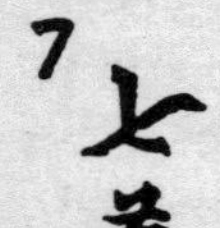

7 Number SEVEN STARS Hope

The Stars represent imagination and literary gifts. It is good to have plenty of ideas, but it is even better when these are linked to practical common sense so that they may be brought to fruition.

8 

8 Number KNOT Difficulties

The knot may be tied, or untied. When linked with the Duck (2 Bamboo), for example, it suggests marriage; linked with the Sword (2 Number) it suggests the severance of present ties. In the central position, it reveals mental agitation.

9 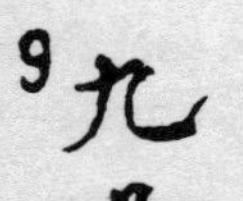

9 Number HEAVEN Temple

This tile suggests perfection in achievement. Its significance as the temple is underlined when it appears next to the House (5 Number) in which case it foretells a wedding. In the East row, it indicates someone interested in religious matters. When associated with 6 Bamboo, the interpretation becomes air travel.

THE HONOURS

These tiles represent the four directions and the three colours – often called 'Dragons' by western Mah Jongg players who are unfamiliar with the names of the Chinese characters.

E 

EAST The Questioner

This tile stresses that the matters suggested by the adjoining tiles relate specifically and immediately to the questioner alone. Often this tile represents success, and the achievement of ambitions. Next to the West tile, it means partnership.

S

南

SOUTH Reward

This is nearly always a fortunate sign, predicting success and recognition. As the answer to a question, the reply can be interpreted as favourable.

W

WEST Objective

This tile can be interpreted favourably or otherwise, depending on where it appears. It also has to be considered in the light of the question, since it can indicate the attainment of objectives, or conversely, an obstacle in one's path. If linked with East, it represents a partnership.

N

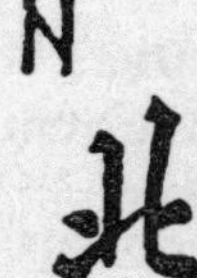

NORTH Obstacles

North represents hardship and difficulties. It is better for this tile to appear in the North, where it means that difficulties have been foreseen and insured against. In the South row, it shows that difficulties have been overcome. It often indicates conflict with authority.

GREEN Commence, Proceed

The Chinese symbol originally depicted an arrow loosed from a bow. Today this tile bears the Chinese character for 'commence' – suitably inscribed in green.

RED Centre, Success

This tile – which shows a red arrow striking its target – indicates that ambitions will be achieved. It is particularly favourable when in the centre of the spread.

WHITE The Unknown

The White tile indicates the unknown, or an uncompleted task. If it is combined with the Pine (2 Circles) it is a certain indication of pen and paper perhaps a letter or document waiting to be signed. If it appears more than once in the spread, this is usually a sign that the person has psychic powers – particularly if Guardian tiles also appear with it. Originally totally blank, the tile is now edged with a simple frame.

THE GUARDIANS

The eight Guardian tiles or cards form a set of their own: many Mah Jongg players do not use them in the game, discarding them as we might the jokers from an ordinary pack of cards. Other versions of the game have regional variations of the eight picture cards shown here. They represent protection and assistance from an unexpected source.

Key: 1-4 red = plants
1-4 blue = seasons

Plum Blossom Love

This card ensures eventual happiness in matters of the heart. A romantic situation may have its current problems, but things will turn out for the better.

Orchid Elegance

The Orchid Guardian protects such valuable items as jewellery, and the well-being of young girls. It shows lost property returned, and improvement in the health of a daughter.

Chrysanthemum Maturity

The Chrysanthemum symbolizes the welfare of ladies of mature years. It shows them enjoying peace, contentment, leisure, and good health.

Bamboo Wisdom

The Bamboo signifies success in examinations, good news in a letter, or documents which bring happiness. It is especially favourable if a Bamboo tile or card is pulled out when this Guardian is in the spread.

Spring Tolerance

This card signifies the need for patience and understanding. It may indicate a long engagement, or warn that safe investments are better than speculations, according to the particular issue in question.

Summer Fertility

There will be ample rewards, but physical effort is needed. More attention to practical matters will bring relief from mental anxiety. This card also indicates recovery from mental illness, or freedom from serious problems such as drug abuse or addiction.

Autumn Promotion

Autumn shows rewards for hard work. There are indications of a happy marriage with many children, or eventual prosperity. If health is the matter in question, this card suggests a sound constitution, but warns of the need for healthy outdoor exercise.

Winter Prudence

Confucius said: 'Continual study and constant practice: are these not in themselves sufficient reward?' this is a sign not to waste one's time in idle pursuits, but to use it usefully and constructively.

NUMEROLOGY

Personal Numbers

It is believed that through numerology – the study of numbers – it is possible to analyse your character and discover your inner self. Numbers, it is said, also hold the key to our destiny, indicating what the future holds for us in every field, including romance, social life and career.

There are many number systems, but most serious students of numerology agree that the only really accurate method of divination is the one used by Chaldeans and the Hebrews' Kabala, many centuries ago. It was these ancients who realized that within each number is a unique resonance, and that every name contains certain identifying patterns, rather like a phonetic fingerprint.

Indeed, in many respects, numbers seem to give things their identity; and so each number is said to have its own character.

Some numbers are considered to have more power than others. Odd numbers are deemed to be 'masculine' and so stronger than the 'feminine' even numbers.

The Life Number

The most basic calculation of numerology involves adding together the figures of your birth date. The result will give your 'Life' number, so-called because it never changes and will be dominant throughout your life, indicating the lessons you may have to learn.

If, for example, you were born on 21 January 1972, your birth date is added up as follows:

$$2 + 1 + 1 + 1 + 9 + 7 + 2 = 23/$$
$$2 + 3 = 5$$

Your birth number, reduced to a single digit, will therefore be 5. This figure is then interpreted according to the attributes and characteristics assigned to it. (These are listed on the chart).

However, should the result add up to 11 or 22, these are not reduced to a single digit as they represent 'Master' numbers and have their own special characteristics, as shown on the chart, too.

Name Numbers

Once the Life number has been calculated, it is time to discover what your name reveals. The table (below) gives the ancient Chaldean – Hebrew Kabala 'code' for converting the alphabet into numbers.

A – 1	H – 5	O – 7	V – 6
B – 2	I – 1	P – 8	W – 6
C – 3	J – 1	Q – 1	X – 5
D – 4	K – 2	R – 2	Y – 1
E – 5	L – 3	S – 3	Z – 7
F – 8	M – 4	T – 4	
G – 3	N – 5	U – 6	

Names are divided into consonants, which give your outward Expression number, and vowels, which reveal your innermost Desire or Heart number. (Again, the table given here lists corresponding characteristics.) Vowel and consonant numbers are calculated separately and then added together to provide a third number – that of Destiny. This reveals how you handle your affairs and the pitfalls to avoid. It is calculated as follows in an example for someone called John Andrews:

```
1   5 5            5 4 2   6 3
J O H N          A N D R E W S
  7              1       5
```

First, add, the consonants and then reduce these to a single digit (unless, of course, they add up to 11 or 22). The result will produce John's Expression number.

$$1 + 5 + 5 + 5 + 4 + 2 + 6 + 3 = 31$$

$$3 + 1 = 4$$

Now add the vowels together.

$$7 + 1 + 5 = 13$$

$$1 + 3 = 4$$

This is John's Desire or Heart number.

To calculate John's Destiny number, add the Desire number to the Expression number.

$$4 + 4 = 8$$

One of the most common problems that occur when calculating name numbers is deciding exactly which name or names to use: registered name, married name, or pet name. The best advice is to use the name by which you are most commonly known, even if it includes an abbreviation or nickname.

The Meaning of Numbers

Consult the chart to discover and analyse those characteristics and attributes ascribed to the numbers 1-9 and to the Master numbers 11 and 22 by ancient magical tradition.

ONE

Expression number (Public face) – Outgoing and confident, you are popular and like to be the centre of attention. You are a natural leader.

Desire/Heart number (Inner self) – Lots of energy and ambition mean you go all out to achieve set goals. You can, however, be complacent in love.

Destiny number (Lifestyle) – A leader at work and at home, you usually like to take charge and rule the roost whenever you can.

Life number (Advice for living) – You can sometimes be intolerant and rather too dominant. Treat others with respect and be more affectionate towards the people around you.

Planetary rulership: The Sun

TWO

Expression number (Public face) – You are happy to take second place, and often provide support for others, but can be over-critical.

Desire/Heart number (Inner self) – Great sensitivity lies beneath your confident exterior. You long for security, and are kind and caring.

Destiny number (Lifestyle) – Calm efficiency and a level-head make you the perfect diplomat. You are tactful and considerate.

Life number (Advice for living) – Keeping things pent-up inside means you can erupt at times and become over emotional. Remember to keep a good balance.

Planetary rulership: The Moon

THREE

Expression number (Public face) – A social creature who likes to be in the limelight, you always seek attention and have plenty of energy.

Desire/Heart number (Inner self) – You are an eternal optimist and have a great sense of humour. Underneath, however, there is a fear of rejection in love or friendship.

Destiny number (Lifestyle) – Creative and full of self-expression, you tend to be successful at what you do: and wherever you go will be a brighter place.

Life number (Advice for living) – You tend to be an idealist and to get carried away at times. Being boastful and conceited are common faults you should try to avoid as you may alienate your friends and relations.

Planetary rulership: Jupiter

FOUR

Expression number (Public face) – Essentially reliable and conservative, you are also loyal and dependable to those you think you can trust.

Desire/Heart number (Inner self) – You are shy and reserved, preferring to take a back seat. A secure and happy home is important to you.

Destiny number (Lifestyle) – You handle your affairs with calm efficiency. Never one to waste time, you get on with the job.

Life number (Advice for living) – Avoid being too set in your ways. Be flexible and try to listen to new ideas when these are presented.

Planetary rulership: The Sun

FIVE

Expression number (Public face) – This number indicates a lively, witty mind. Never sitting still you are renowned for restlessness.

Desire/Heart number (Inner self) – You like to be your own master. This can make you inconstant in a loving relationship.

Destiny number (Lifestyle) – A versatile nature equips you to handle most situations well. You are a good communicator and are best in jobs dealing with people.

Life number (Advice for living) – Stick at what you are doing and avoid flitting from one thing to the next. Take responsibilities seriously.

Planetary rulership: Mercury

SIX

Expression number (Public face) – Outgoing and sociable, you are a happy-go-lucky, popular sort of person. You also like to keep the peace whenever possible, at home and work.

Desire/Heart number (Inner self) – This is the number of love, and your chief concern is for harmony and balance. You also enjoy praise from those around you.

Destiny number (Lifestyle) – You are a great comforter and diplomat, and like to please others. Good with money, you should be successful in business affairs.

Life number (Advice for living) – Your desire for the easy life can make you self-indulgent. Beware of being selfish or too possessive in a loving relationship.

Planetary rulership: Venus

SEVEN

Expression number (Public face) – You may seem aloof as you tend to present a silent face to the world. You are also often labelled by others as an introvert.

Desire/Heart number (Inner self) – Peace and quiet are

important to you, and you tend to be slightly removed from reality. As a result relationships sometimes suffer.

Destiny number (Lifestyle) – As a philosopher, you are always dreaming of a better world. You operate best on your own in a creative job which offers you fulfilment.

Life number (Advice for living) – Try to keep your head out of the clouds, as desire to escape the real world could prove problematic at times when realism is necessary.

Planetary rulership: The Moon

EIGHT

Expression number (Public face) – Determined and energetic, you often seem superior to others. But you do make a good organizer of people and events of all kinds.

Desire/Heart number (Inner self) – You like to be in control of people and situations. You also need security, and are trustworthy and dependable in all circumstances.

Destiny number (Lifestyle) – You are suited to positions of heavy responsibility. Your key words include power and organisation.

Life number (Advice of living) – A tendency to be too pushy or demanding must be avoided or you may start to lose friends.

Planetary rulership: Saturn

NINE

Expression number (Public face) – You are dynamic and have a magnetism that draws people to you. This means you may have many lovers or admirers.

Desire/heart number (Inner self) – Your strong character makes you independent and self-assured. You are creative and like to be kept busy all the time if possible.

Life number (Advice for living) – Greater understanding and self-control will prevent you upsetting those who are close to you.

Planetary rulership: Mars

ELEVEN

Expression number (Public face) – Full of principles, you make a powerful leader. Should anyone disagree, they have a formidable enemy to contend with.

Desire/Heart number (Inner self) – Whatever the opposition, you stick by your ideals. You like to have a mission and fight its cause to the bitter end.

Destiny number (Lifestyle) – Being creative and influential, you are able to persuade people to your way of thinking – a talent suited to teaching and the media.

Life number (Advice for living) – Beware of becoming too obsessed with your ideals; and do not get taken in by charlatans or a bogus goal.

No specific planetary rulership

TWENTY-TWO

Expression number (Public face) – With your knowledge and understanding, people find you a great strength. You are looked up to as masterful in many situations.

Desire/Heart number (Inner self) – This is the number of perfection, and you tend to know that you are special with great potential.

Destiny number (Lifestyle) – You are capable of going far, combining a practical ability with your ideals. You will never pass unnoticed for very long.

Life number (Advice for life) – Complacency is your greatest danger. Do not become self-satisfied with yourself, and always endeavour to fulfil your potential.

No specific planetary rulership

The Fadic Number

The 'Fadic' number, derived from the addition of the 'Life' and 'Destiny' numbers reduced to a single digit or one of the two Master numbers, is often associated with Karma. It is said to provide a clue to an individual's life lesson.

1 The number One is associated with fluctuations of fortune in early life. However, maturity brings more stability and ultimate aims are likely to be realized. Number Ones usually achieve prominent positions and others look to them for guidance. Their organisational skills lead to prosperity and influence.

2 Best working in partnership, Number Twos need the support of others. They excel in jobs where they have contact with the public and tend to become too withdrawn if isolated from normal society. Their initial response to most situations is emotional rather than logical and they can be easily duped by those less honest than themselves.

3 These subjects imbue others with their enthusiasm but, if not tempered by common sense, this trait can lead to unrealistic schemes. Yet their natural optimism is not totally misplaced because they usually enjoy an above average number of opportunities to make substantial gains.

4 Number Fours face a life full of change and uncertainty. Yet, being adventurous by nature, they will delight in meeting each new challenge head on. Independent spirits, their resourcefulness is useful when they are faced with difficulties. But flexibility without control can degenerate into inconstancy.

5 This number is associated with constant movement. Travel and communication usually play a significant role in the Number Five's life, which accords well with a restless disposition. These subjects certainly do not lack initiative, but tend to lack staying power.

6 These subjects seek harmony in all things and willingly subdue their own inclinations in order to achieve this end. Sociable, affectionate, easy-going and considerate, they are very likable and win friends easily, but can be over-accommodating.

7 Challenge is the keynote of this number. Life could become a series of unrelated incidents if the subject lacks a clearly defined goal, but a more decisive Number Seven will grasp opportunities as they arise and turn them to advantage.

8 Stability is the watchword of these practical, reliable and industrious subjects. Number Eights are content to make slow, steady progress and have the patience and persistence to overcome obstacles along the way.

9 The number is associated with enterprise and initiative. Good in times of crisis, these subjects are not afraid to make bold moves even if this arouses opposition in others. Confident and courageous, Number Nines may sometimes take unnecessary risks that do not always come off, so fortunes fluctuate.

11 This is a Master Number and symbolizes creative energy. The subject will utilize this force through work, or use it to inspire others to obtain their goals. This number holds the promise of worldly success.

22 Another Master Number, this one relates to perfection. Idealists, usually with humanitarian instincts, these subjects will strive for an important cause, purpose or duty, often with no thought of reward.

PALMISTRY

The Fingers

Palmistry teaches that the four fingers relate to your instinctive nature signifying hidden facets of your character and talents.

Finger length is important, but may not be obvious. Measure the middle finger from its base in the palm to the tip. Then measure the palm from the top bracelet of the wrist to the base of the middle finger. If the palm is longer, you have short fingers, and vice versa. Roughly equal measurements indicate a well-balanced personality. Short fingers belong to people who act quickly, have plenty of energy, and love new ideas. Those with long fingers prefer to mull things over as a rule.

The length of each phalange of the finger is also significant. In the tables given below 'long' and 'short' are to be interpreted as the length of the section of the finger when compared to other sections of that same finger.

The Little or Mercury Finger

This finger relates to our instincts and ability to communicate. When it leans towards the ring finger, it reveals a sympathetic, kind person. If it stands away from the other fingers, it signals independence and originality.

THE LITTLE FINGER

Top Section

Long Articulate, charming, with strong powers of perception.

Short Indicates shyness, plus difficulties with self-expression.

Middle Section

Long Often the sign of someone who works in the medical profession.

Short Loyalty to others, and a steady personality.

Bottom Section

Long A great need for freedom and privacy. These types are also eloquent.

Short A naive, trusting and possibly impressionable nature.

If it is particularly long, reaching about half way up the top section of the ring finger, it denotes an ability with languages and spoken communication. But when it is set low down on the palm, it signals a lack of self-confidence. If the index finger is similarly low set, then shyness and reticence are very much part of the personality. However, if the index finger is higher, this lack of confidence stems from childhood experiences.

• *Mercury was the Roman god of commerce and trade.*

The Ring or Apollo Finger

This is the finger associated with creativity and self-fulfilment. It represents your artistic attitudes and aptitudes, taste and style. When it is as long as the middle finger (or longer), it indicates a gambler. Such people enjoy taking risks in general. A very short ring finger suggests someone who is not interested in colour or design.

• *Apollo was the Roman patron god of music and the arts.*

THE RING FINGER

Top Section

Long A dramatic personality; someone who probably has acting ability – particularly if the finger has a broad, rounded tip. Length here also indicates creative abilities. If it is thick, these will find practical expression. If thin, the person will be idealistic about art.

Short This type is not at all artistic.

Middle Section

Long The sign of an excellent eye for colour and detail.

Short Difficulty in matching colours, or choosing harmonious shapes.

Bottom Section

Long The sign of refined good taste. If this section is full, it is said to indicate a collector of beautiful things. When it is very fleshy, this person may hoard 'useful' objects.

Short Inability to draw or paint.

The Middle or Saturn Finger

Your middle finger symbolizes your attitudes towards life's basics – earning a living, security, money in the bank and bread on the table. When it is noticeably long, it suggests someone who has very fixed ideas, who may be serious and who often prefers to work alone. A short Saturn finger is the sign of the rebel and eccentric who hates rules and regulations.

When the Saturn finger leans towards the ring finger, it reveals a deep-seated need for security – both emotional and material. These individuals hate arguments and enjoy having people around them. When this finger leans away from the ring finger, it indicates someone who feels a strong need to be alone from time to time.

• ***Saturn was the Roman working deity who helped to create the earth's riches and abundance.***

THE MIDDLE FINGER

Top Section

Long The sign of the detective, researcher and all those who enjoy digging and delving for hidden meanings.

Short These types are submissive, and prefer to work at a slow and steady pace.

Middle Section

Long Practical personalities who are good with figures. Sometimes it indicates an accountant or scientist, especially when it is thin. When full, it denotes a love of nature.

Short May make the same mistake repeatedly. Can be extravagant.

Bottom Section

Long Selfish concern with material security. May be unreliable.

Short Careful with money.

The Index or Jupiter Finger

Your index finger signifies your ego, your sense of self, and how you approach worldly matters. It if leans towards the thumb, it shows an ambitious nature. When it leans away from the middle finger, it denotes an independent thinker. But if the tip leans towards the middle, it suggests great caution.

When it is shorter than the ring finger, it is a sign of low self worth. But if it is as long as the middle finger, the person possesses good leadership qualities.

Remember that the fingers reveal your hidden characteristics while the palm shows the events and direction of your life.

• *The Roman god Jupiter symbolized justice and honour.*

THE INDEX FINGER

Top Section

Long A sign of intellectual abilities, often said to signify a political, legal or religious career.

Short Cynicism, practicality, and a need for material security.

Middle Section

Long A good head for administration.

Short A lack of ambition.

Bottom Section

Long Sporting talents. If it is long and broad, it is also a sign of a good, creative cook.

Short A sensible nature.

Finger Tip Lines

Horizontal lines can sometimes be found on the finger tips, or top section of the fingers. These are often temporary, indicating some current problem, but they fade and disappear as the difficulty is overcome.

Index finger Identity problems; crises in job or career.

Middle finger Difficulties with home, property or financial matters.

Ring finger Unhappiness in a personal relationship.

Little finger Sexual problems; trouble in getting ideas across, perhaps due to lack of confidence or being in the wrong job.

The Thumb

Your thumb represents will-power, reasoning abilities, and levels of vitality. A supple thumb reveals someone with a flexible personality. The stiffer the thumb, the more stubborn the character is thought to be. If the top joint is very rigid, it suggests obstinacy and determination.

Angle Measurement

Another important general character indication may be read from the width of the angle between the thumb and index finger. When the thumb lies close to the rest of the hand, it signals

THE THUMB

Top Section

Short – Weak-willed.
Long – Determination and will-power.
Broad – A practical leader.
Slender – Great charm, and good at communicating ideas.
Full – A steady personality.

Middle Section

This section must be compared with the top section.
Shorter than top section – Someone who acts intuitively, without stopping to look before he or she leaps.
Same length – Logical, reasonable types who enjoy talking things over.
Longer than top section – The thinkers. These types love analysing situations, but find it hard to put their ideas into practice.

The Mount of Venus

This mount is usually read as part of the palm itself, even though it forms the third phalange of the thumb. It contains a wealth of information which will be given in more detail later on.

introversion and a tendency to suffer from stress. The wider the angle, the more out-going the personality is said to be. Sometimes there is quite a difference between the left and right hand. A narrower angle on the left hand would suggest difficulties in childhood which the adult has overcome. On the right, it indicates that responsibilities and restrictions have had a dampening effect on the person's character.

When the thumb is 'waisted' or appears to curve inwards in the middle section, it suggests a tactful person who is careful when dealing with others. A thick middle section reveals someone who often says the wrong thing at the wrong moment.

No analysis of the thumb would be complete without a look at the angles of harmony and rhythm. These are found on the other edge of the thumb, and are formed by the first two joints. The first angle, which is near the wrist, is the angle of harmony. If it is well-formed and pronounced, it suggests a good ear for music, plus a general sense of harmony and balance. The second angle is found at the base of the thumb, and is connected with rhythm and timing. When developed, it indicates manual dexterity; ability to pace oneself and a good sense of timing.

• ***Venus, the Roman goddess of love, symbolized spring and natural fruitfulness.***

The Hand's Shape

One of the most important aspects of the hand which a palmist will take into account is its basic shape. Most hands contain elements of more than one type; but one sort of shape will usually predominate.

Hand shape will give you a useful general impression of a person's character, and provide a good basis for more detailed investigation. So before you begin to scrutinize the lines of the palm, take some time to assess the overall shape of the hand. Is the palm longer than the fingers, or are the fingers longer than the palm? Is the palm wider at the top or at the bottom? Are the fingers thick and broad, or are they narrow and tapering? Are the joints knotty or smooth?

The Elementary Hand

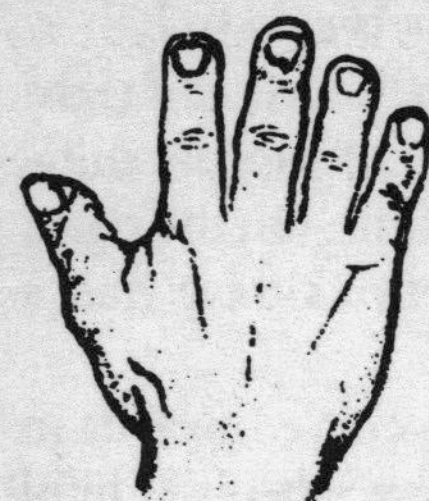

This hand is not a pretty one: the fingers are short and stubby, while the palm is either solid and square, or rectangular. People with this type of hand like to have time to make up their minds. They are often very good with animals and plants, and may be found working in areas where they can be close to nature in some way.

The Square Hand

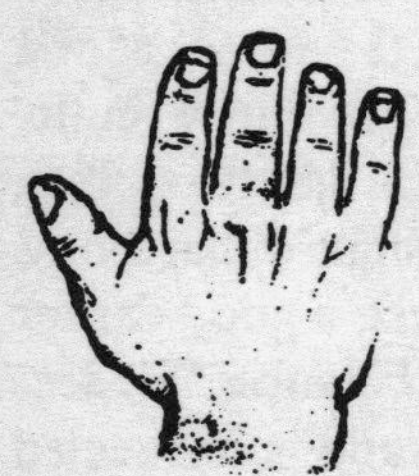

This type of hand is easy to spot, since the square hand contains no extravagant curves. The fingers may seem to belong to a different type, however, and this should modify your conclusions. Basically, the square hand belongs to patient, stubborn personalities who work hard and like to know exactly where they stand. They may also hate sudden changes, preferring a steady routine. They are loyal, but may have trouble showing feelings.

The Conic Hand

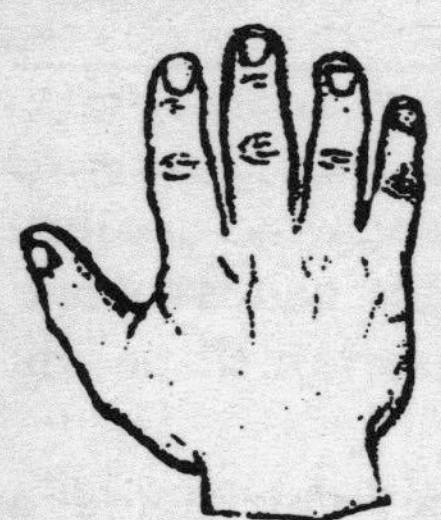

Conic hands are gently rounded, with attractive, tapering fingers which have rounded tips to them. They usually belong to artistic, imaginative people who are invariably charming and have many acquaintances, but few really close friends, since they love variety and are always searching for new ideas. This can make them seem rather superficial and selfish; but, given enough freedom – at work or in love – they are wonderful company and can be generous.

The Psychic Hand

Delicately formed, with slim pointed fingers and long narrow palms, psychic hands belong to the naive and idealistic. Such people often find it very hard to cope with real life, for they are

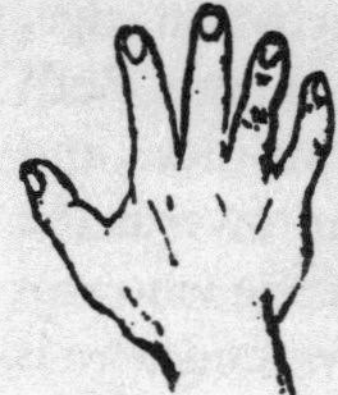

hopelessly impractical in both love and career matters. Dreamers, and often gifted with extra-sensory perception, they usually need someone to take care of them, for they are very vulnerable and can often be hurt.

The Philosophic Hand

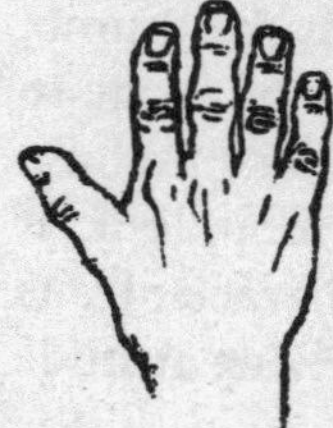

Knotted, bumpy fingers and a rectangular palm characterize the long and bony philosophic hand which belongs to the thinkers of this world – people who like to explore such subjects as religion, politics, and the deeper meaning of life. They need privacy, and dislike practical matters which simply do not interest them.

The Fingerprint

Your fingerprints form a uniquely personal signature that can tell a palmist a lot about you, as well as identifying you to the police.

The study of these subtle patterns is not just undertaken by palmists: psychologists and doctors find that fingerprints can provide valuable evidence about their patients. Indeed, medical research is currently focusing upon the links between these skin patterns and hereditary diseases, as well as some nutritional deficiencies.

The Five Basic Types

Although there are countless variations, experts have identified five basic fingerprint patterns. these are the loop, arch, tented arch, whorl and composite. You will find it easier to analyse your own patterns if you take a print of them, using an ink pad, or even some non-greasy lipstick. This will make the lines on the fingertips clearer, and so easier to categorize.

The Loop

Loops come in two varieties: those which lean towards the outer

edge of the palm, known as the percussion edge; and those which lean towards the thumb. Both types denote an open mind, flexible attitudes, and a love of variety. Loops which lean towards the edge of the palm can suggest someone who will do almost anything to prevent rows, and who is easily affected by others' ideas. People who are easy-going, but also capable of taking the initiative, have loops which lean towards the thumb. Both types are emotional, and may be prone to significant highs and lows in their daily moods.

If you find you have only one loop, look at which finger it appears on. The area of life and character traits this digit represents will be affected by the underlying attitude denoted by the fingerprint loop.

A loop on the middle finger, for example, points to wide-ranging mental attitudes and curiosity. People with this formation enjoy changing their minds, and are wary of those with fixed opinions or particularly stubborn natures.

Someone with a loop on their thumb can be very diplomatic capable of tempering their will-power with adaptability, and compromising with others.

The Whorl

Original thinkers, strong individuals, artists and eccentrics are likely to possess at least one whorl. These types like to do things in their own way, at their own speed and are often very obstinate. However, they have tremendous energy and drive, and are capable of inspiring others with their enthusiasm – when they are not annoying them with their stubbornness.

A whorl on the index finger suggests someone who is happier working for himself or herself. He or she is ambitious, with a strong sense of direction and leadership qualities.

On the middle finger, the whorl denotes analytical abilities, strongly defined opinions, and a marked tendency to think things through step by step.

If there is a whorl on the ring finger, artistic and creative abilities will be expressed in original and unconventional ways. Those who display one on the little finger prefer a quiet life and may seem shy. But do not be misled, for they have deep interests, and will talk freely about matters that concern them – they are simply not interested in idle chit-chat.

The Arch

Arches denote a serious, practical and cautious approach to life. Sometimes people with arches can be a little too sensible, and have a tendency to repress their emotions – ultimately to their own detriment.

An arch on the index finger or middle finger shows someone who finds it hard to express themselves. Although they are persevering, they may lack a true sense of direction. Learning how to overcome inhibitions is very important for these types.

Arches on the thumb often indicate a loyal friend whose common sense approach would be valuable in a crisis. These people are natural counsellors, and may – if other signs confirm this – find much satisfaction in making a career out of helping others to resolve problems.

The Tented Arch

Idealistic, enthusiastic, and often inspired by great causes, those with tented arches can be rather obsessive. They show great emotional energy, and can be quite highly strung.

The index finger is the most common placement for this pattern. Here, it denotes a person who longs to change the world and may become involved with a political movement or charity.

On the middle and third finger, a tented arch points to someone impulsive, whose ideals may be utterly impractical. Musical talent or a love of music is often found too. This will be particularly marked when the arch appears on the ring finger.

This pattern so rarely appears on the little finger or thumb that it is hard to say what it means.

The Composite

A composite pattern consists of two loop shapes, going in opposite directions. It is an excellent sign in those whose work requires them to see all sides of a problem before reaching a firm conclusion.

These types can display great mental flexibility, and are able to see everyone's point of view. However, they can also wear themselves out by looking at every possible permutation, becoming confused and uncertain as a result.

Composites are commonly found on the index finger and thumb. If on the index finger, they may indicate some conflict between daily life and ideals, or personal and practical needs. Such a person may repress his or her true ambitions, or only be able to express them later in life.

On the thumb, it suggests perseverance and an ability to be objective. However, this mental clarity is often accompanied by uncertainty when it comes to very personal matters. This formation may indicate someone who can solve everyone's problems but their own. It may also show a talent for personnel work, the law and management.

The Palm

Look closely at your hand, and you will notice patterns on your palm as well. These are known as palmar patterns and need to be read very carefully. They may confirm some other sign in the hand, or point towards an undiscovered talent or interest in life. These patterns must never be read out of context, but they can be illuminating when looked at with the rest of the palm.

Palmar Loops

Between the index and the middle finger, loops indicate lead-

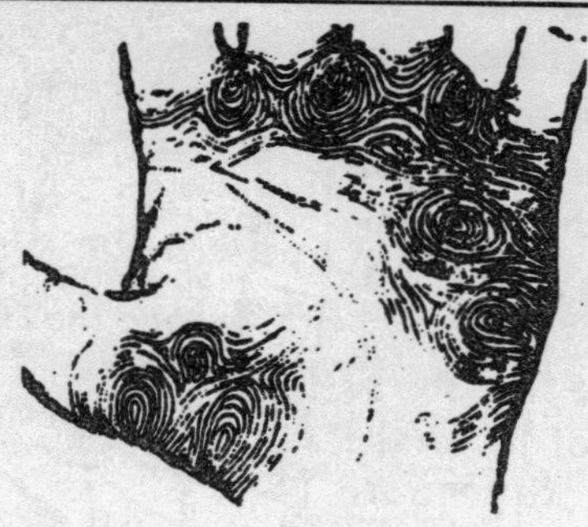

Palmar loops.

ership abilities, charm, and organisational skills. In India, this loop is called the Rajah, and is said to denote 'royal' blood. Loops between the middle and ring finger indicate a desire to help others, coupled with a serious sense of purpose or even a vocation. Between the ring and little finger loops show a quirky sense of humour or great wit.

Loops found on the Mount of Venus are connected with musical talent, or appreciation in a more passive sense.

If a loop lies across the Mount of Luna, curving into the palm from the percussion edge, it may indicate a 'sixth sense'. It also denotes a love of nature, fondness of animals, and potential dowsing ability.

Sometimes there is a loop following the head line down towards the Mount of Luna, or one between head and heart line. This is the sign of an excellent long-term memory.

The Fate Line (1)

The average palm contains a number of minor lines which can reveal some fascinating aspects of personality and destiny.

Also known as the line of Destiny, line of Saturn or line of Career, the Fate line does not appear in every palm. A classic Fate line runs from the wrist up the palm to the middle finger. But it can frequently begin and end in the middle of the palm, making it a difficult line for beginners to find. Once located, it can tell you a lot about someone's career, or lack of it.

The absence of a Fate line means the person is unambitious

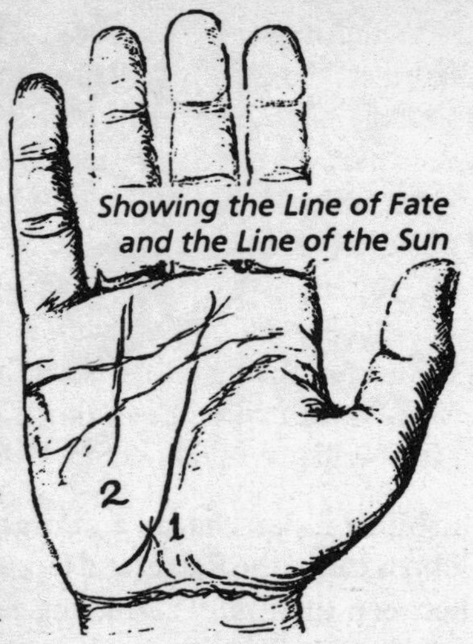

Showing the Line of Fate and the Line of the Sun

and has no great desire to make a mark on the world. Other indications will tell you whether this is through laziness or simply a placid temperament.

A broken Fate line shows many changes of job – the more breaks, the more changes. This can also indicate someone who runs his or her own business, because many different skills are required to keep the show on the road. Working mothers invariably have a fragmented Fate line since they must divide their time between the demands of work and family.

A fork on the Fate line indicates a change of career, perhaps with some kind of study or training period preceding it. But a long, clear line running smoothly up the palm denotes steady progress in a chosen field. Sometimes it can mean great success, too, particularly in the demanding field of sport.

Often the line on the right hand appears different from that on the left. This is because the left hand is believed to reveal your potential at birth, while the right is what you make of this innate ability.

The Line of the Sun (2)

The Apollo or Sun line is a good indicator of how happy someone is deep inside. Some experts maintain that its presence augurs sparkling success. While this can be true, more often it denotes serenity and a contentment with whatever life may bring.

This line is not always present in the palm, but when it is found it is considered to be a partner to the Fate line. It can begin at various places, and is easily confused with the line of Mercury or even the Fate line itself – so look closely before coming to any conclusions.

When it springs from the wrist area and continues up the palm to the Apollo, or ring finger, it is a rare sign of an extremely happy and fortunate life. This sign also denotes early success, possibly in a public area, such as drama.

Sometimes the Sun line begins the Life line from the Mount of Venus (see pages 426-430 for Mounts). This indicates considerable family support in your career, and suggests that family background has been an important contributing factor to success. Rising either from the Life line itself, or the zone of Mars, the Sun line shows that a lot of hard work and individual effort will eventually be rewarded with success.

A Sun line which begins in the Mount of Luna reveals that your career may be in the media, perhaps in entertainment.

If this line is seen starting from the Head line, it is a sure sign of a happy and peaceful middle and old age. It also denotes great direction and determination to succeed in life.

No Sun line at all denotes that life will require hard work. Although success and happiness are within reach, they will not be achieved without a struggle.

The Line of Mercury (3)

Again, this line is not always present in everyone's palm. It starts at the base of the palm, often inside the Life line, and proceeds up the hand towards the little, or Mercury finger. It indicates sensitivity and can highlight a problem with nervous indigestion or any similar stomach complaint.

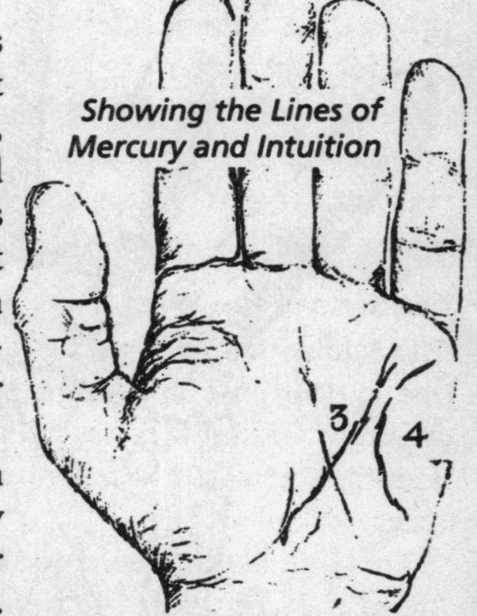

Showing the Lines of Mercury and Intuition

If other indications confirm this, it can also show a tendency towards mild hypochondria or particular care for health. Those with a Mercury line are likely to be highly strung, and should therefore take care of their general health and avoid stress.

The Line of Intuition (4)

This semi-circular line is found on the Mount of Luna, commencing at the outer edge of the palm. It curves in towards the centre and then back, ending near the Mount of Mercury.

A line of Intuition reveals psychic or intuitive abilities. People with this sign often have visual memories and make good judges of character. Their dreams may be predictive or full of insights and they often just 'know' that something is going to happen. If the line is quite weak and appears only on the left hand, it means that the person has inherited a sixth sense but has so far either repressed or ignored it completely.

The Mounts of the Palm

When you look at the surface of the palm, you will see a number of fleshy pads beneath the fingers, at the base of the thumb and along the outer edge. These pads are traditionally known as the *mounts*, and each one represents different character traits.

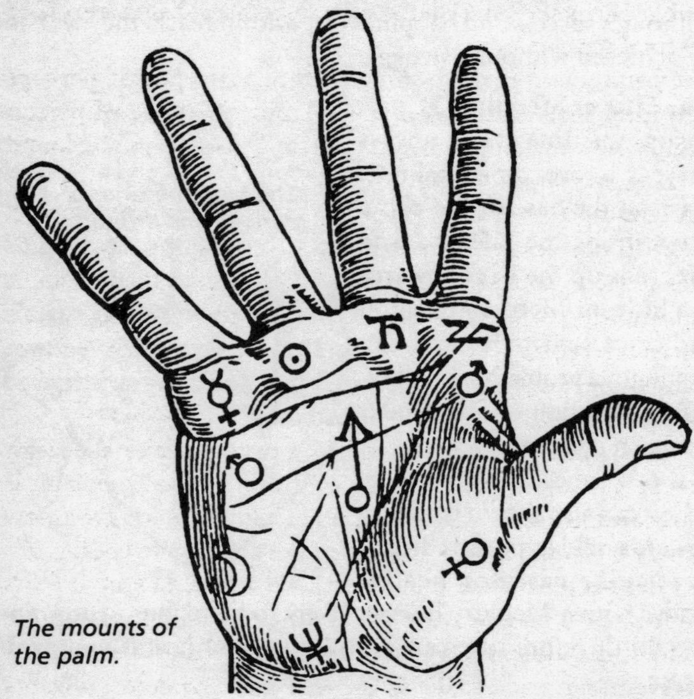

The mounts of the palm.

Close examination of several palms quickly reveals that some mounts tend to be more developed than others. These emphasized areas represent your basic approach to life, while more precise and detailed information is found by looking at the lines.

Bear in mind that you will need to feel the mounts individually to determine their relative size, springiness and development.

Planetary Rulers

The mounts found beneath, or slightly to one side of, each finger are named after the traditional planetary ruler of the finger above. The mount of Apollo, for example, is located beneath the finger of Apollo – more commonly known as the ring finger. Generally speaking, mounts should be well-shaped and firm but yielding. Hard pads suggest a very down-to-earth person, possibly lacking in imagination, but remember that manual work and certain sports can harden the whole hand. Be sure to double-check the lines on the rest of the hand before reaching any final conclusions.

Soft mounts are said to show an unrealistic, poetic, perhaps even idealistic, attitude to life. Certainly, this type of person would not be the kind to spend hours in the garden or be found working on a building site.

A developed mount of Upper Mars reveals moral courage, integrity, and forbearance, while a similar Lower Mars indicates physical courage, assertion and aggressive tendencies. A significantly developed mount of Lower Mars, however, reveals a large reservoir of aggressive physical energy which requires channelling into sport or other exercise. If not, arguments and possibly even violence could be indicated.

The Plain of Mars gives an idea of a person's general energy. This part of the palm has to be analysed by touch, since it is nearly always flat in appearance. Pressing it should reveal how springy it is – the firmer and fuller, the greater the energy.

Other people believe that a firm, well-formed Plain of Mars denotes resourcefulness and an ability to look before leaping. Again, this trait could be confirmed elsewhere in the palm. A soft Plain, however, suggests laziness and a tendency towards self-indulgence. Some palmists divide the Plain into the Quadrangle between the Heart and Hand lines, and the Triangle between the Head and Life lines. These represent sincerity and intelligence respectively.

Mount of Venus

♀ Found at the base of the thumb, this mount indicates the level of vitality and general health. It also relates to the libido, and to a person's ability to express affection. A firm, well developed mount denotes a generous attitude, with potential to enjoy a wide range of physical pleasures. Large, soft Venus mounts traditionally show a sensual person, especially if there are numerous fine lines running across this area. Such people may also have artistic qualities and show considerable talent as dancers, musicians, painters or sculptors.

Where the mount is flat, or lacking resilience, low energy levels or an inhibited, repressed love nature could cause problems. This type of person may be exceptionally self-controlled, or even emotionally cold and distant. Check the Heart line to clarify matters a little further.

Mount of Luna

☽ This mount, also known as the mount of the Moon, is located near the base of the percussion (outer) edge of the palm. It is an indication of imagination, intuition, and psychic abilities, as well as the desire to love and be loved. If well-developed, it reveals a peace-loving personality who is sensitive and probably restless. Many habitual travellers or those with a taste for the exotic have prominent mount of Luna, as do people with a particularly vivid imagination.

Mount of Neptune

♆ This is situated between the mounts of Venus and Luna at the base of the palm. Any development here reveals a certain personal magnetism, coupled with an intuitive ability to relate to others. It can also denote a compelling speaking voice, though many older books do not mention it.

Zone of Mars

♂ This is composed of three areas: the mount of Upper Mars above Luna, the mount of Lower Mars above the mount of Venus, just inside the beginning of the Life line; and the Plain of Mars in the middle of the hand.

Mount of Jupiter

♃ This area, which lies beneath the index finger, is highly indicative of ambition. If very prominent, the person is likely to be rather overbearing and selfish. When rounded and in proportion to the other mounts, it denotes self-knowledge and a well-balanced social life. A flat mount suggests a person who worries unnecessarily and finds it hard to take control of their life. Such a person could also be naive and too concerned with other people's opinions. A hollow mount indicates a tendency to depression.

Mount of Saturn

♄ Found beneath the middle finger, this mount is concerned with a variety of matters including stability, property concerns, study, music, and philosophy. Other signs in the palm must be taken into consideration before deciding exactly which ones apply.

If it is noticeably developed, the Saturn mount provides a warning of moodiness and possible depressive tendencies.

Mount of Apollo

☉ Located beneath the ring finger, the mount of Apollo indicates individual creativity – not just artistic ability, but also how creatively someone lives As well as ruling over music and the arts, Apollo also drove the chariot of the sun daily across the heavens. Consequently this area also represents the 'sunny' or warm side of a person's nature. A well emphasized mount often denotes a happy, generous person, especially if the Venus mount is similarly developed. When very large compared with the rest of the mounts, it shows an extrovert over fond of flattery and attention. An undeveloped mount indicates a tendency to timidity and self-criticism.

Mount of Mercury

☿ Found below the little finger, a well developed Mercury mount shows someone who finds it easy to communicate with others. The more developed the mount, the more talkative and mentally active that person is likely to be. Such people also need their freedom, together with plenty of varied mental stimulation. When undeveloped, the person may be shy and hesitant about saying what he or she really thinks and could possibly lack initiative.

The Nails

The state, shape and natural colouring of your nails can tell an experienced palmist a good deal about basic character traits, as well as your general health and diet. Many doctors examine nails for the same reason, since they can indicate vitamin or mineral deficiencies and weaknesses in certain areas in the body. Lack of zinc, for example, shows up as white spots on the nails.

Naturally, it does not take an expert to know that bitten nails suggest a nervous disposition. Similarly, dirty nails indicate someone who either works with their hands or is not very interested in their appearance. A perfectly manicured set of nails could reveal a variety of character traits, including vanity, fastidiousness, or simply a healthy desire to care for one's appearance. As far as colouring goes, pink indicates an outgoing, well balanced person; white is a sign of cynicism; red shows a quickness to anger; and dark blue or violet nails are a sure indication of poor health.

Nail shapes fall into roughly seven categories, but as with the fingers, it is common to find more than one type on the same pair of hands. The thumbnail, for example, is often a slightly different shape from those of the fingers. In such cases, you must blend and modify the basic meanings given below before deciding on a final interpretation.

Types of Nail

- Large and square – Even-tempered and slow to anger. If nail is deep pink, temper may be explosive once released.

The talon-shaped nail.

The almond-shaped nail.

- Small and square – Critical, fixed opinions on life.
- Rectangular – Peace-loving, preferring open discussion to sulking in private. Often interested in health matters.
- Long Filbert (like the rectangular but broader at the top) – Signals considerable nervous energy. Proud, but with a hatred of arguments. May sulk if hurt, but basically good-natured.
- Short Filbert (a shorter version of the above) – Shows an ability to think quickly.
- Talon – Assertive and energetic in daily life, often at the expense of health.
- Almond – Artistic, affectionate and sensitive.

Health

As we near the end of the 20th-century, medical research is just beginning to confirm something which palmists have known for hundreds of years – that the hand can reveal a great deal about a person's general state of health.

While many doctors now use the condition of a patient's nails as an aid to diagnosis, recent clinical studies have gone even further. Fingerprints, for example, have been shown to reveal genetic problems, and it seems likely that future research in this area will uncover many more diagnostic clues.

A word of warning, however. If you spot something either in your own palm or in someone else's, do not automatically assume the worst. Some signs are temporary, denoting stress or a poor diet, while others simply point to an inherent weakness. Providing people look after their health, there is no reason why anyone's 'weak spot' should ever give them anything other than the kind of minor illnesses we all suffer from time to time.

General Health

The clearest guide to a person's general health is the Life line. Contrary to superstition, the length of the Life line is no reliable indicator of the length of a person's life. A palmist will be far more concerned with its overall appearance and strength.

If the Life line is pale and washed out with many breaks, the person may suffer from a weak constitution, anaemia, or general debility. Such a line is also an indication of a life full of upheaval; breaks can suggest radical changes in direction as well as health problems.

A firm, deeply cut Life line usually denotes good health, and therefore a long life – but there are exceptions to every rule. Never attempt to predict anyone's lifespan, since you are almost bound to be wrong.

Another traditional indicator of general health and vitality is the mouse. Found on the back of the hand, this is the mount formed when the thumb is closed tightly against the index finger. If firm and nicely rounded, the person concerned is

MEDICAL LINES

Three minor lines on the palm are collectively known as the 'Medical Lines' due to their health implications.

The Line of Health
Otherwise known as the line of Mercury or the Via Hepatica, this is a general indicator of nervousness.

Via Lascivia
The Via Lascivia is found at the base of the Mount of Luna where is crosses the palm towards the Mount of Venus. It shows a tendency to allergic reactions, particularly to the chemicals found in wine, beer, medicine, and preserved food.

The Medical Stigmata
The three or four small vertical lines sometimes found beneath the little finger denote healing powers. These could find expression on many levels, from a career in the medical profession to a simple desire to help others.

COMMON AILMENTS

Coughs and Sneezes

Chaining at the start of the lifeline usually indicates a person who rapidly succumbs to coughs, colds and other catarrhal infections.

Very small moons on the nails and *nails which curve around the fingertips* denote a weak chest with possible breathing problems, such as those suffered by asthmatics.

Digestive Problems

A delicate digestion is often revealed by a *small group of fine lines between the lifeline and heart line* which appear close to the line of Mercury (if there is one), around the middle of the palm. Those whose emotions affect their stomach will have such lines, as will anyone with a tendency to nervous indigestion. The lines may also reveal a poor diet, which can be confirmed by looking for other indications – particularly in the nails.

likely to be basically healthy, with the ability to bounce back after minor illnesses. A flabby, small or flat mount shows a more delicate constitution.

Stress Signs

Generally speaking, quantities of fine lines on a palm denote nervous energy, indicating a highly intuitive, creative, and energetic individual who is nevertheless at risk from stress. Such a person would certainly benefit from one of the numerous relaxation techniques available today.

Individual stress points tend to show up as small horizontal lines on the fingertips. The finger involved can give you some clues as to the nature of the problem:

Index finger – insecurity, both personal and for the future.

Middle finger – emphasis on career and money worries.

Ring finger – unhappiness in love, or problems with creative expression.

Little finger – difficulties with communication in relationships.

Nails are another reliable indicator of stress. White spots reveal a zinc deficiency, while noticeable vertical ridges often suggest a liability to allergies (which can be checked by examining the Via Lascivia – see box). Horizontal ridges point to a radical change in eating patterns, such as giving up meat. They can be 'timed' since nails take about 180 days to grow.

Personal Relationships

When palmists are asked to assess how well two people are likely to get on together, they generally start by comparing the general shape of their hands. Hand shape gives an idea of a subject's basic personality, so any signs of compatibility or conflict here will naturally influence the palmist's judgment when it comes to a detailed analysis of the rest of the palm.

Shaping the Future

Square hands are primarily practical, so they get on well with other 'squares' and, up to a point, with the versatile, temperamental *Conic* hand. Square hands are also compatible with their 'higher form' – the longer, broader *Spatulate* hand, which has fingers that widen at the tip and is noted for its creativity.

Adaptable conic types get on well with most people, including themselves. They also make the best match for the delicate, artistic *Psychic* hand which cannot comprehend the square or spatulate hand's practical approach to life in any shape or form. Two psychic types together might make music, but life would take on such an unrealistic rose-tinted glow that in all probability nothing would ever get done.

The *Philosophic* hand, revealed by its knotty finger joints, shows a thoughtful, intelligent nature which might benefit from a more practical, worldly partner. It is certainly no match for the conic hand which displays smooth, tapering fingers, since these suggest impulsive and instinctive behaviour.

SOMEONE SPECIAL?

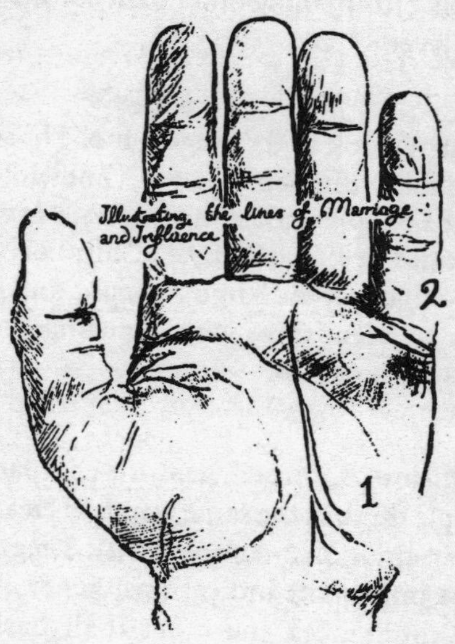

Lines which rise from the Mount of the Moon towards the Fate line (if there is one) are known as Influence lines (1). They can appear quite suddenly, and are said to indicate new relationships.

If the lines appear weak, broken, or have islands on them, then the relationships could be difficult; they are likely to be meaningful love affairs rather than a sign of marriage. However, it is also possible for a weak line to become stronger, paralleling the effect of a deepening attachment.

Should an Influence line join the Fate line, it shows a stable relationship – perhaps involving marriage or living together. A meeting of equals is promised when an Influence line runs parallel to the Fate line, although it could refer as much to a well-balanced business partnership as to a love relationship.

Influence lines can also show the birth of a child. If you spot two, they most probably indicate marriage followed by a child.

Palmists tend to attach less importance these days to the so-called Marriage lines (2) beneath the finger of Mercury (little finger), and some even reject them altogether. The current thinking is that they are an indication of all important relationships – but not necessarily of marriage.

The short, stubby *Elemental* hand is rarely seen in its pure form; when it is, it shows a simple, earthy nature that would have extreme difficulty relating to anything other than a steady, practical hand type on any level.

Finger Friendship

While considering hand shape, look at the fingers too. Those with long fingers are compatible with their own type, but while they may be friendly towards people with short fingers, a love affair between the two could see sparks flying. Similarly, people with fleshy fingers – whatever the length – might find it possible to have light-hearted friendships with slim-fingered types, but they are not really compatible.

On the Right Lines

As far as the lines of the palm are concerned, palmists compare Head lines to see if two people think in the same way, and Heart lines to get an idea of their emotional compatibility. Length and strength are the most important indications; generally speaking, the greater the differences, the more their basic approaches are likely to differ.

As always, though, there are no hard and fast rules and you must use your intuition when assessing the evidence. On the face of it, square hands containing clear head and heart lines – signs of a practical and somewhat serious approach to life – would have little in common emotionally with a temperamental conic hand displaying a flirtatious chained heart line. they may, however, be able to work successfully together, since their different natures would probably complement each other in the context of a purely business relationship.

The Minor Marks

The Palmistry course concludes with a round-up of some of the minor marks and lines which are sometimes found on the palm. As with the major lines and mounts, none of these marks should be interpreted on their own. Use them to confirm indications present elsewhere on the subject's hand.

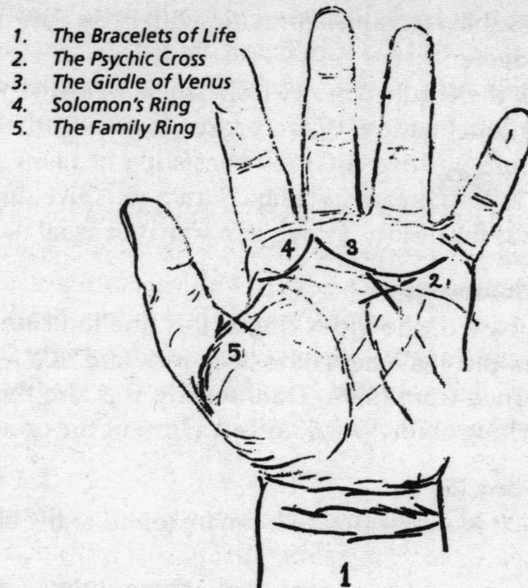

Long Life Bracelets (1)

Well defined horizontal lines on the wrist at the base of the palm suggest a long, healthy, vital life. Some palmists assign 25 years of life to each line of the bracelets, and it is a fact that many people who reach the age of 100 have four lines or more.

A person with three very well defined lines has a sign known as the Magic Bracelet. This shows an ability to adapt physically and mentally to any new situation.

The Psychic Cross (2)

When this rare mark is positioned near the Mount of Jupiter, it shows a person with a purely passing interest in the occult; it could well stop at getting their palm read. Near the Heart line, it reveals someone with a superstitious nature.

If the cross is lined with the Fate line, however, it indicates a person who may pursue psychic interests in their career.

The Girdle of Venus (3)

The Girdle of Venus is a bow shaped line which sits above the Heart line and curves between the gaps separating the third and fourth fingers. A century or so ago, the line was thought to hint at unspeakable lusts and depravities. But these days palmists firmly disagree.

When solid, the Girdle denotes restlessness, sensitivity, and a jealous emotional nature. When broken, however, the indications are more positive; a Girdle consisting of many small crossed lines reveals creativity allied with a sensitive disposition, a fondness for beauty, as well as a warm, sensual nature.

The Ring of Solomon (4)

Found at the base of the index finger, this line indicates that life's problems and challenges have been met, and that lessons have been learned from them. Traditionally, it is also thought to denote teaching ability, wisdom and a love of the occult.

The Family Ring (5)

This line, which is always chained, can be found at the base of the thumb.

Look for lines springing up from the Family Ring into the Mount of Venus – and sometimes beyond. Those which end before, or at, the Life line show family events which have affected the person's life. Any lines which cut across it suggest that family matters have had a dramatic influence on the person's fate.

CHINESE PALMISTRY

The Five Hands

Palmistry is just as popular in China as it is elsewhere in the world: as soon as a conversation turns to fate and fortune, hands are turned and palms inspected. Yet the Chinese approach to hand reading is completely different from the more well known western method. For example, familiar terms such as 'Lifeline' and 'Line of Fate' are not met in true Chinese palmistry. Instead, the ever-practical Chinese divide the palm into regions representing different spheres of the subject's life, then look for marks resembling Chinese characters which show how those spheres might be affected. For example, a sign indicating good fortune in the area of the palm representing children might be taken to signify many sons destined to bring wealth and honour to the family.

Steeped in Legend

The Chinese method has its origins in the legend of the adventurer, T'ai Shu, who lived in the third Century BC and was born with lines forming the Chinese character *Yu* (the name of an ancient State) on his palm. After rising to the position of minister, he later became ruler of the very state whose name was inscribed on his palm at birth.

Fortunately you do not have to be able to read Chinese in order to gain an insight into Chinese palmistry. There are several other methods employed by the Chinese hand-reader which anyone can understand, and it is fascinating to see how this age-old Oriental art compares with its western equivalent.

As in western palmistry, Chinese hand-readers begin by looking at the overall shape of the hands. These are classified according to the five Chinese Elements – Wood, Fire, Earth, Metal and Water – and should reflect the subject's personality (refer to the Chinese Horoscopes section, page 266, for personality profiles of the Five Elements).

Next – and this is an important difference – the reader assesses the 'complexion' of the hand (its colour, fleshiness, relative dryness/wetness) in relation to hand's Element, taking into account the physique and personality of the subject. If there are discrepancies, the reader will suspect a serious imbalance in the subject's mental or physical state.

After considering the shape of the hand, the reader looks at the palm, and imagines it divided into nine regions, each of which is associated with a particular branch of a person's fate and fortune. Regions which are fleshily prominent and healthy-looking reveal good fortune in that particular sphere of life. Those which are sparse augur badly.

Finally, the Chinese hand-reader might look at the fingers. From the lines on them, the reader will aim to pinpoint critical years in the subject's life – ages at which he or she might have experienced (or look forward to experiencing) times of great joy and sadness.

The Five Hands

As in western palmistry, the five hands are seldom found in their pure form – most are a blend of two or more Elements and must be interpreted accordingly.

Even if the shape of the palm does not match the subject's apparent Element type, it is still favourable if the Element(s) suggested by the palm and personality sit next to each other in the traditional Chinese 'productive' order of the Elements – that is, Wood, Fire, Earth, Metal, Water. If the Elements suggested by the palm do not follow this order, the signs are considered to be unfavourable.

The Wood Hand is long and thin with a narrow, oblong palm. Corresponding to the western 'Conic' or 'Psychic' hand, it denotes someone artistic, creative and sensitive.

The Fire Hand is larger, broader and redder than the Wood hand, but still with an oblong palm. Similar to the western 'Philosopher's' hand, it shows a person who lives by their intellect.

The Water Hand is like a strong version of the western 'Conic' type, being shorter than the Wood hand with a noticeably rounded palm. It is said to show a communicative person who likes travelling.

The Earth Hand is similar to the western one – thick, heavy and with a square palm. It is said to denote a country-lover, probably involved in farming, building or similar.

The Metal Hand also has a square palm, but is lighter and more refined than the Earth. Its owner is said to have a talent for business or finance.

The Palaces of the Palm

Chinese hand-readers divide the palm into nine 'palaces', each of which corresponds to a particular sphere of life. The palaces are easily visualized by thinking of the palm as a square divided into nine smaller squares. All the palaces have mystical names taken from the I-Ching.

The palace of *Li* (1) occupies the area just below the middle and ring fingers on either hand. On the left hand, the seven remaining outer palaces then proceed in clockwise order starting with *K'un* (2) below the little finger, *Sun* (8) beneath the first finger and *Ming T'ang* (9) in the centre of the palm. On the right hand they proceed in an anti-clockwise direction.

1 Li *(Fire)* symbolizes the summer when food is plentiful and is said to rule over wealth. The mound here is called *Lu-fong* – the Lucky Mound – and concerns matters to do with the middle 25 years of life. If prominent, it suggests that riches and honours will last throughout life; if weak, wealth gained is likely to melt away.

2 K'un *(Nourishment)* embodies the female principle. The mound here is known as *Fu'fong* – the Happiness Mound –

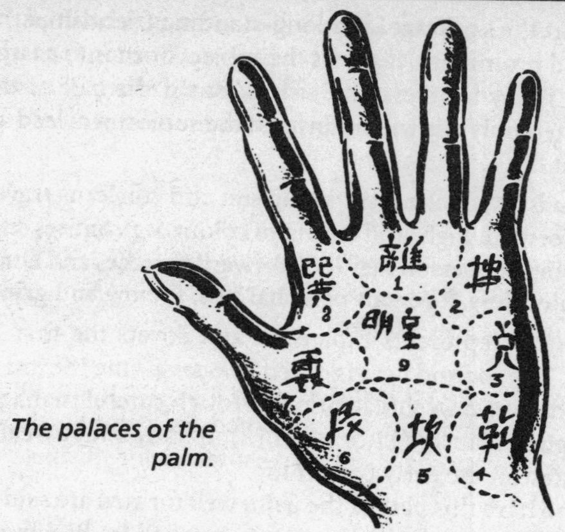

The palaces of the palm.

and shows conditions during the last 25 years of life. If Prominent, it promises many descendants.

For a man, this part of the palm also concerns marriage and love-affairs. For a woman, it refers to traditionally female interests and child care.

3 Tui *(Joy)* is concerned with leisure and retirement. If raised and prominent, it reveals a person who will employ others; riches come through skilful management, or through legacies, marriage or a sudden fortune. But if this area is weak, it can indicate waste and the loss of fortune through idle living.

4 Chien *(Authority)* embodies the masculine principle. For a man it signifies promotion and sons. For a woman, it refers to the husband and father.

If prominent, the bearer will hold a position of authority and have many fine sons. The Chinese consider it very unlucky for this division to be weak, particularly if the subject is male.

5 K'an *(Danger)* symbolizes the north, cold, winter and hardship. It reveals dangers and hardships to be faced in life.

It is more favourable for this part of the palm to be high. If it is marked with a fine, silky texture, it shows an inheritance.

6 Ken *(Obstacles)* is often taken to signify brothers, sisters, relatives of about the same age, and long-standing friendships.

Raised and prominent, it shows the subject born into a large family with many brothers and sisters. But if the ball of the thumb is flat, family ties will be few and the subject will lead an independent life.

7 Chen *(Roads)* symbolizes the rising sun and concerns travel. When well formed, high, and strong in colour, it promises success – an ambitious person may look forward to riches and fame. If thin or colourless, it reveals personal loss, sorrow and grief.

8 Sun *(Growth)* represents expansion and covers the first 25 years of life. The mound here is called *Teh-fong* – the Mount of Virtue – and reveals wealth acquired through careful management. If higher than *Li* (1) or *K'un* (2), it shows that wealth will be greatest in the early part of life.

Those who have this part of the palm well formed are said to be prudent, caring and good natured, and will be highly respected.

If prominent on a woman, it suggests that she will take an interest in her husband's work and share his responsibilities. If it is low, she would be well advised not to play too great a part in his affairs.

9 Ming T'ang is concerned with the general health and day-to-day luck of the subject. The Chinese consider its 'complexion' – which can vary throughout the day – to be of vital importance, though of course, this must be assessed in relation to the subject's normal skin colouring.

A **white or pale** Ming T'ang indicates a life of ease – such a person will not have to work hard for a living. But an excessively pale centre does not necessarily indicate happiness, and losses may well come later in life.

A **yellow or mottled** complexion symbolizes money and is a sign of riches, particularly in middle age. If the yellow hue is lighter than the rest of the palm, it indicates happiness through riches; if darker, the wealth will bring grief.

If the Ming T'ang is **darker** than the rest of the hand, whatever its colour, it is an inauspicious sign. A bluish colour, for example, is said to be an indication of health problems.

KNOW YOUR LUCK FOR THE DAY

The Ming T'ang (centre of the palm) is sometimes examined to find out how a person will fare for the rest of the day. In ancient China, this served as a rough and ready guide for merchants and others who wanted to know whether they should shut up shop early or stay open late.

The Ming T'ang is examined at the Rooster hour – that is, between 5pm and 7pm – and a note made of the temporary colouration. If it is noticeably redder than usual, money is in the offing and trade will be brisk. A palm which is blue or black (i.e. darker than usual) is an unfavourable sign:

- If the dark patch reaches to the *Li* palace (1), there could be physical danger; if it extends to the thumb, parents need help.
- A dark colouration extending to the first finger denotes loss of money; if it extends to the little finger, children or grandchildren may need help.

Obviously, though, it pays to monitor the colouring of your Ming T'ang area over a period of a few days before making any drastic business decisions!

The Temporary Signs

Our destinies change from day to day as we are influenced by people and events around us. Chinese palmists believe that these transitions in our fortunes are revealed by tiny ephemeral marks which often appear on people's hands. Since these can appear overnight and vanish just as quickly, the skill lies in spotting the signs and interpreting them before they disappear from sight.

This is not always an easy task. There are thousands of marks – each imbued with hundreds of subtle meanings depending on their colour, depth and where and when they appear on the palm. For instance, the appearance of the Chinese character for *Woman* is thought to be extremely lucky. However, if it is crossed

WHAT YOUR WRISTS REVEAL

Chinese palmists always study the wrists in minute detail. Symbols of the subconscious mind, they are thought to reveal facets of personality which may be hidden from the world.

A person with thick wrists is thought to be both dynamic and sensual. Thin wrists, however, point to a more sensitive personality who is more inclined towards spirituality and often has an extremely generous nature.

Bracelets – lines that circle the wrist – are also thought to be significant. *A magic triple bracelet* (three horizontal, parallel lines) is thought to be especially fortunate, revealing a person whose intellect and morals will ensure them a happy life. A cross in the middle of this bracelet shows accompanying physical strength and sensuality. Similarly, the *line of jade*, a bracelet which completely circles the wrist, indicates an ability to fascinate the opposite sex.

When the bracelets are chained, this is thought to augur well for both work and earnings – a string of fortunate coincidences may well occur. If they are broken, however, there may be problems.

Bracelets which appear to move upwards towards the palm are said to denote someone who may easily become bored and so yearn for travel and adventure.

by a deep line, the good fortune turns into a warning. When it appears more than once, the meaning changes yet again.

Although western palmists generally tend to overlook these signs, they can add colour and depth to your readings. Some of the most important ones are interpreted below.

Chinese Marks of Fortune

Large Wheel – If this sign is found on the thumb, it shows a lively mind. Elsewhere on the palm it points to psychic powers.

Woman – Expect support from friends and happiness in the family. Thought to be a sign of both wealth and sensuality.

Roof – A temporary setback is around the corner. The wider the angle of the triangle, the more trying it will be.

Fish – A sign of serenity. This mark also promises good fortune, money, and sometimes public honours, too.

Double Boat – A rather unpleasant surprise is just around the corner – but only when this mark is not crossed by others.

Devil – Reveals cowardice, indecisiveness, or perhaps deceitfulness. Fortunately, this is a temporary phase.

Chequerboard – Solutions to problems or a change for the better. But in the palaces of Ken or Chen, depression.

Lotus – When this mark is clearly defined, it shows great intuition, but also a tendency to withdraw from reality.

Elephant Eye – This sign is rarely seen, but is said to point to someone who is loyal, fair and honest.

Lascivious Desires – Thin, close lines on the palaces of Ken or Chen just beneath the thumb show great and long-lived sensuality!

Crescent Moon – Heralds success in love or business. But if crossed by another line, there could be a setback at work.

Ladder of Jade – The sign of a wise, intelligent person. A good omen for those in business, since it heralds success.

Nail – You could soon face an obstacle that will prove challenging. It would be wise not to tackle it head on.

Six Flowers – All round success – be it business, love or social life. This person will be honoured into his or her old age.

Field – Traditionally an extremely fortunate sign which heralds business success and great happiness.

RUNES

The Origin of Runes

The use of rune stones to divine the future is enjoying a remarkable renaissance. This is a very recent trend, particularly outside Scandinavia, where the oldest examples of runic symbols cut into rocks and standing stones are to be found. Part of the reason for this surge of interest may be due to the very simple way in which runes can be used in order to determine trends.

The word rune simply means a 'mystery' or 'secret'. It derives from the Old Norse *run*, Gothic*runa* and Icelandic *runar*; and the root word is usually translated to mean 'whisper'.

Men and Gods

The first rune-masters were those who passed down the mysteries of the runes by word of mouth. But runic characters were carved in stone as a means of communication, not just between people, but between the world of men and that of the gods. Thus, at the mundane or worldly level, Runic was the commercial language of the Germanic peoples of the North, while their tribal shamans used runes for divination and magic.

Runic symbols always represented more than mere letters, for they conveyed concepts that could be recognized and understood by the initiated. They also carried inner meanings which had to be interpreted at a much deeper, subconscious or intuitive level than did the ordinary letters of the alphabet.

Magical Uses

Although it is possible to trace the history of the runic alphabet from surviving rock carvings, there is little remaining evidence of their magical use. This may be due partly to the fact that the runic symbols were etched on to perishable materials such as wood, and were perhaps destroyed once they had served their magical purpose.

We know that divining with runes was a common practice among mediaeval Northern tribes from the literary references found in contemporary texts, but casting the runes probably predates such historical records by many centuries.

Ancient Icelandic literature contains numerous references to the runes and those that used them. According to Norse mythology, the extraordinary, shape-shifting, one-eyed god Odin discovered runes through an act of self-sacrifice. He hung upside down, impaled by his own spear, from the mighty ash called Yggdrasil, or the World Tree, in order to learn the mysteries of life and death. Eventually, he spied the runes below him and seized them. After this ordeal, which lasted nine days and nights, he passed on the secrets of the runes to mankind.

Runic Inscriptions

The earliest runic inscriptions were carved into rock. But, as the Northern tribes were nomadic, more convenient materials had to be found; and so small stones, slivers of wood or bone, and tablets of clay or metal were etched with runic characters. Such variety is the case today, too, for it is possible to get rune sets made in practically any materials – stone, plastic, wood or silver, and even resin or copper. There are also rune cards available, which are similar in appearance to playing cards.

The characters or symbols that comprise the runic alphabet are all composed of straight strokes, probably because it was easier to carve these with very basic tools.

Although the runic alphabet has undergone several changes over the centuries, it is still traditional to use the earliest Scandinavian form, known as the *Elder Futhark,* for divination. This comprises of 24 letters or characters, divided into three groups of eight. The meanings of the individual runes that make up the three 'Aetts' are given at the end of this chapter.

Consulting the Runes

A simple yet effective method of consulting the runes involves the random selection of nine runes. The traditional way to preface this is by shuffling all the runes in a pouch, then casting them upon a cloth or table-top.

The person interpreting the runes then picks them up, one by one, and lays them out in three rows, from left to right, in their correct sequence:

Top row, Freyr's Aett; middle, Haegl's Aett; bottom, Tyr's Aett.

This preliminary exercise is intended to imprint the runes with the personal vibrations of the interpreter and helps to create an atmosphere for successful interpretations.

The runes are then collected up and returned to the pouch for a thorough shuffling before being cast once more on to the cloth. The person who wishes to ask a question of the runes concentrates on the issue in mind, and selects three runes at random from the heap. These are placed in a row, from left to right, in the order selected. This process is repeated twice more; the second row is laid below the first and the last three runes chosen form the bottom line. The remaining runes can be put to one side or replaced immediately in the pouch.

The runes are then interpreted according to their individual attributes and relationship to each other in the light of whatever matter is under consideration. The top row relates to past events or actions; the underlying influences that have given rise to the current situation are reflected by the middle row; and the bottom row indicates the likely future outcome.

Laying out the Runes

An alternative to the traditional method of divination by runes that has already been outlined, is to utilize all the runes for a reading. The runes are selected randomly, one at a time, in the usual manner and laid out like a clock face, starting at the one o'clock position.

The first two runes selected are placed here, the third and fourth are placed at two o'clock, and so on. When this sequence has been completed, the remaining rune is placed in position at the centre of the circle.

Cycle of the Year

The runes are read as pairs: each position relates to one calendar month, starting with the month immediately following the reading at the one o'clock position, then continuing around the circle in sequence.

The 25th rune, in the centre, indicates the pervading influence for the year as a whole and each pair of runes should consistently be interpreted with this factor kept in mind.

Inverted Runes

When interpreting a case, some rune-casters will take account of whether a rune falls upright or reversed. In most instances it is easy to see which way up a rune falls, but in a few, such as *Eoh*, the figure has the same appearance whichever way it is laid or, indeed, which way it is read.

If you wish to note reversed runes in the reading, it is a good idea to mark those that can cause confusion. A small black dot at the top would quickly identify any that were inverted.

In general, reversals indicate a dissipation of the rune's influences. If, for example, an auspicious rune such as *Peorth* were inverted, this would not be interpreted as a bad omen, but simply mean that the benefits would be lessened or delayed. A financial windfall, for instance, would not be less likely to occur because the run was reversed, but the amount of money obtained would be smaller than it would have been had the rune been upright; or perhaps the enquirer may have to wait a while to receive payment.

Different Effects

Conversely, in the case of a basically inauspicious rune, such as *Is*, these influences would be weakened. So a separation from a loved one, for example, may be of shorter duration than if the same rune were upright.

The choice is yours: with a little practice, you will soon be able to decide whether to make allowances for inverted runes and their dissipating influence, or to discount them altogether.

A simple method of divination – employing only three runes instead of the usual nine – is ideal for use when the runes need to be consulted about a specific issue.

The enquirer should concentrate on the matter in question while choosing three runes randomly.

The runes are then laid in a row from right to left in the order selected and interpreted according to their positions.

The Three Rune Spread

Traditionally, the first rune signifies the basis of the matter, the second shows the situation as it exists at the time of the reading, and the third indicates the probable outcome of the events described by the preceding two runes unless action is taken.

However, there is no reason why you cannot alter these meanings to something more appropriate – for example, the first rune could clarify the situation, the second could point to what action is required and the third could tell of the outcome.

Try to see the runes as depicting a short story with a beginning, a middle and an end; this makes it much easier to interpret their message in the light of the query raised. With practice, it should also become easier to adapt the traditional meanings to suit present-day circumstances.

Wyrd

Besides the 24 runes that make up the aetts, a blank rune is normally included in a divinatory set. Known as Wyrd, this powerful symbol represents events, situations or outside influences that are entirely beyond the enquirer's control. Such happenings may change things radically, often leaving the person with no choice.

Wyrd often appears in a rune-cast when an important turning point has been reached in the enquirer's life. He or she may need to take courage in both hands and leap into the void – but the result can only be beneficial.

Freyr's Aett

Feoh: The potential for wealth, in either the material or figurative sense. But this should be used wisely and shared willingly or conflict may arise. New beginnings; perhaps a birth in the family or, more probably, a fresh project or undertaking. Creative energy.

Thorn: Minor problems or petty irritations that can be overcome with a little forethought and tact. A warning to be circumspect in business dealings and emotional relationships as there is danger of rivalry or jealousy. A choice may have to be made.

Rad: Movement and action are indicated. A time of change when plans should be implemented. Travel, especially on business, could prove unexpectedly rewarding. Or there could be a change in the enquirer's domestic situation, perhaps a new home. Deal with official/legal matters now.

Gyfu: This rune often refers to those engaged in humanitarian or charitable works and denotes reward or recognition for past endeavours or a gift from a loved one. Alternatively, it might mean that others will make extra demands on your time and energy. Joint ventures and partnerships are especially favoured.

Ur: Primeval power, essential energy, vitality and virility. The driving force needed to complete a project or fulfil ambition. Change and expansion; justifiable pride; courage and initiative. A particularly good omen for those seeking to advance their careers or social status.

Os: Associated with the Norse god Woden or Odin, this rune signifies divine protection. Often, it refers to an older person, a wise counsellor who can offer advice to the questioner. Intellectual pursuits and communicative skills are favoured. Inspiration.

Cen: A rune of hope and inspiration, indicating that the questioner's present course of action is the right one and will lead to eventual success. It promises protection, guidance and support to those with initiative and is particularly encouraging for anyone who is involved in artistic pursuits.

Wyn: An auspicious rune denoting prosperity, harmony and health. Social life should be very satisfying and a new romantic liaison is a distinct possibility for the unattached; marital relationships should flourish too.

Business prospects are encouraging, with emphasis on wealth and prestige.

Haegl's Aett

Haegl: Unforeseen circumstances may disrupt or delay plans. This is a good time to reconsider aims and, if necessary, change direction. Although hasty decisions are not advised, a calculated risk could pay off. Be prepared for the unexpected.

Nyd: A cautious approach is advisable as this is not a time to seek easy options or to be tempted by get-rich-quick schemes. Think before acting: impatience could lead to errors of judgement and problems. Underlying tensions could erupt if relationships are not handled with tact.

Eoh: A positive attitude is needed in what may be a trying situation. Look to the future rather than regret the past or dwell on present difficulties. A time to make long-term plans and call on inner resources. Changes initiated now will prove beneficial.

Peorth: A pleasurable and profitable period is indicated, so there should be cause for celebration. News from afar brings joy; a happy reunion with a friend from the past. Unexpected good fortune: perhaps a financial windfall, such as a legacy, tax rebate or unexpected gift.

Is: This is known as the ice rune, so patience will be needed. It symbolizes stasis, a time of transition, and may refer to isolation, separation or a parting from a loved one. However, a long-standing difficulty may be resolved with perseverance.

Ger: The culmination of a project; just rewards for past efforts. There will be a chance to complete an important deal or contract. Alternatively, if involved in litigation, expect a satisfactory conclusion. The financial outlook is decidedly promising.

Eolh: Others may try to persuade you to their way of thinking, but you should stick to your principles. Even if the prospects are not encouraging, help could come from an unexpected quarter. A career move made now could prove extremely beneficial.

Sigel: This rune marks a decisive and progressive trend. Particularly favoured are those embarking on a course of study or vocational training. Travel is well starred, especially overseas; health should improve and there is a promise of romance.

Tyr's Aett

Tyr: The courage and enthusiasm to initiate bold schemes is available, giving the promise of success. This rune could also indicate an imminent and passionate affair which will give great happiness; if reversed the relationship could be short-lived.

Beorc: Signifying growth, new beginnings and fertility, this rune can refer equally to the birth of a baby or a successful new business venture. Beneficial changes can be expected to take place at home and at work. Marriage or remarriage is a possibility.

Lagu: Long-distance travel or an overseas journey is probable, either for business or pleasure. The enquirer may be having a testing period; he or she must follow their intuition and be prepared for temporary periods of self-doubt on the journey to success.

Ing: Drawing this rune indicates the end of a cycle. Problems will have been solved or a project will have reached a satisfactory conclusion; it is time to take a break or a well earned holiday. Consolidate resources before preparing for the next cycle.

Eh: A change of residence or job is strongly indicated by this rune. The possibility of travel is also stressed. Success, whether in domestic or business affairs, is well aspected – but only provided that the subject's emotions are kept under careful control.

Man: Conflict with authority, or perhaps a legal problem, is predicted. If reversed there is a danger that others may try to deceive. Young people may break family ties in order to set up home for themselves. A good time to take stock and sort out priorities.

Daeg: An auspicious rune, it can indicate a sudden transformative change in attitudes, circumstances, or lifestyle. This new life could manifest itself in many ways – from going vegetarian, to receiving promotion or moving out of the city to the country.

Odal: This rune refers to money and inherited possessions which the enquirer could receive as a gift. If reversed, there may be disputes of some kind over an inheritance. Family life and issues are well favoured, as are property deals and residential moves.

SCRYING

The Focus

Everybody knows the question that the Wicked Queen in *Snow White* addressed to her magic mirror, but how many are aware what it really refers to? With her famous words 'Mirror, mirror on the wall, who is the fairest of them all?' she was simply practising one of the oldest forms of divination – scrying.

The word scrying derives from the Anglo Saxon 'descry' which today is taken to mean 'reveal'. Practitioners of the art use a transparent globe or a reflective surface which acts as a *focus* for the viewing of visions. Just what they see varies; for some, the images are as realistic as a film, for others, they are much more abstract.

Many objects can be used as a focus – most commonly mirrors, crystals, incense, flames or liquids. However, even everyday items such as magnifying glasses or the backs of watches are said to yield good results.

Scrying probably began with primitive man looking into a pool of water and noticing rippling reflections there. As time passed, he refined his techniques so that eventually scrying was used by ancient cultures the world over from Egypt to South America. Indeed, the name of the Aztec God of magic, Tezcatlipoca, translates literally as 'mirror that smokes'. This reference apparently refers to the initial clouding which occurs in the focus before scryers see visions.

Many famous figures have been linked with the ancient art. The 16th-century French visionary Nostradamus used images which he saw in a mirror as inspiration for his prophetic verses. And 13th-century Franciscan monk Roger Bacon, a pioneer of scientific method, was persecuted for scrying. He owned a bronze head and mirror which apparently spoke to each other and saw 'all manner things'.

English 16th-century astrologer and magician, Dr John Dee, claimed he saw angels in an obsidian mirror and supposedly learned to speak their language.

As an advisor to Queen Elizabeth I, he was consulted before any important decisions concerning affairs of state were made.

So scrying may have played a role in the making of history.

Dee was also one of the first scryers to place his seal of approval on the use of the crystal ball – and laughingly referred to his as a 'shrew stone'.

Some Basic Rules

When most people think of scrying, they immediately imagine crystal balls which certainly have a magical appeal. Naturally, anyone can pay for their fortune to be told, but with a little practice it is far more interesting to do it yourself.

The most common form of scrying uses a static focus such as a mirror, crystal or crystal ball – although the latter can be rather expensive. For those who choose crystals, quartz in its many-coloured forms and black obsidian are the most highly prized. However, any crystal can do the job as long as it is not a man-made one such as Zircon.

The focus should always be kept clean and wrapped in silk or velvet when it is not being used. Mirrors can be wiped with chamois. Crystals, however, should be left in a bowl of spring water overnight. Like a Tarot pack, a crystal or mirror becomes attuned to your personal energies, so never let anyone else touch it – this could affect your ability.

Setting the scene for a scrying session is very much a matter of personal preference. Many scryers, however, choose to work in a dimly lit room with their focus on a black cloth and soft background music playing.

Opening Yourself To Vision

Spend about 10 to 15 minutes unwinding and becoming more aware of your senses. Concentrate all your energies on the focus and after a while you may see a mist forming. For most people this takes several attempts.

Any clouding of your focus is a sign that you are doing well. With more practice, you may see images or patterns in the mist. Different people see different things so do not worry if others' visions are unlike your own.

CATCH A GLIMPSE OF YOUR FUTURE PARTNER

The magical evening of 31 October – Halloween – has long been associated with scrying. Many party games still played on this night are actually derived from the ancient art. For instance, 'bobbing for apples' and 'the apple and candle' are thought to reveal the identity of a future love.

To bob for apples, fill a large tub (bigger than a washing-up bowl) three-quarters full with lukewarm water and add half-a-dozen apples. Everyone playing puts their head in the tub and tries to lift out a piece of fruit using only their mouths. As they remove the fruit, they should watch the surface of the water as the face of a partner-to-be will be reflected in it!

Traditionally, the apple and the candle is a game only for women. Tie an apple to one end of a piece of strong string and a candle to the other end. Suspend it from the ceiling with the candle fixed to the ground so that the apple dangles at about head height.

After spinning the cord, the players try to catch the fruit in their mouths without using their hands. The winner takes the apple and candle to a mirror. There, she brushes her hair in the light of the candle, while eating the apple at the same time. When she has finished, a glance at her reflection may reveal her future husband peeping over her shoulder.

Reading the Signs

Reading the signs which appear in a focus is very much a question of individual interpretation. Scryers, however, have been naturally influenced by the age in which they happened to live.

For example, during mediaeval times when the Church's influence dominated, scryers called up angelic spirits to reveal the future. Nowadays, people rarely see supernatural beings –

in this age of reason they are more likely to see down-to-earth visions.

These can take the form of blurred images, graphic symbols or realistic pictures which often predict the future. In a Society of Psychical Research survey, a certain Miss Goodrich-Freer reported that she had foretold several journeys and events while scrying. According to this study, many others also claimed to have seen a variety of images in crystal balls – ranging from a favourite pet that had died to moving coloured landscapes of exotic unknown places.

Some people, however, prefer to use their focus as a catalyst to trigger visions which they 'see' in their heads. These scryers are often natural clairvoyants.

Colourful Clouds

Before a vision appears, the focus usually becomes foggy and opaque, and often the resulting mist is coloured in some way. Quite a few crystal-gazers never get past this misty stage, but fortunately the colours of the clouds have specific meanings.

If the mists are **white**, they predict happy times are on the way – perhaps Lady Luck will play a hand in events. **Black**, on the other hand, may point to some misfortune. **Green** and **blue** mists indicate positive developments connected with relationships (green) or money and work (blue). **Red** clouds, however, may herald an argument, **yellow** mists, relationship difficulties and **orange**, possible health problems.

Scryers can always ask the mists a direct question – one that can be answered by 'yes' or 'no'. If the clouds rise, the answer is 'yes' and if they descend, 'no'.

Should scryers begin to see distinct images, they often find that the clarity of the pictures varies according to their mood – the happier and more positive they feel, the clearer the shapes that appear.

The images are like Tarot cards, in that they can have two meanings depending on how they are aspected. For instance, seeing an eye can indicate either good luck or impending trouble depending on whether the scryer sees a 'good' eye or an 'evil' eye. Intuition usually helps the crystal-gazer decide whether their vision is positive or negative. Below is a list of some of the most common images.

READING THE SIGNS

Symbol	Positive Meaning	Negative Meaning
Globe	*Travel*	*Stagnation*
Shell	*Wisdom*	*Death*
Star	*Success*	*Warning*
Eye	*Good luck*	*Impending trouble*
Bird	*A message*	*Running away*
Dog	*Trust friends*	*Beware deceitful friends*
Cat	*Good luck*	*Bad trouble*
House	*Well-being*	*Financial problems*
Snake	*Learning*	*Betrayal*
Tree	*Settling down*	*Loss of someone or something close to you*
Wheel	*Travel*	*Injury*
Moon	*Success and growth*	*Failure and misery*

THE TAROT

The Pack

Cartomancy, or the art of reading the past, present and future from cards, can be uncannily accurate, or puzzling and obscure. It is practised both with ordinary playing cards, and with the enigmatic, complex deck known as the Tarot. Once condemned as 'The Devil's Picturebook', the Tarot still alarms, intrigues and challenges people with its powerful images.

Such haunting figures as The Hanged Man, dangling by one foot from a tree, or the grim spectre of Death with his inescapable sickle, can stir up all kinds of peculiar fears and feelings. And this, partly, is what the Tarot is all about. For it is not simply a handy method for telling fortunes.

Occultists, mystics and even some modern psychologists have used the Tarot as a key to unlock secret parts of the mind. In this way, they seek to penetrate the unknown, and to discover hidden messages behind both dreams and events. As you learn about the cards, you will begin to see how all these many facets are linked together, for using the Tarot can help you see more deeply into yourself and others.

Major and Minor Arcanas

Consisting of 78 cards, the Tarot pack is divided into two parts. These are known as the Major and Minor Arcana respectively. The Minor Arcana, numbering 56 cards, looks very similar to the modern pack of playing cards, which is thought to have derived from the Tarot. There are four suits which are as follows: Cups; Wands or Staves; Pentacles or Coins; and Swords. These can be linked to our modern suits in this way: Cups are Hearts; Wands are Diamonds; Pentacles are Clubs; and Swords are Spades.

Each Minor suit contains an Ace, plus nine numbered cards. There are also the court cards: King and Queen, and the Page (or Jack). The additional court cards consist of four Knights. So, as you can see, there is nothing particularly mysterious about the Minor Arcana.

The Major Arcana, numbering 22 cards, is responsible for

the Tarot's mystical reputation. These cards consist of a series of images, beginning with 0, The Fool, and ending with 21, The World. Here are all the important figures of the mediaeval world: The Emperor, The Empress, The Pope, The Devil and The Magician.

Yet there are also more subtle and difficult cards which suggest something deeper going on behind the scenes: The Star, The World, the secretive High Priestess and the triple-faced Moon. Such pictures have little to do with daily life at the time when Tarot first came into being, but seem to hark back to a pre-Christian era, when female goddesses were often more important than their male counterparts, and women were invariably in charge of the magical arts, including divining about the future.

Many experts say that the Major Arcana represents the journey of the soul, from blind ignorance to maturity. Others link the cards with the signs and planets used by astrologers, or with ancient myths and legends. Dozens of different packs are available, each reflecting their designers' beliefs.

Among the best-known and most easily available packs are the Marseilles and the Rider-Waite decks. The Marseilles cards look very mediaeval, while the Rider-Waite deck includes carefully drawn designs which are very pretty. Either would be a good pack for a beginner, for both are very clear.

The Major Arcana

Keywords for the Major Arcana

The keywords which follow show the basic meanings of each Major card. Sometimes the meanings are literal – that is, they represent a person or situation rather than a feeling, or passing mood. But imagination and intuition are needed, or you are likely to miss the more elusive messages.

When cards come out of the pack upside down, they should be left that way for their message is different. These are known as reversed cards, and different keywords apply.

0 The Fool
Innocence; optimism; blind faith; risk.
Reversed: thoughtlessness; a warning to look before you leap; a gambler.

1 The Magician
Creativity; control over worldly events; a powerful person.
Reversed: negative use of power; stopping and starting some activity.

2 The High Priestess
Secrets; intuition; psychic powers; a virgin or a widow.
Reversed: hidden enemies, usually female; superficial people.

3 The Empress
Fertility (either physical or mental); sensual pleasures; abundance; the mother, wife or serious girlfriend; a strong woman.
Reversed: loss; lack of money or comfort; a difficult pregnancy or miscarriage.

4 The Emperor
Ambition; organisation; leadership; a successful man.
Reversed: weakness; lack of will-power or direction.

5 The Pope, or Hierophant

Conventional religion; education; ideas; marriage.
Reversed: eccentricity; rebellion; desire for freedom.

6 The Lovers

Love and romance; sexual attraction; a choice between two distinct paths.
Reversed: a warning to be careful with any new relationship; infidelity; a difficult patch with a partner.

7 The Chariot

Travel, usually on business or for inspiration; success through hard work and personal effort; news from abroad.
Reversed: overwhelming ambition; scattering of energy.

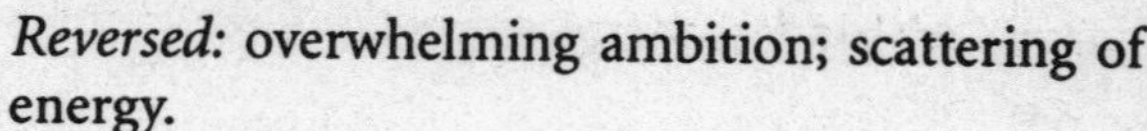

9 The Hermit

A helpful, wise person; the need to be alone; silence is golden.
Reversed: refusing to listen to good advice; inability to settle down easily.

10 The Wheel of Fortune

Unexpected good luck; a sudden turn of events; a fresh start.
Reversed: delay in hoped-for changes; difficulties which are nothing to do with you or outside your control.

11 Strength
Triumph over the negative; courage; working with nature.
Reversed: fear; doubt; loneliness.

12 The Hanged Man
Rebirth; restriction followed by a change of heart.
Reversed: taking the easy way out; refusal to learn.

13 Death
The end of a chapter in your life; new beginnings; major changes.
Reversed: boredom; stagnation; lethargy.

14 Temperance
Peace, or a need for it; the countryside; team work; moderation.
Reversed: quarrels; difficulties at work or within the family.

15 The Devil
Money worries; difficult circumstances; depression; lust; scandal.
Reversed: freedom from care; release; fulfilling and meaningful sexual relations.

16 The Tower

Unexpected upheaval; sudden change out of your control; disruption.
Reversed: inability to welcome change; trying to alter things without much success; lies.

17 The Star

Hope; a light at the end of the tunnel; a need for rest and relaxation.
Reversed: longing for the unattainable; stress; negative thoughts.

18 The Moon

Illusions; the world of entertainment; dreams; depression caused by blocked imagination.
Reversed: nothing is what it seems, so read the small print; having to put something – an ideal, relationship, or dream – on ice for the time being.

19 The Sun

Joy; success; energy; a much loved child; hot countries.
Reversed: happiness in small measure; a warning against going 'over the top'.

20 Judgment

New ideas; fresh vitality; a positive decision is reached.
Reversed: failure; not seeing the heart of the matter.

21 The World
Perfection; completion of a cycle or project; harvest; stability; fame or worldly success without materialism.
Reversed: old habits die hard; difficulty in finishing something properly; mental, physical or emotional exhaustion; success blocked by shyness.

The Major Arcana in Detail

0 The Fool
Ruled by Uranus, planet of revolution, eccentricity and invention. The Fool is a positive card when it falls upright. It can stand for the unconventional rebel, warn of naivety, or foretell journeys – mental, physical or spiritual. It often appears when people are contemplating a major career change and all the risks involved.

1 The Magician
The card of Mercury, planet of communication, the Magician relates to matters of language and the spread of knowledge. The Magician is all about linking ideas, people or events together in a creative way. Here is the power to make your dreams come true, grasp opportunities, see trends and take control. When representing a person, this card denotes an agent, journalist, or 'Mr Fix-It' figure.

2 The High Priestess
The mysterious High Priestess represents the intuitive, often hidden knowledge symbolized by the Moon. She is linked to the powerful Moon goddesses of old, such as Artemis, Isis and Diana. She does not readily reveal her secrets and may stand for untapped psychic gifts, an intuitive woman, or things going on behind the scenes which will be revealed later.

3 The Empress
Here is another aspect of the once-powerful goddess figure worshipped by our ancestors. She appears as the great Earth Mother who rules over abundant crops, pregnancy and birth.

She is linked to Venus, planet of love, unity and harmony, and can represent the conception and birth of an idea or project.

4 The Emperor

Ruled by fiery Aries, the great initiator, the Emperor stands for masculine authority. When this card represents a real-life man, he may well be out of touch with his emotions and very ambitious. When referring to situations, this card suggests growing leadership qualities, or an encounter with a figure of authority.

5 The Hierophant

The Hierophant, or Pope, is ruled by earthy Taurus which is a stubborn, practical sign. This card often suggests solid institutions such as universities, schools and the church. It is the card of teachers and all who open people's minds to a wider world, appearing when you are about to take a course, or further your knowledge in some way. It also represents marriage – an idealized and historical institution.

6 The Lovers

Besides its obvious interpretation as the card of love and romance, the Lovers stand for choice. It is ruled by Gemini, the Twins, and it suggests that there are two sides to every question. The kind of choice represented by this card is often hard to make. The card is telling you to use your intuition to discover what to do.

7 The Chariot

Ruled by the watery, tenacious sign of Cancer, the Chariot stands for progress. But the success promised by this card is hard-won, and will only be achieved by hanging on tightly like the crab which never lets go. The Chariot may also bring interesting news into your life, and it suggests that things are going your way.

8 Strength

The card associated with Leo (the Lion), Strength encourages you to believe in the transforming power of love – even in the most difficult situation. This warm positive card brings light into the darkness, and may represent a brave person who is honest and strong, or nature's healing powers. In some packs this card is number 11.

9 The Hermit

The Hermit, linked to the sign Virgo, the Virgin, gently suggests that it is the right time to look quietly into your heart and mind. You may need to be alone to do this successfully. Sometimes this card represents a wise person who comes into your life and gives you sound advice.

10 The Wheel of Fortune

Ruled by Jupiter, the most expansive planet of the Zodiac, the Wheel of Fortune is very much a card of destiny, fate and karma. A lucky break is just around the corner when you draw this card, and it will probably come in a most unexpected way. This kind of luck is out of your immediate control. It could be a financial windfall, an unusually helpful new friend, or a promotion.

11 Justice

Linked with the star sign of Libra, Justice belongs to the world of logic and legal matters. This card suggests clear decision-making: you are advised calmly to weigh up the pros and cons before proceeding. Sometimes, Justice can also foretell divorce, or the dissolving of a business partnership.

12 The Hanged Man

This disturbingly powerful image is the card of sacrifice, constriction, and – once it has been learned – ultimate freedom. Things may seem stale and unfulfilling, yet you find yourself unable to make changes at the moment. This is not a good time to take decisions. You are best advised to wait, accept the hand fate has dealt you, and rest assured that you will emerge stronger and wiser once the current restrictive influence has passed.

13 Death

Do not be afraid of this card, for although it is powerful and denotes major change, it does not necessarily indicate physical death or destruction – such occurrences are rarely revealed in a Tarot reading. The 13th card is more likely to predict transformation through a loss of some kind, marking the end of a chapter in your life and promising the start of a new phase once you have let the old one go.

14 Temperance

Here, the word Temperance means balance; it suggests the ability to adapt to circumstances or problems. Disputes will be settled now, whether at work or in a relationship. If linked to a person in the spread, this individual will work well with others and bring out the best in everyone. Sometimes a trip to the country or short holiday is predicted.

15 The Devil

This should never be interpreted as an evil card. It simply represents the physical world and the dangers of becoming obsessed with its apparently glittering prizes – wealth, sex, and fame. If referring to an individual, it shows the person is concerned with their own material security and the power of money.

16 The Tower

Total disruption is represented by the Tower. Often such upheavals seem frightening and chaotic at the time, but with hindsight turn out to have a positive side – perhaps offering freedom and new possibilities. Redundancy, sudden alterations in a relationship, or a swift change of home can all be shown here. Look to the surrounding cards for clarification.

17 The Star

The Star brings bright hopes, indicating protection from harm and the promise of rest and healing after a difficult patch. Joy, balance and honesty are the keywords here, whether they refer to work or relationships. This card also denotes nature and animals.

18 The Moon

The card of the imagination, the Moon refers to individual dreams and fantasies. These can be used positively – especially if they refer to any form of creative work or the fulfilment of life-long ambitions – but equally, the Moon warn us that many dreams are only illusions. Sometimes this card also indicates a need for sleep or a tendency towards depression.

19 The Sun
A dynamic and positive card, the Sun lights up any spread in which it appears. It radiates positive energy, denoting joy, ultimate success and renewed vitality. A good social life, surrounding you with warmth and affection, is another indication. A hot country could also be fortunate for you, or there may be excellent news regarding children.

20 Judgment
Any definite decision you come to now will have a beneficial outcome. There may be some kind of awakening – both of mind and body; energy is restored, and so is mental clarity. If you are concerned about someone's health, Judgment denotes a successful convalescence.

21 The World
The World signifies completion: a cycle has come to its natural conclusion, leaving you without regrets or thoughts of what might have been. This card sometimes foretells of a journey, a new home or a new job.

Introduction to the Minor Arcana

Aces (These are equivalent to 'one'). New beginnings; the initiation of ideas; self-motivation; will-power and the ability to create a fresh start.

Twos Harmony, balance and partnerships of every kind, whether in business or love.

Threes Creativity; hope; activity and energy; team work; luck.

Fours Possessions; a sense of security and stability.

Fives Changes; restlessness, or the end of something, sometimes accompanied by regret or loss.

Sixes Travel and movement which may mean a journey, or financial increase.

Sevens Rest; health matters; patience; 'wait-and-see'; or a warning against hasty action.

Eights Strength; business or other responsibilities; positive changes; a new phase.

Nines Completion of a cycle in one's affairs; a feeling of satisfaction; clarifying attitudes or situations; summing up what has been learned or achieved.

Tens Success through transformation; achievement of dreams and wishes; joy; release of energy.

The Court Cards

The court cards can also be grouped in various ways, according to the personality types, astrological signs or physical types they represent. In practice, most readers blend these meanings together, using their individual intuition.

Cups

Physical types and colouring: Fair hair, rounded face and body, dreamy eyes.

Personality types: Emotional, creative, sensitive, sensual, dreamers.

Astrological signs: Water signs – Cancer, Scorpio, Pisces.

Wands

Physical types and colouring: Light brown, reddish or brown hair, well-built muscular body, sparkling eyes.

Personality types: Fiery, energetic, sociable, restless, communicative.

Astrological signs: Fire signs – Aries, Leo, Sagittarius

Swords

Physical types and colouring: Very dark or very fair hair, fine angular features, often tall and slim, piercing gaze.

Personality types: Logical, intellectual, argumentative, unemotional on the surface.

Astrological signs: Air signs – Gemini, Libra, Aquarius.

Pentacles

Physical types and colouring: Dark hair, solid and sometimes squat figure, warm expression in the eyes.

Personality types: Earthy, practical, kind, often well-off, stubborn.
Astrological signs: Earth signs – Taurus, Virgo, Capricorn.

SITUATIONS AND STATES OF MIND

As well as representing actual people, the court cards can also suggest situations and states of mind.

Kings Maturity, material achievements, power.

Queens Feminine wisdom, support, creative achievements.

Knights Changes, the beginning of something starting out.

Pages News, gossip, information.

The Minor Arcana Suit by Suit

The Suit of Wands

Energy, intuition, action and inspiration are the main attributes of the suit of Wands, the Tarot equivalent of the element of Fire in astrology. This suit often tends to relate to questions concerning property matters; creativity, career, and social life.

When a number of Wands appear in a reading, expect an overall sense of increased optimism, movement and activity in your life. But do remember to look carefully at their positions, since reversed Wands can be destructive. A spread with a fair number of reversed Cups – the suit ruled by the Water element – will also diminish the positive qualities of the Wands. Fire and Water do not blend easily.

The court cards are linked to the three astrological Fire signs and may indicate someone born under Aries, Leo, or Sagittarius. Certainly, individuals represented by Wands are fiery, expressive types who need freedom in all areas of their lives.

Ace of Wands Creative beginnings

Career opportunities and bright ideas are starred. You may discover a creative hobby too.

Reversed: *Creative blocks*

Expect delays, especially in matters to do with property, career, or inspiration.

Two of Wands Partners, property

Successful negotiations or deals, and friendships based on mutual interests are all indicated.

Reversed: *Partnership problems*

Unforeseen expenses in business, problems with partners or general delays to any deals.

Three of Wands Developments

Opportunities and finances starred.

Reversed: *Loss of opportunities*

Arrogance, obstinacy or foolish pride could lose you an opportunity.

Four of Wands Harvest, abundance

A well-earned rest, a new home, or inner harmony are possible.

Reversed: *Delayed completion*

Be patient – this card does not suggest failure; simply that the harvest will be delayed.

Five of Wands Creative struggle

A competitive atmosphere prevails. Expect challenges, new ambitions or an upsurge of energy.

Reversed: *Litigation*

Disputes and arguments are likely, although you will probably win through in the end.

Six of Wands Victory

Success is at hand. There will be good news, perhaps relating to work.

Reversed: *Arguments at work*

Be careful of colleagues – someone at work may cause trouble.

Seven of Wands Struggle

You may feel like giving up, but all that is needed is one last push.

Reversed: *Insecurity*
He who hesitates is lost. Fear of failure could spoil your chances.

Eight of Wands Speed, action
News, communication of all kinds, new friends and travel are all possible now.
Reversed: *Disruption*
Do not make any hasty decisions – events are outside your control.

Nine of Wands One last challenge
Recovery from a difficult patch is in sight. You have strength in reverse.
Reversed: *Exhaustion*
Take care of your health – you have probably been overdoing things.

Ten of Wands Career demands
A great deal of hard work is shown here. You may feel weighed down.
Reversed: *Shared success*
A period of hard work is ending. Responsibilities can now be shared.

Page of Wands
An increase in energy, luck with property, possible invitations and short journeys.
Reversed: Delays in communications of all kinds; minor disappointments at work.

Knight of Wands
An impetuous, outgoing young man with a lot of creative energy but little staying power as yet.
Reversed: An untrustworthy charmer – do not fall in love with this character.

Queen of Wands
An independent, hospitable woman. She is passionate in love, but hates possessiveness.
Reversed: An unreliable, possibly jealous woman – often a colleague.

King of Wands

A vital, fiery man who is generous and trustworthy.

Reversed: A narrow-minded, selfish individual who cannot take love seriously.

The Suit of Swords

The suit of Swords has an affinity with the astrological element of Air, indicating mental activity of all kinds. Among the concerns governed by the Swords are legal debates, heated arguments, philosophical discussions, logical planning and abstract creative ideas. Similarly, all forms of written and spoken communication come under the Sword's domain.

On a practical level this Airy suit has links with the law, mathematics, computer and communication technology, travel, and the sciences. The court cards also have strong associations with the astrological signs of Gemini, Libra and Aquarius.

Traditionally the Swords have enjoyed a rather sinister reputation which has tended to obscure their lighter, more positive side; they can, for example, represent a period of learning or fresh ways of looking at things, as well as quarrels and separations. Even so, this suit serves as a timely reminder that thoughts and concepts can shape events in the outside world for good or for ill and that the final decision rests with us.

Ace of Swords Mental power

An extremely powerful card linked to the workings of destiny. This is the time to get new projects and ideas under way.

Reversed: *Imbalance*

Quarrels, the severing of negative links and power games are all indicated. Keep a low profile.

Two of Swords Justice

Affairs are balancing out with the promise that justice will be done. sometimes denotes stalemate.

Reversed: *Slow change*

Release from a situation that has been at a standstill for too long.

Three of Swords Separation

Traditionally the 'broken heart' card it may also indicate a compulsive sexual attraction or 'eternal triangle' situation.

Reversed: *Confusion*

A chaotic situation, resulting from upheaval. However, the situation is not as bleak as it might seem.

Four of Swords Rest

This card can suggest the need for peace, quiet and a good rest.

Reversed: *Exhaustion*

Loneliness, or illness usually caused by stress.

Five of Swords Limitation

A battle is indicated which, if won, will prove a hollow victory. Also limitation and minor setbacks.

Reversed: *Harsh words*

You cannot win any arguments now. Powerful negative feelings may be hard to let go of, but it is better to start afresh.

Six of Swords Travel

Movement, either mental or physical, is predicted. You may be going away, allowing you to enjoy yourself and forget your worries.

Reversed: *Temporary troubles*

Things may seem tough, but you will win through, so keep trying.

Seven of Swords Restlessness

Variable influences with a number of unexpected changes. Theft, especially of ideas, is sometimes foretold. Be cautious.

Reversed: *False friends*

A fast-talking individual may enter your life now. Think carefully before taking their advice.

Eight of Swords Restriction

A solution to difficulties may seem hard to find. Seek outside help.

Reversed: *Release*

New hope, release from problems, and a deserved lucky break. There may be quarrels in a relationship.

Nine of Swords Fears

This card represents an extremely difficult and negative state of mind, but the dark time will pass.

Reversed: *Hope triumphs*

Patience is needed, but there is a light at the end of the tunnel. Blocked emotions are freed now.

Ten of Swords Betrayal

This can represent betrayal of confidence and trust. Words, written or spoken are the most likely cause of the trouble.

Reversed: *The enemy within*

Negative thinking is causing problems, which will continue until there is a change in attitude.

Page of Swords

News, gossip, scandal, and an increase in mental energy are all possibilities here.

Reversed: Someone may be spreading spiteful rumours behind your back.

Knight of Swords

Students, bright young men, or someone rushing into your life.

Reversed: A secretive person who may be lying to you.

Queen of Swords

A lively, intelligent woman who loves to talk. She is emotionally cool and logical.

Reversed: A lonely, insecure and somewhat malicious woman. She is clever and could be dangerous.

King of Swords

A clever, quick-witted man; perhaps a lawyer or other professional.

Reversed: A verbally destructive man who could be very manipulative.

The Suit of Cups

Representing the element of Water, the suit of Cups is primarily concerned with the sensation of feeling, and with the function of imagination in our lives. Every kind of emotion is

represented by this suit – from the most radiant joy to painful sadness and loss.

Cups describe our close relationship – anything from love affairs to marriage, from deep friendships to emotional bonds with children. Even so, it would be wrong to associate this suit only with affairs of the heart. There is a sense of flow about the Cups which affects nearby cards, bringing with it depth, sensitivity and inspiration.

Creativity is another province of the Cups, although here the word means more than simply a talent for music or painting. It is a way of thinking which relies on intuition and imagination – gut feelings – and which can be found in all walks of life.

In other more worldly spheres, the suit of Cups also represents emotional nourishment, nature, the home, pets, and 'creative' businesses of all kinds

Ace of Cups Love and Creativity

Shows a new beginning – creatively, emotionally, or sometimes both. Matters associated with the Cups should flow now.

Reversed: *Unbalanced Emotions*

The Cup, once full of emotional promise, is empty. An affair is ending, creativity is blocked, or there is an emotional imbalance within an existing relationship.

Two of Cups Partnership

Indicates a partnership – either romantic or creative. If other cards agree, it can also denote a particularly happy time socially.

Reversed: *Separation*

Arguments within a relationship are likely, but be cautious; a hasty parting could bring regrets.

Three of Cups Celebration

Generally a sign of some kind of celebration for emotional reasons, such as an engagement. Happiness.

Reversed: *Indulgence*

Over-spending, over-eating, and going out too much are all

likely here. Little harm will result, but you may gain a few pounds.

Four of Cups What do You want?

Indicates fear of emotional pain, or a strong need for security. Boredom could be a problem, but doubt is the most usual meaning.

Reversed: *What does it all mean?*

A frenetic social life as a balk against loneliness. At work there is little challenge or inspiration.

Five of Cups Darkness and Light

Something is lost, but something yet to be dealt with is left over. Despair will give way to hope.

Reversed: *Healing*

Cautious progress forward after a painful time. New opportunities and an end to regret.

Six of Cups Happy Memories

A past lover or friend could reenter your life now. Past efforts will be rewarded at work.

Reversed: *Let go of the Past*

It is time to move on and leave the past behind. Do not be sentimental.

Seven of Cups Confusion

Points of confusion, scattered energy and too many opportunities presenting themselves at once. Wait.

Reversed: *Nothing is what it seems*

Beware of self-delusion and false dreams; objectivity is at an all time low now.

Eight of Cups Movement

Suggests a journey – either physical or emotional. Possibly a situation which was once important is now becoming less consuming.

Reversed: *Depression*

Depression, exhaustion, or an inability to face reality could all be problems. Seek help from others.

Nine of Cups Fulfilment

Everything is flowing wonderfully well for you now. This is an extremely positive card.

Reversed: *Take Care*

Everything may still go well, but do not rest on your laurels or you may lose all you have gained.

Ten of Cups Perfect Happiness

Lasting joy, wishes coming true and growth all round.

Reversed: *Disruption*

A move of home, emotional upheaval, or a sense of loss. The surrounding cards should clarify matters.

Page of Cups Intuition

A gentle child, or the beginnings of a highly intuitive phase in life. Also happy emotional news.

Reversed: *Confusion*

Bad dreams, insubstantial events or lack of coherent information could all be problems.

Knight of Cups Youthful Ideals

A new romance could enter your life with this knight, or he may represent an artistic individual who is just starting out.

Reversed: *A Lost Soul*

Talent and sensitivity are there, but motivation may be sadly lacking.

Queen of Cups Feminine Inspiration

Imaginative, feminine and often psychic, she is talented but could lack confidence underneath.

Reversed: *The Emotional Vampire*

Inclined to manipulate and drain close friends and lovers. She could be emotionally confused or blocked.

King of Cups A Creative King

Often found working in the media or the arts, the King of Cups is moody, emotional and sensitive.

Reversed: *Destructive Fantasies*

Heavy drinking, gloomy moods and sexual infidelity are all indicated.

The Suit of Pentacles

Associated with the element of Earth, the suit of Pentacles signifies material concerns, solid achievement and stability. It is also the 'physical' suit, closely connected to the sensations of touch, taste and smell.

Pentacles bring a sense of structure and reality to a Tarot reading. For instance, their appearance in a spread modifies any plans and schemes denoted by nearby Wands and Swords by indicating that projects will not reach fruition without some solid hard work. This earthy suit also shows an ability to deal with life's practicalities – to work steadily until dreams come true.

In answer to an emotional question, Pentacles indicate an objective, sensible approach. They are not all about dull, hard work either – some cards denote sensual pleasure, others stand for unexpected achievements.

Sometimes called the suit of Coins or Discs, hard cash comes under the Pentacles' domain. Overall, this suit signifies work as opposed to dreamy ambitions; property in the sense of bricks and mortar; worldly status and position; and behaviour which seeks to consolidate and support.

Ace of Pentacles Prosperity

A powerful card indicating financial improvements. Salary increases, gifts or windfalls could come your way. Emotionally, it suggests a stable relationship.

Reversed: *Loss and Greed*

Watch your money carefully – losses are likely. Guard against excess as greed may undermine progress.

Two of Pentacles Duality

Indicates two jobs, changing fortunes, extra work or developing a second string – check the context.

Reversed: *Financial Imbalance*

Financial or emotional ups and downs are suggested. Inconsistency and instability may cause problems in the workplace.

Three of Pentacles Effort Rewarded

Effort and hard work may receive financial reward or recognition. A time for home improvements may be denoted.

Reversed: *Progress Halted*

A fear of failure, lack of application, or over concern with material security could all be blocking progress. There may be some financial delays.

Four of Pentacles Stability

Shows financial stability. Large sums of money are unlikely, but there is enough to feel secure.

Reversed: *Money Miser*

A mean-spirited person or financial anxiety. When describing a personality, it indicates avarice.

Five of Pentacles Lack

Low self-worth or a lack of finances are causing problems. A solution to these should be found further on in the spread.

Reversed: *Regeneration*

Only hard work can improve finances. Any losses will eventually be made good.

Six of Pentacles Gifts

A gift, money or some kind of practical help may soon arrive – or you may be able to assist someone else in this way.

Reversed: *Sharing and Loss*

Financial loss through carelessness is possible. Legal settlements, as in a divorce, will or shattered business arrangement, are also a possibility.

Seven of Pentacles Slow Growth

Indicates a lot of hard work for small gain. There will be a future reward, so don't abandon hope.

Reversed: *Starting Again*

Achievement seems unlikely; it is time to reassess goals. Change in on the way.

Eight of Pentacles Apprenticeship

Denotes a course that teaches new skills or expands your abilities. Financial prudence is advisable.

Reversed: *Limitation at Work*

Work will not be easy – perhaps you are in the wrong job, or your skills are undervalued.

Nine of Pentacles Pleasure

Time to enjoy the fruits of your labours. Sensuality, self-sufficiency, love of nature and happiness surround you.

Reversed: *Security at Risk*

Do not gamble or risk money at this time. Business expansion is temporarily halted, and there may be losses in the immediate future.

Ten of Pentacles Family and Success

Profit is assured from one of two things: family money – perhaps from an inheritance or money from the sale of the family home, or lump sum insurance, bonuses, or tax rebates.

Reversed: *Family Anxieties*

Concern about a family member may be denoted. Otherwise, family restrictions are a problem – expectations, inhibitions or conflicts are all potential problems.

Page of Pentacles Good News

A steady, good-natured child or adolescent. Otherwise, small money gains or good news connected with the family.

Reversed: *Small Restrictions*

Warns against the theft of small amounts of money – perhaps from a wallet or handbag. Unexpected expenditure may arise.

Knight of Pentacles Determination

Sensible, well-planned ambitions will carry this character to the top. He may seem slow, but he is honest and persevering.

Reversed: *Lack of Confidence*

Shows a person who is experiencing career problems caused by a lack of confidence or vision.

Queen of Pentacles Kind and Sensible

A warm, kind woman who loves comfort and is supportive in a crisis.

Reversed: *Selfish and Greedy*

An exceptionally ambitious woman who tends to use people to further her own ends. She works hard, but finds it hard to share good fortune.

King of Pentacles Sensual and Secure
Usually this man has an excellent – if cautious – head for business. He is loyal, sensual and prepared to wait for what he wants.
Reversed: *Boring and Obstinate*
Signals the worst earth sign qualities – he is possessive, mean with money, and afraid of risk.

The Different Spreads

Learning to read the Tarot requires both memory and intuition. Perhaps the best way to become a Tarot reader is to develop your intuition as you study the cards, and learn how to lay them out.

Never forget that your interpretations are not simply based upon what you learn from books; give your intuition a chance to work for you as well.

Preparing for a Reading

Before laying out your cards try to put yourself in a receptive, relaxed mental state. Breathe deeply and rhythmically for a few moments, close your eyes if you like and allow thoughts about everyday matters to simply float away. This helps to set Tarot reading apart from your normal routine, and impresses your subconscious with the idea that it is a special activity.

Choosing your Layout

Tarot reading becomes much easier when you choose the correct layout to suit your needs. Each layout is like a map; sometimes you need an overall view of things, at other times you want to take a closer look at one specific area or question.

It is usually advisable to begin with a general spread, and then proceed to smaller layouts which are designed to answer questions, or concentrate upon one issue at a time.

The Horoscope Spread

The Horoscope spread is a good general layout to start with, since each position highlights a specific area of life. It mirrors the 12 houses of the horoscope; every card relates to its designated area, and is read in this context.

Your first step is to choose what is known as a significator. This card represents you, or the enquirer, and is placed in the centre of the circle. Use one of the court cards for this, selecting it on the basis of gender, and then by astrological sign.

The suit of Wands represents the Fire signs: Aries, Leo, and Sagittarius. The suit of Pentacles represents Earth signs: Taurus, Virgo and Capricorn. Cups symbolize the Water signs of Cancer, Scorpio and Pisces; Swords stand for the Air signs – Gemini, Libra and Aquarius.

Shuffle the Pack

Place your chosen significator on the table, and then shuffle the pack. If you are reading for someone else, ask them to shuffle the cards – making sure some of them are reversed. Once you have done this, cut the deck three times with the left hand and reassemble the cards in a different order.

Now deal them out in a circle, beginning at the equivalent of nine o'clock, and proceeding anti-clockwise around the circle until you have dealt 12 cards.

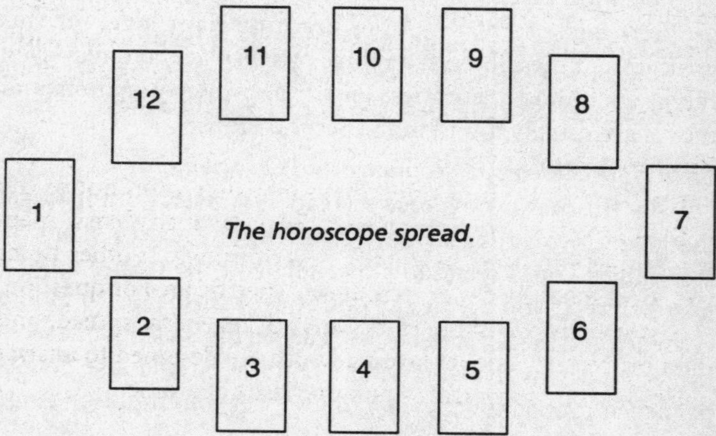

The horoscope spread.

First House: The Self

This position, based at nine o'clock describes your enquirer. It reveals current thoughts and it may indicate challenges and problems. Don't forget to look at your significator to see how this card relates to the qualities shown there.

Second House: Money and Possessions

Finances, material belongings and attitudes towards these matters are revealed here. Cards will refer either to your enquirer's financial situation, or his/her attitude towards it.

Generally, Wands or Pentacles denote practical concerns here, while Cups or Swords represent thoughts and feelings about the material world. Major Arcana cards could reveal attitudes towards talents, abilities, or spiritual wealth.

Third House: Communications

Letters, phone calls, and short visits are all connected with this position. Short journeys, perhaps related to work are also suggested. Cards here should tell you if there is any news along these lines. If a Major Arcana card appears it can tell you a lot about how someone uses his/her mental energy, and how well he/she communicates with others.

Fourth House: Home

This position relates to the home, and feelings about parents, brothers and sisters. Emotions are important here, for this position signifies home as a refuge or safe place, and may even reveal childhood memories. Financial property matters and moves are usually found in the Second House.

Fifth House: Pleasure, Romance and Creativity

Usually this position is easy to read. However, do not forget that many love cards also mean creativity and artistic talent. So a card here could relate to a love affair or the taking up of a new hobby. If you are in any doubt, look at the Tenth House (Career), and the Seventh House (Partnerships). Does one seem more important than the other? Did the First House denote particular problems with work or love? Let your intuition guide you.

Sixth House: Health and Work

This card will relate to day-to-day work rather than long term career, or health matters. Health should be interpreted on mental and emotional levels as well as physical.

Seventh House: Partnership

Look here to find out about joint ventures, business partnerships, husbands and wives and other serious partners.

Eighth House: Sex, Money and Change

This card denotes major endings and beginnings, if any. It can also represent an inheritance or other unearned income; plus revealing sexual matters. The card which appears here should make interpretation simple. An inheritance is normally represented by the Ten of Pentacles; a sexual attraction may appear as a court card, or a Major Arcana card such as The Lovers.

Ninth House: Hopes, Travel and Philosophy

All kinds of travelling are denoted by this position – mental, physical, spiritual and emotional. So cards here could relate to long journeys or periods of study. This house could also reveal future hopes, plans and dreams.

Tenth House: Career

Ambition, attitudes towards realising your dreams, and what interests you in the world about you, are indicated here.

Eleventh House: Friends

Look here for information about social life, colleagues, and group endeavours.

Twelfth House: What is Hidden

Secret fears, unconscious wishes, limitations and repressed urges can all be shown by the card here. Always check to see how it relates to your significator.

The Horseshoe Layout

The horseshoe is a quick and easy layout, designed to answer a clear, specific question. Do not ask questions with lots of 'ifs' and 'buts'; concentrate on a single issue.

Card One: The past.

Past influences which have led to the present situation.

Card Two: The present.

Card Three: Hidden influences.

Or factors you have not taken into consideration yet.

The horseshoe spread.

Card Four: Obstacles.
This could refer to your own thoughts or feelings about your question, or indicate outside problems.

Card Five: The environment.
This covers the attitudes of others, and outside influences upon the question.

Card Six: What should be done.
Your best course of action, or way of looking at the problem.

Card Seven The most likely result.
The possible outcome if you decide to follow the advice given by card six.

A Sample Reading of The Horseshoe Layout

Sally is a young woman aged 24. She wanted to consult the cards about her relationship because, although they had been living together for six months, her boyfriend refused to discuss the subject of marriage. Sally really wanted to marry him, and was understandably worried about her future. Her question was 'Is there any future in my relationship?' the Horseshoe was chosen to analyse the various aspects of her problem. Although she was in some distress when she arrived for the reading, Sally went away feeling that she had received some quite sensible advice.

Card 1 – The Three of Swords, denotes something of Sally's past, and shows that she had been previously disappointed in love. Someone important to her had let her down badly before she met David, her present boyfriend. Her memories of this unhappy episode could be affecting her current relationship and making her feel insecure.

Card 2 *The Lovers* reveals her strong feelings about David, and shows that she feels she must make a choice soon. Certainly, love is uppermost in her mind as she continually mulls over her problems with David.

Card 3 *The Five of Cups* appears in the position of hidden factors. The emotional disappointments suggested by the *Three of Swords* at the beginning are confirmed and strengthened by this card. Sally must let go of the past, and stop allowing her previous problems to affect her love for David. If she does not, she may poison the relationship she wants to flourish.

Card 4 *The Sun*, reversed, suggests that Sally's obstacles are really very small ones. It would seem to be just a matter of time before her wish is granted; positive forces are entering her situation, although there may be a little delay before she achieves what she desires. In the meantime, she will have to be patient.

Card 5 *Justice* symbolizes the views of others, and outside influences. This, amongst other things, is the card of balance indicating that Sally's close friends think she and David make a good couple. As justice also relates to decisions, some of them may be wondering when David will propose marriage to her. It looks as though circumstances favour a fair outcome in the long run.

Card 6 *The Hanged Man* is telling Sally to wait, bide her time, and temporarily sacrifice her insistence upon marriage. If she can compromise for a while, this card promises that changes are on the way. Far from being an alarming sign, the Hanged Man in this context stands for eventual success through the act of self-denial.

Card 7 *The Ten of Cups*, sometimes known as the Wish Card, should lay all Sally's fears to rest. Her dreams of marriage seem certain to come true eventually, and the relationship promises to be a happy one if she decides to follow the advice given by card six.

The Romany Spread

Said to be a favourite of Gypsy fortune tellers, the Romany Spread offers a glimpse into what the near future holds. As this 21-card layout also paints a full picture of the mood and circumstances of the questioner, it can be used to begin a Tarot reading or to amplify other spreads such as the Horoscope.

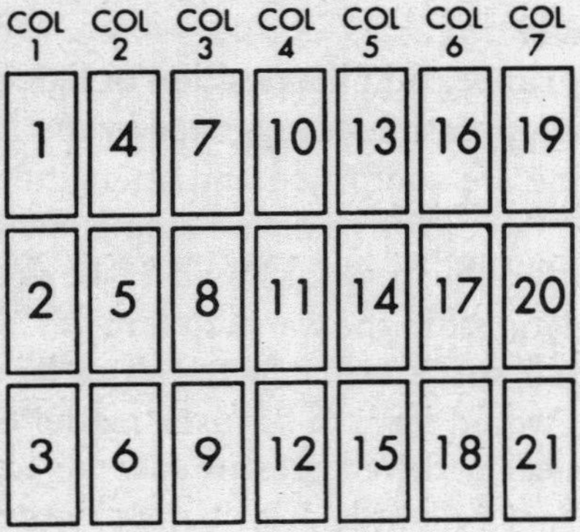

COL 1	COL 2	COL 3	COL 4	COL 5	COL 6	COL 7
1	4	7	10	13	16	19
2	5	8	11	14	17	20
3	6	9	12	15	18	21

Spread One.

This spread can give two very different readings. In the first layout (see Spread 1) which is analysed on the next page, seven vertical columns relate to different spheres of the questioner's life. In the second (see spread 2), three horizontal lines of seven cards represent past, present and future.

Generally speaking, both spreads highlight matters which relate to the next six months or so. If you particularly want to assess how much the past has affected the present, choose the second layout.

Since there is no formally selected significator in either spread, check whether a card representing you – or the person you are reading for – has appeared. If it has, note where it is and which

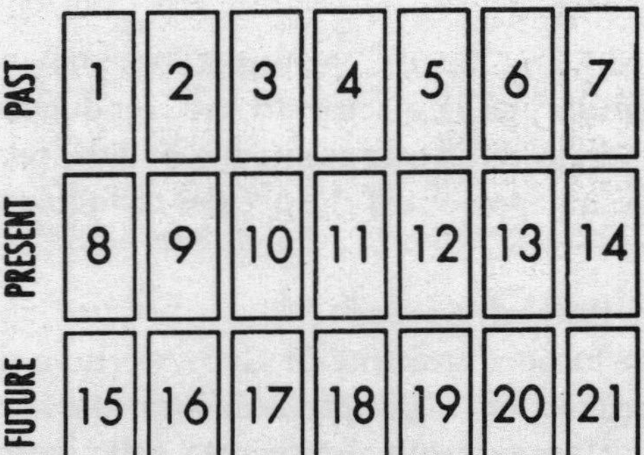

PAST	1	2	3	4	5	6	7
PRESENT	8	9	10	11	12	13	14
FUTURE	15	16	17	18	19	20	21

Spread Two.

cards flank it. The lack of a significator, can suggest detachment from the future.

The next step is to assess the proportion of Major Arcana cards to Minor ones, and decide which suit – if any – forms a majority. Look for resonance and dissonance as well. Now you are ready to begin reading the spread as a whole.

Spread One – A Sample Reading

The questioner, a woman in her late twenties, was uncertain about every aspect of her future at the time of the reading.

Looking at the spread as a whole, we can see that Wands form the primary majority – there are nine altogether. Cups, represented by four cards, are the secondary majority. Unstable emotions are the keyword here, but there is also a liberal helping of creativity and potential. Since Wands deal with practical matters, events relating to the woman's career are likely to be important while Watery Cups show some difficulties in her love life.

Taking a Closer Look

Column 1: The Self

The Four of Cups, Eight of Cups and four of Wands in this position show that unstable emotions are draining the questioner's considerable vitality and creativity. (Cups and Wands weaken one another). But as all the cards here are Minor ones, this state of affairs should be transitory.

Column 2: What is Closest to You?

The Eight, Nine and Ten of Wands suggest a lot of work pressure surrounds this person. She, or someone who is close to her, may be worrying about how they will cope in the future. But overall the outlook is fiery and positive.

Column 3: Hopes And Fears

More fiery creativity in the shape of the Knight and Page of Wands, suggests that the questioner longs to socialize more – perhaps to counterbalance the uneasy emotions in Column 1. The Three of Swords, meanwhile, shows that she may be worrying about a love triangle, or is under stress in her current relationship. Combined with the Eight of Cups, a separation looks likely.

Column 4: What You Expect

The Two of Pentacles suggests that the woman is self-employed or pursuing two careers; a balancing act is called for. This message is backed up by the Lovers, a card which often indicates two paths. The Empress in the middle promises abundant energy and again affirms the creativity of the Wands. The Lovers also links in with the Three of Swords, since it can denote love triangles as well.

Column 5: What You Do Not Expect

Justice at the head of this column confirms that the questioner will have to make a decision of some sort. It lends an air of psychological balance to the battles suggested by the Seven and Five of Wands which accompany it. Creative, property and money matters will be approached logically and calmly.

Column 6: The Near Future

The near future promises to be rather dramatic. The Knight of Swords brings sudden news of an upsetting emotional nature (Five of Cups). But Death counsels acceptance here – an important chapter in the woman's life is drawing to a close. The Five of Cups signals that although something may have been lost, the situation may still be turned to her advantage if she looks to the future.

Column 7: Further On

After a difficult and perhaps depressing time indicated by The Moon, the Knight of Cups brings fresh hope and possibly a new relationship. The Three of Wands shows that a successful person may help the woman through this trying period by offering advice. Further interpretation of this column suggests that a fresh, hitherto hidden, injection of inspiration is likely – especially if the questioner works in the media, arts or any of the caring professions.

The Tree of Life Spread

The Tree of Life spread was inspired by the symbolic Tree of Life or Knowledge, one of the central tenets of the Kabala. The

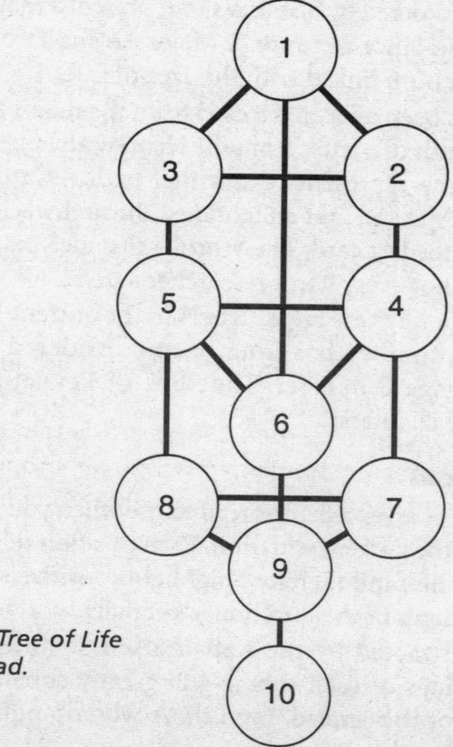

The Tree of Life spread.

Kabala is a mediaeval Hebrew mystical system, a complex collection of philosophies and teachings about God, the universe and mankind's path to enlightenment.

The Tree of Life consists of ten *Sephiroth* (circles) arranged in three columns which are said to represent pillars. Each sphere denotes aspects of God, and by extension, life itself.

On the right hand side is the Pillar of Mercy, which is said to be masculine and active. On the left, the Pillar of Judgment is designated feminine and receptive. Similar ideas are found all over the world in both medicine and divination – yin and yang being a well-known Chinese example. The Middle Pillar symbolizes a connecting principle, which balances and unites the two opposite sides.

The Sephiroth also denote a two-way spiritual path – from God to man and from man to God. Known as the Twenty-two Paths, this is considered by occultists to represent a map of the mystical universe. Since there are 22 Major Arcana Tarot cards, these have often been linked with the Tree of Life.

Each path has been allocated a card from the major Arcana, which corresponds to a letter from the Hebrew alphabet. Since the Major Arcana represents a spiritual path – Card 1, the innocent Fool, is tested and enlightened through each lesson culminating in the last card, The World – this idea is an interesting one. But not every Tarot researcher agrees.

However, because there are 22 letters in the ancient Hebrew alphabet, this number has long been considered both a mystical and magical number. The Book of Revelations, for example, has 22 chapters.

Using The Spread

The Tree of Life is an excellent spread to use when you want an overall view of the current situation. Each position relates to a specific area of life, and therefore highlights positive, negative and neutral spheres of the questioner's activity.

If you are attracted by the Kabala itself, a study of the mystical meanings of each sphere will greatly enhance your interpretation of this spread. Even those who do not sympathize with this system find it works very well too – albeit on a somewhat more superficial level.

What the Positions Mean

Card 1: Kether Supreme Crown

This position relates to the questioner's spiritual world and inner being at the time of the reading. It can also denote attitudes towards these matters, revealing spiritual well-being or otherwise.

Card 2: Hokmah Wisdom

Here we can see how someone deals with their dreams. How much energy do they possess, and how do they use it? What are they responsible for? These are the types of questions to ask yourself when interpreting the card in this position.

Card 3: Binah Understanding

Binah represents understanding in the feminine receptive sense. While Hokmah is active, moving out into the world, Binah denotes potential – and what limits or contains it at this point in the questioner's life.

Card 4: Hesed Love

'Love' in this sense means constructive action, organisation and increase. In the material world it represents finances, practical matters and earthy activities.

Card 5: Geburah Power

Where Hesed builds, Geburah destroys – symbolising the two opposing forces of creation. Here, it relates to challenges in life. Ask yourself how serious any opposition to the questioner's plans might be?

Card 6: Tifereth Beauty

Achievements, image, successes, harmony and order are all attributes of this sphere. It represents the way forward, the questioner's highest aspirations at this time.

Card 7: Netsah Endurance

Here we look at the forces of attraction, and the instinctual nature of the questioner. Both actual relationships and attitudes towards them may appear in this position and if the questioner does not have a relationship in his or her life at this time, then Netsah may denote a past attachment or a future love. Emotional blocks may be clarified.

Card 8: Hod Majesty

Hod opposes Netsah, and therefore represents intellect as opposed to instinct and logic as opposed to intuition. This position denotes worldly affairs, money matters and career in the broadest sense. The questioner's attitude to such things may also be revealed. Check with both Card 6 and Card 2 for a fuller understanding.

Card 9: Yesod Foundation

Rather like the Twelfth House in astrology, Yesod symbolizes what is hidden – in the depths of the unconscious or in real life. Traditionally, Yesod belongs to the Moon and is therefore linked with cycles of growth itself. Its connection with the life force means that this position may also have a bearing on the questioner's physical health and well-being.

Card 10: Malkuth Kingdom

In the Kabala, Malkuth is found at the foot of the Tree. Here it represents earth and roots and so may refer to home, family and important close relationships.

This is a fascinating symbolic position for while it refers to matter, it also symbolizes the spiritual forces of God in the physical world. It is the position of the Shekinah, divine Bride of God. Also said to be the feminine part of God, she was thought to have been separated from her 'husband' and Kabalists believe she must be reunited with God to restore him to wholeness. Through Malkuth, therefore, human beings begin the ascent of the spiritual path – the ladder of the Tree of Life.

A Sample Interpretation of a Celtic Cross Spread

The significator of this Celtic Cross spread – the Queen of Swords – represents a woman born under an Air sign.

Pentacles – the majority suit – show that her problems at work or with money cannot be solved by her usual 'emotional' approach, but only through more practical means.

As Swords weaken Pentacles, the Swords card in dissonance

shows that she may have trouble finding a balance between the conflicting realms of thought and practicalities. But the Nine of Pentacles – the outcome card – indicates that the end result is likely to be extremely favourable.

The Calendar Spread

The Calendar spread in its most basic form contains a card for each month of the year ahead. Shuffle the pack, then lay a clock face beginning at nine o'clock. Work round in an anti-clockwise direction.

A significator can be placed in the centre or alternatively lay the thirteenth card here to indicate a general theme for the year ahead. You can even place both these cards here – do whatever feels right for you.

This spread is most effective when used in conjunction with other layouts. Used after, say, the Celtic Cross or the Horse-shoe, it can help you predict when an outcome is likely to occur. Or use it to begin a reading to find crucial months when relationships or career issues are highlighted.

Look at the Major Arcana cards first when analysing this layout since they show the most important points on the calendar. The more there are, the more important the forthcoming period.

Here is an example of the Calendar spread in action. The questioner is a 26-year-old woman whose life is in a state of flux. The central card influencing the year ahead is the Wheel of Fortune, which indicates further changes. If the questioner can flow with them, the changes are likely to be beneficial ones.

Month 1: The Seven of Cups reversed counsels patience – she should not make any permanent decisions just yet. It also warns against over-indulgence and living in an emotional fantasy world.

Month 2: The Six of Wands reversed backs up the Seven of Cups' message. She still cannot forge ahead and she may have to face problems at work.

Month 3: The King of Wands can be interpreted on two levels. As a career card it suggests either a helpful, dynamic colleague or negotiations of various kinds. With regard to romance, it suggests she may meet someone fiery and creative this time around.

Month 4: The Ten of Cups backs up the last card – either way the King of Wands is a positive contact. Month Four should bring great happiness. A dream may be realized now.

Month 5: The Ten of Wands denotes hard work. The career issue seems to be sorting itself out.

Month 6: Our first Major Arcana card, The High Priestess, falls here. The questioner may begin to explore her imagination, study esoteric subjects or generally get to know herself better now.

Month 7: The King of Pentacles reversed shows that a man may block progress by being obstinate, and afraid of taking risks. Jealousy could also be a problem.

Month 8: The Star reversed reveals a tense time – it may be a good time for a holiday. In love, there may be an upsetting clash of wills – amplifying the message of the King of Pentacles the month before.

Month 9: Things are looking up. The Seven of Pentacles foretells apprenticeship, learning and progress at work.

Month 10: The powerful Ace of Pentacles augurs financial success and emotional stability after the previous months' storms.

Month 11: The Nine of Pentacles speaks of sensuality, happiness, a sense of achievement and fulfilment. It confirms the Ace of Pentacles' message.

Month 12: The year ends happily on the Four of Wands. The questioner reaps rewards for her work and there is a sense of harvest and abundance in her life. The Wheel of Fortune has lived up to its promise. After struggles and difficulties, everything is likely to turn out well.

Other Tarot Timing Devices

Here are two methods you may like to try if the question is 'When?'

The Minor Arcana Method

Each suit of the Minor Arcana is linked symbolically to a season of the year. The list (see below) shows how the twos, threes and fours of the four suits represent particular months.

Shuffle the whole Tarot pack well, concentrating on your question. Cut the cards into three piles and reassemble them in a fresh order. Then deal 13 cards and see whether a month card appears.

If none of the month cards is turned up, deal the same number of cards again. If the same thing happens again, repeat the procedure a third time. If there is still no answer then the issue remains undecided or is unlikely to be resolved during the next 12 months.

Cards For Each Month

Pentacles: Winter

Two – December

Three – January
Four – February
Swords: Spring
Two – March
Three – April
Four – May
Wands: Summer
Two – June
Three – July
Four – August
Cups: Autumn
Two – September
Three – October
Four – November

The Four Aces Method

The four Aces can also be used to represent the four seasons as in the list on the left. Discard the Major Arcana and shuffle the cards thoroughly, ensuring some are reversed. Cut the pack as before and deal 13 cards.

If an upright Ace appears then the answer is yes. Its suit shows the season when your question will be resolved. However, if the Ace is reversed then the answer is no. When no Aces appear in the first deal, try the method again until an Ace is revealed.

The Majorities and Resonance & Dissonance

Before attempting an in depth analysis of a Tarot spread, it is a good idea to take stock of the complete picture before you. Usually one or two suits of the Minor Arcana will dominate.

The one which is represented by the most cards is known as the *Primary Majority,* while the next strongest suit is the *Secondary Majority.*

How the Majorities Work

The majorities point a reading in the right direction by revealing the mood of the questioner and what concerns them – be it their emotions and personal life or external events.

When the majority of cards are from the Fiery Suit of **Wands,** the reading is likely to deal with events in the material world.

Action is the keyword here, and questions concerning career or property will affect the spread.

Earthy **Pentacles** (Coins) also relate to life's practicalities. Hard work and money (or maybe the lack of it) are likely to be the main areas of interest.

Swords represent the Airy realms of thought and communication but they do not necessarily relate to worldly events. Here, moods or attitudes may be colouring the spread.

Watery **Cups** indicate every shade of emotion and feeling, from which spring love and creativity. While such qualities could apply to real-life events, they are more likely to show the questioner's state of mind at the time of the reading.

Resonance and Dissonance

Just as certain Elements in Astrology are more compatible than others, so some suits of the Tarot work together harmoniously and some do not. So, after you have established the majorities in a spread, look for *resonance* (strengthening) and *dissonance* (weakening) patterns in the cards which surround them. While the meanings of individual cards will not be affected, resonance and dissonance may shift the emphasis of an interpretation.

The relationships between the suits are as follows:

- Combinations of **Wands** and **Swords** strengthen each other. They indicate ideas and energy.
- **Wands** are strengthened by **Pentacles** and vice versa. Practical work is fuelled by energy.
- **Wands** and **Cups** weaken each other. This unstable combination shows creative highs and lows, and sudden mood swings.
- **Swords** are strengthened by **Cups** and vice versa. There is a potentially balanced blend of logic and deeper emotion.
- **Swords** and **Pentacles** weaken each other. Such a combination suggests the material world is at odds with the realm of the mind.

For example, when the Ace of Pentacles (indicating financial improvements) is surrounded by Swords, its positive qualities are weakened. But if the Ace is surrounded by Wands, the effects are strengthened and more attention should be paid to its impact on the spread as a whole.

All other combinations are neutral. The suits of Pentacles and Cups, for example, have neither a positive nor negative effect on each other.

Put Yourself in the Picture

The relationships between the suits are very important, so be sure to take them into account when you establish the primary and secondary majorities. Ask yourself whether the suits in the spread strengthen or lessen each other's impact. Does the reading focus on the inner world of emotions (Cups and Swords) or is it firmly rooted in the real world (Pentacles and Wands)? A large number of Swords, however, suggests that negative thinking or an overly logical approach is affecting matters at hand, hence a fresh outlook may be needed.

The same rules apply to individual cards. Ask yourself whether the card you are interpreting is strengthened or weakened by those around it. This could affect the rest of the spread and your chosen significator.

By using resonance, dissonance and majorities before you begin to interpret a spread, you are less likely to get carried away by individual cards and retain a sense of overall perspective.

Some Words of Advice

Most Tarot readers use some form of ritual preparation before a reading, designed to ensure that both reader and questioner are as receptive as possible to what the cards have to say. There are no hard and fast rules about this – the most important thing is simply to relax and enjoy what you are doing. Even so, any ritual is meaningless unless it is infused with feeling, so think carefully about what will get you 'in the mood' and then experiment until you find what works best.

The Tarot is not a parlour game, and neither is a Tarot reading. Keeping the cards in a special place – for example, in a beautiful box, or wrapped in silk or velvet – trains your mind to accept them as a serious tool.

It may also help to have a special place where you always

read the cards. What counts is not the actual place itself, but the act of using it repeatedly for the same purpose – as soon as you sit there, you automatically tune in to the idea of reading the cards. Alternatively, where space is limited, some readers keep a special tablecloth for readings.

Whatever you do, never let other people 'play' with your Tarot pack. After all, you have spent time and energy building up a personal link with the cards which operates on a deep and sometimes unconscious level. The pack represents a symbolic oracle and should always be treated as such.

Respecting the Oracle

In the ancient world, oracles were accorded tremendous respect, and only approached warily on special occasions. The same applies to the Tarot.

Never offer anyone a reading, no matter how tempted you might be. If somebody wants to consult the cards, and knows you can read them, it is their choice. Tarot should not be forced on anyone, even if they like the idea.

If consulted in a frivolous or obsessive manner, the Tarot will most likely respond with a stern rebuff – like Hexagram Four of the *I Ching* (Youthful Folly); *'It is not I who seek the young fool; the young fool seeks me. At the first oracle I inform him. If he asks two or three times, it is importunity. If he importunes, I give him no information.'*

If this seems hard to believe, try it for yourself and see!

Clearing Your Mind

Similarly, you should make absolutely sure that both you and the questioner are clear as to why you are consulting the cards. A muddled or vague state of mind invariably results in a vague or muddled reading.

Spending a few quiet moments together before the reading helps, as does a mental request for the right information – or perhaps the right interpretation. Some practitioners also like to visualize a triangle of light linking them with the questioner: imagine that the point of the triangle is above both your heads, with the base linking your feet. At the same time, ask your higher self for clarity.

Even after the cards have been shuffled, cut and laid out, you may still encounter problems. For example, some people – especially those with a surface knowledge of Tarot – react badly to images like the *Hanged Man* without seeing them within the context of the spread as a whole. Make sure you do not fall into

PROBLEM SPREADS

Sooner or later you are bound to be confronted by a spread so gloomy that it leaves you lost for words. Certainly, it is hard to be cheerful or reassuring when faced with the Ten of Swords, the Tower of Destruction, and the Devil – a combination which on the face of it implies that the questioner is about to meet great difficulties beyond his or her control. You cannot pretend that the cards are not there, nor can you place much of a positive interpretation on a fundamentally negative line-up. However, you can do your questioner a great service by reminding him or her that negative indications such as this will be made all the worse by a negative state of mind. We all face problems in life, but it is how we deal with them that counts – not the problems themselves. Difficulties can also be interpreted in terms of challenges to be overcome rather than unmitigated disaster. Most people react positively to this kind of talk. But remember, if a distraught questioner still believes that his or her life is in ruins, the chances are they need professional help or guidance. As a Tarot reader, you can do no more than direct them to a counsellor or qualified therapist.

the same trap yourself, for it is easy to lay a card like this and mutter dire warnings about sacrifices and blocks. In fact, the *Hanged Man* can just as easily represent a period of inertia or waiting – and even if a sacrifice does have to be made, it is only so that something more life-enhancing can be allowed to take its place.

Things said to people during a reading can affect them subconsciously, so by keeping your messages positive, you can help them turn any setbacks in their lives to their advantage. Besides, there is always a chance you could be mistaken – and the last thing you want to do is inflict your own negativity on the poor questioner!

TEA LEAVES

Preparing the Reading

Tea was first introduced to Europe around the middle of the 17th-century. But for many years, it was a luxury few could afford. So how did the now widespread practice of fortune-telling by tea leaves come about?

Ancient civilisations set great store by oracles, signs and omens – these were read from flights of birds, in the entrails of animals, the weather and practically every manifestation of the natural world. The gods were believed to send messages in this way in order to warn and instruct humanity.

A form of divination similar to reading tea leaves seems to have been practised in Ancient Greece. Known as *Kottavos*, it involved throwing the remains of a cup of wine into a metal bowl. The shape of the resulting splash and the sediment, were then read for omens.

Today, reading the leaves is still a popular domestic art, often passed down from one generation to the next. In countries where little tea is drunk, patterns formed by thick, dark coffee grounds are used instead. Tiny cups of Turkish coffee are used for this, and there are many practitioners – some professional – all over the Middle East. In Western Europe, there are very few professional readers, yet many families boast at least one member, usually female, who can still read the leaves or grounds.

What You Will Need

Obviously, the tea used should be loose, either China or a mixture of Indian and China, and of very good quality. Cheap, small-leafed tea does not form clear symbols and should not be used.

The pot itself should have a wide spout, so that sufficient leaves may be poured into the cup for reading. The right kind of tea cup is important too. It should be china, have a broad top and bottom, and be plain white inside. An old-fashioned breakfast cup will be the best. Mugs are useless: they have perpendicular sides, making it very hard to see the symbols.

The Tea Leaf Oracle

The person wanting his or her fortune told must drink until

there is roughly half a teaspoonful of tea left. He or she should then hold the cup by the handle in the left hand, and swirl it round quite quickly three times in an anti-clockwise direction. The tea cup must then be turned upside-down on to the saucer and left to drain. Serious questioners should concentrate on what they would like to find out. The person who is reading the cup should pick it up after a couple of minutes. If any moisture remains, the cup is replaced on the saucer, stray drops can shift the leaves and alter the pattern. When the cup is completely settled, the reading of the leaves may begin.

The Handle

The handle of the cup represents the questioner. So those symbols falling close to the handle are read as events which will happen directly to him or her, or in the home. The side opposite the handle represents the unexpected, strangers and events outside the home.

The closer the symbol is to the rim or handle of the cup, the sooner the event will occur. Any symbols appearing on the sides of the cup represent the relatively near future – perhaps a fortnight ahead. Signs at the very bottom of the cup point to a month or so ahead at the most. Symbols to the left of the handle represent past events, or influences which are fading. Those to the right are linked with the present and future.

Joys and Sorrows

Tradition states that anything appearing at the very bottom of the cup indicates bad luck or disappointment. Symbols close to the rim are held to be the most fortunate, while those in the centre represent normal life with all its ups and downs. Of course, the actual symbol must be read carefully too. A negative symbol close to the rim would lose a lot of its power, while a positive one found at the bottom would indicate delayed luck, or happiness after a great deal of effort and hard work.

There are a number of superstitions connected with fortune-telling by tea leaves. Some of these are omens, some connected with reading the leaves. Of course, all omens should be taken with a pinch of salt – but they can be fun. And sometimes, when the laws of coincidence are operating in your life, an omen may prove strangely accurate. Here are a few to look out for.

If there are a lot of bubbles on the surface when the tea is poured, some extra money should be coming your way. Money luck is also indicated by a single leaf floating on the surface of the tea.

Before the Reading

A single leaf stuck to the rim, above the level of the tea, reveals the imminent arrival of a stranger. If it sticks out above the rim, this event will be a big surprise to the enquirer. Perhaps romance is in the air, or a long-lost friend is about to turn up.

When there is very little to see at the rim, your enquirer can expect a fairly uneventful time in the immediate future; nothing much will happen for a few weeks or months.

Once the cup is emptied, and has been drained prior to a reading, look carefully to see how the leaves have settled – and how much moisture still remains inside the cup.

The Basic Symbols

The Meaning of Moisture

Moisture traditionally represents tears and invariably refers to the present. There may be some passing sadness troubling the enquirer; symbols and positions should reveal what this is. On a more positive note, moisture tends to change the symbols as it runs around the cup. This means that problems and difficulties are disappearing – and tears will soon dry up.

A mass of leaves is said to augur prosperity and good luck. But this is only true if the heap is seen at the sides of the cup. If the mass falls opposite the handle, there will be some kind of upheaval, probably at work. When a heap of leaves is seen close to the handle, the enquirer may be making trouble for himself or herself and others.

A mass in the bottom of the cup suggests good news which also brings anxiety in its wake. For example, the excitement of moving house, planning a wedding or being promoted is still stressful even though the events are positive ones.

Long or Short Stalks?

Stalks represent people. To identify age, sex, and character you must look closely at the stalk and use your imagination. Does the stalk look strong and upright? Or is it bent and thin? Is it long or short?

Long stalks are said to show male figures, while shorter ones denote females. The relative strength and upright qualities of the stalk suggest reliability, helpfulness and loyalty. Weak, curved stalks reveal deceitful friends or enemies.

People are also often indicated by letters. Such letters are usually very clear, and accompanied by another symbol which can help you decide which area of life the person will affect.

Remember to look at the position this sign appears in: near the handle means matters close to home; opposite the handle, outside events or even foreign countries.

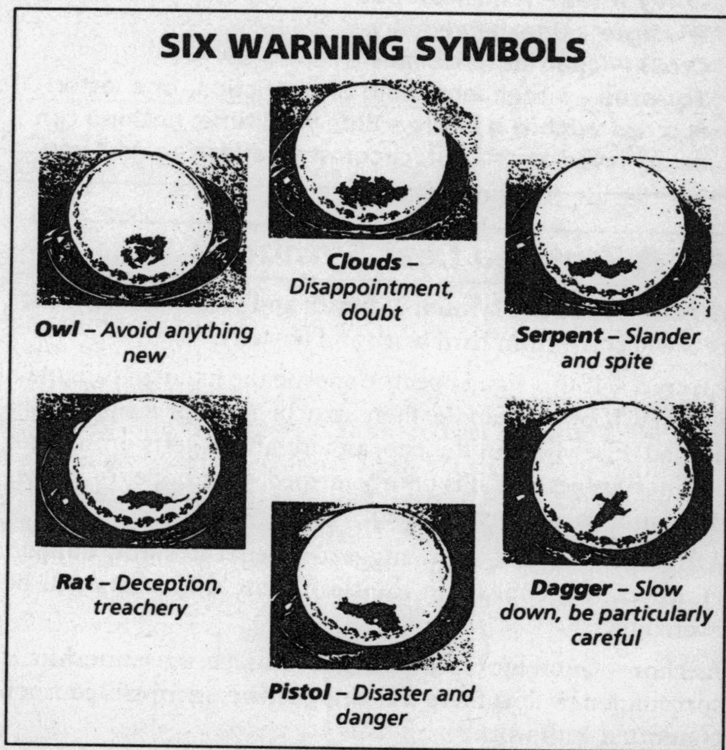

SIX WARNING SYMBOLS

Owl *– Avoid anything new*

Clouds *– Disappointment, doubt*

Serpent *– Slander and spite*

Rat *– Deception, treachery*

Pistol *– Disaster and danger*

Dagger *– Slow down, be particularly careful*

Six Good Luck Symbols

Star – General good fortune
Anchor – Success in business
Bouquet – A happy marriage; loyal friends; appreciation
Clover – Prosperity
Crescent moon – Romance
Bridge – Happy journeys

BASIC SYMBOLS

Dots – Money, a windfall, legacy, or salary increase
Dashes – Energy; a new project
Circles – If large, the end of some matter; if small, news of a marriage
Straight lines – Determination
Wavy lines – A difficult path
Triangle – Unexpected luck
Cross – Quarrels, problems
Squares – Either some kind of restriction, or a letter
A cross within a circle – Bide your time; nothing can be achieved at present; circumstances are against you

An A-Z of Tea Leaf Symbols:

Acorn – A positive symbol of health and future security. Success will come from hard work and tenacity.

Aircraft – If this sign appears opposite the handle, it augurs a journey. If by the handle, there may be news or visitors from abroad. Elsewhere in the cup, an aircraft suggests promotion and new projects. If it is poorly formed, your hopes of immediate success will be frustrated.

Alligator – A bad sign, suggesting enemies and danger. However, if it appears in the clear, these difficulties will be overcome.

Anchor – Good luck, prosperity, and a secure relationship. If surrounded by dots there will be a positive, successful journey connected with work.

Angle – Good fortune, love and peace are on the way. If at the bottom of the cup, it is said to denote spiritual protection and guidance.

Antlers – Trouble, mishaps and minor accidents. This is a warning sign, and these problems will not occur if you take trouble to prevent them, so look carefully at accompanying symbols and the position of the sign. If it is at the bottom of the cup, the matter is in your own hands. If standing clearly alone at the sides, social events will bring trouble in their wake; it might be advisable to cancel.

Ape – A hidden enemy, gossip. A warning to be careful about what you say or reveal to others.

Apple – Vitality and health, also luck in business matters. If this sign is at the bottom of the cup it means recovery from a long illness.

Arch – An opening. If the arch is faint, it means unexpected opportunities. If well-defined, your wishes will be granted soon.

Arrow – News and communications of every kind; look at nearby symbols to decide what kind of news is coming. If there are lots of little dots around the arrow, there is bad news about money matters.

Axe – Problems will be overcome, but not without a fight. It is time to stand up for yourself.

Baby – This can mean a real baby is on the way, or signify the birth of a new business or home.

Basket – Generally, a gift for the home. If near the handle, a pet or baby will prove to be a delightful addition to the family. If at the bottom of the cup, expect finances to fluctuate.

Bat – Hard work or travel for little immediate reward.

Bee, or Bees – A happy omen; if near the handle, a busy social time, lots of news and activity around the home. If away from the handle, a busy time at work which will bring success to the enquirer.

Bell – Most often this signifies news of a wedding, particularly when there are two bells to be seen. Otherwise, good news in general, unless at the bottom of the cup, when the news is not so good.

Birds – Birds in flight mean news from a distance, or journeys. If one appears left of the handle, it means doubtful investments.

Bird's nest – There could be a lucky find; a bargain, or an antique in the attic. Home life will be happy and stable.

Boat – If seen with clouds, a difficult patch lies ahead. If clear, a happy holiday or inspirational trip is in the offing.

Book – A secret will soon be revealed if the book is open. If it is closed, it suggests research and studying. If a stalk or initial is close by, the enquirer is about to get to know a writer.

Boot – If this appears at the top of the cup there will be a swift change of job or home. If it is by the handle, job loss is imminent. If surrounded by little dots it suggests an end to unemployment.

Cabbage – Jealousy. If there are any squares nearby, jealous behaviour may create trouble – check the position to see when this applies to the enquirer, or someone in their life.

Car – Visits from friends.

Castle – Unexpected money luck.

Cat – Generally, deception and lies. If near the handle, however, domestic bliss.

Clock – If close to the top of the cup. this denotes recovery from illness or a difficult patch in life. Elsewhere, it suggests a fortunate meeting and counsels the enquirer to use their time wisely. When in the bottom, a familiar way of life or routine is coming to an end.

Clown – A full and happy social life. Surrounded by clouds – don't overdo it. At the bottom of the cup – doubtful company.

Crescent – If this sign resembles a half-circle, it indicates some kind of offer. The more 'broken' the half-circle appears, the more tentative the approach. The firmer this sign appears, the more it suggests new beginnings, opportunities and interests. When the crescent reminds you of a new moon, it augurs romance – probably within a 'moon month'.

Crown – Success. If close to some wavy lines, there will be some delay, although rewards will come in the end.

Dancers – Good news is on the way. If more than one figure, life is changing for the better.

Deer – Financial difficulties and disagreements at work.

Dog – A lucky sign indicating true friendship and loyalty.

Dragon – Sudden changes and astonishing upheavals which should prove positive, once the dust has settled.

Drum – If at the bottom of the cup, a scandal. If at the rim, success and positive publicity.

Duck – Money through all forms of trade, investment and speculation.

Eagle – Luck and prosperity through a change of home. When away from the handle, foreign connections will prove positive. At the bottom of the cup, this sign is said to foretell the death of a monarch or great statesman – there will be public mourning.

Ear – Interesting news; if at the bottom, scandalous gossip.

Easel – A new job.

Egg – Increase, expansion, new plans and creativity. New undertakings will be successful.

Elephant – Good health, luck and increased strength.

Eye – A warning to look before you leap. Do not be hasty, but try to remain vigilant.

Face – Generally, a friend. If ugly, there may be an upset in a friendship through misunderstandings.

Fairy – A happy love affair begun under unusual circumstances. If at the bottom of the cup, the affair will soon be over.

Fan – Flirtation. Indiscretion is likely if there are wavy lines close to this sign.

Fish – Good news and luck. The time is right to achieve your dreams. If surrounded by dots, there will be news from abroad or the possibility of going to live in another country.

Flag – A friend may prove untrustworthy, take care.

Flock – A flock of animals or birds symbolizes public meetings, demonstrations and large gatherings. Look at accompanying signs to discover their significance.

Flowers – Generally: love, favours, praise and happiness. Specifically: a lily suggests health and self-respect; an iris, a messenger; an ivy leaf, an old friend or lover; violets, happiness to come through realising your ideals.

Garland – A wish will come true.

Gate – Something is barring your way – check the position to see which area of life is affected. If the gate is open, an opportunity will soon present itself.

Goose – A great deal of discussion about something. Mischief-making.

Goat – One goat symbolizes an enemy; a flock indicates a large gathering of people – possibly a public meeting of some kind.

Guitar – A new romance is in the offing.

Gun – Arguments, discord or difficulties.

Hammer – Hard work and struggle is indicated – but with a successful outcome.

Hand – If appearing at the top of the cup, the accent is on friendships and partnerships; at the bottom, this symbol represents an obstinate individual. Look to see where the hand is pointing, as this could be emphasising something.

Hare – Journeys – either for yourself, or the return of someone who has been away. Less frequently, a lucky romance.

Harp – If on the bottom of the cup, this indicates a temporary parting from someone; otherwise, love and harmony is predicted.

Heart – This represents love. If appearing with a ring, marriage; with dots, a wealthy lover; with fruit, a wonderful party.

Horse – Fortunate journeys and short trips.

Horseman – A stranger is entering your life; the outcome is likely to be beneficial.

House – Building success in your work or relationships.

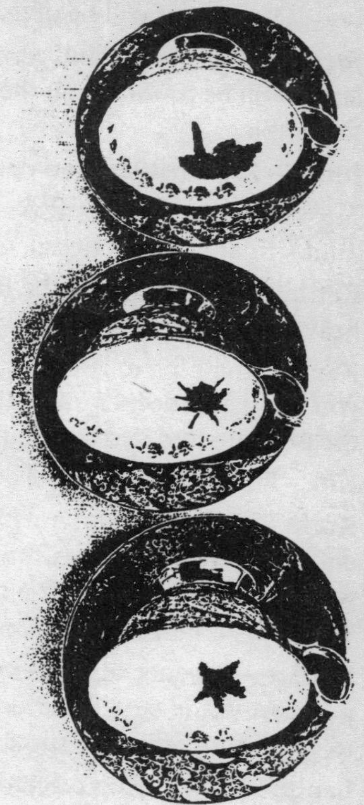

Above, from top:

Ship *– A fortunate omen.*

Spider *– Emphasis on money.*

Star *– Good luck and fortune.*

Above, from top:

Sun *– Good health and love.*

Van *– A change of home or job.*

Wheel *– General progress.*

Ivy – Old friends will be of great help to you now.

Jockey – Speculation and gambling. If clearly depicted, speculation will be profitable; if there are clouds, it is a warning not to gamble.

Judge – Legal matters and documents.

Jug – Good health, but also a warning against excesses of any kind – financial, emotional, or physical.

Kettle – If appearing at the bottom of the cup, domestic upheavals are predicted; if elsewhere, a happy home.

Key – Something to your advantage is about to be revealed, or you will gain a deeper understanding of some situation. Check the position and surrounding symbols for further details.

Kite – Either physical travel or mental exploration is indicated.

Knife – If broken, some conflict or quarrel is coming to an end. Two crossed knives foretell trouble, quarrels and strife; when lying close to either a ring or a heart, a wedding is predicted.

Ladder – Advance of some kind is indicated, depending on its position in the cup. Perseverance and hard work is necessary to climb the 'ladder' of success.

Lamp – A surprising revelation or the discovery of a lost object could be imminent. If located by the handle of the cup, a legacy of some kind is foretold.

Leaves – Joy and happiness will be yours.

Letters – Square or oblong shapes represent letters. If there are dots around them or inside them, the letter will contain money. If there is an initial nearby, this should reveal who the letter is from.

Lines – Dotted lines going from the handle or bottom of the cup to the rim indicate short journeys; wavy lines suggest hold-ups or difficulties when travelling.

Lion – Help from powerful people or distinguished friends.

Man – A visitor is arriving soon.

Mermaid – Temptation – usually of the sexual variety. Someone very flirtatious and compelling could be disrupting your life.

Monkey – Deception in love, or a difficult infatuation.

Mountain – If clearly defined, this suggests happy journeys with friends; if heavy or dark, something is currently blocking your progress.

Mug – Old friends or lovers are coming back into your life.

Mushroom – If clearly defined, a trip to the country is indicated; if upside down, there could be unsettled relationships or separations.

Nail – Teeth could be a problem; there could be a visit to the dentist soon.

Necklace – Broken necklaces foretell breaks in friendships or love affairs; when complete, they signify a gift or an admirer.

Nurse – A need for rest and recuperation.

Oak – A very lucky sign, auguring long life, happiness and success in whatever area it appears.

Oar – Sports and sporting events.

Oval – Jealousy and delays in new enterprises. There may be bad news.

Owl – Beware of starting any new projects; someone could be keeping a secret from you, so keep your counsel for the moment.

Ox – Hospitality and happy social events.

Peacock – A good financial omen. This symbol sometimes suggests the acquisition of property.

Pig – A good relationship with someone, but beware of envious friends.

Pear – Things are looking up financially and socially.

Purse – At the bottom of the cup this warns against loss or theft; if at the top, a small windfall could come your way.

Question marks – Check the surrounding symbols to see what is doubted or questioned.

Rabbit – Success, taking place in a city or town.

Rat – Be wary of others; someone is not to be trusted.

Rider – news coming from some distance; there could be a surprise or unexpected luck.

Ring – This symbol represents marriage. If there are two rings it will be very quick; if dots appear around the ring, it will be a wealthy marriage.

Rocking horse – A renewal of old friendships or love affairs.

Rose – Personal happiness and creativity.

Scales – Usually a legal matter or court case. If there is a sword nearby, the result will soon be known; if the scales are out of balance, think carefully before proceeding.

Scissors – Separation of some kind – check the position.

Ship – Any journey undertaken at this time will be very fortunate. If dealing with foreign countries, in love or business, there will soon be good news; generally, a sign of increase and flow.

Spade – Hard work and persistence will eventually pay off.

Spider – Money is the keynote here. If there are several spiders, money matters will soon be especially important. Spiders also warn against being too open with other people – keep your secrets safe.

Star – If things have been difficult, good luck and fortune will now smile upon you.

Sun – Good health, and happy love affairs are augured. If there are dashes around this symbol, there may be a sudden, positive turn of events.

Tea pot – Consultations and meetings.

Telescope – Adventure and inspiration.

Tortoise – The future is brighter than the present; circumstances will soon be more comfortable.

Trees – If there are several trees, your wish will come true. If dots surround the tree or trees, the country is a good place for you to be at the moment.

Triangles – When upright, these indicate good luck; if reversed, current projects will not be successful in the immediate future.

Umbrella – If open, you can be assured of protection and friends will prove helpful and kind; when closed, make sure you do not ask any favours – you will be disappointed.

Unicorn – Lucky for women; for men it augurs a scandal of some kind.

Van – Signals a change of home or job in the near future. Your place of work may also change.

Vase – Rewards following some kind of sacrifice or compromise. If there are clouds around the vase, you may have to give up something to make someone you love happy.

Wheel – General progress is indicated. This symbol is traditionally said to foretell an inheritance or financial gain of some kind, especially if at the top of the cup.

Windmill – Slow but sure progress is now assured, but do not attempt large, costly moves, they will not be successful.

Wings – Messages and news. The subject matter depends on their position in the cup.

Women – Creativity, fertility and happiness. Several women indicate a scandal or gossip.

Yacht – Pleasure in the company of friends.

Zebra – Adventure connected with foreign people, or travel in far countries.

Index